THE AFRICAN BURIAL GROUND IN NEW YORK CITY

To the ancestors

and

to Alexia

THE AFRICAN BURIAL GROUND IN NEW YORK CITY

MEMORY, SPIRITUALITY, AND SPACE

ANDREA E. FROHNE

Syracuse University Press

For a listing of books published and distributed by Syracuse University Press,
visit www.SyracuseUniversityPress.syr.edu.

ISBN: 978-0-8156-3401-0 (cloth)   978-0-8156-3430-0 (paperback)
978-0-8156-5327-1 (e-book)

Library of Congress Cataloging-in-Publication Data

Available from the publisher upon request.

Manufactured in the United States of America

Contents

Illustrations

Figures

Plates

Following page 232

Tables

Acknowledgments

While my research on the African Burial Ground is located in New York City, it has been inspired, informed, and redefined by people from different parts of the world and many walks of life. I would like to first acknowledge all of the people I interviewed in order to assemble this narrative, the dialogues that I witnessed among New York City activists, the archival specialists who assisted me in numerous institutions, and the ancestors who continued to guide me over the years—from the ones I met in West Africa to those in New York City.

My interviews with artists commissioned to commemorate the African Burial Ground were key in shaping the ways in which I wrote about the pieces and the project as a whole. Thank you to Tomie Arai, Joseph De Pace, Lorenzo Pace, Barbara Chase-Riboud, Houston Conwill, Rodney Léon, and Clyde Lynds.

I am grateful to the entire former African Burial Ground Office of Public Education and Interpretation (OPEI) for their unwavering and unquestioning provision of archives and resources. In particular, former director of OPEI Dr. Sherrill Wilson was always welcoming, encouraging, and open with me in answering questions. Upon the completion of my dissertation, I valued greatly the certificate of appreciation for contributions to the New York African Burial Ground Project that Dr. Wilson awarded me. Former director of memorialization Peggy King Jorde remained an important inspiration throughout my project, and I thank her immensely for sharing her personal insights and including me on mailing lists of all important documents associated with memorialization. I would like to thank staff members in other offices, who shared indispensable government documents, including Amanda Sutphin of the Landmarks Preservation Commission, Pete Sneed, Barbara Gary, Charlotte Cohen, and especially Renee Miscione of GSA, Marcha Johnson of the New York City Department of Parks and Recreation, Susan Harrison of the Art-in-Architecture program in Washington, DC, and former Senator David Paterson's assistant Gina Stahlnecker.

My library research included the New York Public Library (NYPL), the New-York Historical Society, the Museum of the City of New York, Trinity Church Archives, the Municipal Archives, the Municipal Library, the Schomburg Center for Research in Black Culture, and Special Collections at Rutgers University Libraries. In particular, I would like to acknowledge for their invaluable assistance the renowned Alice Hudson, formerly in the Map Division of the NYPL, Eileen Morales at the Museum of the City of New York, and Ron Becker at Rutgers, as well as Mike Klein, with whom I was in email contact at the Library of Congress.

A Gilder-Lehrman Institute Fellowship in New York City in 2006 was particularly indispensable for my manuscript revisions. The primary archives and maps I was free to study at the New-York Historical Society led me to original data and new conclusions that reshaped the final project. A Creative Award from Dickinson College also funded post-dissertation research and attendance at the reburial ceremony in 2003. I am ever grateful to friends who shared their living spaces and intellectual discussions with me on my many visits to New York over the years: Despina Lalaki, Hyun Joo Lee, Ilana Abend, and Michelle Hearne.

Binghamton University's program on the History and Theory of Art and Architecture provided me with an important intellectual space to initially develop this project. I express gratitude to my former advisor, Nkiru Nzegwu, for setting as an example her dynamism in the academy and bringing real-life convictions into her work without fear. Anthony D. King was central in my endeavors to link African art history with studies of urban space and the built environment. Barbara Abou-El-Haj, whom we will miss dearly, was incredibly supportive and informed my work historically and creatively, as did Oscar Vázquez and Jeffner Allen. This project began with Larry McGinnis, who carved a space to make its inception possible and who then validated and expanded my early enthusiasm on the subject. I recognize my former master's advisor Henry Drewal at the University of Wisconsin–Madison, who had and continues to have an enormous impact on the way I research, teach, and talk about African art history with inclusivity, locality, and immediacy.

Great friends and insightful colleagues have sustained this project at its various stages: Penelope Yunker, James Yunker, Raymond Hernandez, Paul Edwards, Onyile B. Onyile, Chloé Georas, Ann Ciola, Fadhili Mshana, Abidin Kusno, Jina Kim, Christine Bianco, Marcia Blackburn, Hong Kal, Colleen McNulty Adour, and Marc Nelson. Salah Hassan's support has been inspirational and valuable since my visiting professorship at Cornell University.

I would like to thank my colleagues at Ohio University for their deep support for, assistance with, and astute advice about this project as they have known me during its revision process: Marina Peterson, Gerard Akindes, Ghirmai Negash, Nick Creary, Nancy Stevens, Steve Howard, Alessandra Raengo, Gillian Berchowitz, Gary Ginther, Kwabena Owusu-Kwarteng, and Ryan DeRosa. I thank the Office of Research at Ohio University for assistance with permissions costs, and the School of Interdisciplinary Arts and Charles Buchanan for generous additional support. And last but not least, I thank my students, virtually all of whom I have taught about the African Burial Ground over the years. Your comments, unabashed remarks, and questions have kept my perspective fresh and renewed my inspiration.

An urban studies reading group at Ohio University reviewed a portion of this manuscript: Mariana Dantas, Marina Peterson, Maria Fanis, Joe McLaughlin. I am grateful for the ongoing advice of Jaap Jacobs, also a member of this group. And finally, I owe an extremely large debt of gratitude to NOLWA (Number One Ladies Writing Agency), a writing support group whose members—African art historians Amanda Carlson, Carol Magee, Shannen Hill, and Cynthia Becker—assisted me greatly during my revision and publishing process. Their ever brilliant comments and more than generous advice were essential for the final formulation of the book! I would also like to add thank you for a separate rigorous peer review from book co-editors Joanna Grabski and Carol Magee, which informed this final project.

In completing the final stages of the manuscript, I am most appreciative of kind, expert guidance from Syracuse University Press, particularly with editors Deanna McCay and Jennika Baines. The astuteness and skill of copyeditor Elizabeth Myers was significant. As cartographer, Amy Rock was unflagging.

I am ever thankful for my family. I would not be who I am today without them: my mother Margaret, my father Vincent, my stepmother Joan, my stepsister Ellie, and my sister Theodora. My daughter's father began this journey offering encouragement and support, and Alexia is witnessing the end result.

THE AFRICAN BURIAL GROUND IN NEW YORK CITY

Introduction

The African Burial Ground is located in the heart of lower Manhattan along Broadway off Duane and Chambers Streets just north of City Hall Park (fig. 1). It is the largest and earliest known cemetery of African descendants in North America. Used approximately from 1712 to 1795, this communal burial space reaches 6.7 acres in size, and it is estimated that more than 15,000 people were interred here.[1]

Long before the cemetery came into use, Africans were first brought to the island of Manhattan in 1626.[2] One known colonial engraving directly illustrates an African presence. By 1790, after Dutch and British colonial importation, enslaved Africans lived in 40 percent of white New York households.[3] By the year 1712 at the latest, a communal African cemetery lay at the edge of town and in a ravine, beyond the surveillance of Europeans. There are no visual representations of the cemetery while it was in use for the next eighty-odd years; yet the sacred site was labeled on four civic maps for reasons connected to city boundaries and land ownership. Then, at the close of the eighteenth century, the African Burial Ground was physically eradicated from existence as Manhattan expanded northward. Several surveys document this division of the African Burial Ground into lots, blocks, and streets between 1787 and 1795, with buildings and streets constructed on it afterwards. Thus, a sacred space was obliterated from visible sight and, over a period of two hundred years, was erased from public memory. During this process, the once-marginalized bodies were gradually covered over by white spaces of the elite government to become what is today the heart of lower Manhattan.

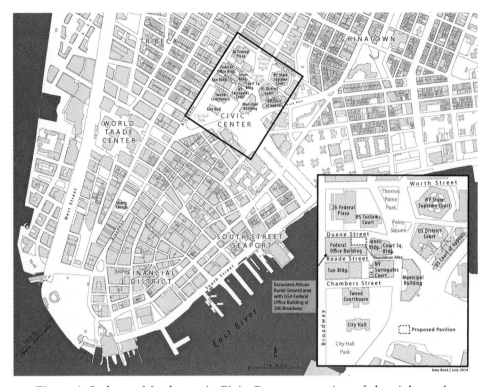

Figure 1. In lower Manhattan's Civic Center, a portion of the eighteenth-century African Burial Ground was excavated at 290 Broadway in the early 1990s. Map by Amy Rock.

Approximate boundaries of the entire African Burial Ground, covering 6.7 acres (outlined in solid and dotted lines, fig. 2),[4] are as follows:

> Northern boundary: Duane Street (north side of the street)
> Southern boundary: Chambers Street (south side of the street)
> Eastern boundary: Centre St/Lafayette Street (west side of the street)
> Western boundary: Broadway (east side of the street)

Republican Alley was virtually undisturbed after it was laid in 1795, and so the burials beneath it remain intact. Because Manhattan was

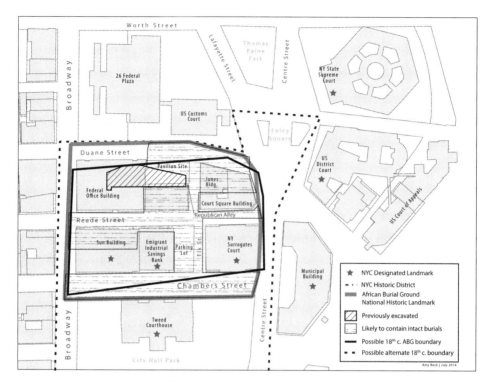

Figure 2. Various boundaries of the African Burial Ground, including excavated land and areas likely to contain intact burials. Map by Amy Rock, adapted from map by Felicia Davis and Lewis Jacobson published in Kaufman (1994, p. 17). Also adapted from map by Kate Frankel, published in "African Burial Ground and the Commons Historic District Designation Report" (1993, fig. 21).

once hilly and then, at the turn of the nineteenth century, was leveled, the burials were covered and protected by 16 to 25 feet of fill, except where foundations, basements, or subways extended into that filled zone.[5]

Once marginalized on the outskirts of the city, today the burial ground is in lower Manhattan's Civic Center (fig. 1), a host of governmental buildings including the Ted Weiss Federal Building, New York Surrogate's Court, Tweed Courthouse, New York City Hall, New York County Courthouse, Foley Square Courthouse, U.S.

Southern District Court, U.S. District Courthouse, U.S. Court of Appeals, One Police Plaza, the Municipal Building, Federal Plaza, the Department of Health, Hospitals, and Sanitation, New York State Family Court, and New York State Department of Motor Vehicles.

The deceased who were buried there faced many challenges and difficulties while they were alive, including malnutrition, lead poisoning, forced manual labor for most ages, and early childhood death. How would these ancestors be treated posthumously? Almost exactly two hundred years after the cemetery was last used for burial, a portion of the forgotten cemetery in Manhatten Burrough Block 154 was exhumed by archaeologists in a sea of disputes, conflicts, and controversies during the 1990s. On top of the burial ground, the federal General Services Administration (GSA) built a $276 million, 34-story office building at 290 Broadway off Duane and Reade Streets (fig. 1 and fig. 3). Initially called the Federal Office Building, the name was changed in 2003 to the Ted Weiss Federal Building after the Hungarian Jewish Congressperson. The rediscovery of the forgotten burial ground was set in motion by legal requirements that salvage archaeology and research be performed prior to any building construction. During construction of this building from 1991 to 1994, digging mistakes were made, such as concrete poured on the eighteenth-century skeletons and mold growth on quickly excavated and improperly stored remains.

From 1991 to 1993, 419 burials were removed from the ground. GSA did not fully perform its lawful obligation to continuously inform and involve its impacted population, African Americans of New York City. Concerned citizens fought and struggled to reverse GSA's treatment of the African Burial Ground through activism, vigils, and demonstrations from the early 1990s into the 2000s. I attended public updates, open houses, and hearings from 1996 to 2003. The activism transformed a once-marginalized chapter in African and African American history into a local and national issue involving mayors of New York City, members of Congress, and presidents of the United States. Following a decade of political battle, as well as scientific research at Howard University, the exhumed remains were eventually reburied on the site in 2003.

Figure 3. LCOR/HOK, Ted Weiss Federal Building (formerly Federal Office Building) at 290 Broadway, 1991–94. Constructed on a portion of the African Burial Ground at a cost of $276 million by the U.S. General Services Administration. Photo by Andrea Frohne.

Over the years, artworks have been commissioned to commemorate the space both in the lobby of the GSA office building and outside of it. Artists such as Houston Conwill, Lorenzo Pace, Barbara Chase-Riboud, and Tomie Arai honor the ancestors through representations of African art and cosmology and African American history.

This book explores the cemetery through analyses of both colonial and contemporary representation. Colonial era maps, prints, and land surveys (some of which were newly uncovered during archival research for this book) visually elucidate forgotten, hidden histories of a mostly enslaved population buried in the African Burial Ground in New York. These documents are considered in relation to slavery, land, production of wealth, and urban development. Contemporary commemorative artworks and personal offerings have become visual representations of the African Burial Ground in the context of honored ancestors and reclaimed sacred space. In sum, I explore the visuality of the African Burial Ground by considering how it was initially forgotten and obliterated and then eventually manifested, engaged, and remembered. A consistently occurring production of spirituality that is African-based is traced through both the colonial and contemporary eras. This spirituality underpins the narrative and the discourse of the African Burial Ground project as a whole.

Generally speaking, the book focuses on the intricate and imbricated issues of space, spirituality, and memory at the African Burial Ground. The history and identity of the space is understood as processes of diasporization, contestation, racialization, and politicization. Through these histories, the space was engaged as sacred—often as African-based—to honor the dead. This space of spirituality is remembered, reclaimed, and reengaged through a pan-African articulation that acknowledges a holistic Africa. I suggest that ultimately the site is incorporated into the New York City and United States body politic. The triangulation of these three notions—space, spirituality, and memory—reveals how the African Burial Ground is represented visually, spiritually, and spatially in New York City.

Space

The African Burial Ground can be understood through studies of space from varying perspectives and time periods. Examples include a geography of racism in the colonial era, with emphases on international maps and local land surveys depicting slavery and European American land ownership. Based on 1990s excavations, a mapping of the underground geography of coffins (stratigraphy) reveals burials three layers deep. Finally, a late twentieth-century contestation of space is detailed to understand an African diasporic site commemorated by over half a dozen government commissioned artworks within New York City.

The African Burial Ground project necessarily grapples with the notion of diaspora in relation to space. It is less useful to talk about one monolithic transatlantic diaspora and more realistic to recognize diasporas of different kinds and types that exist in the plural.[6] The book considers the formation of a New York City African diaspora through the manifestation and representation of the African Burial Ground.

This project is not a search for Africa in the New World. Such research can be found by groundbreaking scholars writing in earlier models of African diaspora studies who traced the transference of specific African cultures to the Americas. As carefully explored in chapter 3, very few of the New York funerary remains can be matched to specific cultures of Africa.

This book instead provides the reverse: it is a looking back from the United States to Africa, with a focus on New York City. How is Africa represented in New York? What are the iterations of Africa in North America? I consider how this particular urban diaspora is articulated, spatialized, and manifested through the lens of the African Burial Ground. My twelve years of primary research in New York City have led me to posit that the burial ground is being reclaimed, and that this reclamation occurs through a homogeneous reference to the African world with less of an emphasis on cultural specificity.

In this way, the book offers an alternative intervention for diaspora studies. At the African Burial Ground, a general Africa is recognized and embraced. Africa must therefore be understood in a general sense. Historian Erik Seeman has identified such a model of scholarship that explores "a broader poetics or sensibility that Africans carried with them when forcibly brought to the Americas."[7] Within a generalized Africa is encapsulated a seemingly romanticized nostalgia of homeland. James Clifford rightfully frames the phenomenon in the following way: "Diaspora cultures mediate in a lived tension, the experiences of separation and entanglement, of living here and remembering/desiring another place."[8] At a time when academic scholarship is conceptualizing the notion of diaspora more along the lines of the transnational, what I found in New York could be understood as essentialized. It is nevertheless through this diasporic identity that empowerment, resistance, and unity were harnessed[9] and garnered toward respectful treatment of the ancestors. It is that general Africa that empowers and resists, which precisely grounds and ties the New York African diaspora to Africa. Indeed, a large percentage of the cemetery population was born in Africa, so the deceased become a direct link between Africa and North America; between Africans and some of the first African Americans; and finally between obfuscated ancestors and descendant New York City diasporans.

This diasporic space saw years of turmoil, activism, conflict, and contestation. Such politicization of space is explored in this book. Chidester and Linenthal emphasize that "ownership [of sacred space] will always be at stake. In this respect, a sacred space is not merely discovered, or founded, or constructed; it is claimed, owned, and operated by people advancing specific interests . . . The analysis of sacred space in America, therefore, will require not only attention to how space has been ritualized and interpreted but also to how it has been appropriated, contested, and 'stolen' back and forth in struggles over power in America."[10] Additionally, Don Mitchell aptly notes, "Indeed, in the contemporary world, there is not a space that is not saturated with the poisoned blood of 'race' through and through."[11] The flows and frictions of the space defined by the African Burial Ground inevitably involve narratives and counternarratives, sometimes with collective resolutions and other times with fragmented dissention.

The word and concept "space" is selected over place for several reasons. Among its many definitions, place is defined as occupied, embodied, and with definite boundaries situated in a specific location.[12] Space on the other hand is characteristically demarcated as ever-mutable, unstable, and in production.[13] As something that is not fixed or static, space is "constructed and produced and is a social experience."[14] Thus, the notion as used here recognizes the indeterminacy of the African Burial Ground. With its immaterial, spiritual component, the physical space necessarily extends to the metaphysical, or the realm of the ancestors. It is a space that is still being defined through the process of reclamation where memories continue to be formulated.[15]

Like the physical and metaphysical space of the burial ground, indeterminacy surrounds birth origins of Africans who lived and died in New York. Few of the funerary remains can be traced to a specific point of origin on the one hand, while a homogeneous process of honoring the dead developed in New York on the other. A great majority of interred bodies were oriented to the west, wrapped in white shrouds and pinned with copper pins, and placed in wooden coffins without any names. Various sacred objects included a shell/nail combination placed on a few coffin lids or conjuring bundles of spheres, quartz, and round disks inside the coffins. One older woman wore around her waist a string of blue and gold beads with cowrie shells, with an unused clay pipe placed beneath her. Two burials contained beads manufactured in Ghana.

Historical documentation offers a general understanding from where in Africa the enslaved originated and what African-based spiritualities were brought to the New York diaspora. When New Amsterdam was under Dutch control (1626–64), the majority of Africans were brought from Angola, the Kongo area, Guinea, Calabar in Nigeria, the Gold Coast (now Ghana), and Curaçao. The

Dutch colony of New Amsterdam was renamed New York City under the British (1664–1776), who transported Africans primarily from Madagascar, Jamaica, Barbados, and Antigua. The points of origin from Africa to the Caribbean under the British included Calabar, Guinea, Angola, the Kongo area, and the Gold Coast. The slave population reached 3,137 by 1771 and comprised 14.3 percent of New York residents. By 1790, blacks comprised nearly one-quarter of the urban population.[16] This proved to be the highest number of enslaved blacks outside of South Carolina during the eighteenth century. Enslaved people in New York City did not work on plantations, as was typical of southern labor, but helped to build the physical infrastructure of the city. As confirmed by the African Burial Ground, ports in the north were spaces of slavery, too.

Spirituality

The production of spirituality at the African Burial Ground has been fundamental to the reclamation and recuperation of the site. First and foremost, as a cemetery, the space is naturally sacred. Second, the site serves as a contemporary space of spirituality, where communication with and veneration of the ancestors has been quintessential for activists, artists, scientists, educators, and the African Burial Ground project as a whole. Activists and concerned citizens called upon the ancestors throughout public meetings, hearings, and vigils related to the site. Shrines were communally built while burials were excavated. Over the years, the ancestors have received written messages and personal offerings from the living that I recorded such as flowers, drinks, fruits, and coins. Finally, the commemorative arts incorporate African spirit worlds into them.

Spirituality of space is a phrase that provides a means for focusing on the sacred space through an African-based lens of the spirit world. It takes into account a personal or collective interaction, recognition, or reference to a spiritual entity in a specific space—that of the African Burial Ground. I purposefully recognize the word "spirit" within spirituality to indicate that the space contains or refers to spirits and also to emphasize interaction between the spirit world and the physical realm. The word *spirituality* is used rather than *religion* so that the concept is not limited to organized religion, or religion as institution, but rather includes a broad spectrum of understanding. In sum, conjoining spirituality with space grounds the metaphysical in the physical space of the African Burial Ground, allowing tensions concerning reclamation, recognition, and respect to emerge.

Because genealogical lineage was fatefully erased through the slave trade, many New York African Americans reconceived all of the deceased in the African Burial Ground as ancestors. It is crucial to contextualize spirituality of space at the African Burial Ground as pan-African. Through such a lens, spirituality is generalized in terms of a homogenous Africa.

In contrast to the New York diaspora, overarching African commonalities differ for how a person becomes an ancestor. Although beliefs and practices in ancestral veneration vary and are not found in all African communities nor practiced by all individuals, typically the person dies a natural death. While living, they should abide by and pass down laws left by their own ancestors, they should bear children to leave descendants, and they should maintain active relationships between the living and the dead.[17] Elders who have entered the next world continue to be members of a family, retain knowledge they acquired in life, and may be reborn into that family again.[18]

All of the deceased in New York have been elevated to the ancestral rank because they or their relatives suffered through the Middle Passage to become the rare yet often-sought direct link to Africa. A portion of the population was born in New York, of whom a high percentage were infants and youth. Additionally, anyone today could be a blood relative of the deceased because of obliterated genealogies. Accordingly, many engaged in the project used the term "descendant," or the "descendant community," of Africans from the burial ground.

Such an understanding of the ancestor originating from a general pan-Africa necessarily becomes a kind of essentializing conception of the spirit world. Any specificity to place or culture is not relevant or even possible. Thus, the ancestors at the African Burial Ground represent Africa as a whole rather than a particular family lineage, masquerade, cultural group, or tradition. The ancestor is instead a link to African identity and memory, with general geographic location being key. As an example, Afrocentric scholar Dona Marimba Richards writes about an African diasporic world view "that inherited its spirituality from the African heritage. . . . African culture is amazingly resilient. In spite of the most culturally destructive force in history, it has not disappeared. We are the bearers of that culture. We are a deeply spiritual people. The powerful indication of our African ancestry lies in our spirituality."[19] The looming presence of the New York ancestors at the end of the twentieth century, so pervasively felt, discussed, and visually represented, reiterates the African Burial Ground as a space of spirituality.

In using the title "ancestor," New Yorkers acknowledge the fluidity between the lands of the living and dead and the possibility for communication between the two. A look at specific African contexts illustrates the tenets of spirituality so crucial to honoring the New York ancestors. The ancestors provide benefits and advice to the living in exchange for being honored with libations and sacrifices. Interaction between the two worlds is fluid and not necessarily separate. Malidoma Patrice Somé, a Dagara of Burkina Faso, explains that "[i]n Western reality, there is a clear split between the spiritual and the material, between religious life and secular life. This concept is alien to the Dagara. For us, as for many indigenous cultures, the supernatural is part of our everyday lives. To a Dagara man or woman, the material is just the spiritual taking on form."[20] W. Emmanuel Abraham writes that Akan practitioners in Ghana do not recognize a bridge or distance between the worlds; rather, the two are part of a continuous reality.[21] The spirit world is not a realm outside or beyond human experience.[22] When an Igbo elder in Nigeria was asked how he could be sure of the reality of the living and dead, he answered, "It is evident," it is a lived reality.[23]

Yorùbá, Akan, and Kongo Cosmologies

This book concerns iterations of Africa in New York that are approached from African world views. In order to conceptually understand the general nature of African-based productions of spirituality at the burial ground, three specific cosmologies of Africa are briefly summarized here to ground the general in specific examples. Yorùbá, Akan, and Kongo cosmologies are relevant because they are powerfully incorporated into the cemetery's commemorative artworks as North American iterations. Also, burials likely contain funerary objects from these areas. Finally, the cosmological frameworks discussed here continue to be practiced and reformulated within Africa as well as its diasporas, including New York, to this day.

Yorùbá, Akan, and Kongo cosmologies are not presented as a truth or as one fixed notion of a spirit world. Also, it is not presumed that all people from the African continent ascribe to indigenous cosmological systems. Instead, interpretations of specific indigenous world views reveal African-based perspectives that are highly relevant to the burial ground. These world views consist of recognition of an ancestral realm, communication between humans and ancestors, and the inclusion of death and rebirth in a cyclical understanding of time.

Yorùbá

Yorùbá-based cosmology is incorporated into a quarter of the commemorative artworks at the African Burial Ground, with a particular emphasis on the crossroads and the òrìshà (deity) named Èsù. The cosmos can be conceived by Yorùbá people as a large crossroads with two general realms that are separate, yet inextricably entwined. *Ayé* constitutes the visible, physical world and *òrun* forms the largely invisible, spiritual realm of ancestors and deities, or òrìshà.[24] The living can request support and guidance from the ancestors, and òrìshà are deified ancestors or are associated with natural forces. The genderless Olódùmarè (or Olórun) is the Supreme Being and creator of both worlds who instructed the òrìshà Obàtálá to leave òrun and create human life in ayé.[25] Major Yoruba òrìshà with specific characteristics and attributes include:

Èsù	crossroads trickster, communicator, mediator
Obàtálá	divine sculptor
Ògún	iron and war
Òshóòsì	hunter
Obalúayé	for sickness and healing
Òsanyìn	leaves and medicines
Oya	the whirlwind and cemetery
Yemoja	river/ocean and motherhood
Òsun	river and love
Shàngó	thunder and lightning

Acts of the òrìshà are the actualization of *àse*, as determined by their personality or *iwa*.[26] Àse is the energy that assists in making things "come to pass," as might be requested in divination. It is defined as a life-force or performative power, and an "essence in which physical materials, metaphysical concepts and art blend to form the energy or life-force that is activating and directing sociopolitical, religious, and artistic processes and experiences."[27] It is present in a variety of things, such as animals, plants, rocks, rivers, humans, prayers, praise songs, òrìshà, òrìshà altars, ancestors, and spirits. Thus àse is an energy of a spiritual nature that exists on earth.

Yorùbá are a people who comprise one of the three largest cultural groups in Nigeria and they live mainly in the southern half of Nigeria and also the neighboring countries of Togo and Benin.[28] They are prevalent in African diasporas as so many enslaved people were taken from this area to places all over the world including Haiti, Cuba, Puerto Rico, Brazil, Trinidad and Tobago, with more recent immigrants to Miami and New York City. Yorùbá cosmology begins with the sacred city of Ife, the ancient ancestral home and the location of the first sacred kingship or *oba*. All other rulers descended from this first oba named Odùdúwà, and the lineage remains unbroken today. According to archaeological excavation, the city of Ife existed at least by 800 CE.

Akan

Akan people (the linguistic name for a group of people who live in central and southern Ghana and parts of Côte d'Ivoire) were brought to New York during the slave trade, as is evident from nine beads that were made in Ghana in Burials 226 and 221 and from the possible presence of a sankofa on a coffin lid on Burial 101. Several of the commemorative artworks revolve thematically around the sankofa. More recently people from Ghana and Côte d'Ivoire have emigrated to New York City during the past century, with continuations of traditions such as swearing-in ceremonies for new *Asantehenes* (rulers) and Queen Mothers in Manhattan.

Akan people recognize a Supreme Being named Nyame, who is the creator of everyone and everything, seen and unseen. Attesting to Nyame, omnipresent and all-pervasive, a proverb states, "If you want to tell God anything tell the wind."[29] Like Nyame, wind is intangible, but its effects are visible all around you.[30] Akan people use this analogy for other spirit entities as well. They are ever conscious of the spirit world, recognizing that spirits, the physical world, nature, and society are dynamically interrelated, whether visible or not.[31]

The essence of Nyame is generally present among humans through the *abosom*, or deities.[32] The abosom were created by Nyame and also have their own identities, as is evident from their shrines and varying modes of human veneration. Some spirits are recognized as dwelling in particular rivers or trees. Stones or living trees and plants are not considered inanimate, but their existence can be defined through the state of being or having *sunsum*. Sunsum is the spirit or essential defining component that pervades both living and inanimate objects and derives from Nyame.[33]

Ancestors are a crucial component to Akan metaphysics. They are honored locally in household shrines and are quite person-like, living close to the realm of humans and continuing to be members of the family left behind.[34] Ancestors protect, watch over, and advise the living, and they can be called upon by trained priests to effect a change or settle a dispute in a client's life. In return, the living offer libations and invite them to participate in family or community affairs.[35] Ancestors can reincarnate if they wish, usually electing to return to their families, although they are not bound to do so.[36] Thus, for Akan people, the spirit world is not a realm outside or beyond human experience. They do not recognize a bridge or distance between two worlds but view the two as part of a continuous reality.

Akan spiritual traditions arrived in the diaspora not only through the slave trade but with contemporary transnational flows as well. An African American renamed Nana Dinizulu consciously sought his identity by regaining lost memories through divination and fostering direct spiritual connections with Africa. He was guided to Ghana in the 1960s to find his ancestral roots and visited the Akonedi Shrine in Larteh for further divination. After some time, he transported shrines to New York and established them there, including a branch of the Akonedi Shrine.[37]

Kongo

Kongo cosmology is incorporated into two contemporary artworks commemorating the African Burial Ground and is likely related to excavated New York City funerary objects such as *minkisi*-like bundles (sacred bundles in containers) in Burial 147, a blue spiral inside the bottom of a ceramic pot in Burial 328, shell and iron nail groupings on top of coffins, and spheres including buttons and round discs in several graves. Also, although perhaps predating the burial ground, three males brought to New York in 1626 with the names Simon Congo, Gratia D'Angola, and Paulo Angola illustrate Kongolese area origins.

Among the Kongolese, *bisimbi* are helpful ancestors. Petitions can be communicated to the bisimbi by means of minkisi, or power objects. Minkisi take the form of containers such as pottery, gourds, shells, or bundles, and they contain grave soil, leaves, white river clay, pieces of iron, quartz, seeds, and stones. Some minkisi, as described above, were likely excavated from the African Burial Ground. An *nganga* or divination specialist who mediates between the land of the living and dead activates the minkisi. It is by this means that ancestors can be asked to alter events within the realm of the living.

Nzambi is the name of the Supreme Creator for the Kongo. Nzambi made all things including the earth, sky, humans, and minkisi.[38] There are two interrelated realms that define Kongo cosmology. Half constitutes the living, and half comprises the dead, with a body of water called *kalunga* separating the two. Kalunga is a supreme force and energy of the universe that creates and transforms. As water, kalunga operates simultaneously as a barrier and as a passage.

Kongo refers to a Bantu-speaking group of people who are culturally, linguistically, spiritually, and historically related. The Kongo was a large kingdom that stretched from what is today Angola to Congo to the Democratic Republic of the Congo (formerly Zaire). Some of the largest numbers of Africans were taken from here to the New World during the slave trade.[39]

Ancestor veneration and cosmologies among Yorùbá, Akan, and Kongo peoples exemplify major conceptual and metaphysical issues surrounding the African Burial Ground project. It is therefore one of the aims of this book to foreground Africa, to maintain it as the focus of the African Burial Ground project. Africa becomes necessarily reconfigured in the New York diaspora in rich and complex ways. For instance, commemorative artworks highlight the Mande Ciwara, Yorùbá Ifá divination tray, Yorùbá crossroads, Akan sankofa, and Kongo cosmogram. Thus, the burial ground is represented as a space of spirituality through honoring the ancestors and incorporating African spirit worlds into the commemorative arts.

The research project that I undertook became a journey yielding a personal story of spirituality. As I began my doctoral studies at Binghamton University, a recurring dream prompted me to visit New York City. I returned with a brochure from the Guggenheim Museum, wherein I saw a small paragraph about the African Burial Ground and a shocking photograph of a skeleton. I made a decision to write on this topic and that night dreamed of entering open graves at the African Burial Ground. In the dream, the skeleton itself was gone from one grave, but its spirit resided there. Another ancestor—an African in New York who had come from Brazil—showed me her grave, which contained a wooden (Christian) cross with her name on it. A month later, I dreamt of more graves, this time at the bottom of the ocean, with additional graves on the beach under the sand. In this dream, an ancestor expressed a strong desire to be buried and great despair that it had not yet occurred. The periodic presence of these ancestors throughout my research helped to keep me dedicated to the project, reminding me of urgent issues at hand.

As recounted in chapter 4, others have communicated with the ancestors from time to time or vice versa. The reburial ceremony in 2003 was especially dramatic with so many focused on honoring and reburying the dead, making the presence of the ancestors extremely palpable during an all-night vigil. Such realities, combined with the representations of spirit worlds in the artworks, become articulations of the interrelationships between physical and metaphysical spaces, or the spirituality of space, at the African Burial Ground.

Memory

With so many gaps in information about the African Burial Ground, concerned citizens and committed government officials fought vociferously for the production of memory at the site. I argue that contemporary commemoration, personal offerings, and political contestation necessarily became a means for representing, recuperating, and recalling the burial ground. I attended hearings, open houses, vigils, and performative events in which it was insisted that the burial ground be discussed, treated, and understood from African perspectives.

I have found that the primary narrative framing the African Burial Ground project as a whole is pan-African, a return to Africa (at times a homogeneous one) that includes and unites arts, cultures, and spiritualities in the diaspora. Many of the commemorative artworks analyzed in chapters 5 and 6 include African arts (Mande Ciwara, Yorùbá Ifá divination tray, Kongo cosmogram, Egyptian neckrest, Akan adinkra) as a means for recalling and extending Africa into contemporary Manhattan. The arts become mnemonic representations of the burial ground itself because there is little or no possibility for its exact reconstruction or reproduction. This parallels Hodgkin and Radstone's assertion that the past is constituted in narrative, but always through representation and through construction.[40]

I argue the African Burial Ground is now inevitably interconnected to the body politic through intricate relationships of space, history, and power. For instance, the final exterior memorial (2007) stands as the first national monument dedicated to people of African descent, thereby rendering it representative of both the city and the nation's historic fabric. This example of shared memory illustrates the tensions over politics of memory, space, and race that played out over decades. It also affirms that people's relationship to the burial ground remains in a state of process and flux as the production of memory, space, and spirituality shift and metamorphose.

The Doctors' Riot of 1788

When the African Burial Ground was still in use in the late eighteenth century, Columbia medical students looted bodies from it, and then from the Trinity Church burial ground a twelve minute walk to the south. The egregious bodysnatching thefts led to the Doctors' Riot of 1788, which encapsulates in a dramatic way the three intertwined themes of space, spirituality, and memory explored in this book. The details of this event illustrate racial contestations over sacred space as mourners attempted to preserve memory of the deceased yet found that their voices were silenced. Africans and descendant Africans submitted a petition protesting against the thefts on 4 February

1788 to the City Council that was never recorded.[41] It stands as one of the very few documents in existence written by eighteenth-century Africans in New York. The document recounts desecration and disregard of sacred space:

> [Free negroes and slaves, in a petition to the common council complain that] it hath lately been the constant Practice of a Number of Young Gentlemen in this City who call themselves Students of Physick, to repair to the Burying Ground assigned for the use of your Petitioners, and under cover of the Night, and in the most wanton Sallies of Excess, to dig up the Bodies of the deceased friends and relatives of your Petitioners, carry them away, and without respect to Age or Sex, mangle their flesh out of a wanton Curiosity and then expose it to Beasts and Birds. That your Petitioners are well aware of the necessity of Phisicians and Surgeons consulting dead Subjects for the Benefit of Mankind, and are far from presupposing it and Injury to the Deceased, in particular Circumstances and when conducting with that decency and Propriety which the Solemnity of such an Occasion requires. [We ask the board to adopt measures] to prevent similar Abuses in future.[42]

Indeed, scientific analysis of skeletal remains excavated in the twentieth century verifies that at least Burials 323 and 364 were disturbed by grave robbers and reburied after dissection by medical students. A freed African American leader wrote two letters to the *New-York Daily Advertiser* to further raise concern in the city. On 16 February 1788, the author asked that, "a stop might be put to this horrid practice here; and the mind of a very great number of my fellow-liberated, or still enslaved Blacks quieted."[43]

The bodysnatching fiasco was no longer ignored when the medical students' ambition took them to Trinity Church to dig up white people's graves in that churchyard. This discovery occurred two months after the African Burial Ground petition, when a boy looking through the window of the New York Hospital witnessed a dissection table and complained to his father.

With tools in hand, the father (whose wife was indeed missing from her grave) and his mason coworkers began what would be called the Doctors' Riot on 13–14 April 1788 involving five thousand people. They stormed the New York Hospital and city jail where medical students were placed for protection.[44] The militia was called upon and eventually ordered to fire. At least three people were killed and several wounded.[45]

Such a circumstance illustrates complex politics of space, race, and power and questions of class and race in both of the sacred spaces. Trinity Church was purposefully built at the head of Wall Street to oversee the financial center, and it remains in a position of power and economic wealth to this day. How is it that a largely European American space of power remains until today sacred and protected so that legible gravestones bear people's names, dates of birth and death, and details of their lives, in contrast to the African Burial Ground where no such records exist? Only grave robbing from the Trinity Church cemetery triggered the Doctors' Riot, although the thefts had been ongoing in the African Burial Ground prior to that. In comparison, the black petition written to beseech protection of a marginalized sacred space from the Columbia body snatchers ended up lost and unrecorded. Such racialization of space would force the question, how would the recently unearthed sacred and historic site be honored and remembered?

Trinity Church historically outlawed African graves (as I discuss in chapter 1) and buried its slave owners. Ironically, the church became a key rallying point for a New York town meeting held in 1992 by local politicians and angered citizens to discuss disrespectful treatment of the African Burial Ground. The community event was an early example of the ambitious struggle and resistance that would continue for roughly fifteen more years toward the reversal of inequity and amnesia with insistence upon respectful treatment and memorialization. Through activism, honoring the ancestors, and the commemorative process that ended in 2007, the African Burial Ground indeed seems to have become a part of the body politic, if tenuously. This book then traces the varied transformations of the space of the African Burial Ground, from when it was first depicted in 1679 by Danckaerts to when the national monument by Rodney Léon opened in 2007, capturing highs and lows, losses and victories, via the intricate relationships of space, spirituality, and memory.

1

Colonial Prints
and Civic Cartographies

Space, Race, and the Colony: Early Africans

During the seventeenth and eighteenth centuries, colonial maps and
prints of New Amsterdam and New York City were produced for
European or local dissemination. The first part of this chapter discusses depictions of a general African presence for a European audience from a European point of view. The history of why Africans
were brought to the area is embedded in the imagery. Shaped by
international politics of space, race, labor, and commodification, the
images encouraged settlement of the land by Europeans and production of wealth by Africans through forced labor. As such, the African
body was erased or marginalized in visual culture of the seventeenth
and eighteenth centuries. A geography of racism emerges through the
exploration of these European colonial representations of early Africans in New York. The visually articulated racism emphasizes the
difficult realities that Africans and people of African descent faced.
Detailed analyses are made of a 1642 New Amsterdam print, the
Visscher Map (1650), and the Seutter Map (ca. 1725–30) in order
to explore visual representation as well as obfuscation of a colonial
African presence. These images offer the only known illustrations of
New York Africans in the colonial era.

The second part of this chapter, in contrast, concerns visual representations produced specifically in New Amsterdam/New York
City for local dissemination. Several maps were drawn to represent

the city. Only four included the African Burial Ground, three of which were produced by local cartographers. Representation of the African Burial Ground space is traced through an analysis of this civic cartography. Also through my spatial inquiry, a history of how the African Burial Ground came into existence is formulated. Each one of these four civic maps—Mrs. Buchnerd's Plan (1735), Maerschalck Plan (1755 and 1763), Major Kirkham's Plan of New York (1807), and Grim Plan (1813, representation of city in 1742–44)—is analyzed in detail to consider how, why, and by whom the burial ground was demarcated.

Arrival of Africans

The first eleven enslaved males were brought to New Amsterdam in 1626. The names of each of the eleven were recorded in 1644 when they requested their freedom from the Dutch West India Company;[1] however, names of the approximately 15,000 people buried in the African Burial Ground remain unknown to this day. Although the eleven may predate the existence of the communal cemetery, their records offer information about the African origins they may have shared with those in the burial ground. Anthony Portuguese, Simon Congo, Big (Groot) Manuel, Little Manuel, Peter Santomee, Manuel de Gerrit de Reus, Gratia D'Angola, Jan Francisco, Little Antonio, Jan Fort Orange, and Paulo Angola reflect the powerful trading alliances that existed between today's Congo, Angola, and Portugal. Because African leaders converted to Christianity, names could have been changed before enslaved people were taken from their African homeland while they were still in the Congo or Angola.[2] The Christianized names include Simon, Paulo, Peter, Antonio, Jan (Dutch for John), and Manuel (variation of Immanuel). Whether the names were changed there or in the New World, at least three if not more of the eleven came from central Africa (Simon Congo, Gratia D'Angola, Paulo Angola). Peter Santomee's name reflects Africa or its early diaspora: Santomee could be the phonetic spelling for the African island of Saõ Tomé, which the Portuguese occupied and the Dutch conquered to use for the slave trade, or it could be St. Thomas in the Virgin Islands.[3]

As well as African origins, Jan Fort Orange's name relates to his experience in the Americas. Fort Orange was the early settlement that would become Albany. After arriving in New Amsterdam, Jan may have moved to Fort Orange.[4] West India Company Africans in Fort Orange were then sent back to New Amsterdam around 1639. The names of Jan's family were also Christianized, with continued central African influence. Upon Jan's return, he married Magdalena Van Angola and they had a child Maria who was baptized in the Dutch Reformed Church. Van Angola may have been one of the first three African women in the area. Three women from Angola were in the colony in 1628 (another of whom was called Mayken).

Enslaved Africans were brought to New York to build the infrastructure of the settlements while Europeans focused largely on the fur trade. New York City came into existence because of the beaver and its fur, which was considered a valuable commodity and the height of fashion in northern Europe. Furs were used as trim on clothing, and as hats and cloaks. Also, beaver oil was used to cure rheumatism, stomach disorders, weak eyesight, toothaches, and dizziness.[5]

The Dutch West India Company (WIC) initiated the settlement by sending thirty families in 1624 to New Netherland to capitalize on the fur trade. These families were mostly Walloons, or French-speaking Protestants. The 110 exiles sailed on the ship the *Nieuw Nederlandt* and settled mainly at Fort Orange (now Albany). In 1625, another fleet of ships carrying forty-two immigrants and livestock arrived. In 1626, the new director, Willem Verhulst, gathered the people scattered throughout New Netherland and brought them to New Amsterdam. The town would be renamed New York City with the 1664 British takeover.

When the WIC realized that new European immigrants were focused on the lucrative fur trade rather than on building the infrastructure of their settlement, it sought alternative means for labor to perform such duties.[6] From 1626 to 1652, the WIC pirated Africans off Spanish and Portuguese ships.[7] Ultimately, piracy would account for between one-quarter and one-third of enslaved people in New Netherland before 1655.[8] As a result, many spoke Portuguese or Spanish. For instance, a 1662 court proceeding in New Amsterdam noted that an enslaved person belonging to Cornelis Steenwijck answered in Portuguese.[9] New Amsterdam in the seventeenth century became a diverse settlement with half of its population originating from places outside of the Netherlands. A traveler in 1643 noted that among a New Netherland population of 904, places of origin included Germany, France, Spanish Netherlands (Belgium), Denmark, Sweden, Norway, and Poland, and at least eighteen languages were spoken.[10]

Geographies of Racism

Africans in Nieu Amsterdam Print, 1642–43

The early engraving depicting the years 1642–43 was one of the very few that illustrated the institution of slavery in the northern United States (fig. 4). In fact, no other views of New Amsterdam or colonial New York explicitly depict, as this print does, enslaved people, 15,000 of whom would be interred in the burial ground beginning roughly three-quarters of a century later. We witness here not only the institution of slavery, but also the involuntary formation of an African diaspora.

In figure 4, two Africans are situated at the bottom left, and two others in the center middle-ground carry the harvest on their heads. This was typically an African mode of transporting objects, and the artist has captured a practice that enslaved people continued in the New World. As will be discussed in chapter 3, researchers found that the necks of both adults and children from the African Burial Ground had borne very heavy loads, sometimes to the point of disfigurement. The cityscape behind the figures depicts the WIC warehouses where Africans lived and labored. Ships stressed commercial success at New Amsterdam's busy port of call. Overall, the scene

Figure 4. Unknown artist, *Nieu Amsterdam*, 1642–43. Copper engraving, 7⁷⁄₁₆ × 9¹³⁄₁₆. In this colonial era print depicting an early African presence, two people are engaged in labor by carrying loads on their heads. This practice was corroborated by skeletal anthropologists who analyzed the deceased in the African Burial Ground. I. N. Phelps Stokes Collection, Miriam and Ira D. Wallach Division of Art, Prints, and Photographs, The New York Public Library, Astor, Lenox and Tilden Foundations.

illustrates labor, commerce, the production of wealth, and colonized territory as a racialized geography.

In the piece, the enslaved are seen as diminutive in relation to the giant Dutch couple in the foreground. The Europeans are fully and well-dressed, while the Africans are bare-chested. This visual representation perpetuated the stereotype of the dichotomy that "primitive" people do not clothe themselves and "civilized" Europeans do. If it were summer, the enslaved may have in fact worked in such clothing, but they would certainly have had to be fully covered during the New York winters. In contrast, the Dutch man wears not only long pants and a long-sleeved coat buttoned all the way to the neck, but also a cloak of animal fur—certainly impractical clothing for a New York summer. Additionally, the Dutchman has his arm extended in a broad gesture that lands in the center of the engraving to survey the wealth: a new colony and Africans working.[11] To complete the scene, he holds a tobacco leaf of the New World in his hand. Processed leaves wrapped around spindles are gathered behind his feet. The artist has shown the wealth of Europeans with key commodities of animal, fur, and tobacco at the expense of the enslaved, thereby constructing the superior and inferior based on class and race.

The *Nieu Amsterdam* engraving was published in *Cities and Costumes of the Inhabited World* (*Orbis habitabilis oppida et vestitus*) by Carolus Allard in Amsterdam ca. 1700.[12] This volume featured views of one hundred cities, many concentrated in Europe. As a kind of encyclopedic book of knowledge, the images conveyed authenticity of people and cityscapes around the world. They were of course constructed and imagined to varying degrees. In fact, the couple and the slaves in figure 4 were recycled to serve as scenes for other geographic places. Engraver Aldert Meijer excerpted and appropriated the New Amsterdam view for the completely different Barbados entry in the same *Cities and Costumes* book. The four enslaved Africans from figure 4 remain visually present in the Barbados view, while the Dutch are transformed to British through a title change; the plate is renamed *English Quakers and Tobacco Planters in Barbados* (*Engelse Quakers en Tabak Planters in Barbados*). Yet another appropriation of the six people shown in this image occurred when Aldert Meijer's Barbados engraving was reworked for new subject matter in Pieter van der Aa's book *Les Forces de l'Europe, Asie, Afrique et Amerique* in 1726. The volume focused on town plans, fortifications, and views of principal cities.[13] To summarize, one engraving directly representing Africans becomes a generic image for the institution of slavery under the British and in the Caribbean, and is reproduced and republished by printmakers throughout Europe for at least a quarter of a century if not more.

As well as illustrating the institution of slavery in the northern United States, figure 4 narrates the very early formation of an African diaspora. Those enslaved by the West India Company worked on six large boweries, or farms, which supplied produce to the colony under the Dutch.[14] They carried animal pelts to WIC ships, worked as deckhands, and loaded and unloaded ships.[15] Some of the enslaved became skilled laborers such as caulkers, blacksmiths, bricklayers, and masons.[16] Others cut wood, erected buildings, split palisades, burned lime, cleared and farmed land, made fences and roads, maintained the fort, and mended oxcarts.[17] Until 1640, European settlers typically hired Africans from the WIC or from one of the few private owners of slaves for seasonal work.[18] This work involved farming, gardening, cleaning, laundering, cooking, raising children, and shopping in the market.[19]

Between 1644 and 1658, an estimated 1,208 Africans were brought to New Amsterdam.[20] After the British took over in 1664, the slave trade increased greatly. In 1703, approximately 700 Africans lived in New York, which was 14.4 percent of the population.[21] In 1746, 2,444 slaves (20.9 percent of the population) and 9,273 Europeans and European descendants lived together. The slave population peaked at 3,137 by 1771. In 1790, 3,470 people, 2,369 of whom were enslaved and the rest free, lived among a total population of 33,131. Nineteen percent of these Europeans/European Americans had enslaved Africans or African descendants.[22] Finally, the black population in New York in 1800 was 5,867, with 3,333 free and 2,534 enslaved.

The Dutch version of slavery in New Amsterdam differed from slavery elsewhere. The Dutch church recognized and recorded African marriages and baptisms. Africans or African Americans could bring cases to court or serve as witnesses against whites.[23] They owned land and bought their freedom from the WIC in old age. Some were paid wages for their work. In fact, five Africans or those of African descent travelled to Holland to resolve their salaries of eight guilders per month, which equaled the low end of white laborers.[24] A stricter and more repressive treatment would develop when the British took control. While the African Burial Ground probably came into use under the British, the two models of slavery accentuate the harsh lives the enslaved experienced under British rule, as will be seen in the following chapters.

Africans in the Visscher Map,
ca. 1648 and the Seutter Map, 1740

Early views and cartography of New Amsterdam and New York City were by and large created and produced in Europe. These visual representations have rarely been critically explored, although they have been reproduced regularly in book publications.[25] Because hegemonic nation-states vied for "New World" occupation, maps were both products and acts of possession, competition, and domination.[26] This imperial, territorializing process[27] resulted in visual representation that depicted settlement and commerce, on the one hand, and advertisement to entice European immigration, on the other. The maps functioned as a visual means to display wealth produced by the burgeoning colonies, which inevitably involved slave labor behind the scenes. Thus, J. B. Harley has famously written that maps are "a socially constructed form of knowledge."[28] Cartouches, scales, compass roses, decorative dedications, and empty space were far from merely decorative, but active elements in this cartographic process that manifested and enhanced political meaning of maps.[29] Through such an analysis, a geography of racism is apparent.

The Dutch cartographer Johannes Jansson created a map that was engraved, printed, and entitled by Nicholas Visscher the *Map of New Netherland, New England as well as parts of Virginia corrected in many places by Nicholas Visscher* (plate 1). This map was so influential that it remained the basis for edited and reworked versions up until 1781, with a total of twenty-six different states.

Created by a Dutch cartographer and engraver, the focus of the map was Dutch. The pinnacle of the cartouche is literally crowned with the Dutch coat of arms. This coat of arms and royal crown protrude into the open expanse of water, rendering them readily visible to claim dominance of the water. Notions of ownership are enacted through renaming of the space so that "Nieuw Nederlandt" and "Nova Belgica" are clearly centralized, and other European names can be seen throughout. This composition contributed to the "visual dimension of possession . . . renaming as it wipes clean one history and rewrites" another.[30] This work then is the mapping of ownership, access, development, and wealth.

The inset of plate 1 depicts New Amsterdam brimming with commerce and an already-built environment to suggest construction, progress, and the potential for wealth. The southern tip of Manhattan is portrayed as a visiting ship would see it from the water, with both the skyline and harbors visible. Native Americans standing on either side of the inset verify the WIC's production of wealth with visual proof of a tangible trading partner on this side of the Atlantic.[31] Wild animals co-opted from an early Blaeu atlas were placed on the main Visscher Map in open, unnamed, unclaimed space to imply a plethora available for trapping and trade.

The visual presence of a commercial company belies its hidden forced labor. The WIC was the largest slave owner during these early years.[32] Its houses are depicted in the inset from the center to the right. Letter I in the inset labels the Pachuys or Packing House that was erected by Stuyvesant in 1649 and used until 1662.[33] The inset also depicts a WIC warehouse to the left (built by Paulus Leendersen van der Grift in 1650) and one to the right (Augustine Heermans had built in 1650).[34] There was additionally a WIC "house of the Company's negroes" where Africans lived (mapped on the Castello Plan, Block M, no. 10). In considering the Visscher Map through the lens of a geography of racism, J. B. Harley's notion of cartographic silence is useful, as he writes of "the dialogue that arises from the intentional or unintentional suppression of knowledge in maps."[35] Africans who had built and would continue to build the infrastructure of New York City were absent, silenced, and only implicitly present.

The Visscher Map became the standard cartographic and visual resource for New Netherland.[36] It was included in a 1655 atlas entitled *Atlas Contractus* by the Dutch publisher Claes Jansoon Visscher.

Alone, the map became a best seller and was reprinted thirty-one times in Holland, Germany, and England from 1651 to 1677.[37] This may be in part because Dutch cartography was considered to be of the highest quality in the early modern era, with its maps of the New World held in the utmost regard.[38] Printing presses in major Dutch cities produced a consistent stream of travel narratives and histories that were disseminated throughout Europe and translated into various languages, including Latin.[39] In fact, in the words of Benjamin Schmidt, the Netherlands set "the geographic agenda for the rest of Europe. Dutch cartography simply dominated the field."[40]

As was common practice, maps were created from copies. Earlier works by Dutch cartographers Willem Blaeu, Joannes de Laet, and Adriean Block were appropriated in part to create the Visscher Map.[41] The geographer de Laet was actually a director of the WIC and a shareholder in a patroonship, or large estate of land in New Netherland. Here, links between the representation of space, production of knowledge, and politics of power are telling.

Another example connects merchant Augustine Heermans to a Visscher Map prototype. The Visscher Map was based upon a prototype map made by a cartographer in New Netherland who was possibly Augustine Heermans.[42] Heermans was one of the most successful merchants of the New World who worked with beaver pelts, tobacco, and indigo.[43] The reason for the existence of this earlier prototype manuscript was to claim possession of land and to press for further delineation of boundaries as part of the colonization process. The prototype map was part of a group of documents called the Remonstrance that was carried across the ocean by unsatisfied colonists in 1649 to request release from Stuyvesant and the Dutch West India Company. One of the complaints was a request to negotiate exact borders between Dutch and British colonies in the area.[44] The resulting Visscher Map attempted to clarify boundary disputes through spatial fixing, although some remained unresolved for over a century.

In 1992, a watercolor drawing made earlier than the Visscher Map was uncovered in the Austria National Library in Vienna

(Österreichische Nationalbibliothek). This drawing was entitled *The City of New Amsterdam on the island of Manhattan in New Netherland (De Stadt . . .)*, or the Albertina drawing. It is very likely that this watercolor drawing is the missing document from the Remonstrance, in which case the view was created in 1648 and would be attributed to Augustine Heermans.[45]

The Seutter Map (plate 2), ca. 1725–30, depicted actual African bodies on its cartouche unlike the indirectly suggested African presence in the Visscher Map. It is the only map I located that directly visualizes Africans in relation to New York City, thereby acknowledging the significant population. The figures are generalized, serving as a decorative element around the perimeter of the view of New York without individuality or local knowledge. Since the map was engraved and produced in Europe, it illustrates a European framing of slavery.

The depiction of Africans around the cartouche in plate 2 illustrates the hierarchy of race that was being constructed at this time during the Enlightenment in Europe. The positioning of the bodies forces the viewer's eye to begin at the bottom left and move up and around to the highest point, which is to King George I or II's throne. This setup mimics charts produced by Enlightenment scientists (now called pseudoscientists) in which the white male or classical god occupied the highest position and non-Europeans were at the bottom, closest to primates. In the plate 2 inset, a divide is created by a standing European figure at the apex, who is then turned 180 degrees away from those below as if to ignore or deny their presence. Primitivized black figures are clothed mainly in fur pelts only to reveal bulging muscles from slave labor. They bear the riches and produce of the colony and are thus inscribed as valuable commodities themselves. Hunched over, they begin at the bottom and climb to the top to bestow products including tobacco leaves, bread (as flour export), fish, pelts, timber, and a barrel onto white classical gods in billowing garments. In contrast to the Africans, the Europeans are fully clothed in classical gowns to represent the imagined, enlightened Greco-Roman basis of white civilization. In fact, the third figure from the end is Mercury, the Roman god of commerce and finance, adorned by a hat with wings and staff with snakes. A chest of coins rests at his feet, suggesting the transformation of slave labor into financial capital. The message could be that prosperous Europeans involved in the slave trade were assured wealth from New York City. The goods will eventually be deposited to the enthroned British monarch at the top. While an African presence and the built environment of Manhattan root the location in New York or the New World, King George at the pinnacle visually emphasizes England. Thus, not only is hierarchy of race visually illustrated, but also the colonization of space.

As well as an African presence, the Seutter Map inscribed multiple European nation-states onto it. The English had taken over land in the northeast, and it was a matter of time before they gained New Amsterdam. Although resistant, Stuyvesant gave up the city peacefully in 1664 to the encroaching English. Upon the takeover, King Charles II of England bestowed virtually all of New Netherland to his brother, James, the Duke of York.[46] The Seutter Map's inset visually recounts the well-known Restitutio, or restitution, when the Dutch briefly recaptured the colony in 1673. Militia are seen along the road in the center of the inset in plate 2. However, when the Dutch and British held negotiations following their war, New Netherland was ceded back to England fifteen months later in November 1674. This occurred because the Dutch Republic willingly exchanged its American colony for England's Surinam in an endeavor to build large sugar plantations there through African slave labor. Thus, intricate global histories are mapped spatially. As will be discussed in chapter 2, the restitution depicted here would have quite an effect on the African Burial Ground because of a dispute over land ownership. During this brief fifteen-month reconquest, the mayor granted part of what would become the burial ground to a family (Van Borsum) that the next British mayor refused to recognize. The burial ground was not mapped by Seutter, although the adjacent body of water was recognized. At the far right of the inset, the letter P identifies the Collect Pond, the water source for the city, which bordered the African

Burial Ground. The water used by the city was labeled, and the cemetery that bordered it was not.

The maker of the map, Matthias Seutter (1678–1757), was a cartographer, engraver, and publisher who lived in Augsburg, Germany. He held the position of official imperial geographer to Emperor Charles VI, and he signed his works under the Latin title that he carried, Sacrae Caesareae Maiestatis Geographus (abbreviated to S.C.Maj. Geogr or SCMG, as inscribed on the cartouche).[47] Seutter published atlases that included *Atlas Geographicas oder Accurate Vorstellung der Ganzen Welt* (Geographical Atlas or Accurate Conception of the Whole World) (1725) and *Grosser Atlas* (1734).

Summary of Africans in Colonial Prints

The *Nieu Amsterdam* print, Visscher Map, and Seutter Map consist of direct and indirect visual representations of an African presence in New Amsterdam and New York City. The works were produced by dominant European powers who sought to visually disseminate the international success of their wealth and power. Geographer James Duncan writes that in considering a geographic site or specific place, the cultural, political, and theoretical sites from which that representation emanates need also be recognized.[48] When this broader context is considered, a discourse emerges that includes spaces of power, weakness, and desire.[49] Duncan's recommendation is particularly interesting because representations of power are often considered, while sites of weakness are not. A rendering of the Other as inferior indeed empowers the Self while it simultaneously mythologizes and weakens the enslaved and colonized. This section's focus on visual culture of an African presence in New York realizes such inequities of power in colonial era imagery.

In terms of geographies of racism, the burgeoning construction of race was visually mapped and articulated through representation of space. This manipulation of space was accomplished through the depiction of racial hierarchy, the use of European language to rename space, and the display of European power to depict wealth and commerce. The Seutter Map and the 1642–43 *Nieu Amsterdam* engraving perhaps most blatantly spell out this mapping of racism. In each of these images a power imbalance was implicitly mapped between the dissemination of commodities, on the one hand, and a labor force facilitating the production of wealth, on the other. Thus, an early construction of race was spatially fixed in colonial visual culture.

Origins of the African Burial Ground

As the population of New Amsterdam grew, a communal cemetery specifically for Africans and people of African descent came into use during the late seventeenth or early eighteenth century. The African Burial Ground was located on the outskirts of town, north of the city-owned Common (today's City Hall Park, fig. 1) near the Fresh Water Pond. There are several factors that brought the African Burial Ground into existence, including the presence of a black neighborhood, the development of Manhattan civic space, and a proximity to Trinity Church, with its Society for the Propagation of the Gospel in Foreign Parts.

A 1679 scene drawn by hand in the *Journal of a Voyage to New York* (1679–80) shows the land that would soon become the African Burial Ground (fig. 5). This image is the closest we come to seeing the land, as no work exists that shows the cemetery while it was in use. The cemetery would soon occupy the left foreground of the drawing, from the windmills and slightly to their north and west. These windmills in the bottom left corner were erected in 1664 and 1677 in what is today City Hall Park just south of Chambers Street.[50] The view begins around what would become Duane Street in the foreground and looks south to the bottom of New Amsterdam, with its fort and flag receding in the distance (just to the left of the center crease).[51]

The Dutchmen Jaspar Danckaerts and Peter Sluyter recorded this area in their diary, the only known seventeenth-century interior view of Manhattan, as they sought a suitable area to establish a religious colony based on the theology of Jean de Labadie. The

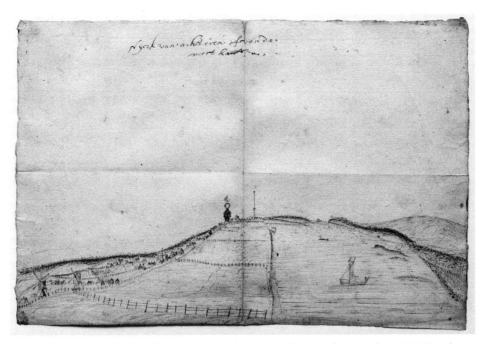

Figure 5. Jasper Danckaerts, *View of New York from the North*, 1679. Hand drawing in Jasper Danckaerts, *Journal of Jasper Danckaerts, 1679–1680*. The journalists described freed Africans living near this land, which would become the African Burial Ground within twenty years. M1979.23.5; Danckaerts and Sluyter journals, 1974.024; Brooklyn Historical Society.

religious reformers did not comment upon what was then known as the "Negroes Burying Ground" as it most likely did not yet exist. Actually, the fact that they did *not* mention the burial ground helps to corroborate that it was not in use or perhaps had not grown to a significant size. However, they did describe the strong African presence in the area. The journal entry for 6 October 1679 reads, "We went from the city, following the Broadway, over the *valley*, or the fresh water. Upon both sides of this way were many habitations of negroes, mulattoes and whites. These negroes were formerly the proper slaves of the (West India) company, but, in consequence of the frequent changes and conquests of the country, they have obtained their freedom and settled themselves down where they have thought proper, and thus on this road, where they have ground enough to live on with their families."[52]

The area was already an African neighborhood in the seventeenth century, as elucidated by Danckaerts along with extant historical documentation,[53] and I maintain must certainly have been key to this site becoming the communal African burying ground. The reason Africans were landowners is that the Dutch West India Company and private enslavers granted what were known as half freedoms, so that they would not have to house or care for the elderly or sick. For instance, Mayken, one of the first three women brought to the colony in 1628 from Angola, was manumitted by the WIC: "An old and sickly negress, Mayken by name, who had served as a slave of the West India Company since 1628, petitioned the provincial authorities for her manumission, which was granted in 1663, or 35 years later."[54] Elderly Africans also purchased their own freedom and earned money by hiring themselves out for work, or could be hired out by the WIC.[55]

Africans began owning land when in 1644, the WIC granted half freedoms to the first eleven males who were brought to New Amsterdam in 1626 after they, along with their wives, petitioned for freedom from enslavement.[56] In 1673, at least twenty-two families lived between the Fresh Water Pond and today's Harlem. A 1697 survey map of Bayard's farm showing land deeded to him by Governor Fletcher, for instance, describes African ownership: one border runs to the "*free negroes' ground*" and from their fence over to Jacob Stillie's land.[57] Thus, the area surrounding what would become the burial ground was certainly an African neighborhood initially, to the point that it was even known as such. Those burying their dead could have felt comfortable in this part of Manhattan. By 1696, land surrounding Fresh Water Pond was being sold to encroaching whites. Additionally, a 1702 statute negated the short-lived land ownership practice: enslaved people manumitted after 1702 could no longer legally own land. Black landowners in this neighborhood held onto land into the 1710s up to the late 1720s.[58] One of the last lots sold was originally Peter Santomee's.[59]

This change regarding black land ownership was just one of several that sadly were enacted under British rule against Africans. It was a marked difference for Africans living under Dutch rule in New Amsterdam. By 1682, a law stated that not more than four slaves were allowed to congregate publicly.[60] Secondly, the British did not recognize marriages and baptisms as the Dutch largely had, and families were separated more frequently. In 1702, a chapter of the New York Colonial laws was written expressly for the regulating of slaves, which included: no buying or selling a slave without the slave owner's permission; punishment of slaves at masters' discretion "not extending to Life or Member"; no more than three slaves gathering together; no attempts to "employ, harbour, conceal or entertain" other people's slaves; and no testifying in court in cases concerning whites but only other slaves.[61] This does not by any means suggest that the laws were followed; black resistance and rebellion were consistently enacted. The fact that each of the laws carried a means of punishment, such as thirty lashings or a fine, indicated that there was a practice of breaking the rules.

It is unknown exactly when the African Burial Ground came into use. It may have been Trinity Church that prompted the inception or increased use of the African Burial Ground. In October 1697, the church issued a statement that prevented the burial of Africans and early African Americans in its cemetery: "Ordered, that after the expiration of four weeks from the date here of no Negroes be buried within the bounds and limits of the church yard of Trinity Church, that is to say, in the rear of the present burying place and that no person or negro whatsoever, do presume after the term above limited to break up any ground for the burying of his negro, as they will answer it at their peril, and that this order be forthwith publish'd."[62] Before this proclamation was made, Trinity Church had owned its land for only five months—from May to October 1697—and no permanent church structure was yet even erected.[63] Within that short period of time, had Africans already been buried on Trinity property? The proclamation seems to suggest that Africans were in fact buried up until this time because it reads, "*after* the expiration of four weeks from the date here of" (emphasis mine). Had Anglicans decided upon a segregation strategy in order to construct a social and racial division? If so, the statement seems instrumental to the formation of the communal African Burial Ground, a twelve minute walk northward. In fact, although unfortunately undated, an entry in Appendix M of "Grants, Gifts, and Loans of Trinity Church" in Berrian's *Historical Sketch of Trinity Church, New-York* (1867) could be the launch of the African Burial Ground: "At one time they [the Vestry] appropriated £200 towards furnishing land for a Negro Burial-Ground."[64]

Even though Africans were ostensibly barred from Trinity property for burial, they were hired as slaves to build the first Trinity Church (completed 1698) at the head of Wall Street. This structure would burn down in 1776, with two subsequent reconstructions. The African laborers were paid to work on the first building, as in this example: "Ordered that Mr. Marston doe pay to ye Negro of Mr. Losseng the Sum of 7-6 itt being for 5 days worke as a Labourer to the Church building" (4 January 1697).[65] Or, private owners of the enslaved received payment from Trinity for "lending" their slaves. For instance, at a meeting of the Managers of the Church on 2 May 1696, it was "Ordered and agreed that on Monday ye foundation be [worked] on towards effecting of which each member present to send a Negro."[66] In sum, Africans were used as a source of labor for building the first Trinity Church before and during the time that the 1697 proclamation was issued. While there was a use of labor, there was a rejection of an equitable religious presence in the Anglican community.

Although ostracized, Africans would be quite closely engaged with Trinity Church through an ancillary organization known as the Society for the Propagation of the Gospel in Foreign Parts (SPG). My research demonstrates that this society was an extremely important link to the existence of the African Burial Ground at the time and for our twentieth century knowledge of the colonial era site.

I suggest that William Huddleston of SPG and Trinity Church was a significant figure leading to the inception of the African Burial Ground. He owned a portion of the African Burial Ground from

1697 to 1702.[67] Huddleston cultivated strong connections with Trinity Church. Most important, he worked as a schoolmaster for the SPG, for which he instructed slaves and their children in reading, writing, and Christianity from 1710 to 1723.[68] He was also elected a vestry man, and a clerk of both the church and vestry for Trinity Church from 1697 to 1714. His son Thomas would take over as schoolmaster upon William's death around 1723, teaching "the blacks in the steeple of Trinity Church every Sunday before sermon and after sermon at his own house."[69] Thus, because the Huddleston family's sympathies lay with Africans, and because Trinity had expelled African burials in 1697, perhaps it was William who suggested, enabled, or turned a blind eye to the initiation of a cemetery on the property that he had inherited that very same year, which would quickly become the burial ground. There may be consolation in knowing that through all of the difficulties Africans experienced in New York, an official who was compassionate to their cause owned a portion of the burial ground for a short time.

The next important link between the SPG and the African Burial Ground is a quote written by the Anglican minister, missionary, and chaplain John Sharpe of Trinity's SPG. In 1712, he wrote specifically about the burial ground that "they are buried in the Common by those of their country and complexion without the office, on the contrary, the Heathenish rites are performed at the grave by their countrymen."[70] This quote by Sharpe has been used to pinpoint the earliest existence of the African Burial Ground because no prior reference has been made in written, mapped, or visual documents. The year 1712 becomes the beginning date of the communal cemetery, since Sharpe is the first to substantiate its existence. However, authors of the final African Burial Ground report contend that by Trinity's 1697 ban, and prior to Sharpe's written 1712 document, "[i]t is likely a cemetery already existed, the one now known as the African Burial Ground."[71]

What prompted John Sharpe to offer his description of the African Burial Ground? He wrote about it on the heels of a 1712 slave insurrection because the SPG had been blamed as its instigator.

Sharpe explains that "[t]he late barbarous massacre attempted by the slaves, April 1712, gave strength at first to this clamour which had a full run for many days. The [SPG] school was charged as the cause of the mischief, the place of conspiracy and that instruction made them insolent."[72] Sharpe's document was to be taken to England to propose three major endeavors: a public school, a public library, and a catechizing chapel for enslaved Africans/African Americans and for Native Americans. Thus, it is in response to this moment in 1712 when the city's eyes and attention were on Africans who were simultaneously marginalized and empowered, having just enacted a rebellion and resistance to increasingly repressive British enslavement, that Rev. Sharpe writes about the cemetery for the first time.

1712 Insurrection

In April 1712, an organized group of Africans successfully staged an actual attack and were subsequently captured. The conspirators of the 1712 Insurrection consisted of a group of twenty-five to fifty, many of whom were Paw Paw people and Coromantee or Akan people of Ghana. Along with two or three Spanish Native Americans, the group plotted to set fire to an outhouse owned by baker Peter Vantilborough in the middle of the night. His two slaves who participated in the revolt were Cuffee (from today's Ghana) and John (a Spanish Native American). When whites ran to quell the fire, they were ambushed, shot, stabbed with swords and knives, clubbed, and hacked with axes. Nine whites were killed and six to twelve more injured.[73] Peter the Porter, owned by Andries Maerschalck, killed Joris Maerschalck with a dagger.[74] Since two members and one slave of the Maerschalck family were involved, this may have strongly impacted the reason why Francis Maerschalck would map the burial ground in his plan of the city.

Of the seventy people arrested as a result of the 1712 Insurrection, forty-three were subject to trials, twenty-five were found guilty, and, of those, twenty-one were brutally executed. The large majority were hanged, three were burned alive at the stake, one was starved to death or slowly burned, and one was broken on the wheel. They were likely buried in the African Burial Ground and killed in its vicinity in the Common. Six others had committed suicide before they were caught. Governor Hunter did not support the high number of executions and stepped in to reprieve the last five, including two Spanish Native Americans named Hosey/Hosea (José) and John (Juan), who were free but had been captured and sold into slavery in 1706.[75] Governor Hunter also saved the purported ringleader, the free Peter the Doctor. The governor's actions invoked dissension from some New Yorkers, and a royal pardon from the queen was sought.[76]

Rev. John Sharpe wrote about spiritually based practices Africans used to protect themselves in preparing for the 1712 rebellion. To begin their plans, they exchanged the blood of each other's hands. The group agreed to secrecy by "Sucking ye blood of each Others hands, and to make them invulnerable as they believed a free negro who pretends socery [sic] gave them a powder to rub on their Cloths."[77] The group was instructed by Peter the Doctor (spiritual specialist or diviner) to rub powder over their bodies to protect themselves from bullets. During the uprising, they were neither shot nor killed.[78] Fein proposed that the powder may have actually been grave dirt taken from the African Burial Ground.[79] Earth from a cemetery would be considered spiritually potent because it is already imbued with activating powers from the ancestral world. Among the Kongo people from today's Democratic Republic of the Congo and Angola, grave earth can be used in *minkisi*, or power packets, that are activated by *ngangas*, or priests. Minkisi-like conjuring bundles were found buried with some of the deceased in the African Burial Ground (see chapter 3), and in Africa minkisi were made and activated in the Kongo at least since 1600.[80] Peter the Doctor would surely hold the status and education of an nganga if he lived in this area of Africa. Earth from the burial ground can hold the potency of the spirit realm and can be activated as minkisi. Such information offers an example of an African-based understanding of the fluidity between the living and the dead. There were in fact a large number of slave rebellion participants who were brought directly from Africa.

Nineteen percent of those involved in the revolt bore African names, including Cuffee (which could be the birth-day name for Kofi or Friday in the Twi language in Ghana), Kitto/Quito, Mingo, Quacko, Quack, and Quash.[81]

Whites wrongly believed that the revolt had been fueled by literacy and catechism lessons given by Elias Neau. Neau had initiated an Anglican catechism school under the SPG.[82] Beginning in 1704, Neau attempted to convert Africans, people of African descent, and Native Americans to Christianity by educating them in reading the Bible, reciting catechisms, and singing from psalm books. He had built up a following of between fifteen and twenty-five consistent participants per year, with others simply attending in order to learn to read or to find reading material. Because they were worked so hard as slaves, "their bodies are fatigued, the attention of their minds cannot be supposed very great, they are then dull and sleepy and obliged to be stirring early to work next morning."[83] Neau taught using a call-and-response method, with which Africans would have been familiar, and he requested that versions of the Lord's Prayer be printed in "Carmantie and Mandingo" languages (from Ghana and the Mande area of West Africa, including Senegal, Guinea, and Mali).[84] Neau also ordered editions of the Lord's Prayer and the Anglican catechism in Dutch, Spanish, and French, thus reflecting the diversity, intelligence, and hybrid experiences of Africans in the New World. His school gained popularity so that enrollment climbed to one hundred, including African and Indian sailors hailing from places such as Bermuda, who would stop in when their ships were docked in the harbor.

Elias Neau's student attendance and their conversion to Christianity became the center of political controversy in an attempt to cast blame for the 1712 rebellion.[85] Whites feared that teaching enslaved people literacy and Christianity would lead to empowerment and freedom. Dealing with the aftermath of the rebellion actually became a troubling conflict among whites concerning the issue of race. Likely concerned about allegations and in an attempt to clear the SPG's name and continue its Christianizing mission, Sharpe in fact visited one of the two who attended the school and had been found guilty in the insurrection: "I went to him after he had hung five days: he declared to me he was innocent of the murder . . . He was often delirious by long continuance in that posture, through hunger, thirst and pain."[86] In reality, it turned out that only two of the accused had attended Neau's classes, and one was then pardoned. Such a case illustrated that people's preconceived notions and racism were dictating the negative treatment of Africans in the community. The continuation and attendance of the school suffered greatly after the 1712 Insurrection. However, Governor Robert Hunter remained a loyal patron and likely kept the school running; he even visited the school with his wife.[87]

The town's dissension against SPG teachings hindered missionary work. Conversely, this helped to retain African traditions, cultures, memories, and spiritualities so that they continued to be practiced, shared, reinvented, and engaged at the African Burial Ground.[88] Indeed, Sharpe revealed through his quote that African-based funerals were performed at the time and lamented that Anglican sacraments were not, when he observed "[t]hey are buried . . . without the office [of Christianity], on the contrary, the Heathenish rites are performed . . ."

Sadly, the city did not question the discontent of its enslaved or consider reasons for the 1712 Insurrection beyond casting blame on Neau's school. Instead, it established even stricter laws following the Africans' act of resistance. Just a few months later in 1712, an "act for preventing suppressing and punishing the Conspiracy and Insurrection of negroes and other slaves" was passed.[89] They could not carry guns unless instructed by the owner. Now, manumission was regulated by the legal system, and an owner had to pay the government £200 plus £20 annually to support the freed person, thus rendering the practice virtually nonexistent. A 1717 revision made manumission more possible, although still difficult up until 1785.[90] Owning any property was again prohibited, forcing even greater dependency on slave owners. In 1713, a "Law for Regulating Negro and Indian Slaves in the Night Time" stated that slaves could not be on the streets an hour after sunset unless they carried a light obtained from their enslavers that would allow them to be seen.[91] This law was enacted to lower attendance to Neau's night classes.[92]

In sum, an early African neighborhood, Trinity Church's proclamation, John Sharpe's quote, and Huddleston's land on the burial ground all offer insight into the instigation of the African Burial Ground. It was a space engaged by Africans for Africans; an area where Africans lived, at least early on, and a space where funerals could be performed, remembered, and reinvented in indigenous African languages.

Civic Mapping of the African Burial Ground

Four civic maps, three of which were drawn by locals, offer varying representations of space of the African Burial Ground. From these maps, complex historical narratives emerge. We are able to see that the burial ground was next to a body of water, was out of town away from European surveillance, and was used as a temporary space of violence during the 1741 Conspiracy, as explained at the end of the chapter. It is posited that these points, along with the above analysis of the cemetery's inception, all contribute to the likelihood that Africans and people of African descent selected and claimed this sacred space as their own.

Spatial representation of the burial ground is further understood through the printing, copying, and disseminating of the maps locally and internationally. Typically a purpose of maps is to render a spatial fixing and to define boundaries.[93] However, in these four cases, the African Burial Ground remains floating and imprecise in terms of its exact location, with each map delineating the cemetery in a different way. Each is analyzed to consider how, why, and by whom the burial ground was represented in plans of the city. Despite its consistent marginalization, these four cartographers remembered and represented the African Burial Ground for reasons I propose below.

In considering cartography, it is important to understand not only what is mapped, but also what is unmapped. Silenced, marginalized spaces can be erased from cartography when those in power control the production of representation to typically focus on spaces of dominance.[94] The features and spaces labeled on maps reveal to us today what producers believed to be politically and historically important, while those who were perceived at the time to be insignificant were excluded and therefore invisible.[95] Politics of power and race played a role in remembering or forgetting the presence of the African Burial Ground in New York City cartography. Therefore, only a very few maps marked its existence.[96] The following maps did represent the site: Mrs. Buchnerd's Plan (1735), Maerschalck Plan (1755 and 1763), Major Kirkham's Plan of New York (1807), and the Grim Plan (1813). Briefly, Mrs. Buchnerd's Plan is the earliest known map of New York City made by a woman. Her representation of the emptiness of space surrounding the cemetery speaks to its undeveloped and isolated nature at this early date. The plan made by local surveyor Francis Maerschalck illustrates the African-built palisade that separated the city Common from the African Burial Ground for a time, and factories that gradually encroached upon the sacred space. The revised and reprinted Maerschalck Plan would be the only mass-produced document to mark the African Burial Ground. Major Kirkham included the African Burial Ground in the logbook of his ship, drawing detailed property lines that would be disputed at length for decades following the closure of the site. Finally, the plan drawn by New Yorker David Grim carried a symbol of execution rather than the name of the cemetery, thereby rendering it as a space of violence. My analysis of these four maps produced by Europeans or descendant Europeans seeks to give voice to the disenfranchised in an effort to understand the African Burial Ground in historical and spatial contexts.

Mrs. Buchnerd's Plan, ca. 1732–35

Buchnerd rendered a pen and ink drawing of New York City around 1732 to 1735 in which she recognized the "Negro Burying Place" (fig. 6). Her hand-drawn map depicting the city in 1735 was the first time that the burial ground was actually represented. She located the "Negro Burying Place" near a windmill just south of the Fresh Water [Pond] and Powder House. It is the same windmill shown in Danckaert's drawing (fig. 5). She included many details that were not represented on other plans of the city, including topographical features and buildings such as the Play House, recreation areas, and the earliest known theatre.[97] This could be a quintessential reason that she mapped the African Burial Ground; it was part of her intimate and firsthand local knowledge of the city.

Although racism, the institution of slavery, and Trinity Church all played a role in the existence of the communal African Burial Ground, it is argued here that early Africans selected their own space for burying the dead, honoring the ancestors, and recalling funerary traditions. Mrs. Buchnerd's Plan illustrates what can be considered several positive aspects about the location of the site. The African burying place was depicted on the outskirts of the city floating in empty space, with few landmarks in its vicinity. Moreover, much of the cemetery actually lay in a ravine. Mourners therefore achieved privacy and seclusion beyond European surveillance. Funerals and communication with ancestors could be performed with relatively minor disturbance or scrutiny. The cemetery was adjacent to Fresh Water Pond, where the land was low-lying and marshy, not ideal for urban development (fig. 6).[98] Although it was a marginalized area of the city because of its low real estate value, this very point probably helped to preserve the sacred land. Finally, its location beside this large body of water may have enhanced spiritual significance in funerary ceremonies. In African cultures (such as Kongo and Igbo) as well as diasporic cultures, water can connote the realm of the dead or the space one travels through to the next world.

Thelma Wills Foote identifies the burial ground as a "semi-autonomous social space" engaged by several generations enacting funerary traditions.[99] Such an assessment is echoed in the passage written by SPG affiliate David Humphreys in 1730. Five years prior to Buchnerd drawing her map, Humphreys described a scene of indigenous African funerary traditions, on the one hand, and a lack

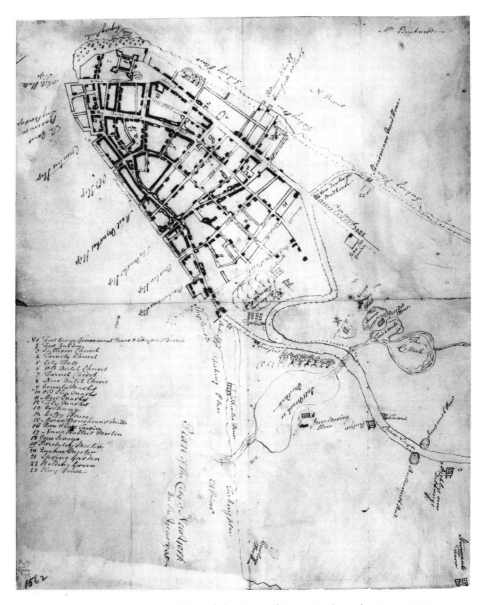

Figure 6. Mrs. Buchnerd, *Plan of the City of New York in the Year 1735*, ca. 1732–35. Pen and ink on paper mounted on linen, 15¼ × 18½ in. The earliest known plan of New York made by a female cartographer. First cartographic representation of the "Negro Burying Place," located on the right side on the crease of the map, just above the swamp. The windmill just below is also depicted in Danckaerts's hand-drawn image (fig. 5). I. N. Phelps Stokes Collection, Miriam and Ira D. Wallach Division of Art, Prints, and Photographs, The New York Public Library, Astor, Lenox and Tilden Foundations.

of Christian sacrament, on the other. In his review of the SPG's work, secretary David Humphreys reported the state of affairs:

> The Negroes were much discouraged from embracing the Christian religion, upon account of the very little regard showed them in any religious respect. Their marriages were performed by mutual consent only, without the blessing of the Church; they were buried by those of their own country or complexion in the common field, without any Christian office, perhaps some ridiculous heathen rites were performed at the grave by some of their own people. No notice was given of their being sick, that they might be visited, on the contrary, frequent discourses were made in conversation that they had no souls and perished as the beasts.[100]

Although the word "heathen" is a biased observation from a Christian point of view, it nevertheless describes indigenous African-based funerals. Along those lines, the sounds, songs, and words were foreign and not European or European American. The quote is not unlike the one made by John Sharpe of the SPG eighteen years earlier. At this space represented by Buchnerd, Africans and people of African descent recalled and reinvented the sacred practices that they remembered, that were passed down to them by family members, or that they learned from others.

The nineteenth-century historian and city clerk David Valentine wrote the third and final existing description of the African Burial Ground, which was published in 1865. It similarly describes African-based funerary traditions in indigenous languages (as "various mummeries and outcries") without Anglican practices, adding that the funerals occurred at night.

> Beyond the Common [now City Hall Park] lay what in the earliest settlement of the town had been appropriated as a burial place for the Negroes, slaves and free. It was a desolate, unappropriated spot, descending with a gentle declivity towards a ravine which led to the Kalchhook Pond. The negroes in this city were, both in the

Dutch and English colonial times, a proscribed and detested race, having nothing in common with the whites. Many of them were native Africans, imported hither in slave ships, and retaining their native superstitions and burial customs, among which was that of burying by night, with various mummeries and outcries . . . So little seems to have been thought of the race that not even a dedication of their burial-place was made by church authorities, or any others who might reasonably be supposed to have an interest in such a matter. The lands were unappropriated, and though within convenient distance from the city, the locality was unattractive and desolate, so that by permission the slave population were allowed to inter their dead there.[101]

Valentine used the word "appropriate," meaning either to take for one's own or to set aside for a specific use or person. Did the government appropriate the land for the Africans? Or did early Africans appropriate it for themselves? In his last sentence, Valentine noted that enslaved people used the land "by permission." This crucial sentence suggested that Africans themselves chose the land and requested permission from the city government to use it. Also, since Valentine stressed that Europeans held no interest in the swampy, undesirable land that lacked real estate value and noted twice that this land north of the city limits was initially "unappropriated," or vacant, then competition for the land would not have existed.

There are a plethora of reasons why early Africans could have selected this area for a communal cemetery. In summary and as depicted in Mrs. Buchnerd's Plan, the location of the cemetery at the northern edge of town was indicative of the marginalized position the freed and enslaved held in society. By being situated along the boundaries of society, they served as a protective buffer against attacks from Native Americans who had been provoked by the Dutch and British. Moreover, the burial ground remained free of urban development up to the later part of the eighteenth century so that it was not engaged by mainstream society. The fact that the space was rarely demarcated in maps of the city suggests an attempt to forget, ignore, or erase it. Nonetheless, an out-of-town cemetery next to a body of water and three written descriptions of the funerals all contributed to an empowered claiming of space for Africans and people of African descent who held spiritually important funerals for their loved ones.

An expanded African population led the British to create laws governing use of the burial ground. The laws offer an idea of how burial traditions were actually being performed. One year after Humphreys's description and a few years before Buchnerd created her map, a 1731 law dictated that only twelve Africans at a time could attend a funeral.[102] All-night funerals with large gatherings of people must indeed have been held at the burial ground if laws attempted to quell them. Official control concerning the burial ground began in 1722, when a law ordered that funerals for African and Native American slaves dying "within this corporation on the South side of the Fresh Water [the exact location of the burial ground] be buried by daylight at or before sunset" or there would be a penalty of 10 shillings paid by the slaveholder.[103] While burials were a time for communal African meeting and mourning, the British attempted to restrict gatherings that were out of town, during the night, and therefore beyond their surveillance out of fear of rebellion.

Not only is Mrs. Buchnerd's Plan the first one to depict the African Burial Ground, it is also the earliest known plan of New York City made by a woman. As a mapmaker, Mrs. Buchnerd experienced her own marginalization. The New York Public Library Print Collection did not acknowledge her as the cartographer, and the map is instead labeled as "anonymous."[104] Although Mrs. Buchnerd signed her name at the top of the plan, Cohen and Augustyn note this could indicate that she was the owner of the map rather than the author. While it would certainly prove unusual for an owner to do such a thing, Cohen and Augustyn point out that her signature matches the handwriting on the map itself.[105] Thus, this stands as the earliest known female-authored map of New York even if there is reluctance to acknowledge it.

Maerschalck Plan, 1755 and 1763

The Maerschalck Plan (*A Plan of the City of New York from an Actual Survey, Anno Domini MDCCLV*) was drawn in 1754 and published in 1755 and 1763. The first version was largely disseminated in New York City (plate 3, detail fig. 7) and the second Maerschalck Plan was reengraved by Peter Andrews and published in 1763 in London in a book collection about American forts (fig. 8).

Of all the colonial archives, the Maerschalck Plan provides the clearest mapping of the African Burial Ground and therefore has been reproduced and referred to numerous times since the late-twentieth-century rediscovery of the site. The spatial complexity in delineating the burial ground's boundaries becomes apparent in the Maerschalck Plan, which also illustrates a tension with encroaching industries. One border of particular importance is the palisade on the edge of town just south of the "Negros Buriel Ground" (fig. 7). Mapped as a zigzagged, unbroken bolded line, a vertical fence of 14-foot-long cedar logs was constructed in 1745 by enslaved Africans of the West India Company.[106] The fence helped to enclose animals grazing in the city's Common. It was also an attempt to protect the town from provoked Native American attacks and from a French attack believed to be imminent. With the palisade constructed as a part of the process of colonization, it was not by coincidence that an African neighborhood and burial ground were also a part of this buffer zone. Africans enslaved to the WIC worked here to build the palisade for a time, and a communal African cemetery that would eventually stretch to nearly seven acres mushroomed from here. In sum, the cemetery's location did not exist randomly.

What might the palisade tell us about the spatial mapping and division of individual burials? Since the palisade was not a permanent fixture, anthropologists on the project suggest that Africans and their descendants buried their dead in the Common before this fence was erected in 1745 and/or then again after it was removed in 1760. Without the fence, the boundaries between the general burial

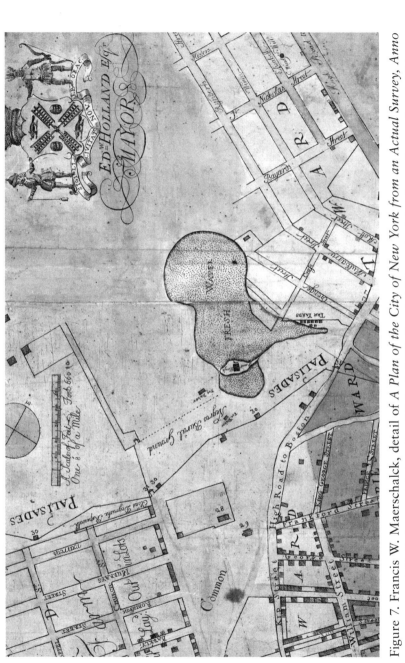

Figure 7. Francis W. Maerschalck, detail of *A Plan of the City of New York from an Actual Survey, Anno Domini MDCCLV*, drawn 1754 and published 1755. Freed Africans had lived nearby, enslaved Africans built the Palisades, and the communal African cemetery that would eventually stretch to 7 acres mushroomed from here. Encroaching industry onto the "Negros Buriel Ground" is evident from two Pot Bakers, or potteries, and Tan Yards. Courtesy of Library of Congress, Geography and Map Division.

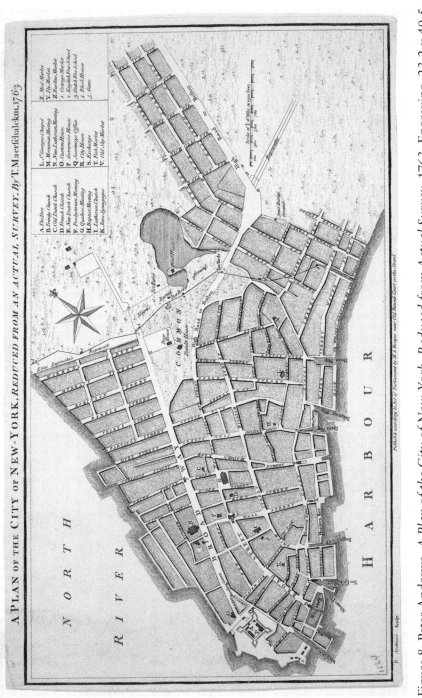

Figure 8. Peter Andrews, *A Plan of the City of New-York, Reduced from Actual Survey*, 1763. Engraving, 23.2 x 40.5 cm. Maerschalck's Plan was reengraved and published in London. The African Burial Ground is again mapped and now presented to an international audience. I. N. Phelps Stokes Collection, Miriam and Ira D. Wallach Division of Art, Prints, and Photographs, The New York Public Library, Astor, Lenox and Tilden Foundations.

ground and the Common were probably not clearly marked.[107] Similarly, it is believed that interments did not occur in the Common during the life of the palisades between 1745 and 1760, since the fencing would have functioned as a physical boundary along the south side of the burial ground during those years. To further support the point that Africans were buried in the Common for periods of time, recall that John Sharpe and David Humphreys both described the burial ground as existing *in* the Common(s): Sharpe wrote in 1712, "They are buried in the Commons . . . ," and Humphreys wrote in 1730, "they were buried . . . in the common field." Although we don't know a time frame to which Valentine referred, it is interesting that in 1865 he wrote "*Beyond* the Commons . . ." (emphasis added). It is perhaps possible to suggest that the African Burial Ground began close to the Common at its southernmost part and expanded to the north, as is substantiated by the relative dating of the excavated portion of the cemetery in chapter 3. Since the palisade was erected in 1745 in order to control animals grazing, and since Africans were likely burying some of their dead here prior to its construction, can we conclude that sacred funerals and grazing animals occurred for a time in the same space? If so, then the marginalization of space for Africans and the burying of their dead would have been extreme up to 1745. Generally speaking, these issues illustrate that the boundaries of the burial ground were in flux during the approximate century when it was in use.

To this day, exact boundaries of the African Burial Ground remain unknown. The impreciseness was even evident on the two versions of the Maerschalck Plan. On the 1755 publication, the name "Negros Buriel Ground" was written only to the west, or left, of the Fresh Water Pond (fig. 7). In contrast, the reworked 1763 version extended part of the respelled name "Negro's Burial Ground" around the Fresh Water Pond to the other side of the Little Collect (fig. 8). On both versions, the far left or western boundary, as demarcated by the words, is Broadway. Indeed, it is believed to this day that Broadway marked the western border of the cemetery.

Another noteworthy contribution that Maerschalck made to his plan in terms of thinking about the representation of space of the African Burial Ground is that he included a short line north of the palisade above the words "Negros Buriel Ground" (dashed in 1755 and an unbroken line in 1763). This line possibly marked the border, pathway, or fence between properties owned by two different families on the African Burial Ground (see chapter 2, as well as evidence of postholes in cemetery map, plate 4).[108] Both of these properties as well as the Common straddled the African Burial Ground, all of which remained mired in land disputes for a century. Maerschalck's two mapped versions alone illustrate the imprecise boundaries of the site and exemplify its fluctuating borders.

Finally, Maerschalck marked burgeoning industries that surrounded and at times encroached upon the burial ground. He labeled the Tan Yards at the southern edge of the Fresh Water Pond, from which animal bones were actually excavated in the 1990s (fig. 7). Also, shards from the Pot Bakers or potteries marked by Maerschalck in the cemetery area were found on and in graves. These industries marked a tension that surely existed between marginalized Africans striving to hold sacred funerals to honor the dead versus businesses who needed Fresh Water Pond water to produce and earn profit. In so doing, the industries polluted Fresh Water Pond so that it ultimately had to be drained at the beginning of the nineteenth century. If the body of water was considered sacred or important in representing the realm of the dead for some Africans, based on their cultural traditions, the ongoing pollution would have been deemed yet another invasion and interruption of sacred space for respecting and honoring ancestors.

Why did Maerschalck map the "Negros Buriel Ground" when so few other cartographers had done so? First, I propose that as a local cartographer and surveyor, he represented on paper the local spaces that he personally knew through his profession.[109] Maerschalck would have known in detail the land surrounding Fresh Water Pond when he personally surveyed its southeast corner in 1744 and then mapped its burgeoning development as seen in both Maerschalck Plans and in a survey for George Janeway.[110] Second, the undeveloped southwest area of the African Burial Ground was involved in several long lasting land disputes of which he would have been aware as city surveyor. To summarize, it is strongly suggested here that Maerschalck mapped the African Burial Ground because he was the city's local surveyor who not only actually surveyed land surrounding Fresh Water Pond, but also had his attention drawn to the African Burial Ground's multiple property disputes between the City and local citizens.

On an even more personal note, Maerschalck could have mapped the site because of a family tragedy related to racial and political urban rebellion. As part of the 1712 Insurrection, a slave of the Maerschalck family murdered another Maerschalck. It is believed that the punished and then executed Africans were buried in the African Burial Ground. Then more recently, two of the Maerschalck slaves were accused of involvement in the 1741 Conspiracy. Although generally speaking the sacred site was spatially and racially marginalized, it seems to have played a significant role in the surveyor's civic life.

One final point supporting my conviction that Maerschalck had specific reasons for mapping the site is that he based his plan on the previously printed Lyne-Bradford Plan of 1730, which did not in fact map the cemetery. Maerschalck must have purposefully added it, as well as the streets that he surveyed southeast of Fresh Water Pond.[111] As was common for that time, Maerschalck reused the copperplate from the Lyne-Bradford Plan and then added his own details.

Maerschalck, and Lyne prior to him, fashioned the city's image as commercial, exemplifying commodity exchange, regional and international trade, and transatlantic travel, all of which involved slave labor. The maps portray heavy naval traffic in the rivers, with piers, wharves, and harbors carefully identified on the plans (plate 3). Both listed the Byards Sugar House, which was the city's first sugar refinery built in 1728. Number 19 in the legend of the 1755 Maerschalck Plan noted the prominent Livingstone family, who made a fortune in the British slave trade. Thus, the maps directly and indirectly represent the undeniable African presence in New York City.

The 1755 publication of the Maerschalck Plan (plate 3) was printed, engraved, and sold by Gerardus Duyckinck. He apparently produced the map as one of several business ventures since he was not strictly a publisher, and he placed an advertisement selling the maps in a 1755 issue of the *New-York Gazette*.[112] Both the Maerschalck and Lyne-Bradford maps bore local seals of dedication to the governor and the city of New York. The seals portray symbols of civic identity and international colonial possession through blades of a Dutch windmill, barrels of flour, beavers representing the first traded commodity, and royal European crowns. The seals are imprinted on the maps on unmarked land to suggest impending growth by a hegemonic power.

The 1755 Maerschalck Plan was reengraved by Peter Andrews and published in a book collection entitled *A Set of Plans and Forts in America. Reduced from Actual Surveys* in London in 1763 (fig. 8). The work was compiled by John Rocque, geographer to George III in England, and published by Mary Ann Rocque in London.[113] Published primarily for an English audience and by the colonizing entity, or English royalty, the 1763 Maerschalck Plan bore printed as opposed to handwritten text, had no ships at all in the water, no city seal or dedication to the governor, and no inclusion of citizens' names of property in the legend. There were, however, several spelling errors that suggest an unfamiliarity with the city and explain the production of the map by a foreign source: "T" instead of "F" for the mapmaker's first name Francis, Maerschalck misspelled as Maerschalckm at the top of the map, "White Hab Slip" instead of White Hall Slip, "Albano Pee" instead of Albany Peers, "Ruger Wharf" instead of Krugers Wharf, "Behmans Slip" instead of Beekman Slip, "Mustarry Street" instead of Mulberry Street, and "Old Street" instead of Mott Street.

Major Kirkham's Plan of New York, ca. 1807

Although it was almost certainly not in use by this time, Major A. Kirkham mapped the "Negros Burial Ground" in his ship's logbook in 1808 (fig. 9). He is the only nonlocal to have mapped the site, aside from the 1763 reprint of the Maerschalck Plan. Born around 1780, Kirkham travelled on the *Royal George*, a war vessel for the British Royal Navy.[114] He maintained a private logbook, which is now housed in the Library of Congress, while on board different ships between 1798 and 1812.[115] One hundred reproductions of Kirkham's Plan of New York were issued by C[harles] J[ames] Sawer of London in 1911.[116] Sawer dated the map to 1807, whereas Kirkham documented his travels to America in 1808, according to his logbook.

Kirkham's Plan is not actually a representation of Manhattan's urban space in 1807. The African Burial Ground closed around 1795 when Chambers Street was laid, and in preparation the city opened a Chrystie Street Burial Ground for Africans in 1795. In comparison to Kirkham's Plan, other maps of Manhattan from around the same time show greater urban development, particularly to the north, and indicate the addition of new streets that are absent in the logbook, especially in the Fresh Water Pond area (see, for instance, the Mangin-Goerck Plan of 1803 or even the Taylor-Roberts Plan of 1797).[117] Kirkham's 1808 date is too late for what he has depicted in terms of urban development and of course the existence of the African Burial Ground. Instead, Kirkham must certainly have used an earlier map of Manhattan as a model. In fact, his hand-drawn map is virtually identical to Bernard Ratzer's "The Ratzen Plan" (1767), and therefore I would argue that Kirkham's Plan is a representation of the city around 1767.[118] It was not uncommon to appropriate an older map in order to produce a new one. Here, almost all of the same landmarks were mapped on both, and the same streets were included or missing on both. The Ratzen Plan had been published in London in 1776 and was then regarded as the finest map of an American city in the eighteenth century.[119] Therefore, Kirkham could have purchased a copy of the map while he was in London since the map was published there.

There is, however, one major difference between the two maps: Kirkham mapped the African Burial Ground (see fig. 9 inset), and Ratzer did not. This means that Kirkham could not have copied the African Burial Ground from the Ratzen Plan, as he had ostensibly copied the other landmarks. Therefore, the following questions must

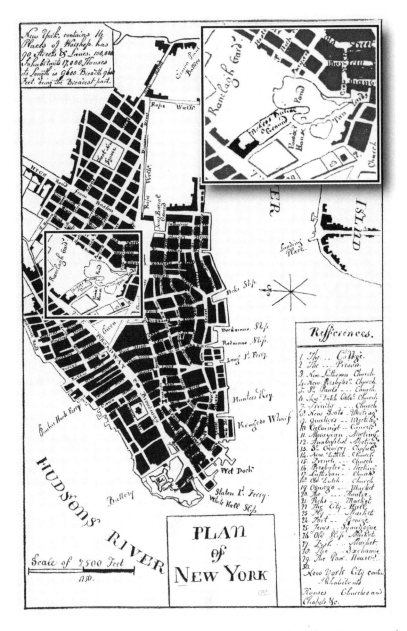

Figure 9. Major Kirkham, R. N., *A Facsimile of a Plan in Pen and Ink in the Log Book Kept by Major Kirkham*, ca. 1807. Black ink on paper, backed with cloth, 50 × 32 cm. Kirkham labeled the burial ground even though it was closed by now. He was a foreigner who nevertheless included the site, although no other cartographers had done so since the reengraved Maerschalck Plan. M33.3.72, neg #89504d. Collection of the New-York Historical Society.

be raised: How did Kirkham know about the existence of the African Burial Ground, especially since it was closed by the time he arrived and was not mapped on the Ratzen Plan or on contemporaneous city maps? Why did he choose to map the cemetery as well as its surrounding private property lines in detail, particularly since he was a foreigner? Kirkham's actual logbook regrettably makes no mention of his map, but in general discusses the times the ship arrived and departed, the ports it sailed into, and the nationalities of other ships that were encountered.

I offer several reasons why Kirkham anachronistically mapped the cemetery. Kirkham's Plan depicts private property lines on the sacred space and structures on or close by it. These borders provide spatial identity to the colonial cemetery and have to a large degree been verified through archaeological excavation as fences. Kirkham was the only mapmaker to delineate the cemetery by actually drawing rectangular borders around it, and he showed the cemetery reaching right to the shores of Fresh Water Pond (fig. 9 inset).

Both the Ratzer and Kirkham maps are important in that they illustrate in detail Teller's houses built upon the cemetery. A few outlined dwellings can be seen along Broadway just above the barracks, which may have been three houses that Isaac Teller built between 1760 and 1765 near what would become Chambers Street. A court case noted, "In May 1768, J. Teller entered into possession of a house which he had built two or three years before on the Negroes' Burying-Ground . . . that he had a fence enclosing the burying-ground, and claimed it as his property."[120] Teller surrounded his property with a fence and charged a fee to enter the land. Thus, the homes would have been built on top of the African Burial Ground. Kirkham mapped the Teller property with its fence between Broadway and the "Negros Burial Ground," as seen just to the left in the figure 9 inset.

Another important property detail that the maps very likely convey is the diagonal property boundary dividing the African Burial Ground in half, which Maerschalck too had drawn. It separated Anthony Rutgers's Kalk Hook Farm (mapped as Ranelagh Gard. by Kirkham) from the Van Borsum family patent, as I will discuss in chapter 2. For

Kirkham, I suggest the fence is represented by the top rectangular line that surrounds the "Negros Burial Ground" (fig. 9 inset). With such intricate detail rendered of this space in Manhattan, it is disturbingly surprising that Ratzer neglected to map the burial ground himself. Why did he eradicate that space from his mapping of the city? Was he only interested in white property ownership, as he mapped many estates, gardens, and property boundaries in detail? Kirkham's Plan similarly offers detailed property information, but with the addition of the African Burial Ground. And perhaps therein lies the answer to the question: Kirkham noted the detailed property markings, somehow understood their relationship to the African Burial Ground, and consequently, added the name to his plan. This relationship between ownership of space and a large, marginalized communal cemetery was significant enough for Kirkham to document.

Grim Plan, 1813

In 1813, David Grim created from memory a map of New York City that depicted the years 1742–44 and was entitled, *A Plan of the City and Environs of New York as they were in the years 1742–1743 and 1744* (fig. 10). Grim rendered detailed information about the city north of the palisades, an area often ignored in cartography of New York City because the town had not fully developed at this northerly point. Generally speaking, this northern area was now owned by wealthy citizens and farmers, which Grim illustrated by drawing farmland, luxurious gardens, and large expanses of property. Number 45 marked Anthony Rutgers's Farm, specifically the estate gardens called Ranelagh (fig. 11). The entire farm was known as Kalk Hook, and the African Burial Ground occupied a portion of it. Like Maerschalck before him, Grim indicated industries around the African Burial Ground. Specifically, Recine & Rips Tan Yard (#40), Corselius Pottery (#43), and Remmey & Crolius Pottery (#44) encroached upon the cemetery area, and ceramic shards and animal bones were dumped into the sacred space, as has been verified by twentieth-century anthropologists and discussed in chapter 3.

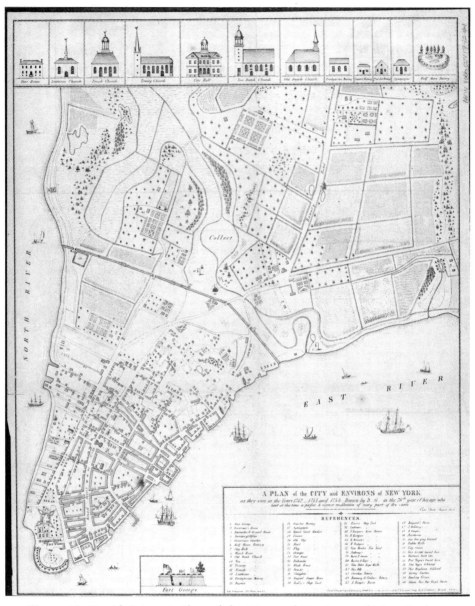

Figure 10. David Grim, *A Plan of the City and Environs of New York as they were in the Years 1742–1743 and 1744. Drawn by D.G. in the 76th year of his age who had at this time a perfect & correct recollection of every part of the same*, 1813. Copied from the original for publication in D. T. Valentine's *Manual*, 1854. Lithograph, 51 × 46 cm. Drawn in 1813, the map chronicles an era several decades earlier, and was then presented to the New-York Historical Society. It includes expansive farms and properties north of the palisades. Courtesy of The Lionel Pincus and Princess Firyal Map Division, The New York Public Library, Astor, Lenox and Tilden Foundations.

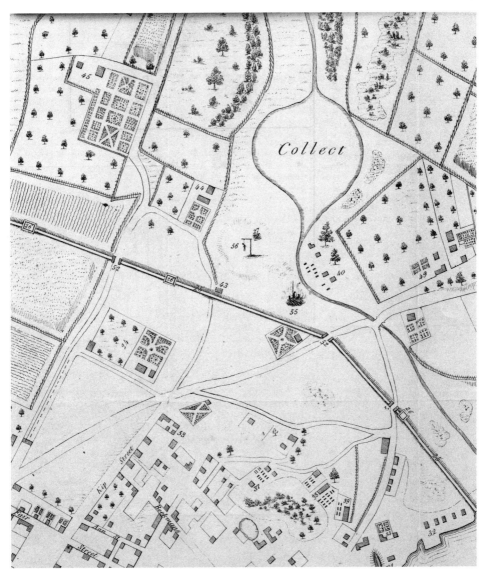

Figure 11. David Grim, Detail of *A Plan of the City and Environs of New York*, 1813. Grim mapped the African Burial Ground (#56) not as a sacred cemetery, but in relation to violence and executions of the 1741 Conspiracy. Courtesy of The Lionel Pincus and Princess Firyal Map Division, The New York Public Library, Astor, Lenox and Tilden Foundations.

Like Kirkham, Grim made this map when the burial ground had already been closed and built upon. The immediate questions, then, are why Grim drew a map from memory and why he used the dates 1742–44. The answers hinge around the African Burial Ground itself.

In the Grim Plan, the African Burial Ground area is not directly labeled but is left unnamed and instead marked in relation to the 1741 Conspiracy and the resulting execution of Africans, who were very likely buried in the African Burial Ground. Grim used two sil-houetted images of black figures; one is hanging from a gibbet and the other burning at the stake (see #56 and #55 in fig. 11). The imagery depicted the gruesome punishment of an ostensible slave rebellion that escalated mass hysteria and executions. Grim's memory of the 1741 drama and trauma dictated his demarcation. He was four years old when the conspiracy occurred, and he was actually taken to view the executions. He later wrote, "I have a perfect idea of seeing the Negroes chained to a stake, and there burned to death."[121]

It can be inferred that David Grim mapped the emergence of a city following its turbulent 1741 Conspiracy while it was still under British rule. In so doing, he took on a role as historian. A 1907 author commented that "David Grim was a man to whose knowledge of early New York every historian and antiquarian is most deeply indebted."[122] Moreover, this map was made for the New-York Historical Society, the oldest museum in New York, which opened in November 1804. A label pasted onto the center of the Historical Society's copy of the map reads, "Presented to the New York Historical Society by David Grim." A publication corroborates this: "David Grim, in his very interesting topographical draft of the city as it was in 1742-4, (done by him when seventy-six years of age, in the year 1813,) is a highly useful relic and gift of the *olden time*. His generous attention to posterity in that gift to the Historical Society is beyond all praise, as a work in itself *sui generis*, and not to be replaced by any other data. He was a chronicle, who lived to be eighty-nine, and to *wonder* at the advancements and *changes* around him! I here mark some of his facts: . . ."[123] The "facts" extend for four pages of text. The author comments elsewhere in the book, "Mr. David Grim, an aged citizen, to whom we are indebted for much valuable *data* given to the Historical Society . . ."[124]

In the Grim Plan of 1813, images of control and oppression are mapped in relation to the African presence in New York, as opposed to the sacred space where the executed were buried. Grim remembered it as a place of violence and execution by first inscribing a small gibbet with a black figure hanging from it for number 56, which he labeled "Plot Negro Gibbeted," and then black figures or silhouettes in flames for number 55, labeled "Plot Negro's burnt here" (fig. 11). "Plot Negro" referred to the 1741 Conspiracy.[125] Relayed by sixteen-year-old indentured servant Mary Burton, the supposed conspiracy by blacks and poor whites who had planned to burn the city cost many in the African community their lives. Indicted Africans and descendant Africans were hanged (#56) on an island between Collect Pond and Little Collect where the city powder house was located (#27). They were also burned at the stake, and this spectacle was held in the Common owned by the city of New York next to the burial ground.

The mapping of the conspiracy illustrates that tensions were high in New York City. The increased black population intensified white fear of local rebellion, which had recently occurred in Stono and Charleston, South Carolina, as well as the earlier 1712 Insurrection in New York.[126] By 1741, nearly one in five inhabitants of New York City was black, and in 1746 there were 2,444 Africans or African descendants (20.9 percent of the population).[127] A string of fires instigated the panic that led to what would become the 1741 Conspiracy. In March 1741, a fire burned Governor Clarke's mansion to the ground inside of Fort George, and the fort itself was burned (#1 in fig. 10). Since the beginning of the New Amsterdam settlement, the fort at the very southern tip of Manhattan had consistently served as the signifier for the political stronghold and military strength of the ruling white power occupying the island of Manhattan. The fort was virtually without fail listed as number one on the legends of maps and views of the city (such as the inset of the Visscher Map, plate 1). Several more groups of fires occurred within a few weeks of Fort George, and ideas of arson and conspiracy developed. Thus, when an Akan man from Ghana named Cuffee ran from a fire, a slave conspiracy was suspected. Certainly there were enough tensions between the enslaved and their enslavers that scholars largely agree oppressed arsonists set a string of fires in retaliation and rebellion; however, plans to take over the city remain unfounded.

The ensuing four month trial through the summer of 1741 recounted a large-scale conspiracy that may or may not have existed, but was certainly fueled by white imagination and hysteria. One of the targets in the trial became the established interracial relationships between enslaved Africans, indentured Europeans, dock workers, sailors, and soldiers.[128] In particular, the white Hughson family, who owned a tavern with a brothel, was arrested before the fires began because stolen goods were reportedly seen in their tavern. The trial also focused on the white sailor John Wilson, along with two slaves named Caesar and Prince, and Prince's white lover Peggy Kerry and mother to their newborn baby, who had all been seen in the Hughson tavern. The Hughson's sixteen-year-old white servant, Mary Burton, had testified as a witness on condition of being freed from indenture. When Burton was questioned about the Hughsons, she had no answers until the court threatened to imprison her. Burton quite likely fabricated her story and certainly created civic uproar. Her statements could not be cross-questioned, as the enslaved under British law were not allowed legal representation. However, many enslavers testified instead that their enslaved were with them during the fires and therefore not guilty.[129] The conspiracy that Burton embellished—that poor whites and blacks had planned to burn down and take over the city—incriminated many townspeople. A few months into the trial, it was decided that a white Latin teacher named John Ury, who was under suspicion of being a Catholic spy, was a leader of the conspiracy. Moreover, the prejudices of elite officials were revealed in the court proceedings, which were published by the New York Supreme Court Judge Daniel Horsmanden in his journal. Judge Horsmanden himself did not believe blacks were capable of developing a conspiracy, and so Ury and the Hughsons became scapegoats as ringleaders of the conspiracy.[130]

Along with Burton, people who were arrested or sentenced to be hung gave up dozens of other names. At one point, just under half of the city's enslaved males over sixteen were in jail.[131] All in all, 160 blacks and 21 whites were arrested. Four whites (including Mr. and Mrs. Hughson, Peggy Kerry, and John Ury) and 17 blacks were hanged, and 13 blacks were burned at the stake. In total, 72 Africans were ostracized from the city and sent to the West Indies and Madeira, where slavery would have been much harsher.

Following all of the executions, Burton began recounting yet more people in connection with the conspiracy. Her naming of prominent white New York citizens took the case to another level. Judge Horsmanden was prompted to close the case quickly so that neither he nor the public would question the veracity of the proceedings. The general New York public, however, had already voiced its doubts when John Ury was accused, and Burton complained of being insulted by people "of both Complexions."[132]

In considering the plight of the accused in 1741, was it possible that Africans slated for execution experienced solace by being in such close proximity to the African Burial Ground (#55 and #56 on the Grim Plan), or in knowing they may be buried there? Was it possible that the city executed Africans on the borders of the African Burial Ground because the area was already understood as an Africanized part of Manhattan?

The spatial location of the hangings, burnings, and burials illustrated an ironic overlapping of race, power, space, and spirituality that involved people of various heritage and class. This complexity therefore demonstrated the inevitable interrelationships of a diverse population, despite issues of classism and racism and imbalances of power. For instance, those linked with the conspiracy were enslaved to families or descendants of families who owned property on the African Burial Ground. These whites included Elizabeth Kiersted, Katherine Kipp, Jr. Hermanus Rutgers, Oliver Teller, and Mrs. Van Borsum, none of whom were slave traders.[133] Other whites who owned acquitted or guilty slaves were wealthy slave traders, including three merchant members of the Bayard family, Abraham and Peter Maerschalck of the city surveyor's family (Francis Maerschalck), Gerardus Duyckinck (who engraved and published the Maerschalck Plan), merchant Adolph Philipse, a Portuguese Jewish merchant named Mordecai Gomez (whose slave hailed directly from Africa with the name Cajoe, or the alias Africa), and merchant Anthony Duane. Anthony Duane's son, James Duane, would have a street named after him that was laid over the burial ground following his tenure as mayor of New York City. Anthony Duane's slave Prince was executed in the 1741 Conspiracy.[134] Prince would thus have a street bearing his master's family name laid over his sacred burial site, close to where he was hanged. Also built over the burial ground, Chambers Street was named after 1741 Conspiracy trial prosecutor John Chambers, who ordered his own slave Robin burned to death, as well as others.

Racism impacted the judgment of the 1741 Conspiracy. Supreme Court Judge Horsmanden wrote a special account in 1744 of the decaying effects on the executed, gibbeted body of John Hughson, whose white skin changed to black, and whose physiognomy, according to Horsmanden, metamorphosed from "Caucasian" into "Negroid" in terms of racial taxonomies developed during this time: " . . . Hughson (who was hung upon the gibbet three weeks before) so much of him as was visible, viz.—face, hands, neck, and feet, were of a deep shining black, rather blacker than the negro placed by him, who was one of the darkest hue of his kind; and the hair of Hughson's beard and neck . . . was curling like the wool of a negro's beard and head, and the features of his face were of the symmetry of a negro beauty; the nose broad and flat, the nostrils open and extended, the mouth wide, lips full and thick."[135]

Horsmanden inscribed the body in relation to notions of racial taxonomies that Enlightenment *philosophes* were using at the same historical moment. In general, intellectuals of the Enlightenment (approximately 1725–1800) privileged reason, the intellect, rationality, empiricism, science, progress, secularism, and freedom. Along with these ideals, the notion of "race" was constructed and defined on the basis of physical observation and hierarchical construction.[136] Work in craniometry and phrenology would force physical appearance to correspond with racial category. Johann Blumenbach, an early developer of the modern racial classification system (1779) viewed Caucasians (white males) as the original, superior race with all others deviating from them. Hierarchy of race, as well as place, was established. David Hume wrote in 1748, "I am apt to suspect the negroes, and in general all the other species of men to be naturally inferior to whites. There never was a civilized nation of any other complexion than white . . . No ingenious manufacturers amongst them, no arts, no sciences."[137] Edward Long justified differentiation of blacks from Europeans because the former were "void of genius, and seem almost incapable of making any progress in civility or science."[138]

Horsmanden's description of Hughson becoming African clearly illustrates the construction and conflation of race and class. The socializing at Hughson's tavern, in which enslaved blacks had melded with the white lower class rather than remaining hierarchically separate, was made visible to New York City at large during the trials. Did John and his wife Sarah receive the ultimate punishment of death because their establishment supported interracial relationships, including sex and friendships, which threatened colonial social order? In fact, Chief Justice James DeLancey commented at the Hughsons' sentencing that they were "guilty of not only making Negroes their equals but even their superiors by waiting upon, keeping with, and entertaining them."[139]

Thus, Hughson's punished and "corrupted" corpse dropped to a lower level from white male to black male in the Enlightenment construction of race. Because Hughson was convicted of a crime as a result of crossing racial lines, his body became black and shared that destiny. In any case, the inscription of blackness onto whiteness reveals the construction of race and the possibility for attachment, detachment, and reattachment of racial identity.[140] Thus, Hughson's body visually depicted the consequence of breaking a racial contract, which was corporeal punishment rendered through spectacle.

The slave trade was reconfigured geographically and numerically as a result of the 1741 Conspiracy. Before 1741, the average number imported per year to New York was 150, and afterward it dropped to sixty per year.[141] Importations from the Caribbean to New York had escalated up until 1741; whereas after that time 70 percent of slaves were brought directly from Africa. The trend is a reverse of the reaction following the 1712 Insurrection. From 1665 to 1712, British traffickers had intensified importation of people directly from Africa by eight times,[142] but this altered with a preference for the Caribbean in response to the 1712 Insurrection.

To return briefly to David Grim, it seems that not only would his attendance at the execution spectacle at age four prompt an impression of the conspiracy, but also his later life experiences may have made him particularly attuned to the intricacies of the pro-ceedings. He worked on a merchant ship for two years in the West Indies, the region from which many enslaved people were brought to New York.[143] He then worked in The Three Tuns Tavern, and as we know, the conspiracy revolved around the Hughsons' tavern. Perhaps because Grim could relate to the conspiracy based on details of his life, he decided to map his memory of the event.

Conclusion

It is unknown exactly why or when the African Burial Ground came into existence. This chapter offers suggestions and also proposes that Africans themselves chose the site for the African Burial Ground rather than have it allocated to them. Points of African agency to con-sider are that the landowners in the vicinity of what would become the African Burial Ground were freed Africans, that the cemetery was located next to a large body of water that could have held spiri-tual significance, that the site was located outside of town away from white surveillance, that Trinity Church discontinued the burial of Africans in 1697 and so a burial space was needed, and that SPG schoolmaster William Huddleston owned a portion of the burial ground area from 1697 to 1702. The cemetery likely came into use before 1712, but definitely existed by 1712 when John Sharpe wrote about it. Sharpe's narrative, along with two others and the British laws enacted later on, offers significant information about actual funerals. They were held in African languages during the night with large groups of people in attendance at times.

The early use of the African Burial Ground is linked to Trinity Church in numerous and powerful ways. It was likely, at least in part, that a communal cemetery began because Trinity proclaimed Africans could no longer be buried in its churchyard in 1697; that two of the only three narratives in existence about the African Burial Ground were written by officials of the church; that the first ever written document (1712) naming the cemetery was by a Trinity church chaplain; that William Huddleston of Trinity's SPG owned a portion of the African Burial Ground, possibly before it was in use; and that the 1712 Insurrection was blamed on Elias Neau of the SPG for teaching Africans to read. These links certainly articulate the tension between the SPG endeavoring to support Africans in a missionary-like way (through conversion and literacy) and other whites who resisted such practices due to fear of black empowerment. To that end, the reason that documents about the burial ground were written by John Sharpe and SPG secretary David Humphreys is because of their great concern that Africans were buried without Christian rites. Sharpe wrote in 1712, the same year as the insurrection, when Christian conversion of Africans was condemned.

Once the burial ground was established, its mapping by a handful of cartographers demarcated an African presence in New York City. It is interesting that the burial ground could never be fixed spatially. Instead, it was located in open space on maps, which would have signified undeveloped land. This "undeveloped space" remained as such for most of the eighteenth century because it was in fact in use as a cemetery for Africans and African descendants. The four mapmakers Buchnerd, Maerschalck, Kirkham, and Grim mapped the site for varying reasons. Buchnerd unmistakably had intimate knowledge of the city for her 1735 map and included other spaces that were infrequently or never mapped by others. Maerschalck was the town

surveyor and so would have had knowledge about the area, probably because of the myriad of legal disputes surrounding ownership
of property, as will be recounted in the next chapter. The map from
Kirkham's logbook, I suggest, was based on the Ratzen Plan of New
York; however, Kirkham added the "Negros Burial Ground," which
was not mapped on the former. Since he spent his life at sea for the
British Royal Navy, how did he come to know about the cemetery, or
why did he map it, complete with fences and property boundaries?
Finally, Grim remembered the burial ground as a space of violence
rather than as a cemetery. He mapped an African burning at the
stake and another one being hanged, two punishments as a result of
the 1741 Conspiracy.

The recounting of the 1712 Insurrection and the 1741 Conspiracy illustrate that certainly suppression and enslavement were
present, but African agency and resistance also played a role in the
colonial New York experience. In sum, the representation of space
through cartography becomes telling in relation to urban expansion,
the vagueness of the cemetery's location, and reasons these four cartographers chose to remember and record the sacred space's existence
in the eighteenth century.

2

Ownership Disputes, Land Surveys, and Urban Developments

Colonial era prints and local maps of Manhattan offered an understanding of an African presence and general mapping of the African Burial Ground, as discussed in chapter 1. This chapter hones in on detailed mapping of the African Burial Ground through land surveys of the cemetery itself from 1673 to its closure in 1795. The end of the chapter recounts urban development on the cemetery from 1795 to the 1980s.

With a paucity of colonial documentation, land survey maps become a significant means for understanding complex histories and territorial tensions at the African Burial Ground. The cemetery and properties adjacent to it were surveyed for two primary reasons: to support urban expansion by dividing lots and laying streets, and to resolve land disputes that in some cases had lasted for more than a century. A tracing of this particular kind of spatial representation of the African Burial Ground reveals the stark tensions between a sacred burial site used by lower class, marginalized Africans and African Americans, on the one hand, and treatment of the landmark as real estate owned by elite Europeans, European Americans, and the city of New York, on the other. While there was by and large an attempt to ignore a colonial African presence, this chapter illustrates that it became repeatedly necessary to acknowledge and document the existence of the cemetery engaged by the African community as space was mapped, delineated, and

75

developed throughout the colonial era. Ironically, documented recognition of the burial ground increased with mapping at the same
time that use of the site was fading. While knowledge about the site
is limited in many ways, a plethora of information exists concerning ownership and conflict over the space.

A survey compiled by Murray Hoffman in the nineteenth century offers layered temporal incarnations in the eighteenth century
to illustrate in a holistic way several land issues surrounding the
African Burial Ground (fig. 12).[1] The survey documents ownership over a 121-year period from 1673 to 1794. These dates included early city land grants and the final planning of streets over
the burial ground beginning in 1784. Hoffman's survey is therefore used as a template throughout this chapter to consider the
treatment of the African Burial Ground space and its surrounding
areas.

In this chapter, to trace the history of the African Burial Ground's
land ownership and development, the land is divided into four
major geographic areas labeled with the numbers that correspond
to Diagram 8 of Hoffman's survey (fig. 12): (1) Kalk Hook Farm,
(2) Corporation of New York, (3) Van Borsum Patent, and (4) Janeway Land. The four areas are threaded throughout the chapter
within three themes. The areas are detailed first in terms of private land and city property beginning in 1673, second in terms of
preparation for development from 1784 to 1795, and third for the
built environment constructed on top of the cemetery from 1795
to the 1980s.

The colonial history in figure 12 can be read in conjunction with
its more contemporary space in the Bromley Map in plate 5, where
the Ted Weiss Federal Building at 290 Broadway would be erected
on modern Block 154. During the time that the Burial Ground was
in use, this block was split diagonally between two landowners (see
dashed line in plate 5): the northern half was called Kalk Hook
Farm (fig. 12, section 1), and the southern half was referred to as
the Van Borsum Patent (fig. 12, section 3).

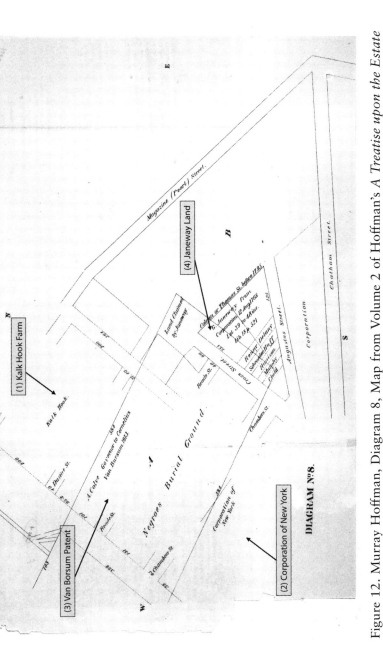

Figure 12. Murray Hoffman, Diagram 8, Map from Volume 2 of Hoffman's *A Treatise upon the Estate and Rights of the Corporation of the City of New York, as Proprietors*, 1862. Black ink on paper, 28 × 42 cm. Survey of land occupied by the African Burial Ground spanning the years 1673 to 1794. The four labeled areas are analyzed in detail in this chapter. M36.5.33, neg. #89503d. Collection of the New-York Historical Society.

Private Lands and City Properties, Beginning 1673

Kalk Hook Farm

The northernmost lot of land depicted on the Hoffman survey was called Kalk Hook Farm (Kalkhoeck, Kalchook, or Calk Hook) (fig. 12, section 1). This farm formed the northern boundary of the African Burial Ground. Specifically, excavations in the 1990s revealed that burials extended 30 to 35 feet into Kalk Hook Farm.[2] Once blocks were formulated by the city of New York, this area became known as the northern half of Block 154 and is still recognized as such today.

The land labeled "Kalk Hook" on the Hoffman survey was initially granted in March 1646 to a Dutchman named Jan Jansen Damen by the Dutch West India Company, which had occupied the land for ten years. Following Jan Jansen Damen's death around 1651, all of this land was divided into four lots.[3] When excavated in the 1990s, burial remains were found here.[4]

One of the four quadrants was owned by Abram Isaac Verplanck but was used by Damen. Verplanck's heirs, who would remain strong Anglican benefactors, then conveyed this area of land to William Huddleston in 1697.[5] Interestingly, Huddleston taught in an Anglican catechism school (SPG) for enslaved blacks and Native Americans from 1710 to 1723.[6] It is suggested in chapter 1 that Huddleston could have enabled the founding of the African Burial Ground since he supported Africans and they were expelled from burial at Trinity Church in 1697. In analyzing the provenance of this land, we see that Huddleston actually owned land on the perimeter of the African Burial Ground, if not on what would become the cemetery itself. Since this was also already an African neighborhood, his proximity to an African part of New York City may have encouraged his position as leader in SPG, or he may have held a particular interest in doing so. Additionally, perhaps Africans buried their dead here because they knew Huddleston to be a friendly and influential neighbor in an area that was already an African neighborhood.

By 1725, Anthony Rutgers had purchased most of Damen's original four lots, and they remained in his family (with a split later to the Barclay family) until they were built over and developed in the 1780s.[7] Additionally, in 1730, Anthony Rutgers submitted a petition to request for ownership 70 acres adjacent to his farm and the Fresh Water Pond because he was concerned that the increasingly stagnant, swampy water was unsanitary.[8] The land was granted to him in 1733 on the condition that he drain the swamp. He had a canal dug to the Hudson River, but when the tanneries found their production disrupted, they successfully petitioned against the drainage canal.

Because Kalk Hook Farm was adjacent to and also a part of the African Burial Ground, the cemetery was integrated into a 1763 survey that is now held by the New-York Historical Society archives.[9] This survey is interesting because, although the African Burial Ground is not depicted on the map itself, the burial ground is referenced in the narrative text inscribed onto the survey. The survey was drawn up after Rutgers's 1746 death because the farm was then divided into three parts for a Rutgers, Leonard Lispenard, and Henry Barclay. Barclay was a son-in-law to Rutgers as well as a minister from Albany who had preached among the Mohawks and later became rector of Trinity Church. It was Henry Barclay's share, or "no. 1" on the survey, that ran along the northern border of the African Burial Ground. The handwritten narrative described Barclay's land as running east "to the Broadway thence across the Broadway and along the Negroes Burying Ground S h2 E 7 chs 83 I to the pond or marsh thence along the pond or marsh."

This handwritten text suggests that, at this point in the 1760s, the cemetery had not yet stretched to or no longer reached into Rutgers's farm (which it did at one time, based on findings made during excavations for the federal office building), but lay to the south of it. The description also suggests that the burial ground reached the shores of the Collect Pond in the 1760s, which would not be the case later on when the expanding tanneries and potteries used the pond for their industries. Finally, the survey noted that the cemetery commenced only after crossing Broadway, which means that the age-old thoroughfare served as the western border for the cemetery.[10] A detailed survey such as this 1763 mapping was forced to acknowledge the presence of the burial ground in its attempt to define the breadth of white property ownership.

Corporation of New York

The land labeled "Corporation of New York" on the Hoffman survey is south of what would become Chambers Street and City Hall Park (fig. 12, section 2). The Corporation of New York, or the Common, referred to municipal land owned by the city. Civic uses through the years included land for pasture, the site for the city Powder House (built 1728), and the area for public celebration of holidays, including Pinkster around the time of Pentecost. Africans were buried in this communal space because a portion of the burial ground stretched into the Common during a period before 1745 and/or after 1760 when no fence separated the Common from the cemetery.[11] Interments in the Common would definitely not have occurred between 1745 and 1760 because a fence (palisade) built by enslaved Africans separated the two areas, as depicted on the Maerschalck Plan (fig. 7) and discussed in chapter 1.

The Common legally belonged to the city as early as the second half of the seventeenth century. Its ownership came about following the 1664 British conquest through the Dongan Charter of 1686, which stipulated that any vacant or unclaimed land belonged to the municipal government. This stipulation was later reinforced by the Montgomerie Charter of 1730.[12] Although the land was in use as a cemetery, no African ever owned the site, and the land remained a de facto possession of the Corporation of New York according to the city. In fact, the area was excavated in 1999 when City Hall Park was redesigned and renovated. Several graves were uncovered at the very north end of the Park, the north foundation of the Tweed Court-house, and Chambers Street. The excavations were hidden from public view by green tarps under the Giuliani administration; the dead were not tested or dated for identity, ostensibly so the city would not be caught in another controversy following 290 Broadway. There was a possibility that the bones derived from a 1736 almshouse that had a small burial ground laid out in this same area of the Common in 1757, or that there was a *"possible"* overlap between the two cemeteries.[13] The final report for the African Burial Ground maintains that the cemetery "probably extended further south" into this very area.[14]

Van Borsum Patent

An area of Hoffman's survey is labeled "A. Colve. Governor to Cornelius. Van Bursum 1673" (fig. 12, section 3). This label existed because when the Dutch briefly regained control of the city from the British in 1673 during the Restitution (as depicted in the inset of the Seutter Map, plate 2), the governor at the time, Anthony Colve, granted several patents of land to civilians. In this case, Governor Colve presented the northern half of the city's Common to Sara Roeloff by deeding it to her second husband, Cornelius Van Borsum. The Van Borsum Patent is outlined by a rectangle on Hoffman's survey and comprises today's southern half of Block 154. Colve's grant to the family was in exchange for Sara Roeloff's assistance in translations between Esopus Native Americans and the city of New Amsterdam during peace negotiations.[15] As is evident from the Hoffman survey and from excavations in the 1990s, the burial ground would come to exist on Van Borsum's plot of land.

Thus, the African Burial Ground land was caught in a dispute at the local level between, on the one hand, the Common Council of New York during the British era, which claimed ownership of undeveloped, unfenced, and unused land (via the Dongan and Montgomerie Charters), and, on the other hand, the Van Borsum/Roeloff family, which had been deeded the land by Governor Colve under the brief Dutch reconquest. The dispute concerning this land would continue for more than a century, not only because local finances were at stake, but also because of claims to colonial leadership and national memory. The city had acted in two directions under two conflicting powers: under brief Dutch control, the governor deeded land to a family in 1673; and then thirteen years later under British control, the 1686 Dongan Charter defined the unoccupied land as the city's. In a larger context, the African Burial Ground would therefore be caught in international politics between the Netherlands and Britain concerning their respective national claims to New World possessions. During these early dates, it is unlikely that the burial ground yet existed or had grown to any communal size.

The Van Borsum story continued after his death. Sara Roeloff became owner of the land in 1680 upon the death of her husband, who willed everything to her.[16] Upon her death in 1693, her estate was divided equally among her eight children.[17] Sara Roeloff had named as executors to her estate her son Lucas Kiersted and her sons-in-law Johannes Kip and William Teller. To add yet another layer of controversy, the 1673 Van Borsum land grant by Governor Colve was reconfirmed twenty-three years later in 1696 by the British governor Benjamin Fletcher. For whatever reason, however, Fletcher "ignored" Roeloff's personal will from three years earlier and instead took the liberty of granting the property in question to the three executors of her estate and "their Heirs and Assignes forever."[18] Had Governor Fletcher deeded the land on his terms in order to maintain male ownership? Or, did he want to reward or favor Kiersted, Kip, and Teller in particular? In any case, a dispute arose over whether these three owned the land, whether Fletcher had perhaps granted them the land in order to serve as executors (on behalf of Roeloff's heirs), or whether Roeloff's children as previously stipulated were the owners.[19] This second dispute remained unresolved for nearly one hundred years. Several times, descendants of Kip and Kiersted visited the Common Council to claim their land. For example, they approached the Common Council in 1753 to request an exchange of the "Negroe burying place" for other city land.[20] The Council of course defaulted to the first dispute by maintaining that the land belonged to the Common, that is, to the City of New York. In fact, in the popular mind, the Van Borsum Patent was considered a part of the public Common owned by the city.[21] Moreover, an act had been passed that attempted to annul the extravagant land grants made by Governor Fletcher.[22] Nonetheless, it is quite possible that these lengthy and unresolved land disputes postponed urban development of this land, enabling continued use of the African Burial Ground.[23] Also, the hilly topography and marshy area surrounding Collect Pond would have made the land difficult to farm or develop.[24]

Further evidence of unresolved land conflicts was documented in December 1760. A prior agreement was made in which Maria Van Vleck and siblings leased from the city for the last nineteen and a half years land south of the palisade that was "three Lots of ground contiguous and adjoining to the Negroes Burying place on part of which said Lots their father [Abraham Van Vleck] built a Potting House pot oven and a well supposing at that time the said lands were his property."[25] To summarize, this portion of land was perhaps initially a part of the African Burial Ground and the Van Borsum patent, was appropriated for use by Van Vleck's pottery factory from about 1741 to 1760, came to be considered part of the Common and therefore city property, and was then reconveyed by lease to the Van Borsum heirs.

Another claimant to the land, Isaac Teller, had built three houses along Broadway near Chambers Street within the Van Borsum patent between 1760 and 1765. Kirkham probably depicted these houses in his plan, as was already considered in chapter 1 (fig. 9). These houses, along with two others just to the north belonging to Ackerman and Kip, were perhaps built on top of graves, and no new burials were dug in this area afterwards.[26] Probably because the burial ground was now Teller's backyard, he attempted to profit from the situation. In the late 1760s, Teller placed a fence around the edge of the burial ground and he then tried to sell plots of land for burials. The court case noted:

In May 1768, J. Teller entered into possession of a house which he had built two or three years before on the Negroes' Burying-Ground and which had, previously to his entrance, been occupied by his tenant; that he had a fence enclosing the burying-ground, and claimed it as his property, and pastured it, and kept the key of the gate leading to the ground, and took payment for the use of the ground . . . ; that he continued in possession afterward . . . until . . . the British army took possession of the house and lot, and during the course of the war; and that while under the dominion of the British, the house and fences were destroyed.[27]

The court case was held in 1812–13 because once again arguments over legal ownership of land arose. When British forces occupied the area beginning in 1776, they destroyed Teller's houses and his fence, and the British began their own small cemetery in the southern part of the African Burial Ground.[28]

Janeway Land

The ownership of the "Janeway Land" lying to the south of the Fresh Water Pond has been traced back to at least 1651 (fig. 12, section 4). Amazingly, this tract of land was also mired in controversy and even involved some of the same people and families of the Van Borsum Patent mixup. Several surveys of the Janeway Land were drawn up by William Cockburn in order to resolve the issue.[29] The Janeway surveys and accompanying documents, which have not been analyzed previously and are presented here for the first time, are of particular significance because of several references to the African Burial Ground.

The provenance of the land is as follows. Governor Stuyvesant granted the patent labeled B in figure 12 to Paulus Schrick on January 31, 1662.[30] Paulus Schrick sold the farm to Jacob Kip in 1661, but also deeded it to his own wife Maria Teller upon his death.[31] Then, in 1698, the City mistakenly conveyed the same four acres to William Janeway.[32] Eventually, William's grandson George Janeway settled the dispute in 1769. Properties and lots would be exchanged by trading five different acres owned by the city.[33] Hoffman has depicted this history on his survey in the triangle (fig. 12, section 4).

The end result of the agreement between the city and George Janeway was surveyed by Cockburn in 1766 (fig. 13). This survey,

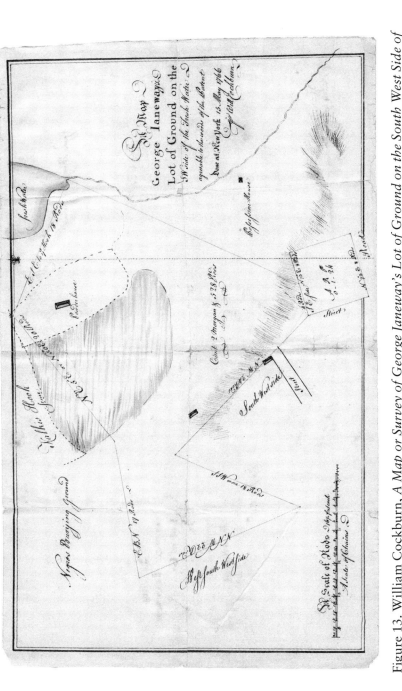

Figure 13. William Cockburn, A Map or Survey of George Janeway's Lot of Ground on the South West Side of the Fresh Water, Agreeable to the Words of the Patent, 1766. Pen and ink on paper, 14⅛ × 18¼ in. This newly found document maps the "Negro Burying Ground," and confirms the existence of a fence running between "Kalkis Hook" and Van Borsum properties. Drawer 8, Folder 5, Item 14 of "The Janeway Papers," Deeds and Indentures Collection. Special Collections and University Archives, Rutgers University Libraries.

which came to light in 2006, adds one more rare representation of the African Burial Ground to the very few in existence. At this time just beyond its midcentury use, the cemetery abutted the southwest side of Collect Pond, as seen in the survey. In figure 13, to the right of the words "Negro Burying Ground" is a label that is particularly noteworthy: it reads, "Kalkis Hook fence." As will be explained in the next chapter, the research team analyzing the burial ground during the last decade of the twentieth century suggested that a fence or fences ran between the Van Borsum and Rutgers properties, cutting the Burial Ground in half for a time.[34] However, the map shown in figure 13, only uncovered in 2006, confirms here for the first time the anthropologists' hypothesis. The fence was standing by 1766, and I suggest was related to Rutgers's land since it was labeled Kalkis Hook after his farm. If the bottom line of Hoffman's rectangle in figure 12 is the palisade, then the top line should be the Kalkis Hook fence that, as can be seen in the top right, corners off the "land claimed by Janeway."

In sum, the Janeway family owned the easternmost portion of the African Burial Ground from around the time it came into existence, in 1698, until 1768, when the city took the land back. Under city ownership, Africans were able to continue their burials for almost another thirty years.

Preparation for Development over the African Burial Ground, 1784–95

Documented frequently toward the end of the eighteenth century, as urban development spread northward, the burial ground was subdivided into lots and sold off. Streets were laid over and structures were built on top of the site. Interestingly, it seems to have been an accepted practice to incorporate cemeteries into urban expansion by building over them or by moving the dead.[35]

Following the 1776 Revolution, a time of peace and economic boom propelled urban development, on the one hand, and the eventual cessation of the African Burial Ground, on the other.[36] The four geographic sections of the burial ground outlined in the Hoff-man survey are again traced during this era of intense development between 1787 and 1795. It would prove to be the final years the African Burial Ground remained in existence and it was quite carefully documented because land disputes had to be resolved and then lots divided, claimed, and sold through the process of surveying, measuring, and finally, mapping. Therefore, historic documents recounting this process bring the burial ground to life for us in the twenty-first century while at the same time, contribute to its erasure at the end of the eighteenth century.

Division of Kalk Hook Farm

Anthony Rutgers's Kalk Hook Farm (fig. 12, section 1) was the first portion of the African Burial Ground to be divided into lots with streets laid over it, as is evident from the 1787 survey (fig. 14).[37] Upon the death of Henry Barclay, Rutgers's land was surveyed, measured, and partitioned into lots by his executors, Leonard Lispenard and wife Mary Barclay.[38] Those lots, as well as surrounding ones, were transferred to Anthony Barclay in 1788 for £5,465. "Negroes Burying Ground" is marked in figure 14, which affirms its partial continued existence at this time. The survey depicts the initial move toward urban development over a portion of the burial ground, instigating the erasure of memory of the site.

What were the implications of dividing sacred space for secular urban development? Did controversy, conflict, or anger erupt? The burial ground had stretched 30 to 35 feet up into the lots of Kalk Hook Farm, as shown in this survey.[39] Were graves still being dug in Kalk Hook Farm, or were they still visited and honored by the living following the drawing up of the survey? What was the response as Africans began to lose engagement with a space containing their loved ones and to witness instead the shrinking and secularizing of the cemetery? It is believed that no structures had yet been built here, but it is possible that a fence or survey posts marking the outlines of lots deterred future burials.[40] We know that a year later,

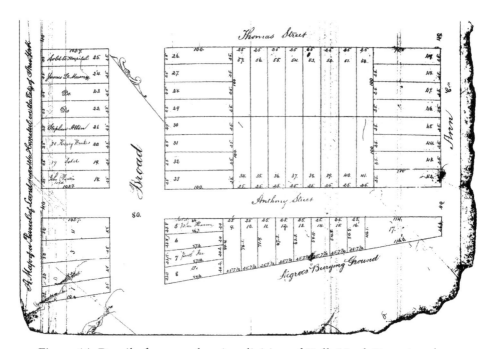

Figure 14. Detail of survey showing division of Kalk Hook Farm into lots, 1787. Microfilm. A portion of the burial ground is divided into lots in preparation for urban development, while half is still labeled a sacred cemetery. Courtesy of the Division of Land Records, Deeds (Liber 46:139).

bodysnatching from the African Burial Ground resulted in the Doctors' Riot of 1788 (see the last section of the introduction), which confirms that the living cared deeply for the deceased and fought to protect them. A colonial African presence is indeed visible politically and cartographically in response to both white medical students and land ownership issues.

A point to consider is that, according to the research team's stratigraphy (spatial and temporal mapping of the graves) of the African Burial Ground, Kalk Hook Farm was actually where the most recent, final burials occurred.[41] Burials in this northernmost section of the burial ground are dated from 1776 to 1795 (see chapter 3). Several deceased were itinerants who came to the city to fight for or against the British. It seems particularly disturbing and emotionally painful that those who had just been laid to rest beginning around 1776 would be built over so immediately, even if their family members did not live nearby (or at least plans were mapped for a move in that direction). Anthony Street (later Duane Street) was mapped in the 1787 survey (fig. 14), and was probably not laid until 1795, when proprietors of adjacent lots were called upon to "dig out and fill in" the street.[42] Also, the Barclays began to sell and lease their lots along Duane Street after this 1787 survey was drawn up. The first structures, however, were built between 1794 and 1799.[43] Thus, the deceased were laid to rest beginning in 1776 up until the cemetery closed, and construction probably began in 1794, meaning that at the very least, the dead remained undisturbed for as much as eighteen years and for as little as less than a year.

It is unknown exactly when the African Burial Ground closed or was no longer in use. However, George Gibbs's survey at the New-York Historical Society verifies that by 1792, the lots were still divided up and unsold, as each 25-foot lot remained empty without the name of an owner added to it. The Gibbs survey suggests that, at least by 1792, Kalk Hook Farm was still free from urban development.[44] Virtually all of the lots on the 1792 survey measured 25 feet, a planning system that aligned with surveyors Goerck and Magnin, who introduced the use of grid-patterned streets to Manhattan and also produced the first citywide survey. This particular block however could not be methodically divided because it existed as a historical reminder of properties owned by two separate families and used by Africans and their descendants. The block was split diagonally for over a century, developed at varying times, and used by Africans to bury their dead.

Anthony Rutgers, who owned Kalk Hook Farm, also owned the Collect Pond area. By the close of the century, the Collect Pond had several problems that must have at least in part affected the African Burial Ground bordering the pond (fig. 13). Burials were closest to the southern side of the pond up until the first half of the eighteenth century, but after that pottery manufacturers began to hem in the burial ground along its eastern side.[45] By the 1780s, the Fresh Water

Pond, or Collect Pond, was severely polluted not only from the tanneries and other industries, but also because it had become a garbage dump. City historian David Valentine noted that "encroachments were daily made on the Fresh Water Pond, and that filth and dirt were thrown into it by persons residing there."[46] John Randel, author of the 1811 Randel Survey or Commissioner's Map, described the Collect Pond: "The Collect was at that time filled up by a collection of spare earth and rubbish &c, carted from the city, which being of greater specific gravity than the debris or mud at the bottom of 'the Pond' or 'Collect' caused it to rise, and mix with the rubbish and stand out, forming a very offensive and irregular mound of several acres; which appeared to me, as seen from Broadway, between which and it there were no buildings, to be from 12 to 15 feet in height above the level of the tide, and of the water remaining in the Pond."[47] The pond was filled in from 1802 to 1812, as ordered by the City Council to facilitate urban development.

A 1798 engraving and watercolor entitled *Collect Pond, New York City* illustrates the African Burial Ground area just after it had closed down (fig. 15). Indeed, it is only one of two views of the African Burial Ground in existence, neither of which was created during the time it was in use (the other is Danckaerts's drawing, made before the burial ground was in use, fig. 5). The cemetery was located on the near side of Collect Pond (foreground of figure 15). The buildings depicted in the middleground on the south shore related to the tanneries that depended on the pond for operation and that had encroached upon the African Burial Ground, using it as a dumping ground for animal bones after the skins were removed. The city prison, named Bridewell (shown to the right of center in fig. 15), was built on the Common in 1775 and most likely disturbed burials in the African Burial Ground when it was constructed.[48] Looking south, buildings and churches such as Trinity Church and St. Paul's Chapel further downtown are visible.

The 1798 *Collect Pond* depicted the body of water from the perspective of one standing on its northeastern shore, either at today's Canal and Centre Streets or at Bayard and Baxter, looking across the

NEW YORK.

Figure 15. Attributed to Archibald Robertson, *Collect Pond, New York City*, 1798. Watercolor and black chalk on off-white laid paper, 17¾ × 23¹⁄₁₆ in. The artwork shows the burial ground area, seen in the foreground, which had closed roughly three years earlier. The structures across the pond in the middleground are the tanneries that used the pond for operation and the burial ground as a dumping site. The Bridewell city prison is to the right of center in the Common. The Edward W. C. Arnold Collection of New York Prints, Maps, and Pictures, Bequest of Edward W. C. Arnold (54.90.168). Photo by Geoffrey Clements. Image copyright The Metropolitan Museum of Art. Image source: Art Resource, NY.

pond to the southwest (fig. 15).⁴⁹ Kalk Hook Farm was to the right, closer to the northwest corner of the pond. The high bluff to the left may actually be the Kalk Hook (chalk or shell hill), for which Rutgers's farm and the Collect Pond were named.⁵⁰ The Collect Pond is rendered serene and scenic. Stokes adds that "[t]his is the only known contemporary view of the Collect or Fresh Water Pond, one of the most picturesque features in the original topography of Manhattan Island."[51] The artist portrayed the site as beautiful countryside where economically comfortable citizens walked idly. At least twenty years earlier, the northern side of the pond was popular for ice skaters, boaters, and fishers, and onlookers would sit on the 100-foot hill to enjoy the scenery.[52] The artist's view was largely nostalgic, as the pond had become so polluted and stagnant that Anthony Rutgers had asked the city to fill it in.

Division of Van Borsum Patent

The southern half of modern Block 154, which was the old Van Borsum grant (fig. 12, section 3), took longer to partition than the northern half. This was certainly not by chance, as development of Manhattan continued around the Van Borsum Patent. One reason for the lag in partitioning this area was the marshiness near Little Collect and Collect Pond, which rendered construction difficult, as well as the pollution within Collect Pond. Another reason was that ownership disputes were still not yet resolved. Finally, an overarching reason the area remained undeveloped for so long was the presence of the African Burial Ground.

Lots within the Van Borsum Patent would be divided equally to all of the heirs by 1795, as depicted in surveys from that year. Two 1795 surveys illustrated this division of lots among the heirs: one from the Bancker Plans in the New York Public Library (fig. 16), and another from the Division of Land Records.[53] It seems that the Bancker survey, created by merchant and surveyor Evart Bancker Jr., served as an earlier draft for the finely finished and tidier Register's Office version. The African Burial Ground was not demarcated on either 1795 survey, since it had now been divided up into lots. Up until this time, final decisions on the legality of ownership had not been clearly resolved. Thus, 1795 most likely marked the latest date for the existence of the African Burial Ground as commercial interests took over and space became a premium. Building began almost immediately following completion of each survey.[54] The title of the survey nevertheless recognized and recalled the cemetery, signaling that it continued to be understood as such in this transitory moment: *Negroes Burying Ground: Drawing of Broadway Block with Lots Numbered.*

The Bancker survey (fig. 16) illustrates the resolution of the disputes surrounding the Van Borsum Patent and who received which lot of land. It served as a partition deed dividing lots among the heirs and claimants to the estate by placing initials of people in specific lots, such as C for Roeloff (later Kip), D for the Teller family, F for

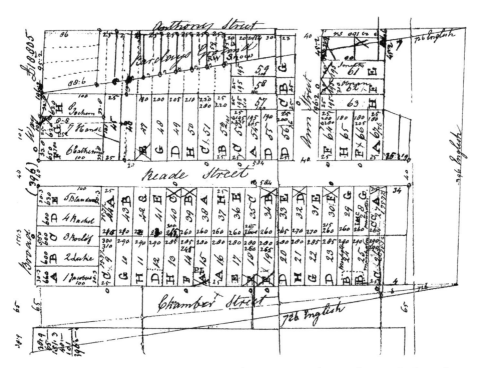

Figure 16. *Negroes Burying Ground: Drawing of Broadway Block with Lots Numbered*, 1795. The burial ground is no longer marked because it has been completely divided up into lots in this transitory time of urban development. A solution to ownership disputes is illustrated. In Bancker Plans, Evart Bancker Jr. Box 1, Folder 44, #3. Manuscript Collections, The New York Public Library, Astor, Lenox and Tilden Foundations.

Van Vleck, and B for Daniel Denniston, whose wife descended from Lucas Kiersted. The choice lots bordering Broadway were decided upon by drawing the names of the eight children of Sara Roeloff for each of the eight lots.[55] City surveyors and assessors divided the other lots, and a fifteen-page document filed in 1833 specified the heirs, including the heirs of Roeloff's executors. The survey contains a few sporadically marked measurements, but actually focuses more on the ownership and monetary wealth of each individual lot in preparation for dissemination.

The Bancker Plans box in the New York Public Library also contains Kiersted's ledger sheets, which list owners matched up to lot numbers and an appraisal of what each lot was worth. It seems that the amounts listed on this ledger sheet in 1784 were then transferred onto each lot of the 1795 survey, with a total of £18,805 handwritten at the top left (fig. 16). The ledger sheet lists, for example, Lot 3 along Broadway to Roelof Kiersted at £600, Lot 7 on Broadway to Hans Kiersted at £620, and Lot 31 along Reade Street to Blandina at £270. Although the burial ground is not mentioned at all, its civic memory remains in the title of the ledger: *Amounts sold for the Appraisement of the lots on the Negroes Burying Ground Kiersted's Lots, 1784.*

Where would Africans bury their dead? In 1794, just prior to the 1795 survey, African and African descendants were able to make their voices heard in a political milieu at a time when industry and urbanization were closing in on their sacred space. On 27 October 1794, the Common Council recorded "a Petition from sundry black men in this City praying the Aid of this Board in purchasing a Piece of Ground for the interment of their dead."[56] Five months later, in April 1795, the Common Council reported back that Chrystie Street from the Delancey estate would be suitable. It was decided that a new African burial ground would open there, that the city would contribute £100 towards the purchase of four lots, each sized 100 feet by 25 feet, at a total cost of £450, and that the city would hold the deed in trust for its users.[57] In June, another petition was submitted by Isaac Fortune and additional free men of color who founded the mutual aid association called the African Society. They requested legal management of the Chrystie Street cemetery, including the collection of burial fees and privileges held by managers of other cemeteries.[58] Trinity Church had already set aside a plot for its black members in 1773 one block west of the African Burial Ground on Reade Street between Church and West Broadway, which remained open only until August 1795.[59] The small plot was then divided into lots and leased.

These petitions would mark only the second time in New York history that publicly voiced statements by Africans and their descendants concerning the African Burial Ground were documented. The first instance was through an unfiled petition in 1788 concerning grave robbing by Columbia medical school (see the last section of the introduction to this book). A cemetery in use for almost a century covering 6.7 acres of space was not documented and archived visually, orally, or textually by any Africans except for these two incidents. Moreover, it was not visually represented by anyone. It was mapped by four cartographers. It was described in written text by two members of Trinity Church's SPG and by a city historian, and it was referred to in the Minutes of the Common Council and Stokes a handful of times. Such was the degree of civic marginalization and racism.

Division in the Corporation

In 1796, the Common Council laid Chambers Street through the African Burial Ground and the Common. In order to do this, the city had to acquire a portion of the African Burial Ground so as to extend Chambers Street east of Broadway (fig. 12 shows Chambers Street had not yet crossed to the left beyond Broadway). However, the Van Borsum land had already been partitioned among its heirs in 1795, as explained above. For a solution, Kip, Breese, Van Vleck, and Denniston sold their land back to the Corporation of New York.[60] Even though the land had been divided up among the heirs, it was still referred to in 1796 during these negotiations as the

"Negroes Burying Ground," as recorded in the minutes of the Common Council. Here, the minutes detail the process for how the city could lay streets over the burial ground: "The Committee to whom the memorial of Henry Kip and others with proposals to settle and adjust the boundary lines between the Corporation and the Claimants of the Land called the Negroes Burying Ground . . . recommend to the Board to agree with them on the following terms viz . . . III. That the Claimants of the said land called the Negroes Burying Ground release and convey all their Estate Right Title and Interest of and in the said Land so to be laid out . . . as a street to remain for the use of a public street forever."[61]

Ownership difficulties did not end there. An additional section of the Van Borsum Patent extended into the northwest corner of the Common on the other south side of the new Chambers Street (see bottom left corner of fig. 12 and fig. 16). This land had been leased by heirs to tenants who had built structures on the land, and so they did not want to relinquish the land without compensation when the heirs attempted to deed it back to the city. This issue was resolved in 1800, and the heirs exchanged their land with the city for lots further east.[62] Goerck's 1796 survey, now held by the New-York Historical Society, illustrates the new "Chamber" Street with the original outline of the Van Borsum Patent as it crossed over Chambers Street and dipped into the Corporation Ground. The survey, entitled *Copy of a Map of Ground in the City of New York (on Chambers, Reade, Anthony/Duane and Broadway)*, was color coded in order to show varying original land grants. The unlabeled and blank Kalk Hook Farm area was pink, the Van Borsum Patent yellow (including the empty triangle in the middle of Block 154 as the unlabeled Alley), and the Janeway Land as pink. The burial ground was not mapped and was very likely no longer in existence.

Division in Janeway Land

Surveys recovered in Rutgers University's Special Collections in 2006 concern the portion of the African Burial Ground known as the

Janeway Land (fig. 12, section 4). In the box was a hand-drawn survey, likely post-1786, recounting a property exchange between the City of New York and George Janeway because the city wanted to square off Janeway's land while gaining access to the Powder House from Pearl Street. The city arranged to give Janeway ten lots of land in lieu of the area surrounding the Powder House. More important for our purposes, the text handwritten on the map goes on to explain that the city also exchanged land with the Kips in order for Africans to continue to use the African Burial Ground (fig. 17).

> Kips Comp: Ground is Laid out between the Red Lines at the Right side of this Plan, out of which they [the Kips] are willing to Leave out for use of this City a peice [sic] of Ground for Negro Burials from the Second prickt Line, In Lieu of [what] the Corporation is to Give them the G[?] of Ground Between the Red and Black lines at the upper part of their Ground—.[63]

In effect, the city requested use of the northern portion of the Van Borsum Patent (close to Kalk Hook Farm) for "The Negro Buryal Place," as marked on the actual survey in figure 17, and offered the Kips land to the south of the Van Borsum Patent. Note that the Kips would still own the land, but the city requested *use* of the piece for the African and African descendant population. According to this document, the city had appealed to the Kips to preserve the African Burial Ground for a time while it planned for urban development.[64]

Building on the African Burial Ground, 1795–1980s

With the complex history of urban development, as briefly outlined below, how is it that so many burials were preserved intact? From the 1790s to 1810, between 16 and 25 feet of fill was placed on top of the graves in order to level a hilly section of Manhattan. The African Burial Ground lay largely in a ravine and therefore had to be filled in to reach grade. The Broadway land was higher and took the least amount of fill, whereas the marshy area near Collect Pond was the

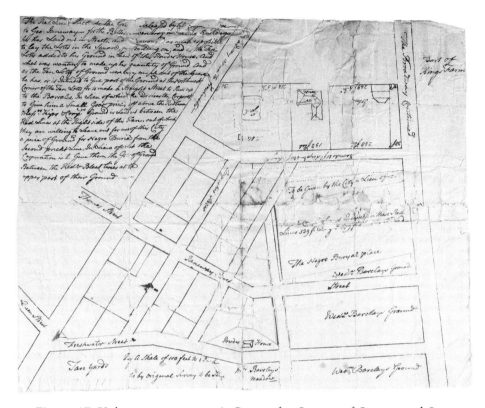

Figure 17. Unknown surveyor, *A Copy of a Survey of Streets and Lots in New York City between Broadway and the Fresh Water, some lots of which are to be given by the Corporation of New York to George Janeway and others to be given by Janeway to the Corporation of New York for the better laying out of streets*, nd. Pen and ink on paper, 14¹⁄₁₆ × 17¾ in. Handwritten text on this survey outlines a request by the City of New York that George Janeway trade a piece of "The Negro Buryal Place." The trade organized land for urban development but also allowed for continued use of the burial ground. The survey is oriented south to north. Drawer 8, Folder 5, Item 9 of "The Janeway Papers," Deeds and Indentures Collection. Special Collections and University Archives, Rutgers University Libraries.

lowest and deepest, requiring up to 25 feet of fill. Each property owner was responsible for bringing his or her own land to grade, and houses had to be destroyed and rebuilt if they were too low. When residences were rebuilt following the leveling (prior to the era of skyscrapers), the foundations and basements typically extended only into the added fill and did not touch the graves. The 16 to 25 feet of fill ultimately protected and preserved many graves until GSA's office building construction in 1991.

Some of the burials were already damaged because the land was built upon prior to the grading.[65] Specifically, on former Kalk Hook Farm, Lots 12 through 17 saw construction from 1794 to 1799, with the first house erected on Lot 12 and others to follow on Lot 15 and 16 (these lot numbers are marked in fig. 16 and plate 5).[66] Tragically, construction of a privy shaft or early toilet on the last two lots resulted in the destruction of half of each skeleton buried there. One is pictured in figure 18. The other was Burial 153 on Lot 15, and the damaged bones were actually found in a pile to the other side of the privy. Similarly, figure 19 shows a nineteenth-century brick drain that neatly punctured through Burial 213. The drain cut the 45 to 55 year old woman through her pelvis to her lower legs. Later, her left arm would be damaged by the office building excavation.[67] These examples illustrate tensions that must have played out between a sacred cemetery versus new real estate. There was a callous disregard for a sacred space used by a marginalized group of people because in order to dig new infrastructure, disruptions of graves would have been evident. The conflict of interest was an eerie echo of what would again occur in the twentieth century.

Buildings of the elite, white government gradually came to occupy a marginalized sacred space. The government district (today known as the Civic Center) eventually built on the African Burial Ground illustrated conflicts of space, class, and race that had been present since the seventeenth century and culminated in New York's present day urban landscape.

The streets that were initially laid down over the African Burial Ground were named after citizens associated with the law,

Figure 18. Burial 297 in situ, ca. 1776–95. A privy shaft, or precursor to the toilet at the back of Lot 16, damaged the entire top half of Burial 297. The legs from below the knees remain. Photo by Dennis Seckler, ca. 1991–92. Courtesy of the U.S. General Services Administration.

government, and Trinity Church (plate 5). Chambers Street was named after John Chambers, an Anglican lawyer, corporation counsel, alderman, and Supreme Court judge between 1727 and 1765.[68] Joseph Reade was a member of the governor's council and/or a warden of Trinity Church. James Duane of Duane Street was a member of Trinity Church who held many prominent positions throughout his life: he was the first mayor of New York after the British left in 1783 (1784–89), an attorney, a U.S. District Court judge, a New York state senator, a delegate to the Continental Congress, and a signer of the Articles of Confederation. Duane Street was initially called Anthony Street, perhaps after Anthony Rutgers of Kalk Hook

Figure 19. Burial 213 in situ, ca. 1735–60. A brick drain was installed during the nineteenth century through the grave of a woman who was about fifty years old. Photo by Dennis Seckler, ca. 1991–92. Courtesy of the U.S. General Services Administration.

Farm, who had owned the land, and was finally renamed Duane Street in 1809.[69] James Duane's father, Anthony Duane of Trinity Church, was a slave trader whose slave Prince was executed in the 1741 Conspiracy.[70] The mayor-to-be, James Duane, lost his parents at a young age and was consequently raised in Livingston Manor by a family involved in slave trading, also of Trinity Church. Robert Livingstone, the third Lord of Livingston Manor, became James Duane's guardian, and James later married Robert's oldest daughter Maria Livingstone. His ties with his father and then with the Livingstone family resulted in familiarity with slavery. The naming of Duane Street over the African Burial Ground becomes a painful and ironic twist, as the enslaved now bear the name of an empowered family associated with the slave trade.

What would be built above the African Burial Ground once it was partitioned into lots and sold off? Initially, the area consisted of a mixture of free African Americans, working class whites, and a growing commercial area. The northeastern burial ground area bordered the most dangerous and poverty-stricken slum neighborhood of New York known as Five Points (at Worth, Baxter, and Park Streets between Broadway and Centre). At the southern end of the burial ground, the upper class presence that would soon take over the area was already visible at Broadway and Chambers Streets with grand dwellings. A testimony given in court in 1812 still carried the memory of the African Burial Ground. It read, "The lots adjoining, and including the premises [of the Van Borsum Patent], and including the African burying ground, for many years since the American war, were regarded as uninviting suburbs. The streets have since widened, the face of the ground wholly changed, and it is now covered with a flourishing population, and elegant improvements."[71] In the space of just one block, Block 154, formerly of Kalk Hook Farm and the Van Borsum Patent, hosted middle class and elites along Broadway as well as the city's industrial core with its working class.[72]

The rest of this chapter explores some of the structures built on top of the burial ground, maintaining the same format as the

Hoffman survey with the four major geographic sections. As this area of Manhattan began to take shape as an urban center, the lots and surrounding streets were divided into city blocks, and each block was assigned a number, which is still in existence today (plate 5). Former Kalk Hook Farm (fig. 12, section 1) became the northern half of Block 154 and the Van Borsum land (fig. 12, section 3) became the southern half of Block 154. The block is bounded by Duane and Reade Streets. The block to the south is Block 153. The block south of that (fig. 12, section 2), which was originally the city's common land and now encompasses City Hall Park, is Block 122. The small block to the east of Block 154 is Block 155, which was the Janeway Land (fig. 12, section 4). All of these blocks exist on top of the African Burial Ground. To construct the office building, the federal government purchased nearly two-thirds of Block 154 at the west end (290–304 Broadway, 28–40 Reade Street, and 72–86 Duane Street).

Block 154—Formerly Kalk Hook Farm and Van Borsum Patent

During the nineteenth century, the African Burial Ground area saw the development of commercial, public, industrial, governmental, and residential structures. Stores from the 1850s remained at numbers 72, 74, and 76 Duane Street until 1991 (when construction began on the office building) (plate 5). A brick building from the Federal era remained at 80 Duane Street, or Lot 12, until 1920.[73] By the 1860s, 5- to 7-story structures replaced smaller frame buildings.[74]

Prior to the Ted Weiss Federal Building at 290 Broadway, the last buildings on the site were torn down in the late 1960s and late 1970s. They took up the left end of Block 154 in plate 5: the 15-story Dun Building (1897) with a brick and granite facade stood at 290–294 Broadway; above the Dun Building in Lot 4, a 10-story building occupied 296 Broadway (1898); and Lots 5 and 6 held a 10-story McKim, Mead, White building at 298–300 Broadway.[75] First known as the Vincent and then as the Fordham Building,

302–304 Broadway in the northwestern corner of Duane at Broadway reached 16 stories. A 5-story brick building at 12 Elm (now Elk) Street had a 17- to 20-foot foundation. All three of these buildings likely decimated burials not only because they were relatively tall buildings, but also because the land along Broadway received less fill for grading purposes than the marshy, low lying land close to Collect Pond. Along Reade Street in Block 154, the address 14–26 Reade Street is very likely to contain intact burials because its basement did not reach the cemetery stratum.[76] The City of New York purchased all of these in 1965 and combined them into one structure, which is today the New York City Planning Commission and the Department of City Planning.

In summary, in the 1830s, the area that the Ted Weiss Federal Building would later occupy on Block 154 had some tenants who both lived and worked there. By the 1860s, 5- to 7-story commercial buildings had moved into the area. By 1875, Block 154 was no longer residential, and at the turn of the century larger buildings up to 15 stories with deep basements were constructed.

Block 153—Corporation of New York

The last known remains from the burial ground were excavated from the Sun newspaper building when it was constructed at the turn of the century, and were then reburied on Allan Street.[77] The Sun Building stood on the western third of Block 153 (the left side of the block) from 1919 to 1952 (plate 5). The City of New York then purchased the building in 1965 for municipal offices and continues to use it today. Prior to that, the A. T. Stewart Building stood here. It was one of the earliest department stores in the country (1845–46, 1850–51, and 1884). Early on, from 1831 to 1832, Aaron Burr lived on the African Burial Ground a few buildings to the east at 31 Reade Street. By this time, Burr's political career, which had included vice president under Thomas Jefferson, attorney general, and New York senator, had ended, and he lived in obscurity and financial difficulty following the infamous duel in which he killed Alexander Hamilton.

Elk Street divided Block 153 into two halves when it was extended south from Reade Street to Chambers Street in 1901 (plate 5). The far eastern half of the block became the Hall of Records (Surrogate's Court) at 23–37 Chambers Street and 1–11 Reade Street when it was purchased by the City around 1898. Because of its deep foundation, there are likely no intact burials remaining. Prior to the Hall of Records, a portion of the block was taken up by the Manhattan Company waterworks, incorporated in 1799. This began as a banking venture for Aaron Burr and others as competition against Alexander Hamilton, and resulted in providing New York's first pipeline water system, which was needed since only one unpolluted source remained.[78] Earlier, during the time the burial ground was in use, the land of the Hall of Records had been associated with the pottery industry and "Pot Baker's" or "Potter's Hill" at the far eastern end of the block. Until 1844, the Crolius family worked just to the northeast of Block 153 at the corner of Reade and Centre Street and within the bounds of the burial ground (see fig. 2, introduction).[79] Additionally, in 1710 Sara Roeloff's granddaughter Maria married Abraham Van Vleck, who had a pottery business on Reade Street and probably leased it to William Crolius.[80]

Block 122—Formerly the Common

Eighteenth-century buildings in use by the civic government on the Common included prisons, a powder house, almshouses, and a magazine for storing ammunition. Specifically, these buildings were as follows: First Almshouse (1735–36 to 1803), Second Almshouse (1796–97 to 1854), New Gaol (1757–59 to 1903), Bridewell (1775–1838), and several barracks in the northern Common. The area continued to develop as a civic and municipal area in the nineteenth century. A new city hall designed by McComb Jr. and Magnin was built on the Common between 1803 and 1811 at the site of the old almshouse and is still in use today, thus rendering the Common the seat of local government (plate 5). Tweed Courthouse, or the County "Courthouse," was built from 1861 to 1872 and is still standing.

Block 155—Janeway Land

The still-standing, 10-story Jones Building (1897–99) and the 21-story Court Square Building (1925) both likely contain intact burials beneath them because several more feet of fill were used to bring this area up to grade (plate 5). In 1981, the City of New York purchased the latter, where it has housed municipal agencies since the 1960s.[81]

Industry became the focus just north of Block 154 on Block 156. By 1818, Worrel and Company, an iron furnace, lay on the northern edge of the former African Burial Ground. Two prominent architectural cast iron foundries operated on Duane Street, one just west and the other just east of Centre Street. Midcentury saw the manufacturing of pianos and silverware as well as printing houses.

Finally, it is believed that there is some potential for burials to exist under the streetbeds of Chambers, Reade, Duane, and Elk Streets because only utility lines are there.[82] Some streets also have sewer lines, but they would not take up the width of the street. The subway tunnels along Broadway and Centre/Lafayette Streets would likely have destroyed burials there.

In summary, the first structures built above the African Burial Ground were frame houses and were then made of brick. Buildings began to take up entire lots, were 5 to 7 stories, and had cast iron and stone facades. By 1870, the area was no longer residential, but had been replaced by 5-story brick offices, small factories, and warehouses. These buildings had subbasements, and some had vaults for coal storage and delivery extending between 3½ and 10 feet deep.

The government expressed a continuing interest into the twentieth century in housing agencies on the African Burial Ground area, the Common, and Foley Square that had surrounded Collect Pond. A 1904 Report of the New York City Improvement Commission strengthened plans for adding more government buildings to surround City Hall Park.[83] Mayor George B. McClellan supported the construction of the Municipal Building near Brooklyn Bridge by architects McKim, Mead, and White (1907–1914). The New York County Courthouse was built north of the Municipal Building from 1913 to 1927. Several proposals followed for government buildings and courts just to the north of City Hall Park.

During the 1960s, it was decided that an enlarged Civic Center would occupy the northern section of City Hall Park and the northern part of what was once the Common as well as the African Burial Ground.[84] Municipal agencies purchased the A. T. Stewart Store and the Emigrant Industrial Savings Bank. Then, in the 1980s, the federal government purchased most of Block 154 for its office building.

Conclusion

A complex spatial urban history unfolded on land appointed for the African Burial Ground. It was a sacred space for Africans and their descendants to bury the dead, while at the same time it became private property owned by upstanding citizens, civic land claimed by the city of New York, dumping grounds for burgeoning pottery and tannery industries, and a grave-robbing site for medical students. The ownership issues centered on and around the burial ground land were local contestations among elite land owners and civic governments negotiating the aftereffects of colonial conquest. The Dutch, during their brief reconquest, created their own rules and dispersion of land that were not acknowledged when the British regained control, as well as vice versa.

In light of all these difficulties, consider the length of time the African Burial Ground existed and the large size to which it grew. Although the edges of its boundaries shifted in relation to surrounding uses and features such as the tanneries, potteries, Collect Pond, and various fences, the cemetery itself held a certain spatial power in that it existed as a nearly-seven-acre African cemetery for virtually the entire eighteenth century. Manhattan expanded around it and north of it before the area itself was covered over and built upon. Additionally, documents repeatedly referred to the space as the "Negroes Burying Ground" rather than by the name of the land owner. The identity of the space was etched in the population's consciousness as the African cemetery.

This chapter has presented a step-by-step documentation of who owned the African Burial Ground, how it came to be owned, and what was then built upon it, using the Hoffman survey as a template (fig. 12). The first section was Kalk Hook Farm (1) owned by Anthony Rutgers, which covered what would become the northern half of block 154, and where burials encroached 30 to 35 feet onto the farm. The second section was the Common, owned by the Corporation of New York (2), where it is believed that burials occurred before and after the existence of the palisades, or before 1745 and/ or after 1760. The Van Borsum Patent (3), mired by ownership disputes that took decades to resolve, took up the southern half of Block 154 where the majority of the burials were excavated in order to build the office building. And finally, the Janeway Land (4) saw land trades between the city and its citizens to correct disputes and to foster urban development, which resulted in continued use of the burial ground.

The proximity of a new government district in relation to the African Burial Ground illustrates struggles over space and race that would only continue to escalate to the present day urban landscape of New York City's Civic Center on top of the African Burial Ground. This delineation of ownership and process of urban development provide a history of the African Burial Ground that tells of conflict and erasure, even as it was used and engaged.

3

Burying the Dead

Skeletal, Archaeological, and Geographical Analyses

While the previous chapter explored the sacred African Burial Ground in contexts of land ownership and the built environment, this chapter lends voice to the deceased themselves from as much of their perspective as possible, as revealed through research conducted over a decade, from 1991 into the twenty-first century.

Exhumed artifacts and skeletons have provided a powerful lens through which to understand the lives and deaths of Africans buried at the African Burial Ground. Skeletal, dental, and funerary remains tell stories about the lives, health, labor, nutrition, spiritual practices, burial customs, mortality rates, African heritage, and New World influences of Africans in New York. The research teams that ultimately carried out the study, led by project director and scientific director Michael Blakey, were particularly diligent and purposeful about analyzing the remains from an African and diasporic perspective so that an African descendant voice came forward from those who lived, worked, and died in New York City.[1] The multivolume final report is available on the internet for public use.[2]

The innovative research opens a window onto people, cultures, and traditions that by force began an African diaspora in New York City. The first section of this chapter considers funerary objects that were excavated, including beads, buttons, and conjuring-like bundles, as well as the spatial arrangement of each grave in the ground, which illustrates important burying practices. In the chapter's second section, skeletal analyses of children and adults shed light on length of life, health, illness, manual labor, and the transatlantic crossing. In the final section of the chapter, DNA analysis is coupled with historical records, offering insights as to where specifically in Africa the deceased originated.

All branches of the research focused on four major directives developed by the teams along with descendant community input: (1) cultural backgrounds and geographical origins of the deceased, (2) cultural and biological changes from African to African American identities and communities, (3) quality of life in relation to enslavement, and (4) modes of resistance during captivity.[3] Through dialogues with each other and with concerned citizens of the African Burial Ground in New York City, the research team pursued the notion of the "democratization of knowledge," in which "descendant or culturally affiliated communities" were involved in discussions and updated on scientific work.[4] These dialogues occurred throughout the African Burial Ground project on a number of levels, including in public updates and open houses, almost all of which I attended.

The remains were excavated between 1990 and 1993 in order to construct the office building at 290 Broadway. For a decade, bones and objects were analyzed at Lehman College in the Bronx, at Howard University in Washington, DC, and in the 6 World Trade Center laboratory, or they were untouched during periods when government funding was cut, as discussed in chapter 4. Following 11 September 2001, some of these funerary objects and archival materials were retrieved, but other items from the World Trade Center laboratory were unrecoverable. Ultimately, the funerary objects, skeletal remains, and coffins were reburied behind the office building at 290 Broadway during a weekend-long ceremony in October 2003.

Archaeological Analyses: Funerary Objects, Body Adornments, and Burial Practices

Funerary remains analysis has resulted in knowledge of how the deceased were buried with coffins, coffin decorations, copper pins, shrouds, and grave markers; of funerary objects such as shells, buttons, coins, pipes, and conjuring-type bundles; and of how bodies were adorned with beads, finger rings, and jewelry. Finally, through a relative dating schema called stratigraphy, all of the graves in the African Burial Ground were divided into four groups and given approximate burial dates based on such influences as surrounding businesses and fence boundaries. The Early Group includes burials up to about 1735 that predate the dumping of kiln waste from pottery manufacturers on the land. The Middle Group ranges from 1735 to 1760, when pottery companies deposited kiln waste, broken vessels, and clay waste into the burial ground. The Late Middle Group lasted from 1760 to 1776 and was contained in the southern half of the excavated cemetery because of a fence that was erected. Finally, the Late Group consisted of burials from 1776 to 1795, which included British occupation, meaning that itinerant Africans from outlying areas came into the city. They are located in the northern section of the cemetery.

With the violent geographic and temporal transplanting of enslaved Africans, cultural practices inevitably changed. African physical environments, cultural accoutrements, and social positions were disrupted. However, African people's deities, beliefs, memories, and knowledge traveled across the Atlantic and were reinvented, reconstituted, and interwoven into New York life. Particular objects, such as plants, ingredients, sculpting tools, and beads, were not available to the uprooted Africans who would then improvise but not necessarily compromise their spiritual expressions. Enslaved people could be isolated from their cultural groups or integrated with people from a myriad of places. This intermixing extended specific cultural and funerary practices within burgeoning communities.[5]

With such variation, it is difficult to assume that one aspect of the New York burial ground specifically derives from one African culture. Even in Africa, one particular culture does not exist in isolation, as there are interactions, intermarriages, interlocutors, trade, and travel consistently occurring between communities, cities, countries, and continents.[6] While archaeological investigations in New

York may not often be able to pinpoint specific cultural or ethnic origins from Africa, a detailed exploration of funerary objects and practices profoundly illustrates that it was indeed a space of spirituality for the eighteenth-century population. The head archaeologist of the African Burial Ground, Warren Perry, and his coauthors write that the "African mortality complex is reflective of the importance and respect of ancestors and is structured by a relation between grave goods and the local cosmologies."[7] It is with these forced cultural concurrences that Africans formulated an African American society in New York through negotiation, cooperation, and reinvention.

A total of 424 graves were identified during excavation, 419 of which contained skeletal remains (some graves contained no surviving remains, as a result of decay, damage, or removal).[8] The burials have been named by number in the order in which they were excavated. Common aspects were shared by almost all of the graves. It was found that 91.6 percent of the deceased were buried in coffins, 97.8 percent had their heads and bodies oriented to the west, and many were wrapped in white shrouds that were pinned together with copper pins or wrapped in winding sheets.[9] Researchers are unclear whether grave markers were typically used because grave markers were found only in the southwest corner of the excavated area, which is where the original ground surface was not disturbed (plate 4). Not many of the burials contained personal adornments or funerary objects. Of those that did, the artifacts included a piece of quartz, a piece of coral, a silver ear bob, buttons, coins, pearlware ceramics, finger rings and other metal jewelry, beads (some of which were made in Africa), shells, pipes, and sleeve links.

Based on the high percentage of similarity among 424 graves over more than eighty years, researchers pondered how there was "an extraordinary degree of homogeneity" and an overall lack of variability considering the widespread geographical, cultural, and temporal origins of blacks in New York.[10] There is no answer, but the final report suggests the 290 Broadway site may represent only a portion of the seven acres, that poverty accounts for the limited number of items in the coffins, that there may have been a kind of burial management system, or that gravediggers could have influenced a general mortuary program. In terms of placing the dead, an orientation with the head towards the west is perhaps one of the first mortuary practices that becomes standardized in the African diaspora.[11] Tradition could also account for the similarities; a practice was in place that newcomers conformed to for whatever reasons.

Coffins

Overall, 352 graves (91.6 percent) had coffins out of a total of 384 graves in which a coffin presence or absence was clear. Of the adults, 85.71 percent were buried in coffins.[12] All of the children were placed in coffins. In general, the most popular three coffin woods were cedar, pine, and fir, and the coffin hardware was almost always just nails. Only Burial 290 was made of the hardwood black walnut. Although not strictly so, coffins changed in shape over time. Many in the Early Group were four-sided and mainly tapered, whereas later groups were hexagonal in shape. The shapes of children's coffins varied greatly, however, likely because they were homemade and so not standardized.[13] In terms of lengths, researchers conclude that coffins were tailor-made to fit the height of the deceased, as there was a high degree of variation in adult coffin size.[14]

Joshua Delaplaine was a successful Quaker cabinet maker, whose career included coffin making, from before 1720 until his death in 1778. The coffins he built for Africans and more than likely buried in the African Burial Ground have been compiled in table 1. An enslaved woman for Christopher Fell received the most expensive coffin at 14 shillings because it was outfitted with the additional hardware of screws, rosin, and black paint.[15] This contrasts with coffins for Europeans, which might have breastplates, lid decorations, linings, and special wood, costing between £3 and £5.

Figure 20 illustrates an actual page from the coffin maker's account book. For the first entry dated 19 July 1755, Caleb Lawrence placed an order for a "rough coffin" for "negro" Joseph Castins for 9 shillings. I suggest that Joseph Castins is the only full first and last

Table 1

Wooden Coffins Made for Africans by Joshua Delaplaine

Date	Person Placing Order	Description	Cost
14 Nov. 1753	Joseph Ryal	"coffin for his negro boy"	10s
22 Jan. 1754	Abraham Leffer[t]s*	"coffin for Jane a negro" (poorhouse)	11s
27 Mar. 1754	Robert Livingston	"a large coffin for his negro"	12s
30 Apr. 1754	Abraham Lefferts	"coffin for Mo[lly?] a negro"	11s
6 Aug. 1754	Christopher Fell	"black coffin for his negro woman rozind & with screws"	14s
20 Dec. 1754	Daniel Gomez	"coffin for his negro woman"	12s
4 Mar. 1755	Caleb Lawrence	"coffin for his negro child"	5s
''	Robert Griffith	"coffin for his negro man"	12s
9 July 1755	Christopher Fell	"coffin for a negro woman"	12s
19 July 1755	Caleb Lawrence	"rough coffin for Joseph Castins negro"	9s
12 Aug. 1755	Estate of Peter Vergerau	"coffin for negro woman w/screws"	13s
27 Aug. 1755	Thomas Dobson	"coffin for his negro girl"	11s
29 Feb. 1756	John Stephens	"black coffin for a negro child"	4s 6d

Source: From Jean Howson and Leonard G. Bianchi, with Iciar Lucena Narvaez and Janet L. Woodruff, "Coffins," in *New York African Burial Ground Archaeology Final Report*, eds. Warren R. Perry, Jean Howson, and Barbara A. Bianco (Washington, DC: U.S. General Services Administration and Howard Univ., 2006), 254. Courtesy of the U.S. General Services Administration.

Note: Africans listed here would have been buried in the African Burial Ground between 1753 and 1756. See Joshua Delaplaine's handwritten record for Joseph Castins in figure 20. *Abraham Lefferts, one of the two city Church Wardens, placed numerous orders for coffins for the poorhouse, two of which were for deceased black inmates.

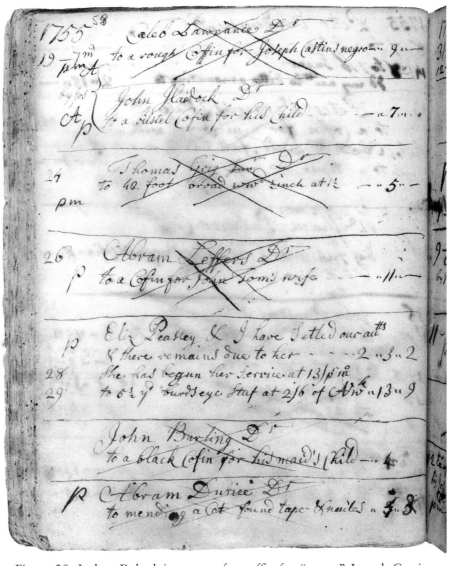

Figure 20. Joshua Delaplaine, entry for coffin for "negro" Joseph Castins ordered by Caleb Lawrence, 19 July 1755. Day book, 1753–56. The first entry, Joseph Castins, is perhaps the only known first and last name of someone interred in the African Burial Ground. Joshua Delaplaine Papers, 1721–1779, Collection of the New-York Historical Society.

name that we know of all the 419 Africans and people of African descent buried in the African Burial Ground.[16]

Because coffins were ubiquitous, the researchers spent time questioning why a few people were not buried in coffins. They concluded that poverty was probably not the reason some lacked a coffin, as some of the deceased who did not have coffins were nonetheless buried with funerary objects such as jewelry. Perhaps a household head of an enslaved person refused to provide a coffin; or alternatively, the mourners resisted accepting a coffin from an enslaver. Most of the thirty-two without coffins were males belonging to the Late Group (plate 4). It seems likely that the economic and social disruptions of the Revolutionary War and British military presence around the dates 1776–83 were major influencing factors. Perhaps there was a shortage of coffins during the war or refugees did not have family to bury them.[17]

Coffin Decoration. Five coffins from the New York burial ground were found with furniture or decoration, which included handles, breastplates, upholstery, and corner and edge lace designs. Because hardware was rare for any coffin in North America prior to 1830, these individuals may have been of high stature.[18] In comparison, metal coffin hardware was found in burials at the Newton Plantation, a contemporaneous cemetery in Barbados, with handles in twenty-three graves and metal plates in another six.

At the African Burial Ground, a twenty- to twenty-four-year-old man in Burial 176 was buried with the most expensive excavated coffin. He was laid into a hexagonal coffin with six handles attached to back plates that were screwed on to the coffin. Two of the hand-wrought iron handles have chevron or arrow cutouts back to back, pointing away from each other.[19] A similarly designed handle was found in St. Anne's Episcopal Churchyard (1692–1790) in Annapolis, which John Milner Associates also excavated. In addition to the handles, the New York coffin lid was decorated with sixty iron tacks, likely manufactured after 1760.[20] The coffin was positioned against what was probably a diagonal fence separating Kalk

Hook Farm from the Van Borsum Patent in the Late Middle Group (1760–76) (see arrow, plate 4). Although honored in death with iron handles and tacks for coffin hardware, Burial 176's skeleton tells the story of an enslaved person. The bones of his lower and upper limbs were scarred as a result of inflammation from bacterial infection or an injury (for either case, this is known as periostitis).[21] The upper limb had a significantly enlarged area of bone due to repeated stress, called hypertrophy, because of forced labor. His skeleton had healed porotic hyperostosis, which are lesions found in the eye orbit, cranium and face, indicating nutritional stress. A history of Burial 176 continues into the twentieth century, when his west end was damaged by the installation of a temporary shelter for archaeological excavation prior to the office building construction at 290 Broadway.

Aspects of the coffin and coffin decoration research were affected by politics surrounding the African Burial Ground. For instance, excavators observed small iron tacks in the coffin lid decoration of Burial 222 when it was still in the ground. However, vandalism occurred, as described in chapter 4, because an ill guard left the site early and was not replaced. The vandals scattered the tacks so that only four were recovered, and the design could not be recorded. Nonetheless, analysts identified the tacks as cast iron and fabricated using a technique patented in England in 1769.[22] Another example is that researchers had set aside unidentifiable items related to coffins (such as corroded screws) on separate shelving in the World Trade Center laboratory when it was shut down in 2000 due to GSA halting the funding. Then, the items were lost in the World Trade Center collapse.

Copper Pins and Shrouds

Hundreds of copper pins, used to hold a sheet, shroud, or clothing on the body, were recovered from the burials (fig. 21). A total of 834 pins were excavated from 210 burials, or 64.6 percent of the burials.[23] However, even more pins were used, as was evident by green stains left by disintegrated pins. The pins were approximately one inch long, made of copper alloy, and drawn with wire-wrapped

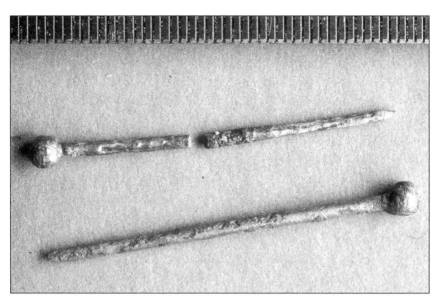

Figure 21. Burial 12, pins, ca. 1776–95. Copper alloy, about 2.2 cm. long. A total of 834 pins held shrouds or winding sheets around most of those interred at the African Burial Ground. These pins were from a double burial of a mother whose infant was buried on top of her. Photo by Jon Abbott. Courtesy of the U.S. General Services Administration.

heads. Such pins were common from the early seventeenth century to the early nineteenth century in this geographic area.

The pins compare with other burial patterns and practices. In Montserrat, skeletons had green copper salts stains from disintegrated copper pins.[24] It is possible that the traditions came from Islamic Africa, in which corpses are wrapped in white shrouds facing east as a general Muslim custom.[25]

The youngest babies in the African Burial Ground were wrapped in cloth held in place by numerous pins. Howson points out that because it seems unnecessary to use more pins for a much smaller body, the pins must have held additional funerary significance rather than just a functional purpose.[26] Two extreme examples are Burial 5, who was between the age of six months and one year and had nineteen pins, and Burial 14, who was up to six months old and had twenty-six pins. A small number of burials had pins only around their heads, mainly at the top of the skull or near the ears (twenty-eight adults and fifteen youths). It is suggested that a piece of cloth may have secured the chin and was pinned at the top of the head to prevent the jaw from falling open. Cloth tying was an eighteenth century English practice, but not with pins. Alternatively, perhaps the pins held the shroud in such a way that the face was exposed at some point during the funeral or wake.

Archaeologists are unsure of the exact nature of the sheet or shroud with which the deceased were buried. An undertaker who advertised in New York in 1768 sold "shrouds and sheets," meaning that they were two different products.[27] A shroud could refer to a type of garment, rather like a nightgown, and a sheet was probably the European and English winding sheet, which was a rectangular cloth that covered the corpse completely and tied above the head and below the feet, with the sides pinned or stitched closed. The cloth could be pulled open to reveal the face. The few textile fragments that could be shroud fragments recovered in association with the pins were made of cotton or linen and were found in eighteen burials.[28]

David Roediger offers a general discussion of slave burials between 1700 and 1865 in the United States that certainly parallel practices at the African Burial Ground, although unfortunately no specific dates, locations, or primary sources are cited. His descriptions included the preparation of a corpse with thorough washing and shrouding, usually in white cloth, frequently done by women.[29] Enslavers often provided wood and nails for coffins, or gave ready-made coffins.[30] Sometimes rum or whiskey, which flowed freely at white funerals, was available.

Robert Farris Thompson has recorded funerary traditions of burying the dead in cloth in the northern Kongo in Africa. A European named Jean-Francois de Rome visited Mbanza Kongo and wrote in his *La fondation de la mission des Capucins au Royaume de Congo* in 1648 that "[i]f the dead person is noble, they wrap the corpse in a carefully sewn white linen cloth; then, having placed him in his coffin, covered with a black cloth, they carry him to the church with a numerous escort. If the dead person is poor, they wrap him in a coarse country cloth, then cover over that with a mat, and in that same mat bury him in the cemetery."[31] Thompson surmises that the cloths for some burials were already being imported.

Asante people in Ghana also followed a tradition of wrapping the deceased in a cloth called *nsaa*. Nsaa, or "northern cloths," were rough, woven textiles made by Muslims. The deceased were wrapped in nsaa before coffins came into use before the eighteenth century, and nsaa were still placed under the dead in 1987.[32] While this camel hair textile would have been coarse, Asante people nonetheless practiced the tradition of wrapping a body before interring it.

Because many of the enslaved brought to New York were from the Kongo and Akan regions, they would have been familiar with the funerary practice of wrapping the deceased. Thus, even if the white shrouds were a European product, the concept would not be foreign, but performed with an African sensibility. Mourners in New York could have performed the tradition, but they only had white sheets available to them on this side of the ocean.

Grave Markers

In the oldest, southwestern area of the excavated burial ground where the ground surface was available for analysis, graves were marked either by a cobblestone outline or with a granite headstone (or both), as depicted in figure 22. Researchers surmise that it is possible external markers were used in other parts of the cemetery as well.[33] For example, Burial 18, Burial 47, and Burial 23 in the southern section had vertical stones at their head, and Burial 194 in the northern part of the Late Group had a part of a vertical wooden cedar post attached to the headboard. Three other grave in close proximity to each other were only outlined with small cobbles. It has been suggested that we do not see other grave markers (or items placed on graves) because the top layer was stripped when earth was cleared with heavy equipment, sometimes to the very tops of coffins because

Figure 22. Burial 47, headstone and cobblestones as grave markers in situ, ca. 1735–60. Granite and cobbles. Photo by Dennis Seckler, 1991. Courtesy of the U.S. General Services Administration.

of pressure for speedy excavation, or that grave tops could have been removed in earlier phases of development as the burial ground was covered over.[34]

Funerals

Ceremonies at the African Burial Ground were typically held at night. When the British overtook New Amsterdam in 1664, they sought tighter control over the increasing number of Africans in New York. They passed laws after the 1712 Insurrection that limited the number of people attending a funeral to twelve and controlled the hours of funerals.[35] Such laws confirmed that funerals with large numbers of people must have been occurring and that they lasted far into the night. Enslaved people were expected to work during the day, and so free time and privacy would be available at night, as observed by

Genovese, "a great many, perhaps a large majority, of slave funerals occurred at night."[36]

In one of the three written narratives of the African Burial Ground carefully analyzed in chapter 1, city historian David Valentine complained about loud "mummeries and outcries" emanating from the site at night.[37] What the European colonists heard, but were not used to, was an African-based funeral of celebration and mourning in indigenous languages. In a description of a 1740 slave funeral in Jamaica, it was written that slaves "sing all the way" to the burying place, and that then, at the site, musicians play drums and gourd rattles and sing again on the way home.[38] Physician George Pinckard noted in late-eighteenth-century Barbados that a female elder and chorus sang and chanted an African song while others danced.[39] Another wrote in 1729 that there was an event of "various instruments of horrid music [and] howling and dancing above the graves of the Dead."[40] Funerals in 1793 were described as athletic, agitated dancing for elders or respected people. Plays were held for these people days after the funeral in which spirits of the dead were called through drumming and singing to possess the performers.

As discussed in chapter 1, the African Burial Ground site was largely free from surveillance and outside of the city limits. Whether the land was chosen or assigned, Africans may have adapted the space to perform traditions of African-based spirituality. For instance, Kongolese Kimpianga Mahaniah wrote in 1977 that cemeteries were generally placed at the entrance and exit of towns for their protection against evil spirits.[41] With the African Burial Ground located on the other side of the palisades away from town, as seen in the Maerschalck Plan (fig. 7), did the palisades serve as a spiritual marker? For instance, during the nineteenth and early twentieth centuries, Yombe people in the Kongo vicinity actually constructed palisades around individual graves. Special shrines would be built for ancestors made of vertically split tree trunks. The enclosure protected the dead from external forces, sheltered the living from powers that might emanate from the dead, and demarcated a sacred space.[42]

Funerary Objects: Coins, Pipes, Shells,
Crystals, Minkisi-like Bundles

Funerary items offer important insight into spiritual links to African traditions. Twenty-six burials, or approximately 7 percent, contained coins, pipes, shells, crystals, and conjuring bundles. We cannot be sure of the symbolism or interpretation of the objects, although comparisons have been made with African American grave sites and an African Caribbean one. Nearly half of these funerary objects were found in the Late Group area of the African Burial Ground dating from 1776 to 1795. Perhaps because relocated and displaced people were coming from out of town during the time of the British occupation, burial practices shifted with new diversity and regional differences.[43]

Many of the objects discussed in this section were not fully studied or recorded and were then lost. As will be explained in chapter 4, this is due in part to the rushed excavation by HCI, the first archaeological team working under GSA pressure. Also, pieces were stored in the World Trade Center laboratory that could not be recovered after its collapse. Some had been photographed, and others were drawn in situ or after excavation in the lab, but then the full set of slides of funerary objects was lost in the World Trade Center laboratory, some of which had not been duplicated. The inability to perform additional research and analysis on some of these items compares to the people buried here, whose history is veiled, partly unrecoverable, or missing.

Copper-alloy coins were definitively found with four of the deceased. The two men and two women were from the Late Group and were adults between thirty and sixty-five years old. The coins were placed over their eyes, which leads to the possibility that this custom began only towards the end of the eighteenth century.[44] A coin from Burial 135 has been identified as a George II halfpenny that was minted between 1729 and 1754, and others are too degraded to identify. This denomination would have been the most common for circulation among Africans. In comparison, single coins were found in eight burials in Philadelphia at the First African Baptist Church cemetery. They were placed over the eyes at the Cedar Baptist Grove cemetery in Philadelphia as well.[45] The practice was performed by Europeans, North Americans, and African Americans.

Clam and oyster shells were deliberately placed on five burials, four of which were in conjunction with a piece of iron on the coffin lids. In varying African and African diaspora traditions, water connotes passage to the realm of the dead, or represents the spirit world itself.[46] An oyster or clam shell from Collect Pond, a nail, and the grave dirt that surrounded the configuration on the coffin lid—all created a connection, perhaps a request to the next world in the manner of minkisi, or power objects, as defined below.

A boy between 2½ and 4½ in Burial 22 was buried with a shell next to his neck, indicating it could have been strung and worn around the neck.[47] Three other coffins each bore a shell and piece of iron placed together on the tops of their coffin lids (it is unknown whether a fourth coupling in Burial 405 was placed on the lid). On Burial 438, a clamshell fragment was positioned directly on top of an iron nail. A few feet away, a complete oyster covered a nail on the coffin lid of Burial 352. A female of an undetermined age in Burial 365 bore a piece of iron (not a nail) that curved around an oyster shell on her lid. The grave was truncated with only the bottom half remaining—the legs, feet, and part of the left hand—and the grave was oriented towards the south, which was highly unusual.[48] All of these shells were lost in the World Trade Center collapse.

Burial 376 was a forty-five- to sixty-five-year-old man buried with the only piece of coral. After a lengthy process, researchers ascertained the coral specifically as *Siderastrea sidereal*, found mainly in the Caribbean, Gulf of Mexico, and Bermuda, and to a lesser degree along the coast of Brazil and the Gulf of Guinea of the West African coast.[49] The piece is missing and presumed to have been lost in the destruction of the World Trade Center.

The objects discussed below seem to have functioned in the manner of *minkisi*-like bundles, or power objects. Minkisi are containers such as gourds or bundles that hold a combination of leaves, medicines, grave dirt, seeds, claws, miniature knives, stones, nails, and/or crystals. Among Kongo people in central Africa, a medicinal expert, or *nganga*, collects, combines, and activates the contents. As well as packets, containers, or wood sculptures, tombs themselves are also minkisi or sacred medicines,[50] thus illuminating the important connection between these funerary objects, the cemetery, and the ancestors. In fact a term for tomb in KiKongo is *nzo a nkisi*, or site of the spirit.[51] Minkisi were made and activated in the Kongo at least since 1600.[52] There is clear evidence that during the 1712 Insurrection in New York spirit-assisted tactics were enacted in the rebellion, and it is proposed in chapter 1 that minkisi were used. This is a rare example in which historical writings verify that a spiritual tradition existed in both Africa and in North America at the same time during the eighteenth century. The spheres, calcite, quartz, spiral design on crockery, and nails or tacks in the New York burials discussed below are found both in Kongo minkisi and later in African American cemeteries in the United States.

The set of objects in Burial 147 was almost certainly a bundle (fig. 23). A fifty-five- to sixty-five-year-old man in the Late Group donned a bundle of pins and tiny copper rings 11 mm. in diameter. Four pins, three of which were in a line along the arm, suggest that the group of rings had been placed in a cloth and pinned to his arm.[53] He may have worn them in concealment while he was living. It is not without significance that the man was one of the oldest of all those excavated.[54] As an elder, he would have amassed the power, wisdom, and experience to perform conjuring and healing for his community. Although he was a person of social and spiritual import, his body still revealed a life of enslavement. The bones of his arms and legs exhibited scarring from infection or injury, and his muscle attachments were enlarged from repeated stress.[55] He had osteoarthritis in all of his major joint complexes and spine. Only the drawing in fig. 23 exists because the in situ photograph was lost in the laboratory after September 11.

Spheres or circular shapes were placed in four graves, which may be interpreted as representations of African-based cosmologies. Burial 375 was a sixteen- to eighteen-year-old woman with a 17 mm.

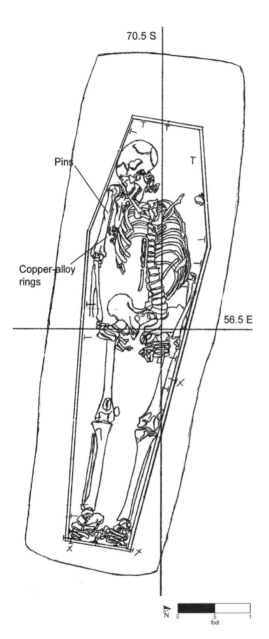

70.5 S

Pins

Copper-alloy
rings

56.5 E

N 0 .5 1
foot

Figure 23. Burial 147, buried with conjuring bundle pinned to the sleeve, ca. 1776–95. A cluster of tiny, copper-alloy rings was enclosed in a cloth pocket or sack and pinned to the sleeve of the man's burial garment. An elder, he lived with enlarged muscle attachments from repeated stress and osteoarthritis. Only a drawing exists, as the in situ photograph could not be recovered from the World Trade Center laboratory following 9/11. Drawing by M. Schur. Courtesy of the U.S. General Services Administration.

marble-like ceramic ball that had a copper band wrapped around it twice. The beautiful object was inserted inside cloth or leather and placed at her hip (fig. 24).[56] The teenager's skeletal condition included periostitis of the lower limbs, or bone scarring, as a result of inflammation from bacterial infection or an injury, and mild to severe osteoarthritis throughout her body. Osteoarthritis is a chronic degeneration of cartilage typically seen in the elderly, and it occurred here as the result of repetitive loading. Burial 410 contained a 3.44 mm. sphere of amber-colored glass. A disk made of mica schist just over ½ cm. in size was included in Burial 135 for a thirty- to forty-year-old male. With its shiny quality, perhaps this disk created flashes of light to catch a spirit's attention or ward away negative spirits who would see themselves reflected, as Robert Farris Thompson famously described.[57] The deceased had two copper coins placed over his eyes.

Figure 24. Burial 375, sphere, ca. 1735–60. Band, ceramic, and copper alloy, 17 mm. diameter. A ceramic ball wound with a copper band was covered in cloth or leather and placed at the hip. Only a teenager, she had osteoarthritis throughout her body from forced labor. Photo by Jon Abbott. Courtesy of the U.S. General Services Administration.

Along these lines, a very small calcite crystal 3½ mm. in size was located in Burial 55, a child between three and five years old.[58] Similarly, Burial 289 was a child between five and nine who was buried with a rounded quartz disc 7 mm. in size. It could have been a game piece, a part of jewelry, a Kongo-derived understanding of nkisi, or a representation of the cosmos. In comparison, quartz has been found in many African American sites, including a cache in the Charles Carrol house in Annapolis dating from 1790 to 1820. The cache included a pearlware bowl with a blue asterisk (probably a Kongo cosmogram) at the bottom placed face down on top of crystals, chipped quartz, perforated disks of bone, pins or nails, stones, buttons, and a faceted glass bead. Riverlake Plantation in Louisiana, which was occupied from the mid–nineteenth century to the mid–twentieth century, yielded crystals and projectile points from underneath houses and in yards.[59] Crystals may have been power objects for an inhabitant of a house and thus buried underneath the dwelling. An African example would be in the northwestern part of Cameroon at Sirak, where millet beer and flour are given as offerings with a piece of quartz to build a new granary.[60] The quartz is then buried under the granary. Robert Farris Thompson posits that crystals visually render the transparency of death because they reveal the other world, just as water does.[61]

Finally, in relation to conjuring-like bundles, a large broken piece of a stoneware vessel was placed on the coffin lid of Burial 328. It had a blue spiral on the bottom of the bowl in the center. The woman was between forty and fifty years old and was placed in a hexagonal coffin. It is likely that the pot was produced at the Crolius-Remmey pottery on Pot Bakers Hill.[62] We have a photograph of the pot in the grave, but the pot was never analyzed in the lab and is lost. There was also a piece of kiln furniture located in the grave, and a George II halfpenny coin was found nearby.[63] Sadly, damage was done to the grave by backhoes scraping down to the top of the coffin and also by a balk on top of it (excavation method of a strip of earth left in place), so that her feet and ankles were removed by the backhoe.

Nevertheless, the pot with its blue spiral design illustrates a very important connection to Africa and African American archaeological sites.[64] Its blue color would symbolize water, which delineates the land of the ancestors. The spiral is a motif that can visually depict the Kongo cosmogram, as described in chapter 5. As well as the Charles Carroll Townhouse in Annapolis mentioned above, another site in South Carolina had eighteen of twenty-eight marked vessels placed underwater, the space of the ancestors. Other pots at the site had crosses marked in the bottom of them. A cross can be a Kongo cosmogram or, turned slightly, an X that marks the crossroads. Thus, upside down or pierced pots would allow for the metaphoric passage between worlds. These examples demonstrate that markings on pots, very similar to those found at Burial 328 in the burial ground, were certainly symbolic and of cosmological significance. In fact, graves in the Kongo bear broken pots, pierced pots or dishes, or shards of pottery. Because of this common practice, Thompson suggests that "broken pottery is virtually synonymous with the image of the cemetery" and operates as a communication between the living and the dead.[65]

Just as New York mourners purposefully placed broken pottery on a grave, such objects are positioned on graves in parts of Africa. The New York practice would have been a continuation in tradition as broken shards were easily at hand from the pottery businesses in and around the African Burial Ground area. In the mid–twentieth century, Mumuye people along the Nigeria/Cameroun border performed men's funerals with *vabo* masqueraders and ceramic vessels. Each pot protects the soul of one who has died that year. The pots are carried to a sacred space and then smashed, thereby releasing the souls of the departed.[66]

Personal Adornments: Beads, Rings, Pendant, Cuff Links

As well as funerary objects, the deceased were buried with personal adornments such as beads, buttons, and jewelry. Personal adornments were largely uncommon at the African Burial Ground, with only twenty-five, or 6.7 percent, of the burials containing them.[67] These adornments were collected or acquired at a variety of times and in places that included Africa, along the routes traveled from Africa to New York, and in New York itself. It is known that glass beads were circulating along circum-Atlantic routes; rings were sold in Africa, the Americas, and Manhattan shops; and a silver pendant could be found in a shop or market stall, or purchased from a mobile peddler.[68] Because of the poverty of many who were buried at the African Burial Ground, the cost of one or two shillings for adornment would likely have been a significant expense.

Beads from Ghana. Of the 146 beads that were excavated, a total of nine were manufactured in and brought from Ghana. They are some of the only known objects brought directly from Africa, through the Middle Passage, and into New York. The beads are a rare to virtually unknown find in North America.[69] How did Africans manage to carry or wear the beads during their transatlantic crossing? For the living, the beads would have been precious objects and mementos of their homeland. Yet, the dead were cared for and honored to the extent that the African beads were buried with them.

All of the nine beads derive from two graves. Burial 226 was an infant under two months of age in his or her own coffin, and was inside the grave site of a thirty- to sixty-year-old man in Burial 221, likely meaning the two shared a social or familial relationship such as father-child or uncle-nephew.[70] Both had their heads to the west, and the baby had straight pins that would have fastened a winding cloth.[71]

Eight opaque yellow beads placed around the infant's neck were made in Ghana through a process of firing glass powder. The method is still practiced today in the Asamong area near Kumasi, and by people in Upper and Lower Manya of the Eastern Region of Ghana.[72] To produce the beads, glass and glass bottles originating from Europe are crushed and pounded into a fine powder, which is then put into clay molds and fired. The molds have holes in the bottom, and a cassava stem is passed through to make the perforation. The beads are smoothed and shaped by grinding after firing.

The ninth bead made in West Africa was a whitish tan cylinder found in the soil just near Burial 434.[73] The burial was only partially excavated because fieldwork was shut down, and the few bones of that burial that had been unearthed were reburied. Then, the bead was lost in the World Trade Center attack.

Beads from Europe. Aside from the nine beads from Ghana, it is likely that the other 137 glass beads were produced in Venice (Murano), a center of bead production and circulation for centuries and across geographies. Murano beads have been found in a variety of other archaeological sites.[74] The beads from the burial ground ranged from opaque black to opaque and translucent yellow, light gold, and light tan. Most of the beads were blue and blue green (from Burial 340), and one bead was made of amber (in Burial 340, possibly from Africa). A few are discussed below.

Burial 187 was a one-and-a-half to four-year-old who had twenty-two small black beads positioned just beneath the pelvic area, probably forming either a bracelet or waist beads around the child's hips.[75] The beads were drawn and cut from glass made in Europe. Deficient tooth enamel (hypoplasia) and undercalcified teeth (hypocalcification) point to the stress endured as a toddler.[76]

Burial 107 was thirty-five to forty years old at death. She was buried between 1760 and 1776 (Late Middle Group) in a hexagonal coffin on an east-west axis, with her head to the west. Coffin nails were found, as well as shroud pins to hold a shroud around her. The burial contained one opaque tubular bead of redwood with a transparent green core that was cased in clear glass. Because the bead was located near her ear, it could likely have been part of the hairstyle to prepare her for burial.[77] As an enslaved woman performing a repetitive kind of labor, the woman had enlarged bones from repetitive stress tensions (significant hypertrophy) throughout her skeleton and mild to moderate osteoarthritis in many joints. In her vertebrae, she had bony projections on joints from repeated and severe stress (osteophytes), pits at end of vertebrae from physical stress (Schmorl's nodes), and bone fracturing from fatigue (spondylolysis).[78]

Two beautiful, large, light-gray, transparent beads with eight facets were recovered from the grave fill of Burial 428 (fig. 25). These beads were lost again in the World Trade Center destruction. Burial 428 certainly suffered under slavery, and her funerary remains were not treated well after death. The skeleton of this forty- to seventy-year-old woman was truncated at the ribcage by a stone wall and a trench constructed by builders.[79] From forced labor, she exhibited significant enlarged bones from repetitive stress tensions (hypertrophies) on her shoulder to elbow bones (humeri); osteoarthritis in her shoulders, back of the neck, and temporo-mandibular joint of the jaw; and bony projections on joints from repeated and severe stress (osteophytes) on the cervical or neck bones.[80]

Rings. A total of five copper-alloy finger rings were found in four women's graves. Two of these rings held insets with glass, known as

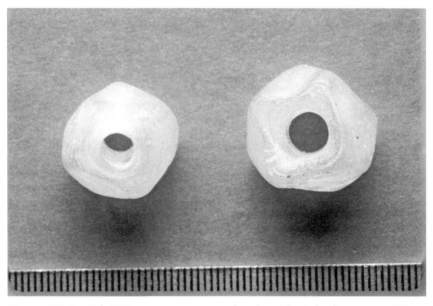

Figure 25. Burial 428, two transparent beads with eight facets, ca. 1735–60. Glass, 8.6 × 9.6 mm. in diameter, ca. 8 mm. long. They were found in the grave fill and then lost in the World Trade Center disaster. Photo by Jon Abbott. Courtesy of the National Park Service.

paste rings. Burial 310 lived to around forty-four to fifty-two years of age, and she was buried with a paste ring rich blue in color on the left hand (plate 6). The second paste ring was worn on the third finger of Burial 242, a forty- to fifty-year-old woman who also had coins placed over her eyes and pins that held her clothing. The center of this ring contained a larger colorless central inset surrounded by three blue glass insets on each side. She was buried north of the fence in the Late Group (post-1776). Paste rings like these have also been found at other North American archaeological sites: Santa Rosa Pensacola, Florida (1723–1752); Seneca and Iroquois sites in western New York (1730–1814); a fort in Michigan occupied by French and British (ca. 1750–1781); and an eighteenth-century Spanish site in St. Augustine, Florida.[81]

African American sites, including the African Burial Ground, yielded copper alloy or silver rings. Burial 377 was a woman between thirty-three and fifty-eight years old. She had three copper alloy rings positioned near her throat, indicating they could have been part of a necklace.[82] Now lost, the rings were photographed in the field and removed, but then were not catalogued in the laboratory, were not accessioned by conservators, and were lost by the time the Howard University Archaeology Team began its work. Additionally, rings that were simply plain metallic bands were found in Burials 115 and 71, both women aged twenty-five to thirty-five.

Silver Bob. A three-and-a-half- to five-and-a-half-year-old child in Burial 254 was buried with a cast silver pendant bearing a pear-shaped dangle. The pendant lay at the child's neck and was likely worn as a necklace (fig. 26). The child was buried directly beneath another child under two years of age, with anthropologists concluding that, "the two youngsters appear to have been placed together in an area crowded with burials."[83]

The silver piece suggests a Native American connection. Silver jewelry in general followed the fur trade throughout upstate New York, the Great Lakes, and upper Mississippi regions.[84] Similar objects that were cut in a conical shape from flat sheet silver, called

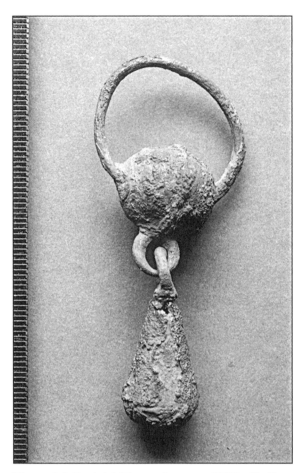

Figure 26. Burial 254, pendant, ca. 1735–60. Cast silver. A three-and-a-half- to five-and-a-half-year old wore this cast silver pendant that may have been made by Native Americans. Photo by Jon Abbott. Courtesy of the U.S. General Services Administration.

bangles and tinkling cones, were common throughout the Great Lakes region and have been found in many 1820 Native American burials from Battle Point, Michigan. Pear-shaped dangles were popular in colonial America and so may have been for Native Americans in the New York region. One that is particularly close to the African

Burial Ground example exists in the Iroquois silverwork collection in the Rochester Museum and Science Center.[85] The collection dates to the second half of the nineteenth century.

Sleeve Links and Cuff Links. Two enamel faces of decorative cuff links were recovered from beneath the left upper arm of Burial 371, a twenty-five- to thirty-five-year-old woman who did not have a coffin (fig. 27). Only the upper body was intact because the rest was destroyed by a very large concrete footing related to construction of the office building in February 1992.[86] The faces of the links were coated in brightly colored blue enamel with a chevron and two dots in white and pink. Because of their location beneath her left humerus, or shoulder-to-elbow bone, they likely did not in fact fasten

Figure 27. Burial 371, cuff links, ca. 1735–60. Enamel face with copper-alloy backs. Coated in brightly colored blue enamel with a chevron and two dots in white and pink, these cuff links were found beneath a woman's left upper arm. Her lower body was destroyed during construction of the federal office building in February 1992. Photo by Jon Abbott. Courtesy of the U.S. General Services Administration.

a sleeve.[87] Archaeologist Warren Perry noted that a women's organization affiliated with the generally male Masonic order called the Prince Hall Chapter of the Eastern Star existed in the late nineteenth century. Archaeologists believed this design to be Masonic during their decade of research, but in the final report they ultimately reject this notion, and we are left with no interpretation of the design.[88] Another enamel face of turquoise, but devoid of any decoration, was found near the chin of Burial 211, a man also without a coffin who was buried in a north-south row of Late Group burials dated to post-1776.[89]

In addition to these two enamel faces, three men (Burials 341, 238, and 392) were buried with octagonal-shaped cuff links made of copper alloy with impressed designs. Finally, Burial 158 had a pair of round, gilded cuff links made of copper alloy worn at his wrists, indicating he was buried wearing a shirt.[90]

Individual Burials

Burial 332. Incredibly, Burial 332 is the only case that provides any indication of a person's name. The initials H. W. and the age thirty-eight were inscribed into the coffin lid with tinned iron tacks, thereby offering us a hint of a name as well as a precise age (fig. 28). He was buried in a hexagonally shaped coffin made of Eastern Red cedar wood that split open lengthwise. A young child in Burial 289 was laid above a part of the grave, possibly deliberately as if they were related.[91] The child was buried with the piece of quartz crystal described above, and two shroud pins. Both graves are circle C in plate 4.

Burial 6. Burial 6 was likely a man between the ages of twenty-five and thirty who was buried in a hexagonal coffin in the Late Group (post-1776) during British occupation. There were eight buttons in the grave, three of which were not related to clothing. The other five belonged to a coat or jacket in which he was buried.[92] These five by and large do not match in size, decoration, or manufacture. Two

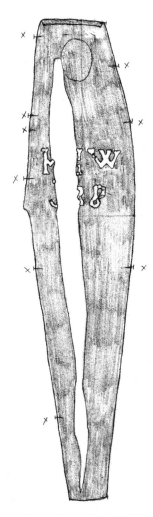

Possible reconstruction of
iron tack lid decoration

Figure 28. Burial 332, coffin lid with initials H. W. and age thirty-eight, ca. 1760–76. This is the only coffin to offer even minimal information about the name or age of the deceased. Each × is a coffin nail. Drawing by M. Schur. Courtesy of the National Park Service.

nonmatching copper alloy gilt buttons were beautifully incised with anchors (plate 7). Buttons with such anchors were used on British naval officer uniforms beginning in 1774. The discovery of the buttons led to a premature assumption that the deceased was buried in a British naval officer uniform from the Revolutionary War, but he was not. Questions about the anchor symbolism therefore arose and remain unresolved.

Was he engaged in the war? Or was he a sailor who had lived his life on the seas? Perhaps the buttons were important spiritually; conceivably as a signifier of water, a type of ideographic marking, or as a return across the water to Africa or the next life.

Interestingly, the same anchor motif was found as a pin or brooch at the Betsey Prince site in Rocky Point on Long Island (fig. 29).[93] The Betsey Prince site was a free black settlement that existed from the 1760s to 1840. Within the context of Christianity, the anchored cross or mariner's cross is connected with St. Clement, who was martyred at the behest of Roman Emperor Trajan and thrown into the sea tied to an iron anchor. If the anchor was understood in this context, the death may well have struck a chord with Africans and their New York descendants who remembered the Middle Passage. It certainly symbolized something specific, whether Christian, water-related, and/or African-based, because the same design was found on two different buttons in the African Burial Ground between 1776 and 1795 and then again on Long Island with roughly contemporaneous dates.

Finally, the person in Burial 6 had filed teeth, which points to a birth in Africa and not in the New World. A chemical analysis (via strontium isotope) also supports his birth in Africa.[94]

Upon his arrival in New York, the young man was forced to work a great deal. He exhibited bone scarring as a result of inflammation from bacterial infection or an injury of lower limbs (periostitis), significant enlarged area of bone (hyptertrophy) also in lower limbs, and osteoarthritis in all lower limb joints and back.[95] He had bony projections on joints from repeated and severe stress on his neck (cervical spondylolysis), and experienced childhood stress including rickets.

Figure 29. Anchor pin or brooch, Betsey Prince site, Long Island, 1760s–1840. The pin was excavated from the Betsey Prince free black settlement at Rocky Point. The anchor is the same in design as on two buttons excavated from Burial 6 at the African Burial Ground (plate 7). Copyright of the New York State Museum, Albany, NY.

Burial 340. Burial 340 is one of the most famous at the African Burial Ground because of its burial contents. The woman held the status of an elder, based on her extraordinary funerary objects and her advanced age, which was somewhere between thirty-nine and sixty-four. She was buried with an entire string of beads and cowrie shells around her waist that rested on her hips (fig. 30). Also, on her right wrist she likely wore a bracelet of forty-one alternating blue-green/turquoise and pale-yellow glass beads. Her incisors were filed to hourglass and peg shapes (by filing or chipping to a point or peg shape), a practice followed in Africa only, suggesting that she was born in Africa and was a survivor of the Middle Passage. Finally, an unused clay pipe was placed beneath her pelvis. Buried with her head to the west, she had been shrouded, as indicated by eleven straight pins mostly around her head, one around the neck, and two on the torso. Burial 340 was buried before 1735 (Early Group) on the far eastern side in what was probably an isolated section of the cemetery (circle D in plate 4). Skeletal analysis revealed a later life of hard labor after she arrived in New York. She had an enlarged area of bone (hypertrophy) as a result of repeated stress on her shoulders and lower arms.[96] She had moderate osteoarthritis in her hip and vertebrae of the neck and lower back. It is possible she suffered anemia or nutritional stress.

In the grave, there were seven different varieties of glass beads of the total 112 recovered, as well as one amber bead with fourteen worn or polished facets, and seven cowries.[97] Anthropologists suggest the multifaceted amber bead could originate from Africa, but it is really unknown, as no exact comparisons for the bead exist either from African or European archaeological excavations.[98] Ledgers from the British Customs House note that these amber beads were shipped to New York and were traded in both Africa and Europe. Another black bead with white, wavy lines correlates with Iroquois sites in eastern and western New York State from 1682 to 1750. Of the 112 beads, 78 percent were blue and turquoise (18 percent were yellow). Stine, Cabak, and Groover explain that "blue is the most consistent bead color present at each African-American site."[99] They reason that African Americans would have had some control and choice in the process of bead consumption.

The waist beads around the pelvis in figure 30 were commonly worn as intimate body ornamentation on the female body and illustrate a cultural continuum from Africa.[100] The National House of Chiefs, Keepers of the Skins and Stools in Ghana concurred: "This

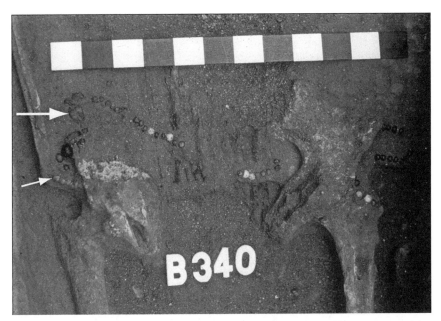

Figure 30. Burial 340, pelvis with glass waist beads, ca. 1712–35. An elder who was born in Africa, survived the Middle Passage, and must have been respected in the community. She was buried with 112 beads, an amber bead of fourteen facets, seven cowrie shells, and an unused clay pipe. Top arrow points to cowrie shell, bottom arrow points to alternating blue-green and yellow beads. Her enslavement is evident from repeated stress throughout the shoulders and lower arms. Photo by Dennis Seckler. Courtesy of the U.S. General Services Administration.

configuration and its burial context are consistent with an Akan-speaking society in which beads are buried with their owner."[101] Waist beads were worn by women historically in Africa as well. In Virginia in 1732, William Hugh Grove wrote that some of the newly arrived, virtually naked boys and girls wore beads around their necks, arms, and waists.[102]

The woman in Burial 340 was interred with a never-used, four-inch-long clay pipe beneath her. Interestingly, there are special pipes called *ebua* made in Ghana only for funerals.[103] The never-to-be-smoked blackened pipes bear figures in mourning gestures. Figurative pipes would not have been available in New York; but mourners may have continued part of the custom by supplying an unused pipe. She somehow warranted this African-based funeral that must have been particularly prized in the New York community.

Two other burials also contained unused pipes. Burial 165 was found with portions of a clay tobacco pipe of European manufacture, and Burial 158 had a piece of an English pipe bowl bearing the letters "IW" buried with him, although it is not clear whether the object was part of the fill or the burial.[104]

A brief consideration of pipes at other burial sites illustrates that unsmoked pipes were of significance and that pipes were funerary objects in Africa. In Barbados on the Newton sugar plantation, a clay pipe was unearthed in Burial 72. This grave, dated between the late 1600s and early 1700s, was for a particularly powerful person who may have been a healer or diviner based on the rich, varied grave goods. The pipe "closely resembles a number of pipes from southern and coastal Ghana that date from the latter half of the 17th century . . . it is almost certainly of African [Ghanaian] origin."[105] Interestingly, the pipe was placed face up with the hole on top in the center of the pelvic area of the body. The pipe may have operated as some kind of passageway or link between the grave dirt (often a potent substance) and his navel (which may be a link to the spirit world just as it was to this physical one).

Unused clay pipes were placed in burials in Jamaica at the Seville Plantation Village (1670–1760). They also were excavated from Elmina, Ghana. In some cases, the pipes were not necessarily unused: an English traveler in Jamaica recorded in 1687 that at funerals, slaves laid the corpse in the grave and then added cassadar bread, roasted fowles, sugar, rum, tobacco, and "pipes with fire to light his pipe."[106] Sites in Maryland and Virginia contained pipes with a Nigerian Kwardata motif dating between 1640 and 1720.[107] In contemporary Ga'anda society, the same incised diamond pattern motif was on a drinking vessel used in an initiation ceremony into adulthood. An archaeological dig at the Houlout cemetery in northern Cameroun (1500–1600) revealed a smoking pipe in a tomb.[108] Thus, pipes in general were funerary objects both in Africa and the New World.

Sankofa Man, Burial 101. Along with Burial 340, Burial 101 is also one of the best known burials because an Akan sankofa may have been tacked into his coffin lid. Now nicknamed Sankofa Man, the sankofa motif underpins the African Burial Ground project and its commemorative artworks in many ways.

The coffin lid's heart-shaped design is possibly a sankofa, which is an ideographic symbol from the Akan linguistic group of people residing in Ghana and Côte d'Ivoire (fig. 31). If it was a sankofa, as identified by the National House of Chiefs, Keepers of the Skins and Stools in Ghana, then the ancestor was buried bearing the proverb "Go back to the past to inform the future." The sankofa symbol is popularly recognized as a bird turned around preening its back feathers; it is also manifested in a heart shape as seen on the outer wall of the final memorial at 290 Broadway in plate 12. In Africa, a sankofa along with other *adinkra*, or ideographic characters, would be worn on textiles to funerals to mourn the dead. Adinkra stamped or printed onto fabric can be worn to important events more generally today.[109] Danquah explains that, "Clearly the use of adinkra cloth and symbols is intended to mark the link forged between the living and the dead, the present and the future, the affairs of the now and the affairs of the hereafter."[110] If Burial 101 bears a sankofa, then the motif brings mourners and ancestors together.

Alternatively, historian Erik Seeman suggests that the interior design of the heart shape is not a sankofa, but rather, the initials of the deceased and his date of death in 1769 (fig. 32).[111] This fits with the relative dating of the coffin, which is ca. 1760–76. Heart motifs with initials or name, and with age or date, have appeared on colonial and nineteenth century coffins.[112]

In my opinion, the final identity or search for origin of the tacked motif is less significant than the power that lies in the representation of the motif itself. People's excitement over the years in finding a direct link to a specific location in Africa fueled and inspired

Figure 31. Burial 101, coffin lid detail in situ, ca. 1760–76. Iron tacks on wood. The tacks famously form a heart-shaped design that might be an Akan adinkra from Ghana that carries the proverb, "Look to the past to inform the future." This man died in his thirties with arthritis, severe cavities, and bone scarring from a bacterial infection. Photo by Dennis Seckler. Courtesy of the U.S. General Services Administration.

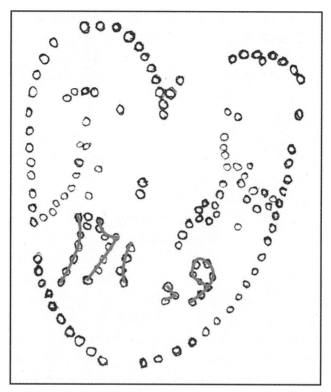

Figure 32. Burial 101, "1769" suggestion for coffin lid. Instead of a sankofa, the year 1769 is a possible interpretation of the tacks for the year the man died. Drawing by M. Schur. Courtesy of the U.S. General Services Administration.

innumerable reproductions of the sankofa, so much so that it became the unofficial motto for the African Burial Ground project as a whole. The sankofa has graced newsletters, websites, coffins for reburying the deceased, and Tomie Arai and Rodney Léon's commemorative artworks (plates 9 and 12), and the symbol's legacy continues, rendering it ubiquitous in commemorating the site today.

The tacked design on the coffin lid of Burial 101 is 1⅖ feet wide and 1½ feet high (fig. 31). The outer heart-shaped part of the design was created with fifty-one iron tacks. Whereas brass tacks were typically used by European Americans, the less expensive iron tacks were used here.[113] The iron could be interpreted spiritually, as it is associated with conjuring bundles. More important, the tacks underwent a tinning process that whitened the tip, giving it a reflective quality so important for creating flashes of light associated with catching the attention of spirits. There was a longitudinal crack or split in the coffin lid made out of larch wood that went through the sankofa. Michael Blakey noted that it could have been ritually cracked or broken purposefully, although it is not known if it was purposeful.[114]

DNA testing was run on this skeleton, and it was found that Sankofa Man's maternal line matches most closely DNA from Tuareg people of western Niger.[115] Researchers are not clear on where he was born because the chemical analysis of strontium isotope levels performed for determining where childhood was spent signaled New York, but his low lead levels and his modified incisors point to Africa.[116] He could have had the tropical skin disease yaws, which would have been contracted in Africa, as evidenced by the malformed tibia or shin bone.[117] Sankofa Man may well have been paired with an infant three to nine months old buried a few inches away in Burial 108 (both are in circle A in plate 4).[118] The small baby's grave was damaged by a backhoe in preparation for excavation, and before that by an old stone foundation on Lot 14.[119]

Sankofa Man's remains also tell a story about his life as an enslaved person in New York City. The labor he performed involved stress to his elbows, as the muscle attachments at the elbows were enlarged.[120] At the time of his death in his early thirties, he already had mild to severe arthritis. His teeth had severe cavities and probably abscesses along with them. Finally, bone scarring existed as a result of inflammation from bacterial infection or an injury on his head and legs (periostitis).[121]

In sum, archaeological analysis of how the deceased were buried with which funerary objects and what body adornment illustrates homogeneity to a certain extent. Even though the African Burial Ground had a large population brought directly from Africa, very little can be attributed to a specific cultural group or geographic place within Africa. Instead, we find similar traditions practiced by different groups of people across Africa, such as the use of pipes, rings, and beads; as well as across its diaspora, with the burial of buttons, shells, quartz, and discs. With such variation, it is difficult to assume that one aspect of the New York burial ground specifically derives from one African culture, and even in Africa itself one particular culture does not exist in isolation.

The examples discussed here instead support the recent scholarship of historian Erik Seeman, who suggests that we take into account instead "a broader poetics or sensibility that Africans carried with them when forcibly brought to the Americas."[122] The above then stand as instances of general, pan-African practices, some of which are understood and remembered, many of which are not. The repeated use of wooden coffins, copper pins, and heads to the west speaks to standards that were practiced and maintained throughout a century of use at the African Burial Ground in New York. The anomalies related to violence, disruption, bodysnatching, war, and other factors outlined later in the chapter also befell Africans and first generations of African Americans.

Stratigraphy: Early, Middle, Late Middle, and Late Group

Stratigraphy, an internal geographical mapping of the African Burial Ground, consists of temporal and spatial divisions at the site by relating the graves to each other (relative dating), to external landmarks, to funerary objects, and to varied coffin shapes. The stratigraphy is a system that allows for a consideration of the graves in relation to each other both horizontally (in terms of proximity) and vertically (in terms of depth). The burials were placed within four major groupings:

Early Group:	c. 1712 to 1735 (51 burials)
Middle Group:	1735 to 1760 (199 burials)
Late Middle Group:	1760 to 1776 (60 burials)
Late Group:	1776 to 1795 (114 burials)

The Early Group includes burials up to circa 1735, which is when pottery factories located at the eastern end of the communal cemetery began heavily dumping their kiln waste into the African Burial Ground. The Early Group graves pre-date this dumping. Because these are the oldest graves, many of them were underneath later ones, were truncated by later ones, or were disturbed by urban development.

The Middle Group dates approximately from 1735 to 1760. Up to this point, the only major construction built in the vicinity was the Almshouse complex, beginning in 1735. By 1741, the famed Corselius/Crolius and Remmey was manufacturing pottery on the far eastern part of the Van Borsum Patent. Several pottery companies used the cemetery as a dumping site for kiln waste, which included broken stoneware vessels, clay waste, and kiln furniture. Enslaved Africans may very possibly have worked for the potters.[123] Shards lying on the cemetery ground were backfilled into the burials during and after the dumping, which dates between 1728 and 1765 approximately.[124] The burial ground was not yet crowded by this time, so the Early Group graves were not greatly disturbed by Middle Group burials.[125]

There are several burial clusters and pairings that have been identified in the Middle Group. For instance, a cluster of graves that may have been purposefully buried next to each other were all burials belonging to children or infants. In addition to being a cluster, Burials 74, 85, 98/100, 103, and 102 seem to run parallel to where a fence or pathway running through the middle of the African Burial Ground would have been (separating Rutgers's Kalk Hook Farm from the Van Borsum Patent), as seen by the cross-hatched post holes, outlined in a thick grey line in plate 4.[126] In another instance along this fence, further to the east, a twenty-five- to thirty-five-year-old woman (Burial 159) was buried with two infants or young children (Burials 161 and 206) on either side of her at the foot of her grave (plate 4, left of 100E beneath postholes).

Another burial cluster is a triple burial consisting of a woman between twenty-five and thirty in Burial 142, who was buried with two infants directly on top of her. One infant was Burial 144, less than two months old, and the other was Burial 149, six to twelve months old. All three were in separate coffins but within the same grave (fig. 33).[127] The three were buried together at the same time.[128] As can be seen by the white dashed lines that outline the coffins, the infants were carefully situated so that all three fit together. They are mapped in plate 4 in the center of the lowest quadrant between 80 and 100E. A couple of other children's graves were between two adults (Burial 347 and 333). If indeed the parents, then the young children were the first generation of an African diaspora in New York.

The Late Middle Group had fifty-six graves assigned to it, with the approximate dates of 1760 to 1776. Construction had increased by now on the Common just south of the burial ground so that the Bridewell jail from 1775 and a cemetery for the almshouse existed (roughly drawn at the top in fig. 17). Although this part of New York City was far less secluded, it was still a space of marginalization because these public institutions were for the criminal, homeless, insane, and impoverished.[129]

Graves were still limited to the southern half of the cemetery because of the diagonal fence or pathway running through the cemetery (thick grey line in plate 4). With this boundary, there was not enough room in the cemetery during the time of the Late Middle Group and so the deceased were added in the empty spaces between the Early and Middle Groups.[130] For instance, a vertical line of burials seems to create a closely knit north-south row in the east central section of the cemetery (short dashed line in plate 4). Because of heavy use and compact space, most of the burials by the end of the Late Middle Group existed only within 1 or 2 feet of each other.

Finally, the Late Group is dated from 1776, the time of the Revolutionary War, to 1795 when the cemetery closed completely. The Late Group graves are the only ones located in the northern section of the African Burial Ground on what was Kalk Hook Farm (plate 4, fig. 12, and plate 5). This area was more sparsely populated because a fence likely ran for a time between the farm and the Van Borsum Patent, as detailed in the previous chapter, which would have prevented earlier funerals from being dug on the north side of it.[131] The

Figure 33. Burials 142, 144, and 149 in situ, woman and two infants, ca. 1735–60. A twenty-five- to thirty-year-old woman with two infants each in their own coffins but the same grave. Photo by Dennis Seckler. Courtesy of the U.S. General Services Administration.

fence's probable postholes were uncovered during excavation (thick grey line in plate 4, dashed line in fig. 7 and plate 5, and diagonal line in figs. 12 and 14). The fence was very likely taken down between 1765 and 1776 during British occupation of the city, making it then possible and necessary (the southern half was oversaturated with graves) to hold funerals in this northern part.[132] Because the northern area is less dense, it is easier to see that graves were organized in rows roughly in a north/south direction that most likely followed contours of the hilly area (see longer dashed line in plate 4).[133] It is also possible that management of the cemetery was more regularized in this late era; perhaps a grave digger spaced the graves apart rather than the mourners.[134] Since these graves were dug during a time of war with itinerant men travelling to New York, there would have been fewer kinship associations among the graves.

The highest number of coffinless graves (twenty-one out of thirty-two) in the African Burial Ground is located here in the Late Group. This was during the time of the Revolutionary War and a seven year long British occupation of the city. Africans and African descendants from outlying areas were attracted to work for British forces as they were offered freedom. Thousands came from surrounding areas and other colonies, and it is believed that some of these people, who had no one to bury them or at least no one to order them a coffin, were buried here. This situation is clearly verified in a New-York Historical Society document: "An aged gentleman tells me he remembers when the site of this granite hotel [Astor], was still a commons, or open field, on which the negroes from Virginia, inveigled thence by Lord Dunmore, in the revolution, were encamped. They got the small-pox, died in great numbers, and were buried in the negro ground, in the rear of Chambers street."[135] This extremely important, not yet quoted information cites the precise location of the Late Period African Burial Ground and attributes the coffinless mass burials to a smallpox outbreak. Additionally, a shortage in wood for fuel and building may have meant coffins were not easy to come by. These notions are supported by the coffinless being adult men who could have been soldiers or refugees, rather than women or children.

None of the children in the African Burial Ground were coffin-less, but thirteen youth in the Late Group were buried as spatially detached or isolated. They do not seem to be associated with adults and one area had three babies in a space that may have been spe-cifically set aside for children (Burials 183, 184, and 186, circle B in plate 4). Because the children are largely still associated with the north/south rows, it is possible there was a connection with adults but they were kept spatially apart.

The soil of some of the graves in the northern area contained animal bone and horn remnants, mostly of cows. It seems that waste from tanneries had already been dumped, and then twenty-two graves were dug and the animal bones became part of the backfilling to close grave shafts. The Late Group contained a higher number of people buried in street clothes although others were still shrouded. Also, miscellaneous items, including coins, shells, and pipes were more prominent in the Late Group than in earlier groups.[136]

The Late Group contained a few inexplicably unusual burials that had encountered violence in some way. Burial 364 had a twenty-five- to thirty-five-year-old man with no coffin whose bones were taken apart and put back together incorrectly.[137] The forearm was placed where the lower leg should have been, and the lower leg was placed alongside the upper part of the leg. Both forearms had been severed with a sharp blade just before or just after his death. Did this dismemberment occur on a cadaver that was stolen and partially dis-sected by the Columbia medical students, as recounted in the intro-duction? If so, perhaps the body was then discovered, retrieved, and reburied.[138]

Burial 323 was a nineteen- to thirty-year-old man whose cadaver received post-mortem surgery. The top of his skull was completely sawn off, and it was then placed in his arms. The body was positioned with the head to the east rather than the west and was without a cof-fin. The unusual or inauspicious burial could have undergone dissec-tion or an autopsy.[139] Sectioning the cranium was typically performed in autopsies of the eighteenth century. Not only does this body seem to be a victim of Columbia medical students' bodysnatching, which ended in 1788 as described in the introduction, but he was excavated not long after burial since he is dated to the Late Group (1776–95).

In considering the stratigraphy of the African Burial Ground, it is evident that landmarks and socioeconomic histories of the area influenced burial conditions and locations. For instance, tanning yards and pottery manufacturers on the sacred land resulted in animal bones and pottery shards in the grave fill. Also, two fences—one in the south between the Common and an unexcavated section of the cemetery, as described in chapter 2, and another that ran diagonally between two properties through the middle of the excavated cemetery—influenced where the burials were positioned and determined the intense crowding in the southern half of the excavated site.

Skeletal Analyses: Lives and Deaths of the African Burial Ground Population

Much of the skeletal analysis provides a painful and at times tragic view of life, labor, disease, and malnutrition experienced by those buried in the African Burial Ground. In addition to determining the age and sex of the deceased, bone analyses revealed delayed development in bones, infection, arthritis, lead poisoning, malnutrition, and injury as a result of repetitive forced labor. The majority of those who died before eight years of age were born in New York.[140] Conversely, many who survived to adulthood were born in Africa, with early lives that were strong, healthy, and well-nourished, and then experienced great hardship in New York City. Ultimately, the findings offer insight into the lives first of children and then of adults who were buried at the African Burial Ground, shedding light on experiences related to slavery in New York and the first African Americans in New York City.[141]

The Short Lives of Children

Those who were younger than fifteen years of age at the African Burial Ground had a particularly high mortality rate. Perhaps one of the most shocking statistics ascertained from skeletal analysis is that 55.3 percent of the interred children had died by age two. The majority of these babies died in the first year of their life, at 39.2 percent.[142] The following skeletal analyses reveal the enormous difficulties that the young faced during their childhood. The traumas were literally etched onto physical bodies: birth in New York City or Africa, healthy African childhood, Middle Passage experience, malnutrition and stunted growth, tooth infection, and the grim effects of forced manual labor.

Children eight years of age or younger were very likely born in New York.[143] The stresses of forced labor and malnutrition point to the fact that those who were born in New York had extremely difficult lives and low survival rates. Of the New York born children under six and a half years of age, 70.8 percent exhibited dental defects in crown developments and tooth enamel (dental hypoplasia) as a result of infectious disease, systemic metabolic stress, and insufficient protein, calcium, or carbohydrates.[144] While those under eight were born in New York, children in Africa as young as nine years old were put through the grueling Middle Passage. High stress was found among children between ages nine and sixteen, which researchers associate with surviving the Middle Passage and living in New York.[145] Forty-four percent of those who did survive would then die between the ages of fifteen and twenty-four because of the impact of life in New York.[146] Conversely, people who lived to old age exhibited far less stress between the ages of nine and sixteen because they had spent their healthy childhoods in Africa.

To the surprise of the researchers, the teeth of those born in New York contained extremely high levels of lead. The amount of over 100 parts per million would have created "neurological and behavioral consequences."[147] Those with modified (filed) teeth who were born in Africa contained low levels of lead. Beyond knowing that breastfeeding passed lead into infants, the researchers are unclear what caused such lead pollution in colonial New York, the source of the pollution, and how much of a factor lead poisoning was in early deaths.

The bones of children younger than fifteen offered information concerning disruptions in growth and development. Thirteen children had sixty-one lesions in total in the eye orbit, cranium, and face that are often related to nutritional deficiencies and disease processes; anemia would be the most common example (porotic hyperostosis).[148] Just over half of the thirteen lived with chronic infections. The young population was clearly "not reaching its growth potential."[149]

Abnormal bone structure, or morphology, was also found among youth younger than fifteen years of age. Forty children out of forty-eight, or 83 percent, exhibited abnormally shaped long bones,[150] meaning they likely had rickets. Specifically, vitamin D deficiency inhibits the absorption of calcium into the bone matrix, which results in softer, weaker, more pliable long bones. The skeletal system has a reduced ability to resist bending stress imposed by load-bearing work, or even normal activity, with permanently bowed legs as a consequence.

Effects of labor taken into consideration with bone pathologies illuminated the individual and collective experience of slavery in New York. Out of forty-eight individuals under the age of twenty-five, nineteen (or 39.5 percent) bore evidence of biomechanical stress indicators.[151] This stress occurred from labor involving load bearing action and/or repetitive motion and included excessive arthritis or skeletal fractures in children. Five children had fractures, eight had signs of arthritis, sixteen experienced long-term biomechanical stress, and eleven went through acute events of intense physical activity. Thus, "these individuals are a clear example that enslaved children in New York City engaged in strenuous physical activities."[152] Eight of the nineteen children lived only to the ages of four to ten years old. Some as young as four showed biomechanical stress, illustrating that children were forced into slavery and physical labor in New York from a very young age.

Child labor was also evident through the premature fusion of the suturing of the bones of the head, a pathology that existed in fifteen of forty-eight children (31.3 percent), three of whom were under the age of six.[153] This condition, called craniosynostosis, demonstrates that the children were already carrying heavy loads on their heads by the age of four or five. Such labor is visually evident in the only colonial era print depicting the institution of slavery in New Amsterdam and New York, with Africans carrying what they have harvested on their heads (fig. 4). Because of this premature suture closure in children, the brain was prevented from normal growth and so skull bones were misshapen. Lab director and osteologist Mark Mack offered the comment that capitalism was literally built on the heads of these children.[154]

Burial 39 was one such child, a six year old who lived with premature closure of the cranial sutures in combination with fusion of the cervical (neck) vertebrae.[155] Another example of a child with craniosynostosis was Burial 17. Between four and six years old, the child had several other conditions that included rickets, a cleft palate, a missing central incisor that never grew in (hypodontia), and deficient and undercalcified tooth enamel (known as enamel hypoplasia and hypocalcification, respectively).[156] The grave is one example of overcrowding at the African Burial Ground because Burial 10 was added above the child, cutting into her or his grave shaft. Moreover, a separate, earlier Burial 26 existed underneath a slight portion of the child in Burial 17. The vertical spatial analysis reveals three layers of burials here.

Infant mortality is painfully evident from the excavation of shared graves containing mothers and their newborns. As seen in figure 33, Burials 12 and 14 contained a thirty-five- to forty-five-year-old mother with an infant who was either a newborn or less than six months old on her torso. The infant was in a coffin just on top of the adult's in such close proximity that the decay of wood probably resulted in the collapse of one into the other.[157] The baby had meningitis and cranial periostitis, which is bone scarring as a result of inflammation from bacterial infection or an injury. They were buried at the same time. One more example is Burial 335 and 356, which was a twenty-five- to thirty-five-year-old mother holding her newborn in the crook of her right arm, both inside of one hexagonal coffin.[158] In all, twenty-six graves were shared.

To conclude the childhood skeletal analysis section of this chapter, it is clearly evident that infant mortality was high. Newborns and children at weaning age in particular had "high levels of new infection, anemia and other indicators of poor nutrition such as growth retardation and stunting."[159] There was little evidence of healed lesions or other pathologies in children, meaning that the New York–born children did not tend to experience an extended diseased state, on the one hand, or recovery from disease, on the other. Instead, they died of acute disease and/or nutritional stresses in a shorter amount of time. The enslaved population was not heightened through fertility or natural population increase. Instead, the continuing supply of human captives "render[ed] the enslaved disposable."[160]

Demographics and Mortality Rates of Children and Adults

In all age groups, general demographic information could be discerned from 301 of the 419 who were excavated. Mortality rates were found to be highest for infants who were newborn to six months of age; next highest were adults aged between thirty and thirty-four; and the third highest mortality rates were among adults aged forty-five to forty-nine (fig. 34).[161] Female adults died most frequently between the childbearing ages of thirty and thirty-nine (37.6 percent), and the mortality rate of male adults was highest from ages forty to forty-nine (34.3 percent).[162] Researchers suggest that these patterns might result from either a higher enslavement of captives in these age groups in general, or else a higher proportion of recently arrived captives in these age groups who could not adapt to the poor living conditions in New York. If women lived beyond age forty, it is likely that they could live until fifty-five or beyond sixty.

Few demographic comparisons could be made with other cemeteries because of the lack of records, particularly with any cemeteries containing European or European American populations, since so few from that era have been excavated and analyzed. Because material evidence did not exist, researchers accessed written records of Trinity Church in order to compare mortality information between

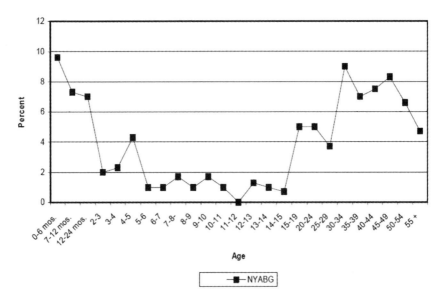

Figure 34. New York African Burial Ground mortality rates. Mortality rates were found to be highest for infants who were newborn to six months of age. Courtesy of the U.S. General Services Administration.

the two cemeteries, which were contemporaneous and located in lower Manhattan within a fifteen-minute walk of each other. Many of those buried at Trinity Church were likely owners of the enslaved at the African Burial Ground.[163] However, unlike the African Burial Ground, the cemetery at Trinity Church is available to its public to this day with gravestones bearing detailed epigraphs. They include the name of the deceased, birthdate, death date, birthplace, number of years alive, family members, and perhaps their profession in life. For instance, one I read explained, "Here lies Robert Crannell and Catharine Wife of Robert Crannell. Deceased Jany 26 1761 aged 65 years and son Thomas."

The ages at death among the white Anglican population in New York were found to be virtually an inverse of the African Burial Ground mortality rates. For the Trinity Church cemetery, 327 deaths were recorded (187 adults and 140 children) between 1700 and 1777. The one hundred males demonstrated moderate death rates at middle age but died primarily later in life, living even into their eighties and nineties.[164] Trinity Church mortality rates for newborns to five year olds were similar to that of the African Burial Ground at the rate of 85 percent, or 119 children of 140 children. A dramatic decline was observed in death rate for Trinity youth aged five to fourteen. In sum, English men and women "lived to old age up to ten times more often than did Africans."[165]

Adult Health at the African Burial Ground

Adult life in New York was no easier than childhood experience. Traumas and health problems point to a difficult life for adult Africans living in colonial New York. One example is a high rate of tooth loss, caries (cavities from dental decay), and abscessed teeth. Of 166 adults with dental remains, it was found that 72.9 percent of males and 84.3 percent of females had at least one carious tooth.[166] Painful abscesses appear to have been largely left untreated. Researchers note that the diet of colonial New Yorkers, such as corn or wheat flour, sugar, and molasses, contributed to the development of caries because it was high in carbohydrates. They comment, "In addition to other hardships, it appears that individuals from the ABG had to endure the pain of dental pathologies and possibly changes in diet due to decreased ability to masticate [chew]. The overall high rate of dental pathology may reflect deficiencies in diet and dental hygiene. These results provide additional evidence of poor dietary regimens, unhealthy living conditions and lack of dental care that characterizes the quality of life for the majority of those who lived in bondage."[167]

Bone analysis of adults sheds light on their nutritional inadequacies and infectious diseases. Of the 358 adults who could be examined, 306 individuals had at least one bone pathology, and just over half of the entire group experienced infectious disease that resulted in periostitis.[168]

The condition of porotic hyperostosis offers further information about lack of nutrition in the adult African Burial Ground population. It is reflected in the lesions found in the eye orbit, cranium, and face that are associated most often with anemia, scurvy, rickets, and infection. Of the observable 275 crania, close to half (47.3 percent) exhibited this porotic hyperostosis.[169] Sadly, the pathologies discussed here merely illustrate the "tip of an iceberg" for disease and ill health that would not have shown up on the skeleton itself.[170]

Adult Forced Labor

Several factors in the skeletal analysis told the story of adult forced labor of the African Burial Ground population. The physical manifestations of slavery borne on the bodies resembled southern plantation slavery in many ways.[171] The effects of biomechanical stress were examined through a variety of skeletal factors in adults age fifteen or greater. Of 187 individuals who were analyzed, sixty-three exhibited osteoarthritis, the form of arthritis characterized by chronic degeneration of cartilage of the joints, suggesting that repetitive loading affected the cartilage tissues.[172] While arthritis is typically found in the elderly, people between fifteen and twenty-four years of age at the African Burial Ground were afflicted with the condition due to excessive mechanical stress. Forty-five percent of those within this age group had osteoarthritis in their lumbar vertebrae, or lower back. Arduous physical labor such as carrying, bending and lifting, and dragging heavy objects would be examples of activities likely to have caused this. Osteoarthritis in the lower limb and ankles points to high stress perhaps from walking on rough earth or climbing stairs or inclines while carrying loads.

The neck was also a site demonstrating the effects of mechanical stress under slavery. Cervical osteophytosis, or the condition of bony projections on joints that cause limited joint motion coupled with pain, points to the fact that forty-four adults underwent repeated and severe stress to their necks.[173] The older they were, the more frequently this became apparent as the stress, such as compression of the neck during milking or the extension of neck for fruit picking, was repeated over time. Four people exhibited moderate to severe osteophytosis without arthritis in their backs, suggesting that loading of the shoulders and head would have placed excessive stress localized in the neck. The mechanical strain to the neck proved so great that seven people had fractures in their cervical (neck) vertebrae.

The identification of Schmorl's nodes is another indicator that points to stress. Schmorl's nodes are slightly depressed pits found on the ends of vertebrae as a result of pressure of cartilaginous protrusions on the discs between vertebrae.[174] Under general circumstances, the nodes develop in relation to age degeneration. Extreme physical stress is evident in the African Burial Ground population, with nodes appearing most frequently in those between the ages of twenty-five and thirty-four in all vertebral regions. A total of thirty-four individuals bore the nodes, out of 187 who were tested.

Four burials (11, 37, 97, and 107) exhibited a complete separation or fracture in the lumbosacral region of the back, which is in the small of the back and the back of the pelvis between the hips (fig. 35). This spondylolysis is typically due to fracturing from fatigue. These four burials with spondylolysis also experienced heavy stress on their bodies overall. Burial 11 was a thirty-five- to fifty-year-old man with many stress lesions (over a third of his thirty-three muscle and ligament attachments) from carrying or heavy lifting. He also had osteoarthritis in his neck, hip, and elbow.[175] He had osteophytosis on his vertebrae, while hypoplasia was evident indicating childhood stress through dental analysis.[176]

Another factor pointing to heavy labor at the African Burial Ground was the evidence of repetitive stress tensions (hypertrophy) in the area where the elbow flexes.[177] This suggests labor related to excessively repeated back and forth motion of the arm and forearm, as in work performed by masons, bakers, and farmers. There were also repetitive stress signs related to supination, or a type of rotation

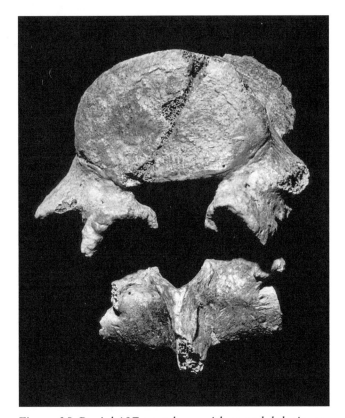

Figure 35. Burial 107, vertebrae with spondylolysis, ca. 1760–76. A view from above of a thirty-five- to forty-year-old woman's vertebrae. There has been a complete separation or fracture in the lumbosacral region, which is in the small of the back and the back part of the pelvis between the hips. Courtesy of the U.S. National Park Service.

involving the hand. Supination is performed by twisting the forearm in order to open a jar, to sew, to weave, as well as to pick citrus fruit, paddle a boat or canoe, or employ heavy tools for reaching into furnace irons.

In sum, researchers conclude that the most consistent results from their research on skeletal indicators illustrate that "strenuous labor began at an early age for at least some individuals, based on the presence of osteophytosis, osteoarthritis, enthesopathies, and Schmorl's nodes in the youngest age category of 15–24 years."[178]

Violence

Finally, fractures were present, which speaks to the violence experienced in slavery. It is particularly telling that many fractures (approximately 80 to 90 percent) occurred at or around the time of death, meaning that they were related to the cause of death, particularly in the case of fractured skulls. Researchers suggest that those with extremely high numbers of fractures were not accidents, but likely reflect beatings or murders of enslaved people.[179] A total of 198 fractures were found in forty-one males and females.[180] Most of the fractures in males were in the cranium (23.5 percent) followed by the ribs (11.4 percent). Females exhibited the most fractures in their femurs or thighs, and crania.

Burial 205 was a female aged between eighteen and twenty with the highest number of fractures at or around time of death; she had thirty-two throughout her body in the arms and legs, vertebrae, and skull.[181] She was buried in the northern half of the cemetery, placing her in the Late Group in terms of chronology, in a clearly north-south running row of burials. Her grave was dug in the area of an animal waste dump and a ceramic dump as evidenced by the grave fill, which contained a high amount of bone and shards, including stoneware, delft, Staffordshire slipware, and Chinese export porcelain.[182] She was laid in a hexagonal coffin built with nails, and ten copper alloy pins indicate that she was shrouded.

Other graves with a significantly high number of fractures included a male aged fifty or older with twenty-three fractures. A healed fracture in his left collarbone occurred sometime during life, with other broken bones closer to time of death in the arms and legs, pelvis, and vertebrae. Three youths aged ten to fourteen had fractures, with Burial 180's being the most severe. He or she, an eleven to thirteen year old, had eighteen breaks throughout the skeleton all around the time of death, including all four limbs, the pelvis, and the cranium.[183] The child had periostitis on the lower limbs as well as rickets, and was born in New York.[184]

Burial 25 speaks to another act of violence because she was shot. She was twenty to twenty-four years old and 5 feet 1 inch tall, with a flattened lead musket ball lodged beneath her fourth left rib in her ribcage (fig. 36). She had also received a blunt force trauma to her face multiple times (perhaps from a rifle butt), and a spiral fracture in the right forearm that typically results from violently twisting and pulling the arm. A small amount of bone remodeling is evident, indicating that she lived for a short time after she was beaten.[185] In terms of her life under slavery, her lower arm bones (ulnae) were scarred where muscles attach at the elbows because she had performed habitual activity using these muscles.[186] Her coffin was placed above an older man, aged fifty to sixty, in Burial 32 so that the coffins were aligned with each other suggesting a deliberate co-interment. Sadly, she was also disturbed in death because she was truncated by a stone

Figure 36. Burial 25, musket ball in fourth left rib in situ, ca. 1735–60. A twenty- to twenty-four-year-old female who had been shot and her body beaten. Photo by Dennis Seckler. Courtesy of the U.S. General Services Administration.

foundation that cut the entire burial at the bottom of the femurs leaving her with no ankles or feet.[187]

Culturally Modified Teeth, Dental Health, and New York Stresses

A total of twenty-six people interred at the African Burial Ground had culturally modified teeth, the highest number excavated from an African diasporic population.[188] Cultural modification of teeth reflects a form of body beautification. It is performed in parts of Africa but was not continued in the New World following the Middle Passage,[189] which means that these twenty-six people with filed teeth were born and raised in Africa. The designs include hourglass, wedge, wave in anterior teeth, chipping and filing, bluntly pointed incisors, and pointed incisors. In all, ten different styles were identified that do not belong to any one ethnicity in particular because people in different cultural groups in Africa used and continue to use many styles.[190] The deceased were over thirty years old, and their teeth were likely modified during their adolescent years in Africa.

For example, the upper middle incisors of Burial 23 (buried with a headstone) were chipped and filed into an inverted "V" or wedge shape. Burial 151's joint in his left jaw was dislocated from trauma, and he had all four of his upper incisors filed into points.[191] Interestingly, Burial 23 was one of the earliest burials (Early Group), and Burial 151 was one of the very last interred (Late Group), signaling a broad continuity in body beautification across tradition, temporality, and geography in Africa.

One extraordinary find was in Burial 137, which contained a whole tooth and a partial tooth belonging to a pig.[192] The tooth was tested to determine geographic origin, and its high strontium isotope ratio indicates that it actually belonged to an African born pig, specifically from Ghana. Researchers have not attempted an interpretation beyond these scientific findings. The remains of the human had been severely crushed and fractured at some point, and the cranium was missing.[193]

In concluding the skeletal analysis portion of this chapter, it is clear that the adults' bones and teeth "bear witness to the stresses of malnutrition, infection, poor medical care, lead pollution, over-work, and injury" once they were brought to New York. Children eight years of age and younger in the burial ground were born in New York. However, research attests that the adults interred in the African Burial Ground by and large were not born into slavery, but originated from Africa where they had lived healthy, nutritionally sound lives as children.

Geographical Analyses Origins of the Deceased

DNA Testing for Origins

Despite the amount of intricate, complex, highly advanced research performed over the course of a decade, we still know where only a very few of the deceased came from specifically in Africa. Research-ers selected twenty-eight adult skulls for a craniometric analysis. They found that most were clearly Central and West African, four to five were in the range of South Africa, one was close to Native Amer-ican, but overlapped with another who was European.[194] Four were closer to European than African. The craniometric method does not allow for defining narrow geographic areas or specific ethnic groups.

In preparation for comprehensive DNA testing on the remains, forty-eight skeletons were tested in 1995 in order to ascertain their matrilineal line. About 2 mm. of bone had to be cleaned, resurfaced, and broken into small pieces for the test.[195] This bone was then placed in liquid nitrogen and pounded into a fine powder. Ultimately, mater-nal genetic affinities were found with Yoruba, Fulbe (Peul), Hausa, and Mandinka people, among others (table 2). Many hurdles were encountered, such as an inadequate database on African genetics and the fact that no databank for African DNA existed at all. An advi-sory board was formed from 2000 to 2002 so that the first human DNA bank of Africans could be created.[196] As of 2004, the bank con-tained over four hundred samples and was affiliated with UNESCO's

"Route of the Slaves" project. Another challenge was that by 2000, GSA had cut research funding on the African Burial Ground project, as explained toward the end of chapter 4. Consequently, no DNA testing on any other skeletons was ever performed. DNA has been taken from the rest of the remains in the hopes that this research may one day be conducted. As well as ascertaining geographic locations and ethnic identities, such testing would reveal potential biological relationships in clustered graves or shared graves, for example, between parents and children.

Historical Documents

The DNA testing performed on the small sample of forty-eight at the African Burial Ground offers an idea of the varied origins of enslaved people brought to New York. Historical documents shed additional light on the origins of the deceased in the African Burial Ground in a general sense. It is not easy to correlate specific cultural presences from Africa to New York, or to identify precise African identities or cultures in New York. But a look at the historical documentation begins to show similarities and patterns so that we can have a general understanding, particularly of an African-based spirituality. It illuminates the degree of complexity and negotiation that must have occurred among Africans in New York. This information then paves the way for understanding one of the oldest African diasporas in North America, which continues to exist in New York City to this day.

Dutch Slave Trade. For the earliest era of slave trading to New Amsterdam, a large number of Africans hailed from Angola, as is evidenced in the names of several of the first eleven males.[197] Because the Dutch usurped Portuguese areas of control, many of the first Africans came from the same areas the Portuguese traveled, such as Elmina and Sao Thome as well as Angola and the Kongo.[198]

A direct form of slave trading developed between the island of Curaçao, thirty miles off the Venezuela coast, and New Netherland

Table 2
Molecular Genetic Affinities of Forty-Eight Individuals
Whose DNA Was Tested at the African Burial Ground

Burial Number	Tissue Site Sampled	mtDNA Haplo-group	Geographical, Country, and Macroethnic Genetic Affinity
1	R. Radius	L2	West/Central AFRICAN
6		L2	West Africa, Benin (Fulbe peoples)
7	Not Indicated	L3	West Africa, Niger
9	R. Radius	L2	West Africa, Benin (Fulbe peoples)
11	R. Ulna	L2	West/Central AFRICAN
12	Not Indicated	L2	West/Central AFRICAN
16	R. Ulna	L2	West/Central AFRICAN
20	R. Fibula	L2	West/Central AFRICAN
25	R. Ulna	L3	West/Central AFRICAN
32		L3	West Africa, Niger
37	R. Fibula	L2	West/Central AFRICAN
40	R. Fibula	L3	West Africa, Niger
47	R. Ulna	L2	West Africa, Benin (Fulbe peoples)
49	R. Fibula	L2	West/Central AFRICAN
51	R. Fibula	L2	West/Central AFRICAN
56	R. Radius	L3	West Africa, Niger
58	Not Indicated	L2	West/Central AFRICAN
63	Not Indicated	L2	West/Central AFRICAN
67	R. Radius	L2	West/Central AFRICAN
71		L2	West/Central AFRICAN
73	R. Radius	L2	West Africa, Nigeria (Yoruba peoples)
76	R. Fibula	L3	West Africa, Niger
89	R. Ulna	L1	West/Central AFRICAN
97	R. Ulna	L2	West Africa, Nigeria (Fulbe peoples)
101	Not Indicated	L3	West Africa, Niger
105	Not Indicated	L1	West/Central AFRICAN

Table 2
Molecular Genetic Affinities of Forty-Eight Individuals
Whose DNA Was Tested at the African Burial Ground (Continued)

Burial Number	Tissue Site Sampled	mtDNA Haplo-group	Geographical, Country, and Macroethnic Genetic Affinity
107	R. Fibula	L2	West Africa, Nigeria (Hausa peoples)
115	R. Fibula	L3	West Africa, Niger
122	R. Ulna	L2	West Africa, Nigeria (Hausa peoples)
135	R. Fibula	L2	West//Central AFRICAN
138	R. Fibula	L2	West Africa, Senegal (Mandinka peoples)
144	Not Indicated		West/Central AFRICAN
151	R. Ulna	L2	West/Central AFRICAN
154	R. Fibula	L3	West Africa, Niger
158	R. Fibula	L2	West Africa, Senegal (Mandinka peoples)
171	R. Ulna	L1	West/Central AFRICAN
176	Not Indicated	L2	West/Central AFRICAN
180	R. Radius	L2	West Africa, Senegal (Mandinka peoples)
194	Not Indicated	L2	West Africa, Nigeria (Fulbe peoples)
219	R. Fibula	L3	West Africa, Niger
226	Not Indicated	L2	West/Central AFRICAN
233	Not Indicated	L2	West Africa, Benin (Fulbe peoples)
242	R. Fibula	L2	West Africa, Nigeria (Fulbe peoples)
310	R. Rib	L2	West/Central AFRICAN
335	R. Ulna	L2	West/Central AFRICAN
340	Not Indicated	L2	West Africa, Nigeria (Fulbe peoples)

Source: From F. L. C. Jackson, A. Mayes, M. E. Mack, A. Froment, S. O. Y. Keita, R. A. Kittles, M. George, K. Shujaa, M. L. Blakey, and L. M. Rankin-Hill, "Origins of the New York African Burial Ground Population: Biological Evidence of Geographical and Macroethnic Affiliations Using Craniometrics, Dental Morphology, and Preliminary Genetic Analyses," in *The New York African Burial Ground Skeletal Biology Final Report*, edited by Michael L. Blakey and Lesley M. Rankin-Hill (Washington, DC: General Services Administration and Howard Univ., 2004), 1:194. Courtesy of the U.S. General Services Administration.

(the general area, including New Amsterdam, which was colonized by the Dutch) from around 1647 to 1664.[199] Peter Stuyvesant was director-general of both New Netherland and Curaçao during this time period, so he was instrumental in contriving a trading relationship between the two places. Curaçao and its neighboring islands Bonaire and Aruba could offer horses, salt, and slaves in exchange for New Netherland flour and grain. The West India Company performed the bulk of the trade, but allowed private trading between the two areas as well.[200] Between 1659 and 1664, at least 438 enslaved people, or an average of eighty-seven per year, were transported from Curaçao to New Netherland.[201]

What were the origins of the people who were taken to Curaçao and would then find themselves in New Amsterdam? During those early years of the seventeenth century, Africans by and large originated from the Angola and Kongo region.[202] Overall, more than 70 percent in New York in 1664 bore their country as a last name: Angola.[203] Dutch Reformed Church records illustrate the predominant Angolan presence: of the fifty-two spouses married between 1641 and 1664, twenty-eight names were Angola or a derivation of it. Examples include the marriages in 1641 of Anthony Van Angola and Catalina Van Angola, and Lucie D'Angola and Laurens Van Angola.[204] One person was named Van Loange (Loango), another de Chongo (Congo), as well as a Van CapoVerde (of Cape Verde) and Van St. Domingo. Enslaved people in the colony had received Portuguese or Christian first names. This is likely because the Portuguese in Angola had named and Christianized the Africans prior to importation.[205] Other names revealed the prevalence of Africans from the Guinea coast. Lewis Guinea and Jan Guinea were among the eight people who requested full freedom from the WIC in 1664.[206]

English Slave Trade. The trading company, principal traders, and place of embarkation for the slave trade shifted with the 1664 change of political power in New York when England took over. Jamaica, Barbados, and Antigua replaced Curaçao as central trading depots with "seasoned" slaves.[207]

Amazingly, beginning in 1686, Africans were taken from the southeastern African island of Madagascar and sailed around the bottom of South Africa. It must have been one of the longest journeys in the Middle Passage. New York merchants set up a trading relationship with nearby pirates, selling liquor and gunpowder to sustain them on the small island of St. Mary off Madagascar.[208] These pirates sold to New Yorkers in return East Indian goods as well as captured Africans. The Philipse family of Philipsburgh Manor (a successful patroonship) outside of Albany was particularly involved with this direct trading until 1698. Samuel Burgess sailed the *Margaret* to Madagascar for Frederick Philipse. As Captain Kidd's ex-crewmate, he took many voyages to Madagascar selling guns and liquor to pirates there in exchange for gold and Africans. Captain Kidd himself lived in New York City from around 1691 to 1695, and married a woman from there.[209]

Up until the end of the seventeenth century, enslaved people usually arrived from the Caribbean in small shipments.[210] Wilson records at least 630 in 1659.[211] Prior to 1742 under the British, up to 70 percent of Africans arrived from the Caribbean and the Americas. It was because of the 1741 Conspiracy, as explained in chapter 1, that peoples' attitudes towards slave trading in the Caribbean altered, and Africa was preferred thereafter. Between 1700 and 1774, at least 6,800 enslaved people were brought to New York.[212] Of these, 2,800 were imported directly from Africa to New York and 4,000 were imported indirectly from the Caribbean to New York.

Lydon's table reveals that between 1715 and 1764 the largest number of ships arriving in New York came from Jamaica (with many of the numbers occurring before 1743).[213] Of the total, 15.3 percent came from Barbados. Other islands included Antigua, St. Eustatius, and Bermuda, as well as South Carolina.

In summary, under the Dutch (1626–64), the majority of people came from Angola, Guinea, Calabar, the Gold Coast, and Curaçao. Other places included Sao Thome, Cape Verde, and Brazil. During British rule (1664–1776), people came to New York City from Madagascar, Jamaica, Barbados, and Antigua. In fact, in runaway slave advertisements in New York between 1726 and 1814, people were described as hailing from Madagascar, Guinea, Jamaica, and Barbados. Their points of origin from Africa to the Caribbean included Calabar and the Bight of Biafra, Guinea, Angola, and the Gold Coast.

Conclusion

To conclude, the three major sections of this chapter consider burial items through archaeological analysis, health and sickness through skeletal analysis, and geographic origins through DNA and historical documents, including the global shipping routes through which Africans were brought to New York. While the data can be frustratingly inexact at times, or not deeply interpreted at others, a new comprehensive understanding begins to emerge about the deceased in the African Burial Ground. No matter how little their wealth, mourners honored their dead with objects valuable to them—some carried all the way from Africa via the Middle Passage, others obtained in New York. These objects may have represented African cosmologies, customs, or symbolisms, or else were valuable clothing adornments, or they may have carried a myriad of other interpretations. The chapter offers information about the lives, deaths, and spiritual practices of the deceased, giving them a voice that has not been heard before now. As Michael Blakey explained, "We can, in a sense, go back to the actual ancestors themselves and glean from what they have left us in their material representation as much of their experience as we can find."[214]

Many times, the recognition of this is painful, with skeletons offering evidence that their former bodies were pushed to the maximum in terms of the forced labor they performed to support enslavers' families or to build the infrastructure of New York City. This, combined with poor nutrition and high lead levels, resulted in stressed and at times diseased bodies. It was very difficult for New York City children to survive such hurdles. Those who were brought to New York at a later age on the other hand had lived very strong and healthy childhoods. Some Africans came as far away as Madagascar, while many others were brought through the Caribbean including

Curaçao, Barbados, and Antigua from their departure points along the Gold Coast of West Africa and the Congo and Angola of Central Africa. People with these varied identities, practices, languages, and cultures developed an early African diaspora in the city of New York as they performed, remembered, and invented expressions of spirituality at the African Burial Ground.

4

Contemporary Politics and Grassroots Efforts

It was an arduous and contentious process that enabled the archaeological analysis outlined in chapter 3 to be performed. That process is detailed here through a chronology of events with a narrative about difficult tensions, competing voices, and counternarratives that arose through the years from 1988 to the reburial in 2003.[1] Complex questions about who formulates memory, how, and for whom, were confronted through an exploration of conflicting agendas between the General Services Administration (GSA), civic government agencies, New York City African Americans, and research professionals working on the project. Based on a variety of voices that I heard, recorded, and researched at the African Burial Ground, I witnessed concerned citizens who at times worked together and at times splintered into groups, rendering a seamless collective memory of the site an impossibility. In reality, blended discourses and negotiated agendas from personal, civic, and national narratives have combined to define complex ways in which the African Burial Ground is recognized and remembered. I argue that what was initially a nearly forgotten and then clandestine discovery has since entered the United States' national memory and New York's body politic.

The detailed chronological narrative in this chapter demonstrates contemporary battles over space, politics, and spirituality. In a complex unfolding of events, GSA came to learn about the burial ground between 1988 and 1991 when the land was purchased, the Environmental Impact Statement was released, and archaeological testing was finally performed to uncover actual burials prior to any construction on the office building. Although a primary myth about the African Burial Ground is that it was accidentally and suddenly "discovered" by construction workers building the office, details here counter that notion by illustrating that GSA followed the proper step-by-step procedure and laws for digging into New York City ground, and in doing so gained knowledge about the historic site early on.

In this chapter, the burial ground narrative has been divided into three overarching phases. Phase one concerns grassroots activists, many of whom were African American, who endeavored for years to reverse GSA's questionable treatment of sacred space. GSA did not always include and inform African Americans of New York City about the African Burial Ground, which was its lawful obligation. The controversy reached a height in the early 1990s when bones were damaged in a digging accident, had concrete poured on them by construction workers, were excavated too quickly, and then were improperly stored in cardboard boxes so that mold formed on them. Committed activists in turn engaged New York City government officials, who listened closely to their constituents.

Phase two of the narrative concerns government intervention and African American participation in the project from 1992 to 1996. In July and September 1992, Illinois representative Gus Savage held Congressional hearings that resulted in several reversals that ultimately led to African American scientific control of the remains, reburial of the bones and artifacts on the site, suitable memorialization of the cemetery, and abandonment of a proposed pavilion where a concentrated number of burials lay. Resistance to GSA, on the one hand, and commemorations of the site, on the other, were carried out through an African-based discourse of spirituality in which a demand for respectful treatment was wrapped up in honoring the ancestors, calling on the spirit world, writing messages to the dead, and leaving offerings. This complicated melding of politics and spirituality has actually become a means for constituting the African Burial Ground. The grassroots efforts gradually transformed what was once a historically dispossessed space into a remembered and reinvented place in downtown lower Manhattan. Today, the area between Duane and Reade Streets just off Broadway acknowledges a once oppressed and marginalized eighteenth-century people now located in the crux of contemporary, mainstream New York City. It has been a slow, painstaking process, which included budget cuts that closed down the project in 1999 and loss of some funerary objects and archival material in the World Trade Center attack. Eventually, all of the remains were returned from Howard University following scientific analysis and reburied behind the Ted Weiss Federal Building at 290 Broadway in 2003.

Phase three of the burial ground narrative concerns commemoration and reburial negotiation from 1996 to 2003. In the end, the African Burial Ground was indeed memorialized, honored, and reclaimed in the twenty-first century. How did that occur? The contested issues illustrate how a marginalized space—a space in production—garnered attention to involve the New York City mayor's office, members of Congress, the Manhattan borough president, and presidents of the United States. The government, typically understood as a hegemonic entity, fought within and against itself by challenging GSA in order to demand proper treatment of the African Burial Ground. Through its contestation, disputation, and marginalization, the African Burial Ground today is necessarily situated within the national and civic body politic. These varying discourses countered and conflicted with each other at the African Burial Ground to arrive at uneasy solutions.

Phase One: Grassroots Struggles for Respectful Treatment of the Burial Ground, 1988–92

Acquiring Land for the Office Building

GSA, the federal agency that owns the African Burial Ground land, first came to learn about the existence of the burial ground as it prepared to construct its office building between 1988 and 1991. GSA provides for more than one million government employees nationwide, supplying office furniture, computers, equipment, travel and transportation arrangements, information technology solutions, and network services, as well as buildings, leases, and property developments for government agencies.[2] The office in New York is a regional branch (Northeast and Caribbean) of GSA, with Bill Diamond as its then–regional director, that is umbrellaed under the national GSA office in Washington, DC.

GSA purchased two plots of land in lower Manhattan in December 1990 for the construction of a federal office building and a federal courthouse. Amazingly, both of the sites were ultimately of major historical significance, causing history to be reconceptualized in new ways. After mandatory salvage archaeology and research were performed prior to any building construction, it was found that the land for the federal courthouse at 500 Pearl St. in Foley Square (now Daniel Moynihan U.S. District Court) rested on a portion of the historic Five Points site (fig. 1, between Worth and Broadway). Five Points was known as the poorest, most dangerous neighborhood in nineteenth-century New York City, where many immigrants resided. It is beyond the scope of this project to further follow the Five Points story, the artifacts that were excavated from that site, or the construction of the Foley Square U.S. Federal Courthouse that was built there.[3]

The second plot of land designated for a federal office building at 290 Broadway was situated on a section of the eighteenth-century African Burial Ground. The 34-story office building that would eventually be built on top of the African Burial Ground would house U.S. Attorney offices, an Environmental Protection Agency regional office, and the IRS district office.[4]

In 1987, GSA made it known to Congress that it was interested in purchasing these two plots of land in lower Manhattan from the City of New York. Then, on 1 March 1988, GSA accordingly submitted to the House of Representatives a prospectus that was written before an environmental impact statement revealed that an African Burial Ground might exist. Congress accepted the prospectus for purchasing land without the knowledge of any cemetery.

GSA became aware of the burial ground within the year and did not inform Congress.[5]

1989 Memorandum of Agreement

Before GSA could commence any construction work on the building, it had to follow laws that would protect the site should anything of historical importance be found. If anything were located, it would become the full responsibility of the owner of the property, in this case GSA.

GSA had to first comply with the National Historic Preservation Act of 1966, as well as the Advisory Council on Historic Preservation (ACHP), which is a group created under the preservation act in order to implement the act. In turn, ACHP advises how the property owner might assist in meeting responsibilities and obligations related to issues of historic preservation that might be found.[6] If there is a risk of adverse effects to historic property, then a Memorandum of Agreement (MOA) must be drawn up to ensure a mandatory consultation process with the public. GSA's minimal work with the public would become a point of great contention through the years.

On 15 March 1989, prior to the sale of land, GSA and ACHP signed a Memorandum of Agreement. It seems clear to me that GSA was now aware that the burial ground existed. Although the historic cemetery was in fact *not* mentioned by name in the MOA, the document discussed plans for archeological investigation, stating that the property might be eligible for listing on the National Register of Historic Places (which is a reason that an MOA is drawn up).[7] The New York State Historic Preservation Office (NYSHPO), which also participated in the process, refused to sign the MOA because it believed that GSA had not at that time properly followed its responsibilities set out in Section 106 of the National Historic Preservation Act. NYSHPO's signature line on the MOA was simply left blank. Instead, the executive director of the ACHP Robert Bush wrote to GSA asking for a new MOA or an amendment to the existing one.

Since GSA did not know about the Burial Ground when submitting its prospectus to Congress earlier in March 1988, I conclude that sometime between that time and the March 1989 MOA a year later, they had become aware that the African Burial Ground existed from analyses of extant historical maps and colonial documents. However, GSA and the rest of the world would not yet know if actual remains were present until physical archaeological testing was performed in May 1991, after the December 1990 final sale of land.

Environmental Impact Statement

Before the signing of the 1989 MOA, GSA hired their prime contractor, Edwards and Kelcey, to draft an environmental impact statement (EIS) in 1988, as pursuant to the instructions in Section 106 of the National Historic Preservation Act and the National Environmental Policy Act.[8] Edwards and Kelcey, in turn, subcontracted a company called Historic Conservation and Interpretation (HCI) to conduct a study that provided detailed historical information about the African Burial Ground and to determine the potential for existing remains.[9] The HCI document, called the *Stage 1A Cultural Resource Survey*, was released in September 1989 and revised in May 1990. It was this text that revealed in writing the existence of the African Burial Ground on the plot of land at 290 Broadway.

Edwards and Kelcey completed the *Foley Square Project Draft Environmental Impact Statement* (EIS) on 7 July 1990, five months prior to the sale of the land. This EIS document was disseminated to two hundred federal, state, and city agencies and community organizations, and public hearings were held concerning the draft. Through all of this, no comments were made about the African Burial Ground. Out of an entire two volumes, two to three pages of readable script in the draft EIS were devoted to the African Burial Ground in the ten- to fifteen-page cultural resources section.[10] Discussion of the burial ground in this document was embedded in concerns about the impact of the intended office building on traffic, water, pollution, and the population in the area.

Finding the Bones

General Services Administration followed through with the purchase of two plots of land on 12 December 1990 for $104 million from the city of New York. The Broadway block sold for $54.2 million. Because the city was the seller, both Mayors Koch and Dinkins were aware of the historical documentation that located an African cemetery on the site prior to the sale of land.[11] No testing had yet been performed to ascertain whether burials were indeed intact because GSA did not own the land up until now.

Beginning in September 1988, prior to the sale, GSA had already begun to secure an architect to design the office building. The entire architect selection process lasted over two and a half years.[12] A commission was awarded in April 1991 to the architectural firm Hellmuth, Obata and Kassabaum (HOK) for design, to general contractor Tishman Foley Partners for calculating costs, and to the developer Linpro New York Realty for hiring subcontractors.[13] These would be among the federal government's earliest design/build competitions.[14]

Since GSA now owned the land following the sale in December 1990, it could perform its mandated archaeological testing to discover if sensitive, physical remains from the African Burial Ground indeed existed. However, it is questioned here why GSA first commissioned the architects for the office building in April 1991 and then, six months after the sale of the land, conducted archaeological testing in May 1991.

To do so, in May 1991 GSA again contracted with Edwards and Kelcey, who in turn subcontracted HCI to archaeologically test and physically excavate an area. HCI used its backhoe to dig 30 feet deep in order to reach culturally sterile soil.[15] Intact burials were indeed located in situ on 20 May 1991. In retrospect, HCI owner Edward Rutsch recalled, "There was no doubt about what it was."[16] Rutsch first located ceramic shards, and then a skeleton. He backfilled what he unearthed and reported his find to GSA.[17] GSA pressed HCI to estimate the number of existing burials.[18] So Rutsch had to dig again using his backhoe. As Rutsch himself was aware, use of large machinery would have violated archaeological protocols in potentially sensitive areas. He located more skeletons, as well as shroud pins.

A site supervisor from the initial digging wrote that, although GSA knew about the possible presence of a cemetery early on, the agency had delayed physical investigation of the site to such an extent that, when the bones were finally unearthed, "there was little time left before construction was to begin."[19] The supervisor (Philip Perazio) commented, "This mess is entirely of the GSA's own making . . . it is an example of how a federal agency can get itself into a tremendous amount of hot water by trying to sabotage the 106 process."[20]

May 1991 was the date by which HCI's physical testing definitively confirmed that the African Burial Ground was virtually intact 25 feet below ground, at least in this particular section of the nearly 7-acre communal cemetery. The find would lead to a full-scale excavation four months later, beginning in September 1991.[21] GSA decided on its own that a full excavation of all burials would be performed in order to lay the foundation and underground parking garage for the federal office building. The New York African Burial Ground Archaeology final report published in 2006 noted that GSA's adoption of full archaeological excavation as the mitigation strategy was not in accordance with procedures.[22] Amazingly, within a month of the full scale excavation, construction began on the office building in October 1991, and from that point on, building was concurrent with excavation of the burials.

It is important to point out that the media have repeatedly recounted either that the burial ground was uncovered by *construction workers* or that the remains were *accidentally discovered*.[23] As explained in detail above, claims of any kind of "discovery" of the cemetery are erroneous because the parties involved knew what was at stake at least from 1989. GSA actually possessed knowledge about the eighteenth-century cemetery even *before* the land was purchased, because the proper salvage archaeology procedure had been conducted even if the reporting of it had not. The unearthing of bones was no accident, but rather a confirmation of both the environmental impact statement and HCI's salvage archaeology report.

After HCI relayed to GSA its testing, the information did not immediately become public. Up to and through this time, the broader public did not have any knowledge that the African Burial Ground existed or that it was about to be built upon. Only governmental agencies and their subcontractors knew that they were digging into a colonial era African cemetery from 1712, and through this secrecy they perpetuated the amnesia that had been in place for two hundred years. Such denial of history proved detrimental to relations with citizens of New York City and went against the MOA and Section 106. Of great insult was the fact that, when bones were first found in May, GSA put ACHP on hold by suggesting they did not know whether the bones were human.[24] An archaeological worker at the site observed a general attitude of "we need to figure out how to get this done right before it is publicized and before we have officials making decisions, because then it's going to be a mess."[25] Hence, the *New York Times* did not report that human bones had been found until one month later on 15 June 1991.[26] GSA Regional Administrator Bill Diamond held a press conference at the site on 8 October, the same month that construction on the building began.

Up until the public press conference, GSA controlled and disallowed a production of memory at the African Burial Ground by suppressing the knowledge it had obtained. To the extent that GSA did not properly carry out its Section 106 responsibilities, no one else could participate in reclaiming, remembering, and defining the space. It would take grave mistakes on the part of GSA for others to begin to insist upon an alternative narrativizing of memory.

Excavation and Improper Storage of Remains

Overall, excavations were conducted from 12 September 1991 until their suspension on 29 July 1992 (fig. 37). After the prior archaeological testing and fieldwork from July 1990 until 29 July 1991, owner Edward Rutsch of HCI hired the Metropolitan Forensic

Anthropology Team (MFAT) to analyze burials because of the density of burials and because HCI was a small company. MFAT was a European American team that had no experience with burials, African Americans, or skeletal biology. At this juncture, it was a tragic move on GSA's part to allow largely European American archaeological teams the control over an African and African American space. The palpable implications were that not only was black history once again controlled by white people, but also that through an opaque veil of secrecy, it was again being erased by white people. Thus, in this early stage of the project, memory at the African Burial Ground was being shaped and produced by European Americans.

The full excavation of burial remains commenced on 12 September 1991, and by 15 September it was apparent that a large number of burials were intact. The team excavated an average of two to

Figure 37. Excavation of burials under white tent at 290 Broadway, 1990–92. Excavations were conducted from 12 September 1991 until their suspension on 29 July 1992. The digging overlapped with construction of the Ted Weiss Federal Building, built from 1991 to 1994. Courtesy of the U.S. General Services Administration.

three deceased humans per day and was working eleven hours a day for seven days a week. When Dr. Michael Blakey later took on the research aspect of the project, he noted that many of the skulls had been damaged due to hurried excavation.[27] On 5 December 1991, building project manager John Rossi called for accelerated speed in excavating. Dunlap reported in the *New York Times*, "By using what he called the 'coroner's method,' [project manager] Mr. Rossi said only one day would be needed to clean a skeleton, remove it and place it in a box still surrounded by soil. It now takes three to five days to remove a skeleton."[28] The term "coroner's method" of inquiry was particularly outrageous in relation to excavating the remains and would be cited often by concerned citizens at various public meetings. They also latched onto the notion that the expertise of the archaeological team was in criminal investigations rather than cemeteries or African American sites.

Although the order to expedite excavation was not given, at least officially, the quantity and rapidity of excavated remains proved too much for MFAT and HCI to handle under the initial expectation set by GSA, which was that the teams would excavate a total of only ten burials.[29] The excavated remains were being stored in a three-room lab at Lehman College in the Bronx, the site contracted by HCI to house the remains. HCI therefore wrapped the deceased and their funerary objects in newspapers and left them in cardboard boxes until the local MFAT could clean, study, and interpret everything. During this time, mold formed on the bones, irreparably damaging some. GSA's prime contractor, Edwards and Kelcey, commented, "We were digging them out faster than [storage] cases could be made."[30]

The African American community did not trust the storage process and wanted to view the situation. "We kept asking [MFAT], 'Can we go up there?' And that involved more waiting, more delays . . . It wasn't that we were against Lehman, we just wanted to see how our ancestors were being stored" explained Miriam Francis.[31] African American anthropologist Michael Blakey pressed MFAT to allow him entry into the storage area to view the conservation techniques. Deterioration had indeed occurred through mold growth from improper environment control. In particular, some of the eighteenth-century bones were stored without air conditioning for many months, and the gymnasium where remains were stored did not have temperature controls. Moreover, heavy bones had been placed on top of more fragile remains, and other bones were overpacked in cabinet drawers.[32] Also, some windows were not blocked to prevent ultraviolet rays from harming the remains.

On 16 December 1991, spurred by the difficult situation with GSA and by the outrage of people in the New York City community, Senator David Paterson established a task force to monitor the excavations and follow up on problems.

1991 Memorandum of Agreement

Government agencies became increasingly uneasy and called for an amended MOA in the fall of 1991. In light of the actual disclosure of the remains, the 1989 MOA was finally amended and signed by GSA, ACHP, and the New York City Landmarks Preservation Commission (LPC) on 20 December 1991.[33] In general, LPC preserves New York City's historic and cultural heritage. The Chair of LPC explained that, under the MOA, "it's the Landmark's responsibility to provide technical guidance to ensure preservation of archeological resources impacted by the Foley Square project."[34]

The new 1991 MOA contained a requirement detailing public involvement: community groups, organizations, institutions, and local professional organizations would participate in reviewing plans for the analysis and reburial of the remains. Under the sections on public involvement and site interpretation, the amended MOA called for an on-site memorial, an interpretive center within the building, and a documentary video funded by GSA. However, because public involvement was previously stipulated by Section 106 and should have been part of GSA's agenda from the start, GSA was already in violation of the MOA.[35] Beginning in March 1992, GSA worked to amend this by holding open meetings with the public.

Archaeological Mistakes

Errors occurred when building construction continued concurrent with the excavation that had commenced in October 1991. The major mistakes included demolition of several burials on 14 February 1992 due to a digging accident, and damage to about twenty burials when concrete was poured on them. Dan Pagano, an archaeologist for the Landmarks Preservation Commission, happened to discover HCI archaeologists sorting through jawbones and leg and arm bones outside of the excavation area when he was photographing the site with a telephoto lens. With an out-of-date map, construction crews had used a backhoe to lay a concrete footing for the tower.[36] At this point, GSA Regional Administrator Bill Diamond stopped construction in the areas where archaeologists were working so that burials would not be further damaged.

Not much had been written by the media following the initial "discovery" of the burial ground. However, this digging accident prompted a "story" steeped in controversy. Peggy King Jorde, assistant to the mayor's office, recognized that "it really did not hit a lot of people until after some of the remains were destroyed. And then it just hit the papers. And there was this hysteria about what the government was actually doing."[37]

Another episode occurred at the site on 6 March 1992. Archaeologist William Henry reported to Federal Protective Services that vandals had broken into the excavation site, disturbing six burials, damaging skulls, and stealing teeth and pelvic bones.[38] This vandalism occurred because one ill guard left the premises, a second guard skipped the 9:30 p.m. round, and then all rounds halted at 10:00 p.m. due to rain.

Public Anger and Activism

As community members' distrust in GSA accelerated, they began to monitor the excavation and construction sites themselves. It became increasingly important for descendant African Americans to participate in the unfolding history of the African Burial Ground by preventing degradation to the ancestors and by fighting for African American participation in the project. A long and bitter battle ensued primarily with African Americans reclaiming a history and identity of the space through an African-based perspective. The competing voices resulted in tensions, conflicts, anger, and eventually, rewritten memory.

Activists included Elombe Brath, Chair of the Patrice Lumumba Coalition, who was made aware of a rumor that concrete would be poured on 20 March 1992. He, activist Sonny Carson, and members of civic organizations physically blocked the concrete trucks from entering the site for the day by sitting in front of them at the gate entrance. As a result, meetings were agreed upon with GSA. In his written statement for the Congressional hearing that would be held in September 1992, Elombe Brath shared his hopes that, in resisting improper treatment of the African Burial Ground, activists would help to bring "this matter to a conclusion that will reflect the majesty and historical significance of the lives of these remarkable African people who struggled for dignity and laid the foundation for the struggle for basic human rights that continues to this day . . . Mr. Chairman, we could not guarantee that those who reposed at the site in question received justice 200 years ago because we were not there. But we are here today, and it seems that they have arisen from their slumber to put that awesome responsibility on us now."[39]

African Americans, concerned citizens, and Senator David Paterson's Task Force began to formulate demands for respectful treatment of the dead. These entreaties were publicly expressed at a hearing conducted by Councilperson Wendell Foster at city hall on 21 April 1992. A combination of community leaders, activists, and elected officials attended, including Councilperson Adam Clayton Powell IV, Senator David Paterson, and city council members Kathryn Freed, Tom Duane, and Wendell Foster. For three hours, more than two dozen speakers pressed the government to rebury the remains. Paterson added that "[t]he way the GSA has handled this burial ground symbolizes the desecration of black people."[40]

On 23 April 1992, a historic City of New York town meeting was held at Trinity Church for the African Burial Ground. This church was the very institution that had ostracized Africans three hundred years earlier, in 1697, from its still-extant cemetery. The town meeting was cosponsored by LPC, Senator Paterson, city council members (including Kathryn Freed), Manhattan Borough President Ruth Messinger, and the Mayor's Advisory Committee. New York City councilperson Adam Clayton Powell drew applause when he lamented, "You do not disturb the deceased. You leave our people alone. You should let them rest in peace. At the very least, we should do everything we can to stop the construction of this building."[41] In his riveting speech, Reverend Herbert Daughtry of the House of the Lord Church exclaimed, "Had it not been for the bodies and labor of our ancestors, there wouldn't have been a United States of America."[42] He reminded the audience that they could be the descendants of those in the burial ground, and he insisted upon a proper memorial.

Public dissatisfaction concerning the policies of GSA and MFAT escalated to outrage as tensions grew over secular space versus a sacred, historic cemetery. Activists protested vehemently against disrespectful treatment and against GSA's reluctance to recognize or commemorate the sacred site that it had disturbed. Urban designer Herman Howard responded, "Someone's going to tell you that the remains of your ancestors are not more important than getting up this office building?"[43] Journalist and OPEI public educator Emilyn Brown understood that everything the interred "had lived for and possibly died for was being minimized for the sake of a building."[44] Donna Cole, a full-time employee at OPEI, lamented, "So what if you paid X amount of dollars for it? Once you discovered it was a burial ground, you basically should have left it alone."[45] Along with others, Miriam Francis challenged European American control of the project: "If it was an African find, we wanted to make sure that it was interpreted from an African point of view."[46]

Mayor Dinkins established a Mayor's Advisory Committee in April 1992 comprised of concerned citizens in the community.

Howard Dodson, director of the Schomburg Center for Research in Black Culture, was made chair of the advisory committee. He compiled a list summarizing peoples' discontent with GSA, stating that it had "violated the sensibilities and sensitivities of contemporary African Americans, the sacredness of the burial ground site, and the rights of those interred there to rest in peace":

Specifically, the General Services Administration has:
—Knowingly initiated construction of the Federal Building without apparently seeking an alternative site as required by law
—Conducted the excavation without benefit of an approved research design in violation of the terms of the memorandum of agreement
—Damaged remains of up to 20 burials through construction in an unexcavated site
—Submitted an archaeologically unprofessional and culturally insensitive draft research design that reflected a general lack of appreciation for the historical and cultural significance of the find
—Refused to consider reinterring the human remains in the Federal building site
—Refused to consider providing adequate space and funding for an appropriate memorial museum in the Federal building
—Refused to consider redesigning the pavilion to accommodate some of these functions
—Continued to excavate human remains over the protests of African-American and concerned New Yorkers.[47]

During the controversy, it was regional administrator Bill Diamond of GSA's northeast office in particular who resisted the descendant African American community and local politicians. Diamond explained the "feeling was that while the cemetery had existed, it was no more in existence."[48] He reasoned that "We, that is GSA, have been instructed by the Congress, by law, to construct an 850,000 square foot office building on the site and we have no alternative but to do so unless we are instructed by Congress not to do so."[49] As recounted earlier in this chapter, the reverse was true: GSA had approached Congress to request construction of the building in its March 1988 prospectus. Diamond acknowledged the differences between concerned citizens and GSA, stating, "I'm hoping that the community will buy into the American system of settling differences peaceably."[50]

Reinterment of the remains at 290 Broadway was a major issue that could not be agreed upon. As early as 1991, Diamond explained, "We [GSA] are committed to re-interment of these remains to an appropriate site."[51] He proposed Trinity Church Cemetery in Harlem. A spokesperson of GSA added, "We see on-site reinterment as inconsistent with the use of a federal office building."[52] In a public meeting in June 1992, Diamond expressed his willingness to contribute $250,000 to an interpretive display within the office building, an appropriate plaque on the exterior of the building, and again, reinterment of the remains in a public park 50 yards away, off of federal land.[53] By removing the deceased from the space, an African presence would be erased, African American engagement of the space obstructed, and visibility of the burial ground diminished. So contentious was the issue that a solution would not be arrived upon until fifteen years later.

It is instructive to compare this early difficulty in bringing the African Burial Ground into the body politic with the final early twenty-first-century moment when the secretary of the interior, the mayor of New York City, and the president of the United States eventually and readily embraced the burial ground as part of the nation's identity at the 2007 dedication of the final exterior memorial. The journey through conflict, tension, and the production of counternarratives was long, slow, and arduous, but it is a telling case study in dealing with histories of racism, slavery, activism, politics, and acceptance on all sides.

Interestingly, William Diamond was the instigator and leader in the removal of the *Tilted Arc* sculpture by artist Richard Serra just across Duane Street. *Tilted Arc* was commissioned by GSA's Art-in-Architecture program (described at the beginning of chapter 5) and was installed in 1981 on the plaza behind the Jacob Javits Federal Plaza building, right next to the African Burial Ground. Diamond and the panel he appointed successfully removed the arc in 1989, thereby igniting a now-historic national debate about the public's role and voice in public art. Within two years, he had embroiled himself in yet another controversy over control of space. His resistance to recognizing the African Burial Ground as sacred would lead to national repercussions that involved the identity and history of an entire population of New York City African descendants.

Lack and Rejection of GSA Research Design

The 1991 Memorandum of Agreement had stipulated that HCI prepare a research design for the 290 Broadway site and the courthouse site by 10 January 1992. In terms of the excavations, the absence of any design glaringly highlighted a lack of purpose, the absence of research questions to pursue, a lack of direction for research preservation, and even the potential destruction of significant archaeological information. HCI's project archaeologist, Edward Rutsch, explained he was too busy to create a plan: "Many times it was expressed to me [by GSA] that millions of dollars of public money were being lost. There was terrific pressure to get the excavation done—to finish it."[54] HCI was working seven days a week with overtime every day.

GSA presented a research plan to ACHP in April 1992, three months late, which was thereupon rejected immediately. On 10 June 1992, ACHP responded in its letter that the design was "a hastily prepared and incomplete document which fails to outline the measures which will be taken to ensure the proper treatment of archeologically significant areas of the project sites."[55] Additionally, ACHP needed an explanation for the analysis, curation, interpretation, and final treatment of the remains. They made several recommendations for how to involve the public (as required in the amended MOA and Section 106). A revised version was requested by 16 July.

Progress toward Research Design
with Newly Appointed John Milner Associates

On 1 July 1992, ten months after excavations commenced and after the majority of the 419 skeletons were removed, GSA responded to grassroots pressure and directed Edwards and Kelcey to replace MFAT and HCI with another team. This switch occurred only after GSA had received extensive comments on their research design submission. John Milner Associates (JMA) of West Chester, Pennsylvania, excavated only for roughly the last month of the project. Nevertheless, the archaeological team replacement was extremely important because of JMA's prior experience working with cemeteries and with African American sites. The company had overseen excavation on the nineteenth-century First African Baptist Church burial ground in Philadelphia and it had employee diversity. JMA would ultimately provide quality level conservation and interpretation of the already largely excavated remains.

After the change, GSA directed JMA to write a new research design that would address concerns pertaining to science and to involve the community as necessitated by Section 106. The design was to be ready ninety days from the end of July.

Still No Research Design

An ACHP meeting with the Mayor's Advisory Committee on 13 July 1992 led both groups to believe GSA was operating without clear understanding of why more skeletons were being excavated or how they would be studied, and without an appreciation for African Americans' concern for proper treatment of the remains.[56] ACHP asserted that "all work should be suspended" until GSA considered preserving the remaining burials, resolving where to rebury the bodies, recognizing the significance of the site, and finally, writing its research plan. JMA answered that they would need six to eight weeks longer to draw up the revised research design and reported that no analysis of remains had yet been performed. The next set date for a finished research plan was 16 October 1992.[57]

The Turning Point: Gus Savage's Hearing

The general public pressured GSA to terminate excavation of the remains, particularly in the area where a pavilion was planned on a small plot of land behind the office tower (fig. 1). The architectural plans called for a 4-story pavilion connected to the office tower that would house a cafeteria, day care center, auditorium, and pedestrian galleria. But the largest concentration of extant burials—an estimated two hundred—was in this southeast area, and local New Yorkers did not want any more of the bodies disturbed. GSA and the architects maintained that all of the burials would be removed unless Congress intervened.

Mayor Dinkins took up activists' concern about excavating this heavily concentrated area of the cemetery. Dinkins wrote a letter to William Diamond on 16 July 1992 requesting that GSA "suspend all excavation and construction activities in the Pavilion area . . . Options for completing the building without further excavation must be examined."[58] The next day, on 17 July 1992, Dinkins called upon Congressperson Floyd Flake in the House of Representatives because he recognized that "Congressional action is necessary . . ." The letter closed with, "As I am sure you recognize, it is important that we intervene in this project before any further destruction takes place at this important site."[59]

Throughout my research, I repeatedly heard comments about the important role David Dinkins played as mayor. Without a black mayor, it was understood that African American interests would not have been as strongly represented. Dinkins and assistant Peggy King Jorde successfully realized grassroots community work into governmental action.

Diamond's reply by letter to Dinkins was that GSA would be excavating an additional two hundred bodies in order to build the pavilion. Diamond could discern "no basis for discontinuance of ongoing excavations," explaining, "I would not be put in a position of abrogating important government contracts because of political pressure."[60]

Finally, former Illinois representative Gus Savage, who chaired a congressional committee that oversaw GSA, took decisive action.[61] Defense attorney and civil rights leader Alton Maddock brought an article in the *New York Times* concerning the burial ground to Gus Savage's attention. Because GSA could not enact the requests made by Dinkins, the mayor had gone to the press with his demands, and Savage read about those demands in the newspaper.[62] When Savage knew that skeletons were being exhumed daily, he acted immediately by organizing a hearing within two days. He flew to New York City and, on 27 July 1992, heard testimonies at the Court of International Trade in New York City. Savage was able to affect change because he was part of a parent committee to GSA (Subcommittee on Public Buildings and Grounds, of the Committee on Public Works and Transportation in the House of Representatives) that controlled the agency's funding. As well as appropriating funds to GSA, the role of this subcommittee was to begin the approval process for any major construction, repair, or leasing of federal office space for GSA. In fact, Savage's subcommittee had authorized the federal office building funds prior to his assuming the role of chair. Savage explained in the hearing that, "whatever Congress authorizes, it can de-authorize. And if this Subcommittee and its parent Committee is dissatisfied with how things are proceeding when we return to Washington tomorrow, we will proceed to exercise in whatever way necessary that authority."[63]

In a prepared statement read during this hearing, Public Buildings Service Commissioner Milton Herson explained perhaps the crux of the GSA issue: loss of time, money, and construction plans. Dropping the proposed pavilion site would result in a loss of $40 million: $5 million in interest payments, $10 million in land acquisition costs, and $25 million in initial construction payments.[64]

Finally, William Diamond was questioned during the hearing. He maintained that excavations should not stop and that he had not recommended suspension to the central GSA office in Washington, DC, despite the immense pressure put on him. Congressperson Owens summarized Diamond's testimony: "the official position of GSA and the Bush Administration is that if they want any changes made, if they want any modifications in this building, Congress is going to have to do it, because the administration's position is: We will not do it."[65]

Savage ended the 27 July hearing before Noel Pointer, Kent Barwick of the Municipal Art Society, Elombe Brath of the Patrice Lumumba Coalition, Robert MacDonald of the Museum of the City of New York, or Howard Dodson of the Mayor's Advisory Committee and Schomburg Center gave their statements. Savage reasoned, the "hearing is going no further because this regional director is opposed to responding to the wishes . . . that were expressed here today and has been in violation of Section 106 as well as a memorandum of agreement."[66] Savage first ordered GSA to prepare an amended prospectus immediately. He then explained that all pending GSA requests to his subcommittee, including lease renewals and construction projects, would not be approved. "And don't waste your time asking this subcommittee for anything else as long as I'm chairman, unless you can figure out a way to go around me! I am not going to be part of your disrespect."[67] The courtroom erupted in celebratory cheers. Three days later, the excavation on the pavilion site was shut down.

Phase Two: African American Participation and Government Intervention, 1992–96

Significant Changes

The day after the hearing, Savage telephoned and then met with federal GSA administrator Richard Austin in Washington. Austin agreed to terminate the excavation immediately.[68] Two weeks later at a banquet, Gus Savage began a speech by saying, "For those of you who may not know, excavation has ceased forever on the burial site."[69] The archaeological site closed on 9 October 1992. President Bush signed Public Law 102-393, which ordered GSA not to build on the proposed pavilion site.

Next, Savage traveled back to New York City with the director of ACHP Dr. Robert Bush and GSA Administrator Austin to meet with Mayor Dinkins and other civic leaders in Gracie Mansion. They reviewed and authorized the execution of the following changes: excavations would be halted, and research would include top African American scientists; GSA would establish and fund a federal steering committee to ensure African American involvement and to "provide recommendations on the future of the site";[70] and a memorial would be made with community involvement. Another significant result of the meeting was that GSA directed Linpro New York Reality, Inc., to alter the contracts so that the pavilion adjacent to the office building was deleted, the office tower redesigned, and the foundation stabilized to accommodate the modification. Savage added that he would expedite the designation of a historic landmark by contacting the secretary of the interior, which he did by letter on 26 August. Finally, GSA had begun production of a documentary video for national distribution, written by Christopher Moore and directed by David Kutz.

Yet another major breakthrough occurred on 31 July 1992. The Senate Appropriations Committee allocated up to $3 million for protection and memorialization of the African Burial Ground within the 1993 Treasury, Postal and General Government Appropriations Bill. Initially, Diamond had suggested the meager amount of $250,000 for an exhibit within the office building.[71] However, Senator Alfonse D'Amato of New York requested the $3 million because, as he explained, "It is essential that we provide for a significant reinterment of all the skeletal remains at the site. At the same time, we must protect and memorialize an important cultural and historic legacy of our city."[72] The Senate then accepted the bill in the beginning of October 1992, and finally President George H. W. Bush approved the $3 million allocation.

Ultimately, civic, state, and federal government levels enabled effective transformation in response to powerful guidance from grassroots activists. Finally, if not historically, African Americans from this point forward would be involved in handling the remains and deciding on the future of the African Burial Ground, including reburial, memorialization, and scientific research. The next sections of this narrative chronicle these changes brought about by Savage's two hearings. Slowly, a reclamation and reconstitution of the African Burial Ground began to occur.

New Scientific Leadership

Dr. Michael Blakey, one of only a handful of African American physical anthropologists, was contracted with GSA as scientific director of the skeletal remains on 18 September 1992. He and the remains would be based in Washington, DC, at the historically black Howard University, which was contracted with GSA on 16 August 1993.[73]

The African American descendant community charged that scientific study could give voice to the ancestors only when African and African American scholars were involved in all aspects of the project. Warren Perry, who would become the archaeological director, explored the importance of this: "Questions of who gives voice to the past, who defines the problems, and how they are analyzed and interpreted are matters of critical social importance. The African Burial Ground project will for the first time represent a voice of African descendants analyzing and interpreting the scientific materials."[74] OPEI director and anthropologist Sherrill Wilson commented, "We're changing the way African burial sites will be handled in the future . . . we're saying respect our history, respect our past. Taking the remains from a white archaeological firm and putting them in the hands of a black institution had never been done before."[75]

Blakey's initial primary role was to complete the research design by 16 October, which he and JMA finally and successfully accomplished on 15 October 1992. Blakey's academically innovative, African-based perspective on the construction of race met with conflict in the scientific community. After all of its missed deadlines and failed drafts, GSA sent the research design out for comments. Additionally, MFAT director James Taylor shared the design with 120 of his colleagues in November 1992.

Most of the critiques of Blakey's design concerned the issue of testing for "race," which became a major difference in research methodology between MFAT and Blakey. According to MFAT's early research, 7 percent of the excavated remains were European. The plausibility of the presence of a few Europeans compelled many to insist upon testing for "race." For instance, Madeleine Hinkes of the U.S. Army Research, Development, and Engineering Center (RD&E) Center in Natick, Massachusetts, commented, "I am greatly perturbed by the apparent assumption that all remains are Negroid. Such assumptions are the bane of good science. There needs to be much more emphasis . . . on racial assessment."[76] Marc Micozzi, Director of the National Museum of Health and Medicine of the Armed Forces Institute of Pathology in Washington, DC, wrote, "No mention is made of conducting an assessment of race on each individual skeleton . . . The lack of race assessment in the research design is a significant omission."[77]

However, Blakey and others purposefully resisted a racial approach because it was already historically documented extensively that the cemetery was African. Blakey explained that "[t]he only use of [typing by race] is to reinforce the notion that races exist, for the purpose of maintaining the structure of a racist society."[78] As Michigan State University anthropologist Norman Sauer explained, "race" is merely a sociological construction: "races in the sense of the 'big three or four' are not a reflection of natural biological groupings, but naive 'taxonomic' categories handed down from the 18th century. That they are used today for socio/political reasons is unarguable."[79] Sauer maintained that a labeling of the bodies as black or white would offer little "understanding of the history of the population(s) represented," but rather, that a consideration of *specific areas in Africa* or elsewhere that were home to a large number of early Americans would be invaluable.

As well as objecting to the theoretical premise of testing for "race," Blakey questioned the reliability of postcranial, mensurational methods for determining "race." Mensurational methods involve the direct measurement of bones and or teeth for this purpose. Blakey's newer methodological approach was significant because it rejected the Enlightenment era racializing practices and ideologies. The Enlightenment-derived racist system, which categorized and mythologized race, divided people into groups based on physical characteristics and head size and then constructed a hierarchy from lowest to highest. Instead of testing for whiteness or blackness, Blakey's research plan focused on ascertaining specific African origins through DNA testing and innovative chemical analysis in order to identify from where within Africa the enslaved originated.[80]

The Federal Steering Committee

As well as Dr. Blakey's involvement, another breakthrough in the project was the formation of a Federal Steering Committee, as agreed upon by Gus Savage and chartered by the federal government in October 1992. This committee was comprised of community members (many of whom belonged to the previously established Mayor's Advisory Committee), politicians, and professionals.[81] The committee made recommendations to GSA and to Congress, and it served as a liaison to the New York African American community to ensure Section 106 responsibilities were carried out. Howard Dodson, the committee's chair, explained, "We are advisors to both GSA and Congress. The idea is not to be an advisory to GSA, but a watchdog over GSA."[82] The group began meeting at the end of 1992 and lasted until 1994. After a plethora of recorded meetings open to the public, the steering committee recommended to Congress and GSA a set of seven resolutions on 6 August 1993.[83] These recommendations derive largely from the 1991 Memorandum of Agreement and the Mayor's Advisory Committee:

I. Establish a world class museum and research center of African and African American history and culture within the National Historic Landmark.

II. Erect memorial(s) within the landmark area.

III. Instigate a signage program interpreting the history and culture of African peoples in the landmark area.

IV. Install memorial art work and exhibit of the excavation in the lobby of the office building.

V. Reinter the remains in the former Pavilion area. Construct a temporary memorial during research and a permanent one after reburial.

VI. A sacred international service accompanies the reinterment.

VII. The three million dollars be used towards the design and realization of these projects.

Through hard work and continuous pressure, all of the resolutions save one were eventually met. The reversal of so many of GSA's early actions is remarkable, and the implementation of these recommendations by GSA is equally extraordinary. Resolution one, for a museum devoted to Africans and people of African descent in New York City, remains the farthest from actualization. The six realized directives demonstrate negotiated manifestations of an African-based discourse that has become a part of formulating and narrativizing the site.

Additional Archaeological Mistakes

Although Savage resolved many immediate issues with GSA, additional digging mistakes and conflicts with the community would continue. On 13 February 1993, Consolidated Edison electric company attempted to install electric transformers for the Department of General Services about 200 yards southeast of the excavated Burial Ground.[84] A trench was dug on Chambers Street 13 feet deep in which, once again, funerary remains were disturbed. The digging up of bones was initially witnessed by Eric Byron, who, ironically, was an employee of New York Unearthed, an archaeological museum at the South Street Seaport Museum. Con Ed refused to stop working for several hours until LPC notified them.[85] In the meantime, state Senator David Paterson's special assistant, Gina Stahlnecker, had arrived. She called the police, noting that the large hole was "chock-a-block with bones" such as broken jaws with teeth, chips of bones, and teeth. Byron added, "There were piles and piles of dirt with bones popping out all over the place."[86]

The unearthed soil was deposited at the west end of Chambers Street on the fenced-in playground at Stuyvesant High School. The dirt mounds were removed by a subcontractor and taken to a recycling lot near a Con Ed depot at West 29th Street. An archaeologist and Stuyvesant science students salvaged seventeen boxes of remains, which were stored in the Tweed Courthouse basement and later moved to Brooklyn College. Although it is believed the bones would have yielded little scientific information due to their excavation and treatment thereafter, they were still considered sacred. During hearings and OPEI open houses over the years, the descendant community repeatedly inquired about the remains, asking questions like "Where are they?" and "Are they actually at Brooklyn College?"[87]

One year later, yet another "accident" occurred when Con Ed and a subcontractor were repairing a steam line. On 5 February 1994, cranial bone fragments, animal bones, and a human femur bone were dug up and found lying in piles of earth on Reade Street near Broadway. Peggy King Jorde kicked a pile of dirt to find the femur bone.[88] She stopped the workers and their digging. Jorde explained to a reporter, "More than ever it is critical that there be a protocol in place in this area, even in the place of emergencies." LPC had reviewed the job and issued a permit to Con Ed for "minor work dated 2/2/94," but that permit did not expire until 2 February 1998! Dr. Wilson, head of the OPEI office questioned, "What kind of emergency lasts for four years?" She commented that "Con Ed is suffering from selective amnesia."[89]

Historic District Designation

The designation of the burial ground as an officially recognized site of historic importance was another major accomplishment that grew out of the Gracie Mansion meeting with Gus Savage. The City Landmarks Preservation Commission's unanimous 8–0 vote designated the African Burial Ground and common historic district as a New York City historic district on 25 February 1993. The city council unanimously confirmed this on 2 June 1993. The boundaries of the historic district include the 6.7-acre area of the entire African Burial Ground, reaching from the southern tip of City Hall Park up to Duane Street and over to part of Foley Square (see introduction, fig. 2). In response, Councilperson Mary Pinkett of Brooklyn said, "And after you buried them, you didn't give a damn. Not only didn't you give a damn, but you built parking lots over them. . . . This is enough. You can't walk over the bodies of our ancestors anymore."[90] The historic district designation protects the area from any kind of future digging. All alteration, demolition, or new construction must initially be reviewed by LPC.[91] In order to prevent incidents like Con Ed's February 1992 and 1993 mistakes, LPC would also produce a map of archaeologically sensitive places in the district with restrictions on them. Despite these measures, there was the February 1994 incident described above. In addition to being confirmed as a city historic district, the African Burial Ground was designated a National Historic Landmark by then–secretary of the interior Bruce Babbitt on 19 April 1993.

Office of Public Education and Interpretation

On 20 May 1993, GSA's Office of Public Education and Interpretation of the African Burial Ground opened under Dr. Sherrill Wilson, an urban anthropologist and ethnohistorian. Virtually all of the archives, including newspaper articles, government documents, laboratory photographs, and transcripts of meetings, were housed in OPEI's World Trade Center 6 office. OPEI's office next moved to

Varick Street, and then within the office building at 290 Broadway. At the time of publication of this book, all archival documents and images are housed at 26 Wall Street in Federal Hall National Memorial, the National Park Service headquarters for seven of their sites.[92]

OPEI offered a powerful voice for the African Burial Ground from a prominent position in mainstream society in lower Manhattan. Throughout the years, it continually trained volunteers who devoted hours of their time to learn about the burial ground and in turn educate others. It provided incredible outreach opportunities to New York City schools, church groups, and community groups. Program offerings throughout the 1990s included slide presentations, video viewings, educational symposia, folders filled with educational material, tours of the commemorative artwork, and vigils at the African Burial Ground. By the fall of 1999, OPEI had reached more than one hundred thousand individuals with public information. They produced a quarterly newsletter containing summaries of reports from the scientific laboratories, current updates about the site including religious events, history of Africans in New York City, politics surrounding the project, poetry and short stories by children, bibliographic resources, and book reviews. The newsletter had a distribution of at least fifteen thousand copies internationally. OPEI has been transformed into the interpretive center within the lobby of 290 Broadway.

Transfer of Bones to Howard University

In December 1992, the Federal Steering Committee officially recommended that the remains be transferred to the historically black Howard University for study under Michael Blakey and his team. ACHP agreed, and between August and November 1993 the bones were shipped out of Lehman College in the Bronx to Howard in Washington, DC.

The move bore both spiritual and political significance with the transfer from European American to African American oversight. During a public forum at city hall, it was noted, "I think that you can't minimize the spiritual dimension of this whole thing and, you know, while the scientific analysis is clearly important, I think we would be remiss to let these remains . . . leave this area without some type of spiritual ceremony . . . so I think you've got to balance the spiritual aspect with the scientific."[93] In early November 1993, several hundred people gathered to ceremonially bid the last bones farewell. Priests of Christian, Islamic, and Yoruba spiritual practices congregated in the Mariner's Temple Baptist Church. The high priest Nii Ako of the Ga Adangbe Kpee people led a song, "Singing Spirits from the River Nile, Joining with Us Today."[94] Blakey, the new scientific director, spoke to the overflowing sanctuary: "our job [as researchers] is to sit at the feet of those that were enslaved. Our job is to restore them to who they were: their origins, age, culture, and work, and to restore their identities, which were buried and seemingly disguised from us forever."[95] With these words, he incorporated the main points of the finally completed research design into a spiritual context.

At the other end, in Washington, DC, a day-long event called "The Ties That Bind" was held at Howard University on 5 November 1993. Dr. Blakey, Senator Paterson, Dr. Howard Dodson, and Dr. Joyce Ladner were among those who recounted past difficulties and future plans for the African Burial Ground. Prayers were said by Okomfo Aba Nsiah Opare, the senior priestess of the Bosum-Dzemawodzi Shrine (Ghanaian based) in New York. Howard University and St. Augustine gospel choirs performed. Finally, there was a gala reception replete with impromptu drumming and dancing.

Blakey noted that there was a "sense of triumph for everyone" during the celebrations.[96] He also recognized it as a "healing process" that followed New Yorkers' struggles to properly involve African Americans in all aspects of the burial ground project: "We were not just celebrating the ancestors which was important enough and not only celebrating the triumph that the community had achieved in fending off the federal government's attempt to desecrate the site more but I had the sense that we were in the process of continuing the construction of our culture; that this was a proper way for an African Diasporic people to proceed."[97]

Honoring the Ancestors

"Walking through the lobby, it is impossible not to think of the dead beneath one's feet and—by extension—of the nameless and unremembered dead all over Manhattan. It is as if these African dead have claimed an otherwise anonymous Government building as their own."[98]

Not just during the transferal of bones, but throughout the years, recognition of a sacred space and of the ancestors was continually stressed during hearings, vigils, protests, demonstrations, and interpersonal discussions. This was played out through an African-based discourse of spirituality in which ancestors were called upon, messages were written to the dead, and offerings were left in public spaces. African American activists in particular created a powerful countervoice that challenged GSA's approach.

This complicated melding of politics and spirituality actually became a means for constituting and defining the African Burial Ground in the present. For example, Chief Alagba Egunfemi Adegbaloa from the African village of Oyotunji in South Carolina expressed it in this way: "I feel if any good is to come of this finding of our African Ancestors, we need to stop associating them with just the physical, economical, or social situations. We need to open our hearts and minds to the real situation, which most have been avoiding, and that is the spiritual aspect of the African presence."[99] In another comment, Glen C. Campbell added, "The concept of holy place and space is critical to balancing the soul of the African American community . . . The site under consideration is a cemetery; nothing else. It should therefore be treated as a cemetery."[100] Jazz violinist and activist Noel Pointer characterized the importance of spirituality: "There is a slogan that seems to be going around the community right now that is borrowed from an old Negro spiritual that says, 'Some of them bones is my mother's bones come to together for to rise and shine; some of them bones is my father's bones; and some of them bones is mine.' So there is a sense of a very, very personal connection that our community has with the African burial ground that goes deeper than all the academics, that goes deeper than all the politics that are coming out."[101]

Slavery, history, spirituality, and politics blurred together. Activist Onaje Muid explained at a public forum, "I am appalled that the federal government built on land that is the ancestral burial land of my people. Those Africans were captive in this country and never had a voice. You must talk about the pain, the degradation. They gave their lives in the most desperate way so that I can be here today."[102] Senator Paterson spoke of the occurrence in sacred terms in which he considered the unearthing a "spiritual accident . . . We might not know where our great, great grandparents are buried, but these are their representatives. These are our ancestors, and we must do everything we can to make sure they're treated with respect."[103] He expanded upon the notion of communication between the living and dead on the television broadcast of *Like It Is*: "I believe that our ancestors are crying out to us from their graves, that we not let them be disrespected in their death, the way they probably were in their life."[104]

Physical spaces related to the African Burial Ground were activated for communication with the spirit world. For instance, an altar was set up at Lehman College, where the remains were stored. People visited the bones to pay their respect or perform ceremonies. Due to the influx of visitors, MFAT opened a repository where people left offerings, including drawings, shells, mementos, candles, and dried flowers.[105] At the excavation site, an altar was erected with two bottles of Florida water, a sweet potato, plums, a calabash, sunglasses, and a cup of coffee.[106] A shrine at the excavation contained flowers, fruit, pinecones, a glass container of water, and large clay vessel. It was attended to by Alagba Egunfemi Adegbalola, a priest of Oyatunji village in South Carolina who explained, "All around the world, you do not violate the cemetery. It is our last place to rest."[107]

A powerful twenty-six-hour vigil demonstrated the ways in which political activism and spiritual engagement of the ancestors were performed in tandem. The motivated public was compelled to continue their work as issues remained unresolved. The vigil began on 9 August 1992 at noon and finished the next day on Monday at 2:00 p.m. at the World Trade Center outdoor pavilion and at the African Burial Ground.[108]

Spiritual practitioners at the vigil were Muslims, Christians, Native Americans, Yorubas, and Khemetics of Egypt. Throughout the day and night, there was drumming, singing, African dancing, and pouring of libations to the ancestors. The Northeastern Indigenous Society comprised of Native American nations participated, as well as members of the Delaware Matinicock and T'Ono O'dham nations, and one descendant of the Blackfoot and Mosquito. Also, the Sen Ur Semahj of the Shrine of Ptah attended. One woman fell back into possession by a spirit. A member of Asante royalty from Ghana poured a libation to honor the dead. The pantheon of òrìshà, or Yoruba deities, was called upon to look over the living and dead. A strong, cleansing rain poured down on the crowd during the Black Rock Coalition's performance of "Redemption Song" by Bob Marley. The vigil then carried on under the shelter of the Court of International Trade.

Other events have been held over the years to define the African Burial Ground as a space of spirituality for communicating with the deceased buried there. For instance, a second annual commemoration event was held at Lehman College on 11 December 1992, at which Nana Kwabena Brobbey Dankwa, the Asante ruler of Ghana presiding over the northeast United States, began by pouring a libation as drummers accompanied him.[109] At another event, held on 6 June 1992 in memory of the South African Soweto Demonstrations, a sign explained that apartheid parallels the racism experienced in New York City.[110]

A special delegation of Africans gathered at the burial ground on 4 August 1995 as part of a purification ceremony that began in Ghana. Chiefs, Queen Mothers, and Delegates of Ghana travelled to the United States and poured libations to the dead to honor and seek atonement, in part from African rulers who had sold them to slave-holders.[111] Nana Oduro Naumapau II, the president of the Ghana National House of Chiefs, also asked for investments in Ghana: "We want African Americans to come home to build their own country."[112]

As well as large organized events, smaller prayer vigils were held by OPEI on the grassy plot of land that would have housed the pavilion. Director Sherrill Wilson would typically say a few words to honor the ancestors outside behind the building, ask if anyone would like to speak, and then hold a moment of silence. Participants wrote messages to the dead on cards handed out to them, as occurred in a prayer vigil on 8 April 1999. Entitled "A Tribute to the Ancestors of the African Burial Ground (Duane and Elk Streets)," the card instructed, "Write a message to your African Ancestors on this card and have it acknowledged at the African Burial Ground Ceremony and Prayer Vigil." The cards were then laid on the ground on a ring of flowers in front of the participants, and all cards were saved to be reburied with the remains.

One prayer vigil was particularly memorable. At an educator symposium held at 26 Federal Plaza on 20 November 1999, artist Lorenzo Pace spoke about his commissioned work *Triumph of the Human Spirit* in Foley Square, and he performed on his flute in honor of the dead. The symposium ran late, but it was decided that the evening prayer vigil would still be held. However, the lock to access the fenced area had just been changed, and OPEI had not been given the new combination. Already at the site, visitors decided to create their own version of a vigil outside of the property on the sidewalk in the dark. They stood on the other side of the locked fence to perform a beautiful "Giving Thanks Tribute" as they sang and lit candles in memory of the dead. In the face of restriction and limitation, the groups of people had succeeded in manifesting a spirituality of space to honor those who came before them. At another open house on 20 May 2000, the day had turned into a long one, and it was decided that people would not make the fifteen-minute walk from the World Trade Center, where the open house was held, to 290 Broadway for a vigil. A priest and his companions spontaneously took out their drums in the room and began drumming.

Completed Office Building

Despite GSA's complaints and fear that costs would be excessive and time lost because of the African Burial Ground, the building project finished in December 1994 according to schedule (fig. 3). Although the burial ground set the project back eighteen weeks, Tishman accelerated erecting the building's steel frame and made up the time. Other costs were offset by the elimination of the pavilion. The project manager, John Rossi, added that in his thirty-year career with GSA, it is rare for large government projects to finish on time: "This was a first for me."[113] Thus, a new skyscraper now rested on top of an eighteenth-century African Burial Ground, 419 funerary remains were excavated, and African American involvement was solid amidst continuing tensions and negotiations.

Phase Three: Commemoration and Reburial Negotiations, 1996–2003

The first part of the narrative concerning the African Burial Ground had come to a close. The remains had been rediscovered, unearthed, fought for, and relocated in order to be studied from an African-based perspective. Gus Savage's hearings concerning battles over space, "race," and ancestral honor served as the culmination of public protest. The office building was completed. The latter era from 1996 onward saw negotiation and activism geared towards meaningful memorialization, the eventual reburial of the remains at 290 Broadway, and the final opening of an interpretive center within the office building. Embittered conflicts remained ongoing between GSA, scientific researchers, memorialization organizers, and members of the community.[114]

Four main directors were funded and contracted through GSA in order to carry out different aspects of the burial ground project.

Physical anthropologist Michael Blakey became the overall project director, and continued his 1992 appointment as scientific director. He and his team at Howard University cleaned, recorded, analyzed, and wrote about the bones. In August 1996, Dr. Warren Perry of the University of Connecticut was appointed to direct the archaeological branch of the project. This study concerned funerary objects, body adornments, and spatial analysis of the graves. Perry and his team, working in a laboratory in the World Trade Center, documented, cleaned, and wrote about the artifacts, and they also created a groundbreaking database with a three-dimensional view of the coffins in relation to each other in situ. The third director, Peggy King Jorde was contracted by GSA in October 1996 to head the memorialization, interpretive center, and reburial aspects of the project. She organized the interpretive center and exterior memorial competitions and prepared a reinterment ceremony. Jorde had served as special advisor to Mayor Dinkins and was a project planner in the mayor's Office of Construction prior to that, at which point in time she brought the burial ground issues to the attention of the mayor.[115] Finally, urban anthropologist Sherrill Wilson headed the outreach office, OPEI, which provided exhaustive archives and offered outreach programming for schools and the community. They facilitated important open houses on occasional Saturdays during which knowledge could be shared and debated among professionals, community members, and GSA officials.

GSA Closes Down the Project

Three of these four directors faced a hiatus as GSA cut off funding in the late 1990s, which resulted in a shutdown of the African Burial Ground project. The reduction and cessation of funding consumed the agenda of organized events. In May 1998, GSA requested a new budget proposal from Dr. Blakey detailing the work at Howard not yet completed. Initially, GSA had agreed to a $10 million proposal in 1992, with the funding allocated not all at once but on a task-by-task basis. By 1998, the project had used half of its projected budget, $5.2

million, most of which had gone to salaries. In response to GSA's request, Blakey and Howard University submitted a second budget in 1998 for completing DNA analysis and chemical studies on the bones, as well as for comparative analyses against other skeletons. These final groundbreaking studies would reveal specifically from where and of which ethnic groups in Africa the deceased had originated. GSA thereupon withdrew funding because the DNA work was "experimental" and not normal procedure for mitigation.[116] The full genetic research would indeed never be conducted. Thus, prior to reburial, DNA samples were taken for possible future testing. GSA's funding for the burial ground project would end on 30 April 1999 before research was complete, the memorialization carried out, or the reburial performed. Blakey commented, "GSA expects it to go away, if they wait it out."[117]

In light of the lack of funding, citizens expressed deep concerns at the November 1998 open house hosted by OPEI: Who would see the memorialization process through? Who would present the research Blakey and Perry had overseen? How would the bodies be reburied? Sherrill Wilson commented, "I'm often asked who will tell the story of the African Burial Ground. Will it be told by the GSA as an administrative function or by African-American scholars and members of the New York and larger African-American community?"[118] With the end of funding near, Jorde's office was operating at 50 percent by January 1999 and her three-year contract was slated to end in October 1999.[119] However, the memorialization work was two years behind due to delays.

In order to raise public awareness about events surrounding the burial ground, a community hearing was organized for 23 January 1999 at the Schomburg Center in Harlem by a newly formed group called Friends of the African Burial Ground. The group was founded by Ayo Harrington in the fall of 1998 due to growing concern about the status of the project. Harrington invited GSA representatives to the hearing in the hope that they would report on the burial ground and respond to the community's concerns and questions. Harrington received a fax the day before the hearing noting that no GSA person would attend. She commented that, contrary to their MOA and Section 106 responsibilities, GSA had not held any public forums to communicate with the public or to solicit comment since 1994.[120] During the hearing that I attended, the chairs on the auditorium stage with the place names for GSA officials remained conspicuously empty.

Lisa Wager's Appointment over the Project Leaders

Toward the end of 1998, GSA appointed Lisa Wager executive project director over Drs. Blakey, Perry, and Wilson and Peggy King Jorde, although her expertise was not related to the burial ground. It was during this time that I witnessed the directors, and Blakey in particular, forced into a situation where they themselves became politically active. Blakey published an explanation of events, an update of scientific research, and an appeal to the community on 28 February 1999 in *About . . . Time Magazine.*

> For the past months it has appeared that GSA is 1) imposing less qualified GSA employees over qualified African-American consultants, 2) discontinuing African-American involvement except for a recently assembled "National Management Team" of GSA officials and 3) is reneging on funding for important research that is necessary to complete the research design that GSA is obligated to implement under the Memorandum of Agreement. The continued authority of the existing project directors to implement what we all promised we would do will be wiped away by this Spring unless the public reaffirms its desire to have us complete the job that the descendant community negotiated with GSA in 1993 . . .
>
> In other words, if GSA is to support the tasks it approved in order to construct its building in 1993, then only you will make it so, now or never. It is your tax money, it is your project, these are your ancestors and descendants who are affected by these decisions. I want you to know, however, that we have been and remain scholars in service to you, our ethical client.[121]

Lisa Wager faced an enormous amount of pressure from the New York City community, which was enraged that she was put in charge of the entire project. People telephoned her, visited her, and wrote letters to GSA. Perhaps the situation reached its pinnacle at a public forum at the Mariner's Temple on 8 April 1999. The purpose of the hearing was to introduce five short-listed teams for the interpretive center competition. Instead of addressing the finalists' designs for the interpretive center, the audience directed their attention to Wager for most of the hearing. Artist Lorenzo Pace walked to the front of the church and leaned forward to calmly raise the question, "Why still the bad blood?" [between GSA and the community]. Others yelled, demanding answers about the lack of funding to complete the project and the pending reburial date that never seemed to arrive.

Still others pointed out that Dr. Blakey and Dr. Wilson had boycotted this public forum and had instead written a letter to Peggy King Jorde the previous day, which was photocopied and made available to everyone at the hearing. The letter explained that GSA's hiring of Lisa Wager was the reason for their absence: "We will not, however, aid the GSA in its present effort to tokenize competent African American leadership while it places the project under a Euro-American Executive Director who has been the overseer of violations of public agreements and obstruction of the goals which the black community established for the African Burial Ground. The African American community is currently being duped by the GSA and we are committed to minimizing our presence as a smoke screen for the GSA."[122] A person in attendance named Ken Fitch spoke into the microphone: "I am protesting the absence of Dr. Blakey and Dr. Wilson. This is a matter of great concern; without historical and scientific dialogue, there can't be honesty."[123] People's anger rose to a furious pitch as they yelled in outrage. Wager eventually walked to the front of the room to say a few words. She answered that the funding [cuts] of the project had not been resolved and that GSA was doing its best.

Friends of the African Burial Ground held another meeting at the Schomburg Center on 24 April 1999. Here, the audience called for

Wager's resignation. Earlier, on 15 March 1999, Friends of the African Burial Ground leader Harrington had written a letter to Congressperson Charles Rangel. She explained that Wager's title had been "specifically created for a GSA non–African American employee" and that this act "reveals GSA's contempt, disrespect and unbelievable insensitivity to the spirit of the African Burial Ground . . . We want the title eliminated immediately."[124] Wager resigned on 12 May 1999.

GSA's Bill Lawson Offers Short-Lived Hope

Within ten days of Wager's departure, GSA brought on board a new deputy regional administrator named Bill Lawson as well as an associate regional administrator named Ronald Law. This time, GSA hired African Americans who spoke positively about the project and made an effort to work with the community. Memorably, a GSA update on 2 October 1999 was the first organized by GSA since the Federal Steering Committee had disbanded in 1994. Bill Lawson addressed the audience by saying, "I'm asking you to accept my apology on behalf of this agency."[125] People listened closely, but were filled with skepticism. Blakey responded to Lawson by saying he was thankful he had the chance to hear an apology from GSA for the first time, and from "someone who was brought into GSA in part by you [i.e., the audience]." Lawson continued: "GSA has been derelict and there has been fighting along the way—You will see we are supporting this project . . . Ron and I are turning it around." He added that GSA would be held accountable for its actions, and that the project was taking too long. He also empathized, "I know you are tired of rhetoric."

A small group in the audience expressed their anger over delays, stalling tactics, and the need for a prompt reburial. A group called the Committee of Descendants of the Afrikan Ancestral Burial Ground called for immediate reburial of the excavated remains. The group's leader, Ollie McClean, explained she had sent a letter to Bill Lawson dated 27 September 1999 demanding that the dead be reburied during Kwanzaa in December. Now that GSA had purportedly taken the side of the community, the Committee of Descendants directed antagonistic comments towards Dr. Blakey, suggesting that he was hoarding the remains and postponing reburial on purpose in the name of science. Blakey, who was in attendance, patiently explained that his work had been completed long ago and he was only awaiting funding for DNA analysis, the final leg of the project.

Memorialization was also an issue for the Committee of Descendants' members. Jorde had adamantly insisted that the exterior memorial on the former pavilion area be in place *before* bodies were reburied, as that was a concern among activists. But GSA was two years behind in short listing teams for the memorial competition. The committee members then turned on Jorde and suggested that she was dragging the project out so that she could retain longer employment with GSA and earn more money. Bill Lawson attempted to step in a few times and redirect the blame towards GSA. He asked that they hold GSA accountable for the delays, and said Blakey was taking criticism that should be directed toward him.

In frustration, the descendants group asked the audience: "Who wants the burial tomorrow?" No one in the Schomburg auditorium moved or offered support.[126] This heated interaction illustrated that, with activism and resistance, individual voices and collective groups strived for varying outcomes. Factions occurred, anger and frustration were taking over, and patience was spent. The major issues of reburial, memorialization, and just treatment of a sacred site seemingly could not be realized no matter how much energy was exerted towards the cause.

Sadly, Lawson would not follow through with his commitment. He left within six months of beginning the job, again with no explanation from GSA to the community. Neither Lawson nor GSA notified anyone about his change in position in January 2000, and then word of mouth spread about a going-away party held for him.[127]

Twenty-First-Century Politics

GSA officially closed down the project, locking the laboratory doors of the World Trade Center on 1 February 2000.[128] The laboratory would be completely destroyed on 11 September 2001. In September 2000, Congress authorized GSA to spend or borrow the money necessary to memorialize and reinter the dead, which President Bill Clinton signed into law on 21 December 2000.

Blakey spoke impromptu from the audience at a 10 March 2001 update, reiterating that GSA must fund the African Burial Ground project to completion, as mandated by Congress. Following Blakey's comment, an unintroduced woman (Cassandra Henderson, recently hired by GSA for public relations) stood up and asked, "Michael, will you take questions?" Because she was new, she was unaware that three of the four project directors, who held PhDs, were customarily addressed as "doctor." The audience took this opportunity to express displeasure over the many new hires who had no history with the project, even if the hires were African American people this time. Several in the audience commented on the unprofessional nature of the situation, complaining that this second new person had not even been introduced.

GSA's Ronald Law then presented another new hire, Lana Turner, as the consultant for reinterment and the exterior memorial project. I asked about her position in relation to Peggy King Jorde, who had been the longstanding director of memorialization and reinterment. Throughout the afternoon, many questioned Law about Jorde, commending her for her devotion and deep understanding of the project. Confusion spurred anger, as Turner did not know her own telephone number when asked, nor the beginning date of her contract. She suggested that today might be the first day, but she didn't really know.

On 5 February 2001, the *New York Daily News* published an article, written as an exposé against Blakey, which proved so controversial that it sparked a renewed interest by the press in the burial ground, although now from a negative standpoint.[129] Its author, Robert Ingrassia, reported that GSA was in the process of auditing Blakey's expenditures, implying that the researcher had mishandled the funds. In a rebuttal article printed in the *New Amsterdam News* in March 2001, Blakey explained that audits were a normal routine for the project and had been performed before.[130] He was quoted as saying, "There is no evidence whatsoever of mismanagement of funds," explaining that every aspect of the project was negotiated with and agreed upon by GSA. Objections to funding DNA analysis, the final leg of research, were expressed by Ronald Law, who reasoned in the article that, "It's not part of our mission . . . The DNA research, as sexy as it is, is quite costly."

Interpretive Center and Exterior Memorial Design Competitions

Wrapped up in the reclamation of memory and question of how to represent the African Burial Ground were politics of space, race, and spirituality. As well as budget holdups, the major stumbling blocks in the second half of the 1990s included delays with design and construction of the interpretive center inside the office building lobby, an exterior memorial on the former pavilion site, and an international reburial.[131]

GSA launched open design competitions for an interpretive center and exterior memorial, as stipulated in the amended 1991 Memorandum of Agreement and the community-derived Federal Steering Committee recommendations to Congress in 1993. The process formally began on 13 March 1997 when announcements for both the interpretive center and exterior memorial competitions were released, with solicitations for the former sent out 13 September 1997. At a February 1998 symposium for competition teams interested in either project, speakers foregrounded the significance of spirituality and the honoring of ancestors. David Rice, member of the Organization of Black Designers, addressed the audience saying, "I think it is very important to ask what are we remembering here?" He explained, "Somehow [people from the 18th century] made their presence known to us, this is the spiritual component. We have to give a voice to the nameless, faceless people."[132] Dòwòti Désir, independent curator of the Public Art Project, corroborated Rice's view by stating, "Our ancestors have revealed hidden truths, they demand the rewriting of history." Finally, Schomburg Center director Howard Dodson, who had also chaired the Federal Steering Committee, impressed upon the audience that the African Burial Ground is an "extraordinary collective space . . . it should be infused with spiritual power that is there, not just what is under our square, but where 20,000 human remains' voices speak."

Later, at a forum on 8 April 1999, Pastor Bill of St. James Apostolic Church asked, "Can these bones live? If you are the instruments to make this [interpretive center], then it is the greatest honor. You are working with spirit." Another speaker noted, "Do not forget this is sacred ground." Oneid Mouid added, "I am appalled that the federal government has decided to build on the Burial Ground of my people . . . Remember that Africans never had a voice. You become their voice."[133]

For the designs, the answer for some lay in an Afrocentric pan-African discourse. As the design competition brochure explained, "Given the space constraints, the [interpretive center] objective is to interpret or 'tell the story.'"[134] Addressed as a sentinel and an elder, Adunni Oshupa Tabasi expressed her deep concern that, since the competitions were open, anyone could be selected to commemorate the African Burial Ground. She impassioned, "I want to state my open disapproval, and that I object to the open competition. Let the truth and horror be told by Africans who know and who have studied, from the 14th century to the present."[135] Miss Dicks, another sentinel and elder, corroborated this view by asserting, "We do not need outsiders to do this for us; it should be for and by Africans." The exchange illustrated the inevitable tensions and countervoices permeating the African Burial Ground project; namely that concerned citizens often held views that were in direct opposition to GSA. Dr. Henrik Clarke's recent widow, Sybil Williams Clarke, was quoted in the press concerning the same issue, "What we're insisting on is that this is sacred ground." She added that any memorial should, "record and tell our story—our story, told by us: not by the enslavers or the children of our enslavers."[136]

By the spring of 1999, an advisory committee had composed a short list of five teams to design the interpretive center for GSA.[137] At this point, and as a result of community activism, the general public became more involved.[138] It was decided in February and publicly announced in March 2000 that IDI Construction Company was the competition winner.[139] On 17 June 2000, IDI held a formal presentation of their design for the public at the City University of New York. Their plan would be historical, political, interactive, and spiritual, including space for an altar and place to leave offerings. With IDI team member Atim Oton leading the presentation, the audience again did not respond to the design. Instead, they spent most of the time expressing anger and frustration because they were disenfranchised, with GSA in control of the memorialization and no reburial of the excavated remains in sight. One question concerned the size of the 2,000-square-foot space that the interpretive enter would occupy: "Who agreed to this tiny space? It is a disgrace." Miss Dicks reiterated, "We don't want this [interpretive center]. It's not related to the community. And I don't care when it opens. I just want the reburial."

The historian on the team, Dr. A. J. Williams-Myers of the State University of New York at New Paltz, attempted to bring the presentation around to a positive note for African Americans by saying, "The story needs to be told by us. Will you tell the story?" A member in the audience answered that the ancestral spirits were waiting: "I have spoken with them, they have spoken with me."[140] A priest from Oyatunji seated next to me responded quietly with incredulity that he too had spoken with the ancestors, but only through divination. Once again, and despite the anger, spirituality was an important component in the politics, narrative, and contestation of the African Burial Ground.

It had taken three years to get to this point. The interpretive center design competition had progressed slowly, but it now came to a complete halt due to GSA's budget issues and refusal to fund DNA testing, as explained above. As an educational center, it was imperative that the interpretive center contain scientific information. Yet, IDI could not be given the archaeological and skeletal content in order to move forward with the design component because Drs. Blakey and Warren no longer had contracts with GSA, and their research was not in final written form.

IDI was eventually forced to pull out of the project, as they were held in limbo for so long. It would ultimately be the National Park Service (NPS) that implemented the design and construction of the interpretive center years later. OPEI functioned as a temporary interpretive center inside of the building with assistance from the Schomburg Center until February 2006.

The National Park Service entered into an interagency agreement with GSA in September 2003 to complete the interpretive center and the exterior memorial.[141] Funds for the projects were appropriated by Congress in 2003. Much later, on 27 February 2006, NPS sent out a presolicitation notice for the design of the interpretive center, and on the following day sent out an entirely new request for proposals with a deadline of May 2006.[142] The square footage of the center was expanded to 8,780 square feet instead of the formerly proposed 2,000 square feet. Architectural build-out proposals, interpretive media proposals, and audiovisual aspects would be submitted for the development of exhibits. A team called Amaze was selected, and an open house for their project was held 25 April 2007. The visitor center inside of Ted Weiss Federal Building opened in 2010.

Bones in City Hall Park

During the employment of Executive Director Lisa Wager, project funding cuts, and the first interpretive center competition, yet another controversy had emerged. After the digging accidents of 1993, 1994, and 1995, bones were once again uncovered from February to July 1999. This time, the digging occurred in City Hall Park, which was being renovated to reproduce its nineteenth-century appearance at a cost of $25 million under Mayor Giuliani. Bones were found at the park's north side and next to Chambers Street (figs. 1 and 2).

According to oral history rumors at the time, the Giuliani administration did not want to risk more controversy, especially related to the African Burial Ground, and so none of the bones were tested for identification. We still to this day do not know whose bones they are.

Some insisted the graves were from a 1736 alms house formerly on this land, or from a prison. Others compellingly argued they were part of the African Burial Ground.[143] The African Burial Ground final report agreed that "the cemetery probably extended further south than the [National Historic Landmark] boundary" (fig. 2).[144] The excavations I witnessed to the east along Centre Street in 1999 were always hidden behind large green tarps.

Twenty-five graves in all were identified in City Hall Park, primarily of women and children. There were also secondary burials, meaning they were initially interred elsewhere, and then moved to a second site. One area contained twelve infants, and three other areas had twelve adults each.[145] Excavation of these burials occurred without analysis under LPC. Many other still-intact burials in City Hall Park were left untouched in areas where there was no digging for the renovation. Thus, portions of City Hall Park constitute an unmarked cemetery.

The Long Awaited Reburial, October 2003

After twelve years above ground, the deceased were finally reinterred in the fall of 2003 onsite at the African Burial Ground. The reburial was a victorious and momentous occasion. It was a highly visible event that rightly reflected significance for the deceased as well as for African Americans in the city. The *New York Times* ran the story with a large photograph on its 4 October front page, and traffic along Wall Street and Broadway was detoured or altered. Dr. Howard Dodson and the Schomburg Center facilitated the reburial procession and ceremony. Four coffins with the remains of an adult male, adult female, young girl, and young boy traveled from Howard University through Baltimore, Wilmington, Philadelphia, Camden, Newark, and Jersey City before arriving in Manhattan during five days of "The Rites of Ancestral Return," which ended on 5 October 2003.

The rest of the coffins arrived in New York City by water at South Street in a small fleet of vessels on Friday, 3 October. Historically, this would have been the site of the colonial slave market, where some of those about to be reburied had originally docked in New York. This time the arrival was celebratory and honorary, with hundreds if not thousands of school children among the audience. Invited presenters spoke from the pier: New Jersey Secretary of State Regena Thomas, New York Secretary of State Randy Daniel, Honorable David Dinkins, Reverend Herbert Daughtry, Dr. Kofi Asare Opoku, Mayor Michael Bloomberg, Congressperson Charlie Rangel, State Senator David Paterson, Manhattan Borough President C. Virginia Fields, Councilperson Charles Barron, Dr. Howard Dodson, Dr. Michael Blakey, Dr. Sherrill Wilson, and GSA Regional Administrator Stephen Perry.

The coffins traveled by land in several horse-drawn carriages to 290 Broadway. A parade processed along the thoroughfare consisting of drummers, pall bearers, the six horse-drawn wagons with the coffins, a brass band, flag carriers, community groups, project researchers, Freemasons, and the public. The crowd walked all the way up Wall Street, turned north, and then walked along Broadway (where one lane of traffic was closed) for fourteen blocks. On arriving at the African Burial Ground at 290 Broadway, the four coffins that had traveled up the coast were transferred into a limousine hearse to drive through each of the five boroughs of New York City.

The rest of the coffins, 419 in total, were unloaded at the office building (fig. 38). Each of the remains was laid in a wooden coffin that had been hand-carved in Ghana and was lined with kente cloth. The small coffins were incised with varying adinkra symbols, including the now well-known sankofa.[146]

During all of my years of research at the burial ground, the mass funeral was the most spiritually open moment, with accessibility to the ancestors and to the land on which they were buried and about to be reburied. On 3–4 October 2003, visitors could move in, out, and around the GSA property at any time of day or night; they could leave any object as an actual offering that would not be discarded; and they could even sleep in sleeping bags during an all-night vigil prior to the funerary ceremony the next day.

Figure 38. Coffins handmade in Ghana unloaded on Duane Street at 290 Broadway for reburial, 3 October 2003. Each was carved with an adinkra and contained the bones of one of the 419 ancestors. After years of activism and the Federal Steering Committee's recommendation to Congress, the remains were successfully reburied on the land that was the eighteenth-century communal African Burial Ground. The Supreme Court and the Federal Courthouse are in the background. Photo by Andrea Frohne.

Attendees began to leave offerings that accumulated through the day, into the night, and during the next morning prior to the funeral (fig. 39). There were flowers of varying colors; fruits such as mangoes, pomegranates, red apples, and a pineapple; messages written to the ancestors; and bottles of water and one of rose water, for libations. Coins were placed on top of some of the coffins. One person left a Butterfinger candy bar as food for the dead.

Performances by varying community groups throughout the all-night vigil exemplified a kind of invention of spirituality. Bits and pieces of traditions were drawn from different places and cultures in Africa and the United States as part of the formation of an African Burial Ground diaspora. One person conducted a naming ceremony far into the night, calling out an African, specifically Swahili, name for each of the deceased 419. There were dance groups such as Shepsu Day with Shrim Sa and Amen Amakhu. I saw an elderly

Figure 39. Offerings placed on coffins after all-night vigil prior to reburial, 4 October 2003. Fruits, flowers, coins, and a Butterfinger candy bar were left for the dead on their final journey and passageway to the afterlife. Photo by Andrea Frohne.

woman fall into spirit possession as she performed on stage with other women, who then supported her as they continued dancing. A man recently arrived from Côte d'Ivoire who did not speak English was asked to perform an impromptu divination on the ground, which he did with little translation provided afterwards. These reinventions in New York City of pan-Africa contribute to the reclamation, representation, and remembering of the African Burial Ground. Ghanaian kente cloth, ancient Egyptian ankh, and the Swahili language, for example, become signifiers representing Africa as a whole.[147]

The vigil continued into the next day, and some who had spent the night now rolled up their sleeping bags, while others just arriving passed by the coffins, again leaving more offerings. For the public tribute, two large screens visually projected performances to thousands congregating in Foley Square beside Lorenzo Pace's sculpture fountain discussed in chapter 6. The afternoon lineup included the Harlem Boys Choir, a talk by Amadou Diallo's mother, an extraordinary poem recited by a five-year-old named Autumn entitled "Flying on Ancestral Spirits." Reverend Herbert Daughtry reread his dramatic speech presented in Trinity Church during the decade-earlier, critical years of activism. Native American Hubert Frances traveled from Canada, and with wisdom he gently advised the audience to mentally leave the ancestors here, allowing them to continue their journey in the spirit world, rather than carry them with us in our thoughts as we walked away from 290 Broadway. It struck me that he imparted rules and guidelines concerning the spirit world that were otherwise not widely known or shared among the descendant community. Just before the actual reburial, Maya Angelou adapted a rendition of "Still I Rise" specifically for the African Burial Ground: "You may bury me in the bottom of Manhattan. I will rise. My people will get me. I will rise out of the huts of history's shame."[148]

For the final phase of the burial, attendees surrounded the now-closed black gates at 290 Broadway. Only drummers and selected invitees entered through the gates to the grassy area for the actual and final reburial rites (fig. 40). Intense chanting, singing, and drumming accompanied the individual coffins, which had by this time

been placed into four large wooden crypts, as they were slowly low-
ered into the ground along with all of the offerings and messages that
had amassed over the past two days. The burial was the culmination
of the two day event.

In some respects, the reburial was a city-wide triumphal closing
chapter to the two-decade-long struggle for respectful recognition
and sacred treatment of the African Burial Ground. Yet the final
honoring of the ancestors was intermixed with anger over slavery,
over GSA's disrespect for the dead, and over still-apparent racism.

It is the production of this complex narrativization, along with its
counternarratives, that would eventually situate the African Burial
Ground within the national and civic body politic. Along those
lines, State Senator David Paterson remarked at the reburial, "This
is American history. This isn't just black history. The burial grounds
are just a tool in which American history is told in the right way."

Figure 40. Drummers lead the burial procession, October 2003. Photo by
Andrea Frohne.

He added, "This is secret, unknown history that is finally being told. Finally."[149] After it had been largely forgotten for two hundred years, the sacred burial ground saw a reclamation at the end of the twentieth century and the beginning of the twenty-first century through the intricate interlacing of spiritual concerns bound up in the political. The combination became a means for constituting the African Burial Ground through artistic commemoration.

5

Early Commemorative Artworks, 1992–1995

African-Based Spirituality

As unresolved tensions continued in New York City and archaeological research progressed on the funerary and skeletal remains, it became increasingly clear that commemoration and memorialization were of utmost importance at the African Burial Ground. The project anthropologists revealed details about the eighteenth-century lives, deaths, and spiritual practices of the deceased; and the maps, prints, and land surveys disclosed colonial uses of the space. But whose voices could come forward and how would the ancestors be honored at the dawn of the twenty-first century?

The answer reveals itself via three major categories of artworks: the first is art initiatives by the public; the second is art commissioned by the government; and the third is private offerings. Government commissioned artworks are subdivided into two categories based on when, how, and why they were funded: Round one commissions (discussed in this chapter) were awarded in 1993 and occurred through the standard Art-in-Architecture building requirement; Round two commissions (discussed in chapter 6) were made possible in 1995 by special congressional funding in response to public pressure for increased recognition of the site.

All of the commemoration projects would have to be rendered without realistic reconstruction or reproduction because no visual data existed about the cemetery's appearance, boundaries, or names of the deceased. As a result, the artworks have become central to recognizing the site, contributing in powerful ways to an invention of memory at the African Burial Ground.

In particular, production of spirituality is key in visually commemorating the dead. An African-based visual vocabulary has facilitated a civic reclamation and recuperation of the African Burial Ground. Specifically, artists incorporated African arts and cosmologies into their works as a powerful means for representing the African Burial Ground. A multiplicity of African cosmologies and cultures are depicted in the artworks, including the Akan sankofa, Gullah ringshout, Kongo cosmogram, and Yorùbá crossroads. As explored here, Africa necessarily becomes reconfigured in the New York diaspora in rich and complex ways. The following analyses of the early commemorative artworks reveal these processes of spirituality and memory in production at 290 Broadway.

Two key ways the production of spirituality occurred are, first, through artistic representations of African spirit worlds, as described above, and second, through rendering the African Burial Ground a space of spirituality.[1] Communication with and veneration of the ancestors was key. The manifestation of a space of spirituality was fostered by rendering literal depictions of the ancestors, as in works by Gayle and Brown, and by infusing the sacred into the 290 Broadway block generally. Expressions of spirituality are seen on construction fences covered with school children's interpretations of the colonial burial ground, through personal offerings left on the grounds, and by the inscription of spiritual systems on the office building floor.

All of these artworks then express iterations of Africa in North America as a means for honoring the burial ground. In tandem with representations of African arts and spirit worlds, African American history is also visually recounted in the commemorations. Several works illustrate New York City black history in particular. In sum, the commemorative artworks document the formation of a particular diaspora—a New York City African diaspora—that is linked directly to the African Burial Ground, with all of its complexities, struggles, losses, and victories.

Interestingly, a few of the commissioned artworks are less related to Africa or are not made by African descendant artists. A non-African-based approach at times raised concerns or invoked anger, resulting in important conflicts and consequences that are explored here.

Art Initiatives by the Public

David Rashid Gayle, *The African Burial Ground*, 1992

In *The African Burial Ground* (1992), artist David Rashid Gayle expresses tensions between the U.S. government and African ancestors occupying the same urban space (fig. 41). The work petitions for ancestral guidance in the face of the overwhelming difficulties outlined in chapter 4.

Gayle was the first artist to publicly create a work of art for the cemetery. He was approached by burial ground activist and renowned jazz violinist Noel Pointer at an art exhibition in the early 1990s while exhibiting a piece that honored his late brother. Pointer spoke with Gayle about the African Burial Ground and invited him to make an artwork for the site.[2] The artwork would be used to rally grassroots support and would eventually become a focal point when it was installed and unveiled at the Howard University "Ties That Bind" event honoring the arrival of African Burial Ground skeletal remains from New York City in November 1993.

The project would launch Gayle into an intensive and lengthy investigation, including a research partnership with Amal A. Muhammad, as Gayle began to question, "How do you depict this?"[3] There were no historical images of the colonial cemetery or an African presence to guide Gayle. Gayle adds, "I was born in New York. I never knew the history of slavery in New York." He began with an appointment to access the burial ground excavation site. Gayle walked and then lay down on colonial era earth for a "transformative experience."

In his painting, Gayle used his family as models to portray ancestors (fig. 41). The adolescent figure on the far left bearing the

Figure 41. David Rashid Gayle, *The African Burial Ground*, 1992. Acrylic and collage on board, 30 × 40 in. Ancestors rise above the Supreme Courthouse, with four of the pillars replaced by bones. Candles in an "×" shape mark the Burial Ground, mapped in the foreground of the painting. Collection of the artist. Courtesy of the U.S. General Services Administration.

shackles of slavery is his son; second from the left is his wife, born in the southern United States; and third from left is his mother, from Jamaica.[4] The women wear the white shrouds with which we know a majority of the deceased were interred, as described in chapter 3. The figure on the right was a model from West Africa whom Gayle did not know personally. He wears the pan-African kente cloth, suggesting his status as an activated ancestor and a life formerly lived in Africa. These four figures of varying generations and locations simultaneously represent deceased ancestors and living African diasporas.[5] For Gayle's family, specifically, this includes bloodlines from Africa, the Caribbean, Scotland, China, India, and New York City.

The four diaphanous ancestors hover above the Supreme Courthouse (1919–25) at 60 Centre Street, which fills the middle of the painting (fig. 2). The neoclassical-style, Enlightenment-era architecture in lower Manhattan's Civic Center was based on ancient Greece to further American democracy. The inscription across the entablature of the actual building and in the painting is taken from the beginning of George Washington's 1789 letter to the Attorney General: "The True Administration of Justice is the Firmest Pillar of Good Government." How has justice, wrapped up in American national identity, functioned for the ancestors buried here? Gayle defamiliarizes these ideals by exchanging four of the Corinthian columns for African bones and leaving six intact. Such a substitution begins to illustrate the permeation of an African presence in New York City, forcing questions such as, Whose space was this? and Whose labor was at work during the colonial era?[6]

As Gayle worked on the African Burial Ground in these very early years, he was met with the question, "Where is it, where is it?" in conversations.[7] This prompted the map in the foreground of the painting, which illustrates that any of these blocks may be covering sacred ground. Three buildings—26 Federal Plaza and U.S. Customs Court at the bottom left, and the Tweed Court House on the right—are filled in with American flags. City hall, at the far bottom right, and the L-shaped archaeological dig in the center are covered with Ghanaian kente cloth. The African textile specifically refers to the

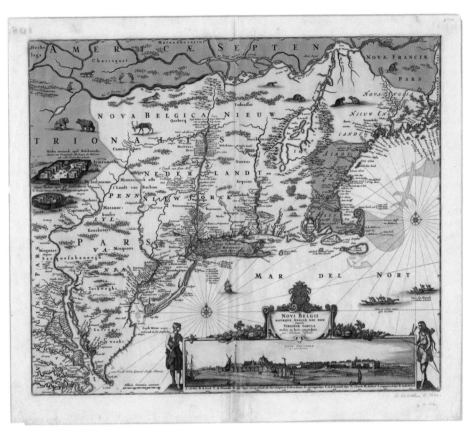

Plate 1. Nicholas Visscher, *Novi Belgii Novaeque Angliae nec non partis Virginiae tabula*, ca. 1684. Hand col. copperplate engraving, 46 × 55 cm. The inset illustrates the burgeoning colony, including the Dutch West India Company row of houses where enslaved Africans worked. E-US-[1684]. Fl.RA; Brooklyn Historical Society Map Collection.

Plate 2. Matthias Seutter, *Recens edita totius Novi Belgii: In America Septentrionali siti*, 1740. Hand col. copperplate engraving, 50 × 58 cm. Printed in Europe, Africans of colonial New York are used as decoration for the inset, bearing the riches of the colony they have produced through the institution of slavery. E-US-[1740].Fl.RA; Brooklyn Historical Society Map Collection.

Plate 3. Francis W. Maerschalck, *A Plan of the City of New York from an Actual Survey, Anno Domini MDCCLV*, drawn 1754 and published 1755. Col. copperplate engraving, 47 × 86 cm. The "Negros Buriel Ground" is clearly marked outside of town on the far side of the Palisades, near Fresh Water Pond. It was situated in a low-lying area away from urban surveillance. Courtesy of Library of Congress, Geography and Map Division.

Plate 4. New York African Burial Ground archaeological site plan. A stratigraphy, or internal geographic mapping of 424 graves with temporal and spatial divisions, including the horizontal and vertical layout of burials in relation to each other. Vertical lines show possible north/south rows. From left, circle A is Burial 101, B shows three isolated infants, C is Burial 332, and D is Burial 340. Courtesy of the U.S. General Services Administration.

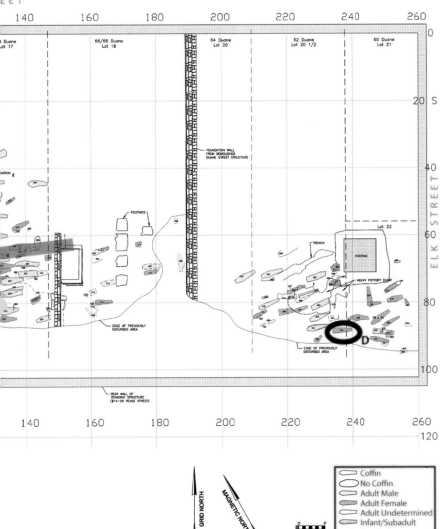

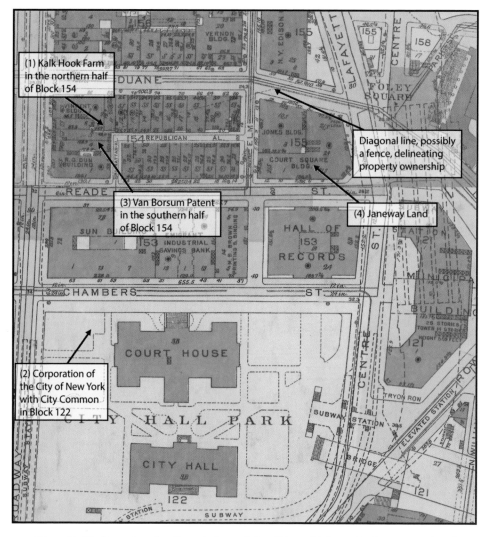

Plate 5. G. Bromley & Co., *Atlas of the City of New York, Borough of Manhattan*, 1934, plates 6 and 8. Detailed building construction, lot numbers, block numbers, and street addresses covering the African Burial Ground earlier in the twentieth century. Block 154 would be excavated for construction of the federal office building. Reprinted/used with permission from The Sanborn Library, LLC. The Lionel Pincus and Princess Firyal Map Division, The New York Public Library, Astor, Lenox and Tilden Foundations.

Plate 6. Burial 310, paste ring with blue insets, ca. 1735–60. Cast copper-alloy and glass. The center glass and one side inset are missing. A woman of about fifty years old wore the ring on her left hand. Photo by Jon Abbott. Courtesy of the U.S. General Services Administration.

Plate 7. Burial 6, anchor button, ca. 1776–95. Cast copper-alloy, gilded both sides, 17 mm. diameter. One of five nonmatching buttons from a man's coat or jacket that suggests connections to water or the Revolutionary War. The motif matches an anchor excavated from the free black Betsey Prince site on Long Island (fig. 29). Photo by Jon Abbott. Courtesy of the U.S. General Services Administration.

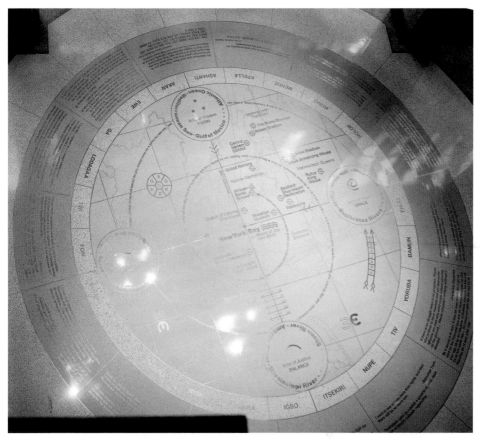

Plate 8. Houston Conwill, Joseph De Pace, and Estella Conwill Majozo, *The New Ring Shout*, 1994. Terrazzo and brass, 40 ft. diameter. An artwork laid in the center of the federal office building lobby floor. Its complex geospiritual mapping is based largely on the ring shout and the Kongo cosmogram connecting Africans, African Americans, New York City, and the African Burial Ground through music, dance, and poetry. Details include a blue outer ring of New York State African American ancestors, a circle of African nations, global bodies of water, a map of New York City, and a spiral ending at the African Burial Ground. Photographs in the Carol M. Highsmith Archive, Library of Congress, Prints and Photographs Division.

Plate 9. Tomie Arai, *Renewal*, 1998. Silkscreen on canvas, 7½ × 38 ft. The work spans the wall across from the elevators in the office building lobby. The left pillar contains the heart-shaped sankofa and names of the first eleven Africans in New York, the right pillar illustrates the slave trade surrounded by pieces of African textiles. The apex bears a Yoruba Ifá divination tray with objects from the African Burial Ground. Photographs in the Carol M. Highsmith Archive, Library of Congress, Prints and Photographs Division.

Plate 10. Detail of Tomie Arai, *Renewal*, 1998. Apex contains a Yorùbá Ifá divination tray with objects excavated from the African Burial Ground. The reproduced Maerschalck Plan (1755) shows burial pins on the left and Burial 315 on the right, with arms crossed over her chest. The cover of the court case proceedings from the 1741 Conspiracy lies to the left. Photographs in the Carol M. Highsmith Archive, Library of Congress, Prints and Photographs Division.

Plate 11. Lorenzo Pace, *Triumph of the Human Spirit*, 2000. Black granite, 60 × 62 ft. Located half a block away from the federal office building, the sculpture fountain was funded through Percent for Art. It is based on the female Ciwara from Mali and honors diasporic Africans. Photo by Andrea Frohne.

Plate 12. Rodney Léon with AARRIS Architects, *The Ancestral Libation Chamber*, 2007. Black granite, 100 × 250 ft. This national monument, managed by the National Park Service, was the final work to officially memorialize the site. It is comprised of a Door of No Return entryway graced by the sankofa. The circular, descending ramp bears symbols connected to an African experience from Haiti, Congo, Nigeria, Cuba, Ghana, etc. The last symbol on the right, for Legba, is a gateway between physical and spirit realms. Closest to the ancestors at the bottom, Africa is centrally mapped with its surrounding global diasporas. Photographs in the Carol M. Highsmith Archive, Library of Congress, Prints and Photographs Division.

black mayor David Dinkins within the locus of power at city hall, and the actual exhumation of Africans and African descendants.[8] The ideals the U.S. flag upholds are juxtaposed against and in tandem with the textile more generally representing Africa and pan-Africanism.[9] Gayle maps a tension articulated between "Africa" and "America" to represent the very real politics that were at stake at the African Burial Ground after it had been uncovered.

This artwork interjects a space of spirituality into Foley Square not just with the undeniable presence of ancestors but also through a double row of candles that crisscross to create an "X" shape in the foreground of figure 41. For Gayle, "X marks the spot" while it also forms a cross over the site.[10] His forty-four candles denote the year 1644 when eleven Africans requested and were granted freedom from enslavement.[11] Freed Africans lived in this very area, as detailed in chapter 1. Additionally, the candles are a clever manifestation of the crossroads, an African cosmological delineation of the intersection between the living and the dead. In particular, they are known in the Yorùbá spiritual system as a place where a decision is made and a road taken. The deity Èsù is strongly associated with the crossroads and can be found there; he is a mediator, trickster, and clearer or obstructer of paths, carrying messages from one world to the next. The crossroads that rest on the foundation of the office building that was literally being constructed by GSA as Gayle painted his artwork relayed a question during what was the early stage of excavation and civic conflict: How will controversies over respectful treatment of the urban, sacred space be resolved? Will the course of history change? Will the road be smooth or bumpy, clear or obstructed?

Through candles (frequently placed on òrìshà altars in diasporas), it could be interpreted that Gayle petitions Èsù for guidance and the ancestors for wisdom. This communication rests on the streets of urban Manhattan, above the earth of the graveyard, the tangible material closest to the next world. Although polemical, potential for guidance is nevertheless already present: we have the white justice system as a neoclassical courthouse, with African Burial Ground ancestors looming above. All carry the wisdom, history, and knowledge to guide the city in its decision-making processes. In 1992, the outcome over the sacred urban cemetery was still unclear. It would actually take the conjoined forces of the government with activists engaging African-based spiritualities to affect change over the next fifteen years. Gayle's artwork offers rich, spatiotemporal layers of colonial histories and contemporary politics connecting African ancestors with African diaspora descendants.

Children's Interpretive Project, 1992

The Children's Interpretive Project was the first public art project to commemorate the African Burial Ground. Toward the end of the time that the federal office building was under construction in 1992, members of the community and Ellen Anderson in particular decided that the site should be represented more as a sacred African cemetery and less as a space of development. As developer, construction manager, and property manager of the project, Linpro New York Reality, Inc., sponsored an Awareness Through Art program.[12] Hundreds of school children (nearly one hundred classes in New York City) and members of community groups were given kits consisting of a 4 × 8 plywood panel, paint, brushes, drop cloths, sketch books, crayons, and background information on the African Burial Ground and Africans in colonial New York. The panels would be nailed onto the fence that surrounded the worksite at 290 Broadway.

Initially, Linpro sent out a notice that the themes for the art to surround the work site were: (1) the building under construction, (2) people of New York, or (3) burial grounds. Parents of school children wrote letters to Senator David Paterson concerned with the nonspecificity of the criteria and the disregard for Africans/African Americans and the African Burial Ground itself. Paterson wrote a letter to GSA regional director Bill Diamond protesting these themes and explaining that he "expects a new and more sensitive mural project description be distributed."[13]

Thus, students who created the murals across New York City were educated about the African Burial Ground and an African presence in colonial New York City. Final topics included living in diverse communities, African identity, the ancestors, slavery, New York's early history, and scenes of the burial ground. The brightly colored, dynamic murals initiated memorialization on the site. As the public passed by the construction space, they witnessed a reclamation of memory at work from children's points of view.

The African Burial Ground Competition Coalition, 1992–94

Several New York City organizations that came together in the spring of 1992 recognized the need for commemoration before any official commemoration had yet occurred.[14] The African Burial Ground Competition Coalition decided that an idea competition would be held in which the winners' projects would not be realized but published in a book. The president of the New York Coalition of Black Architects, Bill Davis, saw the competition as a means for venting strong emotions and passion during this early phase of the project.[15]

By the 14 January 1994 deadline, approximately 170 projects from around the world had been submitted. After intense deliberation, the jury selected four first award winners and four second award winners.[16] Much to the chagrin of the African American public, none of the eight finalists was African American. The committee had endeavored to make the event inclusive, had prescribed a nominal entry fee of twenty dollars, and had worked as a blind jury. This situation exposes the sensitivity and difficulty in commemorating a space that has been denied historically and contemporaneously. Whose voices represent the past, and whose pasts are represented? Nevertheless, entries from across the country and as far away as Australia illustrated that the African Burial Ground carried national and global significance.

Art Commissioned by the Government, Round One

The first three artworks in the lobby of 290 Broadway were part of a routine procedure for commissioning public art in newly built federal architecture with funding from the Art-in-Architecture program.

This program was established in 1963 following recommendations from President Kennedy's Ad Hoc Committee on Federal Office Space, which noted, "where appropriate, fine art should be incorporated into the designs of Federal buildings with emphasis on the work of living American artists."[17] To this end, GSA allocates half of one percent of the estimated construction cost of each new federal building for commissioned, site-specific art by contemporary artists.[18] The commissioned artist works with building architects and community advisors to integrate the piece into the final architectural project. Ultimately, the artworks in GSA buildings are meant to augment the civic meaning of federal architecture and showcase contemporary American art.

The Art-in-Architecture program did not specifically mandate commemoration of the cemetery. As a result, the artists incorporated the African Burial Ground to varying degrees in their site-specific installations. The process for commissioning the first three artworks in 290 Broadway followed the typical Art-in-Architecture procedure. Approximately five thousand artists who were on the Art-in-Architecture registry were contacted about the commissions for 290 Broadway, and then those who were interested applied. A panel recommended a short list of artists from the GSA registry in November 1992.[19] GSA made a selection from the short list and contracted an artist for a design, after which the panel reviewed the design and submitted a recommendation back to GSA.[20]

In the end, GSA commissioned the following artworks in 1993: Houston Conwill, Joseph De Pace, and Estella Majozo Conwill designed a cosmogram named *The New Ring Shout* to be laid into the ground (installed 1994); Roger Brown composed a mosaic for the interior (installed 1994); and Clyde Lynds created a fiber optic relief entitled *America Song* for the entrance of the building (installed 1995).

Houston Conwill, Joseph De Pace, Estella Conwill Majozo,
The New Ring Shout, Installed 1994

Houston Conwill, Joseph De Pace, and Estella Conwill Majozo designed *The New Ring Shout*, a 40-foot handmade cosmogram of terrazzo and polished brass that was laid into the floor of the central rotunda at 290 Broadway in 1994 (plate 8). It manifests a pan-African space of spirituality by representing several African cosmologies and African American histories. Multiple spiritual systems interlace through and among each other to become a polydimensional mapping of cosmological flows and transspiritual space between Africa, its diasporas, and Western Europe.

As the title indicates, the piece is founded on the ring shout, one of the oldest African-based performances existing in the United States.[21] With basic elements brought from Africa, the ring shout consists of call and response singing of "shout" songs, polyrhythmic stick beating, clapping, and perambulation. Famously performed by Gullah people on the Sea Islands of Georgia and South Carolina, this spiritual practice, known as shouting, most often occurs during or following a Christian prayer meeting, lasting long into the night. Participants move counterclockwise with increasing speed and intensity. A typical shout in the Sea Islands was documented in 1932: "Just as a whirling dynamo generates a magnetic field, so this vibrant circle varying in diameter according to the endurance of the participants turning on, and on, and on seemed to create a desire which could not be satisfied until each one yielded to the irresistible urge [to join the circle]."[22] With the word "new" in its title, *The New Ring Shout* evokes transcultural reinvention of African spiritual practices, rendering the piece a "new world cosmogram."[23]

As well as a ring shout, *The New Ring Shout* is based on the Kongo cosmogram of central Africa in today's Congo Democratic Republic, the Republic of Congo, and Angola. The artists composed a cosmogram by intersecting a vertical and horizontal axis (+), and then a second cosmogram as a spiral made of words. These various African cosmogram motifs are drawn in figure 42. Robert Farris Thompson rendered the Kongo cosmogram well-known in African and African American studies through his influential, still-in-print book *Flash of the Spirit*, which the team used in part to develop their design proposal for *The New Ring Shout*.[24]

Figure 42. Various versions of the Kongo cosmogram. Adapted by Amy Rock from Robert Farris Thompson and Joseph Cornet, *The Four Moments of the Sun: Kongo Art in Two Worlds* (New Haven: Eastern Press, Inc., 1981), 28.

The cosmogram, according to Thompson, illustrates a fluid, cyclical connection between realms of the living and dead. The horizontal axis creates a boundary called *kalunga*, a line of water and passage between the living who occupy the upper half and the dead who comprise the lower half.[25] In *The New Ring Shout*, the artists named this boundary the "Hurston Line" after anthropologist Zora Neale Hurston (plate 8). The vertical line connects the realm of the living with the dead. It is a path of power lying between the worlds.[26] The vertical line is named the "Hughes Line" for author Langston Hughes. Hurston and Hughes were key figures in the Harlem Renaissance in New York City and were close friends for a time, collaborating on a play and producing the literary magazine "Fire!"

Four large disks on the end of each axis list twelve bodies of water from around the world (table 3). The Mississippi River, Pacific Ocean, Niger River, and Ganges River, for instance, mark migratory flows that people have used through the centuries to travel, immigrate, trade, and create diasporas (plate 8). The team explains that the piece "presents a rechoreographing of history tracing a cultural pilgrimage and contemplative metaphorical journey of transformation along the twelve global water sites."[27] In terms of metaphysical mapping, the disks mark precise places or ritually designated points where a Kongo spirit may land when it is called to communicate in the physical world.[28] Called *dikenga*, these "four moments of the sun" or "singing the points" on the Kongo cosmogram mark the four phases of life, beginning with birth and moving counterclockwise through life, death, and rebirth.[29] Thus, the artwork depicts cosmological time with African Burial Ground ancestors in the spirit world and humans at various life stages in the physical world.

Additional spiritual systems beyond the Kongo are incorporated into *The New Ring Shout*, rendering it what I call a transspiritual space, with several spaces of spirituality combined into one. The two axes also refer to Esu-Elégba Yorùbá crossroads of Nigeria, which, like the Kongo diagram, embody continuous interconnection between the world of the living and dead.[30] The crossroads are not unlike the ones Gayle depicted with candles in his acrylic painting.

A spiral song line wraps around the two + axes, which is yet another incarnation of the Kongo cosmogram (plate 8 and fig. 42). Structurally, the songline is African and Kongolese, with the coiled song lyrics singing primarily of diasporas. The songs map historic struggle, artistic expression, resistance through pan-African activism and history, and freedom from slavery (table 3). *The New Ring Shout*

Table 3

Bodies of Water and Song Lines in *The New Ring Shout*

Bodies of Water	*Music Titles in the Song Line*
Caribbean Sea	"Oh Freedom"
Ganges River	"Amazing Grace"
Pacific Ocean	"Go Down Moses"
Stono River	South African National Anthem
Amazon River	"Redemption Song"
Mississippi River	Black National Anthem
Euphrates River	"We Shall Overcome"
Niger River	Chinese National Anthem
Nile River	"Montuno"
Atlantic Ocean	"Man is Out of Sync"
Mediterranean Sea	"Nwèl Inosan"
Gulf of Mexico	"God Made Us All"

252 • The African Burial Ground

provides a means for linking people with the very history of slavery upon which the building rests. For Houston Conwill, it is a "way of connecting people to what has happened . . . People have to deal with what the building is on."[31]

The beginning of the spiral song line refers to the moment when slavery has just been abolished. "Oh, Freedom," translated into Krio/Creole here, gives voice to enslaved diasporic Africans: "O Freedom! O Freedom ove me •en befo I be a slabe I be berrit een my grabe." A post–Civil War African American Freedom song, its lyrics include,

> Oh freedom / Oh freedom / Oh freedom over me
> And before I be a slave/ I'll be buried in my grave.

The second song represented is "Amazing Grace," written by an English ex-slave trader in 1725 after converting to Christianity, and the third, "Go Down Moses," is a spiritual that recites the verse from Exodus 5:1, "let my people go." The song was famously sung by Paul Robeson, an African American ancestor quoted directly in the outer blue ring of *The New Ring Shout*.

Next the song line bears an excerpt from the South African National Anthem, the first stanza and chorus of which was written by Methodist mission school teacher Enoch Sontonga in 1897. The African National Congress adopted and added to the piece, which is today sung in Zulu, Xhosa, Sesotho, Afrikaans, and other languages. The anthem stands as a symbol for South African independence and resistance to apartheid, since it was frequently sung at antiapartheid rallies. Interestingly, Sontonga's death parallels to some extent the story of the African Burial Ground. Upon hearing of the composer's unmarked grave in 1995, Nelson Mandela pushed for its rediscovery and, after a series of research investigations, the cremated remains were located and declared a national monument. Thus, a once marginalized moment in history caught up in issues of national identity, race, and politics then becomes representative of those very issues burdening the nation state and body politic. At the monument dedication, Mandela declared, "In paying this tribute to Enoch Mankayi

Sontonga, we are recovering a part of the history of our nation and our continent . . . Our humble actions today form part of the re-awakening of the South African nation."[32] The first verse, the first two lines of which are in *The New Ring Shout* in Zulu, read:

Nkosi Sikelel' iAfrica
Maluphakanyisw' uphando lwayo

God bless Africa
May its spirit rise high up

Continuing along *The New Ring Shout*, the song line moves to the pan-African message put forward by Jamaican reggae artist Bob Marley, whose "Redemption Song" calls for "songs of freedom" as part of the process of decolonization to "Emancipate yourselves from mental slavery." The next line is taken from the beginning of the Black National Anthem, "Lift Every Voice and Sing," written by Harlem Renaissance poet James Weldon Johnson in 1900 and set to music by his brother John Rosamond Johnson. The NAACP adopted the song in 1919, and later sculptor Augusta Savage created the 16-foot-tall sculpture *Lift Every Voice and Sing* as a commission for the 1939 World's Fair.

Lift ev'ry voice and sing,
'Til earth and heaven ring
Ring with the harmonies of liberty

Immediately following that is the song, "We Shall Overcome," which was composed in part as a gospel song by Reverend Charles Tindley and then became a protest song and key anthem for the civil rights movement. The artists next included a portion of the Chinese National Anthem, which has a long and varied political history, including a ban during the Cultural Revolution. It describes sacrifice for national liberation and resistance against imperialism: "Arise, ye who refuse to be slaves; / With our very flesh and blood Let us build our new Great Wall! / . . . Arise! Arise! Arise! Millions of hearts with one mind."

The song line then moves into the African diaspora with the song "Montuno," by Cuban guitarist and composer Juanito Marquez. The title refers to a technical aspect of Salsa music, with its African-derived call-and-response in which the solo leads and the chorus or instruments respond (coro-prégon). The song line excerpt, "No tiene fronteras! Es libre" translates into:

> It [this montuno] has no borders . . . (coro/response) It's free
> It has no flags . . . (coro/response) Its everyone's

The composer Marquez himself had lived in exile since 1969, and thus recognized firsthand the importance of art and culture as transnational. The group named Harmony sings, "Man is out of sync / Racism can be cured if we just think."

The second-to-last song, "Nwèl Inosan," or "Innocent Christmas," is in Haitian Creole and was performed by the group Boukman Eksperyans. The name Boukman honors Boukman Jetty from Jamaica, who initiated a slave rebellion in Haiti in 1791, and Eksperyans refers to Jimi Hendrix's important album "Experience."[33] The lyrics written in Creole on the ring shout are *"Nwel la rive / Fok nou pa pedi lespwa nou/ Lespwa lavkap jeme pou nou ka inite,"* which says that Christmas is arriving and calls for people not to lose hope, but to stay unified. The group's most famous song and album title, "Kalfou Dangere" (Dangerous Crossroads) (1992), illustrates the strong Kongo presence in Haiti and the importance of crossroads in the African world: "Liars, you'll be in deep trouble / At the crossroads of the Kongo people."

Finally, the song line ends with the 1943 calypso song "God Made us All" by the Trinidadian nicknamed Pretender, who dealt with social injustices in his music. This song put forward the revolutionary notion of equality among all people: "Hoping some day that both black and white will stand up by each other and unite." This last verse of the song line is a reflection of *The New Ring Shout* piece as a whole, which is designed to engage all people: "Our works are intended to open the exclusivity of the historical canon to multiple perspectives, each ethnic, racial, and cultural group speaking for itself—a declaration of cultural interdependence."[34] The artwork is formulated as pan-African and global while specifically connected to the African Burial Ground. Thus, the songline spiral ends on the mapped African Burial Ground, literally marking the physical space beneath our feet.

In keeping with the transspiritual aspect of *The New Ring Shout*, there are additional cosmologies subtly intertwined.[35] The piece is based on the medieval labyrinth laid into the floor of Chartres Cathedral in 1200 that was a pilgrimage site for undertaking the metaphoric journey of the maze, at times with dance, through hell to heaven or through the Holy Land to Heaven. The team points out that Chartres was erected on a Druidic power space once associated with the Black Virgin.[36]

The inner, central circle of the artwork contains a map of New York City, a city impacted by transnational migratory flows (plate 8). The Kongo cosmogram, imbricated within the map, is brought out of Africa and into America; it is repositioned in the new local reality of New York City, just on top of the African Burial Ground. Specifically, the artwork links colonial African Burial Ground ancestors, some of whom were Kongolese, with today's New York City inhabitants.

Spaces of global flow and large multicultural gatherings, particularly pan-African, are marked on the New York City map in plate 8 with minicosmograms to map both physical and metaphysical space (table 4). One is in the center, marking "New York Bay," the collective term for the bodies of water surrounding New York City and the opening to the Atlantic Ocean. These waters bore the ships of the settlers, the slave trade, early Native Americans traveling in the area, and immigrants arriving throughout the centuries. The global flows have facilitated the creation of diasporas and diversity in New York. The Statue of Liberty and Ellis Island stand as supreme examples of this global flow. The United Nations concerns diversity in relation to national politics and identity. Two more signposts in *The New Ring Shout* mark Shea Stadium and Yankee Stadium, areas of large gatherings that are denoted to emphasize places where humans and nations are brought together.[37] These arenas were located in the Bronx and in Flushing, two outlying areas with large Latin American and Asian diaspora neighborhoods to which the rest of New York City once traveled to attend the mainstream American sport of baseball.

Several museums are included on the map. The Tibetan Museum is included for its recognition of political issues and as representative of Asian cultures. The Brooklyn Museum was the first U.S. space to

Table 4

New York City Sites and African Nations in *The New Ring Shout*

Sites Mapped in New York	*African Nations*
Statue of Liberty	Igbo
Ellis Island	Itsekiri
Garibaldi/Meucci Museum	Nupe
Bedford-Stuyvesant Restoration	Tiv
Bronx Museum	Yoruba
Yankee Stadium	Bamun
Central Harlem District	Tikar
Brooklyn Museum	Fulani
Louis Armstrong House	Wolof
Rufus King House	Kono
Weeksville	Mende
United Nations	Kpelle
Shea Stadium	Ashanti
Tibetan Museum	Ewe
	Ga
	Twi
	Fon
	Batawa
	Edo
	Hausa
	Idoma
	Igbira

exhibit African art, and the Bronx Museum is a community museum specializing in Latin American as well as African and Asian arts. The Garibaldi/Meucci Museum is marked specifically to remember two nineteenth-century Italian immigrants who lived in exile on Staten Island. Meucci invented the telephone before Bell, but could not afford the patent. He immigrated to Cuba and then to Staten Island, where he hosted the Italian national hero Giuseppe Garibaldi. Garibaldi had played a key role as a general in the Risorgimento (Italian unification and liberation from 1750 to 1870), and prior to that had lived as an exile for fourteen years in South America fighting for liberation in Brazil and Uruguay.

Finally, several of the mapped sites are particularly significant in African American history. Weeksville was a village in Brooklyn founded by African American land investors and political activists beginning in 1838, eleven years after the abolition of slavery. By the 1850s, there were over five hundred residents in the thriving, self-sufficient community of today's Bedford Stuyvesant. The Louis Armstrong house honors the great jazz musician who lived in New York. The Bedford-Stuyvesant Restoration project began as a federally supported model of community development initiated by Senator Robert F. Kennedy. Both criticized and praised, the project brought together a white power structure of the business world with black community leadership and restoration. The Rufus King house marks the life (1755–1827) of an active politician, New York State senator, and abolitionist who was one of the earliest political leaders to argue openly against slavery. Finally, Native American names of regions interspersed throughout the map remind us of an indigenous presence.

There are additional symbols included in this map that bear personal significance for Houston Conwill. This improvisational aspect of *The New Ring Shout* can be likened to art historian Richard J. Powell's philosophical notion of a "blues aesthetic," in which a syncopated rhythm is layered over a fixed and standard composition.[38] Conwill explains that he works in this aesthetic, much like the process of performing blues music.[39] Conwill hopes the symbols are open to many interpretations concerning ideas of journey, return, life, and wisdom.

The entire piece is framed by blue to symbolize water and the ancestral space of the Kongolese. Quotes by fourteen famous deceased African American leaders connected to New York State are inscribed within the blue frame (plate 8). The knowledge, education, and accomplishments of these ancestors guided Africans in New York City and elsewhere to combat racism, inequity, and injustice, and to create arts, speeches, education, and political movements that brought about major changes. Their words are written in English and then translated into a different foreign language to suggest inclusivity and global outreach. The quoted leaders include abolitionists, civil rights leaders, Afro-centrist historian Yosef ben Jochannan, and pan-Africanists. Marcus Garvey's Garveyism inspired Rastafarianism, and John Henrik Clarke was a historian who founded Black and Puerto Rican Studies at Hunter College (he was involved in activism at the African Burial Ground until his death in 1998). The humanitarian Clare McBride Hale founded the Hale House in 1969 on 122nd Street to care for children of AIDS-infected and drug-addicted mothers.

The quotes in the outer blue ring read:

I want to see women have their rights, and then there will be no more war. —Sojourner Truth (translated into Gaelic)

If there is no struggle there is no progress. Those who profess to favor freedom and yet deprecate agitation are men who want crops without plowing up the ground . . . Power concedes nothing without a demand. —Frederick Douglas (translated into Baule)

When I found I had crossed that line, there was such a glory over everything. I am free and they shall be free. I will bring them here. —Harriet Tubman (translated into Spanish)

To speak of a 'philosophy' that is solely the development of one high-culture or civilization is to be totally ignorant of human migrations and amalgamation down through the centuries. —Yosef ben-Jochannan (translated into Tagalog)

Everyone living together in peace and harmony and love . . . that's the goal that we seek, and I think that the more people there are who reach that state of mind, the better will all be. —Rosa Parks (translated into Japanese)

You cannot subjugate a man and recognize his humanity, his history and his personality. —John Henrik Clarke (translated into Chinese)

We hold them and rock them. They love you to tell them how great they are, how good they are. Somehow even at a young age, they understand that. They're happy and they turn out well . . . I'm not an American hero. I'm just a person that loves children. —Mother Clare McBride Hale (translated into Korean)

When we let freedom ring, when we let it ring from every village and every hamlet, from every state and every city, we will be able to speed up that day when all God's children, Black men and White men, Jews and Gentiles, Protestants and Catholics will be able to join hands and sing in the words of the old Negro spiritual, 'Free at last! Free at last! Thanks God Almighty, we are free at last.' —Martin Luther King Jr. (translated into Hindi)

'Love thy neighbor' is a precept which would transform the world if it were universally practiced . . . loving your neighbor means being inter-racial, inter-religious and international. —Mary McLeod Bethune (translated into Zulu)

I'm for truth no matter who tells it, I'm for justice no matter who it is for or against. I'm a human being first and foremost, and as such I'm for whoever and whatever benefits humanity. —Malcolm X (translated into Hebrew)

I know there is race prejudice, not only in America, but also wherever two races meet together in numbers . . . I do not give it heart room because it seems to me to be the last refuge of the weak. — Zora Neale Hurston (translated into Arabic)

Save us, World Spirit, from our lesser selves, Grant us that war and hatred cease, Reveal our souls in every race and hue. —Marcus Mosiah Garvey (translated into Greek)

There must always be a remedy for wrong and injustice. —Ida B. Wells (translated into Italian)

The artist must take sides. He must elect to fight from freedom or slavery. —Paul Robeson (translated into French)

Adjacent to the blue ring are names of twenty-four African cultural groups or nations (table 4). The ethnicities point to African derivations as well as descendant diasporas.

A separate poem written by Conwill Majozo constitutes part of *The New Ring Shout.* It was printed in a brochure available onsite. The poem titled *The New Ring Shout* invokes both personal and polycultural spiritualities. Conwill Majozo describes looking to the past, to the ancestors, and then to ourselves in order to connect all three. The poem bears a pan-African focus while it extends to other cultures like the artwork it is based upon. For instance, it cites Dogon people of Mali, "Here is mandala of memory— Here is Dogon drum—"[40] and the verse "till the tom-tom cries," a direct quote from Langston Hughes's 1925 piece "The Negro Artist and the Racial Mountain," which resounded in the pan-African world because so many literary figures took up the metaphor of the tom-tom, particularly Négritude authors Senghor, Césaire, and Damas, as well as Créolité writer Glissant.[41] Conwill Majozo calls for a connection with the soul, particularly in the last stanza, "Recognize the parted self. Dance and deliver!"[42] Through relating with the ancestors, learning from New World intellectuals, and performing the unbroken ring shout, there is renaissance, rebirth, remembering, and reunification.

Ultimately, *The New Ring Shout* artwork employs several kinds of mapping that connects the African Burial Ground, Africa, and the formation of new diasporas. A transspiritual mapping of spirit systems, including the Kongo cosmogram, Yorùbá crossroads, ring shout, Christian cross, and Chartres maze, produces a spirituality of space on the floor of the office building. This is interwoven with geopolitical mapping systems to locate us in New York City and to recall Africa.

The New Ring Shout was activated as a space of spirituality during a dedication of the 290 Broadway art works in October 1998. The leader Dòwòti Désir, now titled Manbo Asogwe, poured a libation on the cosmogram, and she greeted guests, artists, the spirit world, and ancestors of the burial ground. This spiritual leader called upon the trickster lwa (Haitian deity) Papa Legba, who resides at the crossroads. This call added yet another transspiritual layer to The New Ring Shout because she engaged the space in terms of a Vodoun world view, reconceptualizing the crossroads as Papa Legba's terrain. She explained later that GSA may have invited her as a Haitian and a priest to meet the public's needs, but her very presence and engagement of the spiritual world "once again subverted the whole [GSA] process" in the typically ambiguous manner of Papa Legba.[43]

A performance series was held on The New Ring Shout during Black History Month in February 2000 and 2001, sponsored by a partnership between GSA's Office of Memorialization and the Metropolitan Transit Authority. School groups attended, and employees stopped on their way to and from offices to enjoy such sounds as the kora, saxophone, and Brazilian guitar. Project Executive Peggy King Jorde specifically organized this series to encourage people to "reclaim the site as sacred" by visiting 290 Broadway and engaging the space as a "living memorial," even if the excavated deceased were not yet reburied.[44]

Roger Brown Mosaic, Untitled, Installed 1994

While The New Ring Shout concerned Africa and diasporas directly, Roger Brown's mosaic linked deaths of people with AIDS to deaths of enslaved Africans buried in New York City. Brown connected two different historic moments with suffering, marginalization, and censorship of information. At this early stage in the project, there was no guideline calling for a commemoration of the site. Such a situation illustrates the politics of space and memory at stake and the tensions over acknowledging and honoring the site.

The *Untitled* mosaic by Roger Brown is positioned in the eastern wing of 290 Broadway at the Duane Street entrance (fig. 43). This 14

Figure 43. Roger Brown, *Untitled*, 1994. Glass mosaic tiles, 14 × 10 ft. This mosaic explores death in New York City in relation to colonial slavery and contemporary AIDS. Photographs in the Carol M. Highsmith Archive, Library of Congress, Prints and Photographs Division.

x 10-foot mosaic made of glass tile depicts a mélange of skulls and faces piled beneath icons of New York City: Brooklyn Bridge, twin towers of the World Trade Center, and the Empire State Building. The faces below the skyline can be seen as suppression of history or the deceased who helped to build the city. Brown has integrated the AIDS epidemic with those buried in the cemetery. He described both as victims of suffering, a "mosaic of death heads in memory of those of all races who have suffered and died too soon."[45] He explained, "My theme uses the gaunt faces of AIDS victims interspersed by race and contrasted to the skulls of the slavery victims found in the Black cemetery. The city rises in the background as if growing out of the heap of human misery left behind."[46] Some of the multicolored heads below the city are still living, but living with death close by. They inhabit an intermediate space between the living city above and the skulls below.

Roger Brown (1942–1997) was a leading painter in the Chicago Imagist style, a kind of realism based on naïve art done in a flat, stylized treatment of form. Originally from Alabama, he focused on American landscapes and cityscapes. His art graced the cover of *Time* magazine in 1990 and 1993, and he created a mosaic of Icarus and Daedalus for the façade of the NBC Tower on LaSalle Street in Chicago.

How have viewers responded to Brown's mosaic? I observed tours given by OPEI from 1998 to 2001, during which tour leaders successfully and creatively directed analyses of the artworks to an African-based subjectivity focused on the African Burial Ground. Chandra Pittman asked her tour group in November 1998 why some skulls were interspersed among living heads and vice versa. A child proposed the idea that the living and dead coexist among each other. This interpretation aligns with an African-based metaphysical understanding that intercommunication and interaction exist between ancestors and humans. The leader then linked the heads to the New York skyline to tell a neglected history about enslaved Africans building the infrastructure of New York City. The tour group raised the sensitive question about why the mosaic was installed so high toward the ceiling and in an out of the way corner where neither employees nor the visiting public travel. They noted the mosaic might not even be seen because of its height and wondered if it was meant to be hidden and kept out of the way on purpose. Perhaps like the disease itself, the subject was not put on central display but rather pushed to the side.

Clyde Lynds, America Song, Installed 1995

Clyde Lynds's *America Song* is a relief sculpture just outside of the main entrance of the office building at 290 Broadway (fig. 44). The 23-foot-high, 10-foot-wide piece is constructed of reinforced concrete, granite, stainless steel, fiber optics, and electronics. Fiber optics cast within the concrete panels create beads or points of moving light. *America Song* is a memorial in the form of a stele or stone monument carved for the dead.

America Song posits a memory of slavery in relation to American national identity. Beneath a 15-foot bird's wing, an excerpt from a song by an anonymous African American poet reads:

I want to be free.
Want to be free—
Rainbow round my shoulder.
Wings on my feet.

Lynds explains about the text in the artwork, "These words, in combination with a metaphor for freedom—a wing—emphasize all people's desire for freedom" so that *America Song*, "must also speak universally to all Americans but include a strong reference to the site's history."[47] The piece offers an emotional memory of slavery in honor of the deceased buried in the African Burial Ground specifically.

The generic wing[48] as a universal symbol of freedom may also suggest the American eagle. The wing is accented by rays radiating from the bottom upwards to suggest the Statue of Liberty's crown or the sunrise on a silver dollar (fig. 44).[49] Ultimately, a tension

Figure 44. Clyde Lynds, *America Song*, 1995. Reinforced concrete, granite, stainless steel, fiber optics, electronics, 23 × 10 ft. Installed outside the office building main entrance, this relief sculpture juxtaposes patriotic symbols of democracy against text composed by an enslaved African American denied freedom. Photographs in the Carol M. Highsmith Archive, Library of Congress, Prints and Photographs Division.

arises between patriotic symbols of American democracy juxtaposed against text composed by an oppressed slave denied the freedom and justice espoused by the founding fathers. Indeed, *America Song* raises questions of freedom, subjugation, and American identity with its location on the wall of a government building erected on top of a cemetery of enslaved and freed Africans. Further questions emerge because Lynds purposefully designed the public art piece to fit within the rubric of "traditional concepts of sculpture for a Federal building."[50] He points out that government buildings typically bear quotes by historically significant people. Yet his quote is both anonymous and representative of the marginalized who were historically eschewed from the body politic. Thus, an alternative interpretation of the piece is that struggles to escape slavery are a part of America's song, history, and government.

The Art-in-Architecture Committee, composed in part by members of the community, argued that the anonymous poet be relabeled "African" rather than "African American," as written in Lynds's design proposal.[51] This designation, they explained, was part of the process of reclaiming African identity and heritage, a remembering literally at stake since GSA's early 1990s attempt to suppress the rediscovery of the African Burial Ground. Thus, members of the panel shunned the label "American" as part of a returning-to-Africa ideal. Conversely, the artwork might be understood to link African with American through American national identity. Such inevitable tensions between politics of race and national identity lead to the questions, does the commemoration interject an African and/or African American presence into the body politic, and does it bring a black presence onto the face of a federal building?

The OPEI site tours opened interpretations beyond the above analyses. In keeping with the artwork, tour leader Chadra Pittman creatively brought agency to voices excluded from the hegemonic notion of American democracy. In May 1999, I listened as she asked visitors, could the eagle wing be Native American? This interesting question brings the power and spiritual significance of the eagle in terms of Native American cultures on a par with the icon of the United States. Although historically the U.S. government had attempted to disempower such nations, a Native American presence is indeed a part of *America Song*, as they were the first "Americans." Pittman then asked what the semicircular rays radiating from the bottom might bring to mind. The audience suggested the sun, and the crown of the Statue of Liberty. Rather than press ideals of democracy, Pittman reminded the audience that the first version of the Statue of Liberty was an African woman.[52] Finally, she related the anonymous quote to the anonymous dead who were and are buried in the cemetery beneath our feet.

In its simplicity, the piece evokes a wide variety of interpretations. Dòwòti Désir offered the notion that Lynds makes a concentrated effort "to speak to the lost dreams and privileges of that ancestral community."[53] Désir correlates the visibility of the piece at night with the importance of night for eighteenth-century New York Africans, as a time when people could commune at the burial ground and honor their traditions and their dead. Also, people escaping their enslavers traveled at night by following the stars. Lynds indeed evokes the night sky, as shifting fiber optics create a starlit sky along with a sliver of a concrete moon in the upper right section of the piece. OPEI employee Marie-Alice Devieux, who led a site tour in November 1999, added to her audience that the piece "gives a hopeful feeling to the building."

Private Offerings

While the artworks themselves had the potential to render and represent spaces of spirituality, the question remained, how effectively could they be engaged and experienced? The commemorations presented some obstacles for the public. After the 1995 Oklahoma City bombing, the office building itself enforced restriction and controls so that visitors could not readily walk into the lobby to view the artworks without first facing metal detectors and security guards. Taking photographs was prohibited without special permission, as the act could ostensibly contribute to terrorism. The interior lobby with artworks was completely inaccessible after hours and on weekends until an interpretive center/visitor center opened in the mid-2000s.

Similarly, until the exterior memorial opened in 2007, the grassy area with two hundred unexcavated burials behind the office building was encaged by a metal, locked fence. Attached to the fence was a sign, "No Trespassing. Violators will be Prosecuted." Inside the fence, signs marked "the African Burial Ground" with a brief description for viewers and passersby (fig. 45). People only encountered text to interpret the space standing outside the fence.

It was outside of this fence surrounding the grassy area along the sidewalk that personal offerings were left through the years. This alternative reclamation of space converted a secular office building to a space of spirituality. Private offerings that I found left at the site over the years also become a way to counter government commissioned art. This comparison brings forward a tension between the institutionalized commemoration discussed above and articulations of private memory.

The following multifarious offerings exemplify the necessity for recognizing, remembering, and reclaiming the burial ground. They can be understood through African-based conceptions of the ancestral realm. On several occasions before the 2007 exterior memorial was constructed, I passed the fence to discover informal personal offerings that, by honoring the dead, also demarcated the space as sacred. On 23 February 2000, two glass jars of water were filled with white peonies and left up against the chain link fence behind the office building (fig. 45). The visitor intended for the flowers in full bloom to remain there for more than a day since they had water to sustain them. This aesthetically beautiful offering was left to activate a sacred space spiritually—a cemetery that naturally warranted flowers for remembering the ancestors. Another time, in June 1999, I found that an orange had been left alongside the fence. Later, in May 2000, there were three apples, one yellow between two red ones. Fruit is a typical offering placed on altars or left for deities, particularly practitioners of Santeria, Candomblé, and Òrìshà worship. In

Figure 45. Offerings, 2000. Gifts were left over the years at the fence surrounding the former pavilion to honor the dead and demarcate the space as sacred. Photo by Andrea Frohne.

another instance in June 1999, I witnessed a schoolteacher walk his entire elementary school class to the fence, talk to them briefly, and then pull out a paper bag of fruit. He handed the fruit to the students and then instructed them to place the fruits on the ground alongside the fence. In effect, he was teaching his entire class to honor their ancestors by depositing fruits as offerings. The next day when I returned, the offering had been cleared away.

In fact, all of the objects described above were gone by the next day; objects seemingly discarded on the ground countered Western aesthetics of a pristine lawn. These gifts used to spiritualize a sacred space were held in tension with secular, urban space practices regulated by the hegemonic entity holding the means to control that space. Random objects left for the dead do not conform to the norm in the controlled shaping of American urban space.[54]

Nevertheless, one person was successful in leaving an offering for longer than a day. Tied into the fence behind the office building were two slim handmade brown pouches about one and a half inches long covered with white squares of fabric and connected by a leather cord (fig. 46). One pouch faced outwards to Elk Street, and the other was tied to look inwards into the cemetery. The small, barely noticeable pouches remained threaded through the fence for many months during the spring of 2000. Were they small minkisi, sewn closed, concealing empowered contents? Were they handmade gris-gris with protective verses from the Qur'an inserted inside? We may not possess specific answers for the personal contribution; but its purpose to recognize and honor the dead was enacted.

Such practices are certainly not limited to the African world, and can be contrasted with other government-related sites. For instance, the Vietnam Veterans Memorial and the initial memorialization at the World Trade Center after 9/11 are accepted spaces of national and personal mourning. These two examples are offered not to compare actual events, but to illustrate the fundamental, if not universal, human aspiration to honor the dead. In memorializing the loss of life, people leave offerings such as flowers, candles, and written messages to the dead. Why is this practice accepted for some spaces and not others?

Figure 46. Small handmade pouches, 2000. These objects were looped into the fence behind the office building, successfully and clandestinely recognizing the ancestors for several months. Photo by Andrea Frohne.

Visitors from all around the world travel to the Vietnam Veterans Memorial in Washington to remember the dead at any hour, night or day. Many of them communicate with the deceased through messages and gifts left at the wall. Articles are cleared away twice a day and placed in a storage space after they are tagged and catalogued. However, this was not always the case. The U.S. National Park Service, which maintains the memorial, initially gathered up the objects, such as letters, toys, badges, medals, liquor, tobacco, marijuana, personal memorabilia, photographs, and Easter baskets, and classified them as "lost and found."[55] This illustrates the authorities' initial inability to recognize the memorial as such; a space for remembering and communicating with the dead. But by the sheer magnitude of the number of objects left as offerings, they were forced to reconsider the "classification" of the objects. Now, visitors simultaneously "leave a piece of memory" and articulate a part of history.[56]

The World Trade Center disaster invoked a natural and national (as well as international) need to leave offerings to the victims. Candles, messages, flowers, flags, and photographs appeared all over New York City in public spaces where thousands pass, or in remote places such as the Staten Island shoreline looking towards Manhattan (fig. 47). Like the African Burial Ground, a metal fence separating Ground Zero from the public prior to development became

Figure 47. September 11 shrine on Staten Island looking towards Manhattan, October 2001. Photo by Andrea Frohne.

the focal point for visitors and mourners. They continued to bring memorabilia, leave flowers as offerings, and write messages on the fence itself at Ground Zero.

The aesthetics of "order" that were briefly overturned during the intense personal and public mourning have since been restored by and large. By July 2006, official signage attached to the fence read: "Please understand all articles left behind must be removed" and "Please do not write anywhere on the viewing fence" (fig. 48). Again, I scrutinized the space for evidence of offerings and have photographed ribbons, carnations, gum wrappers, small messages, and a pair of tiny Christian icons threaded through the fence.

At 290 Broadway and now at Ground Zero, spiritual engagement and reclamation of the space have been suppressed, and offerings

Figure 48. Metal fence along West Broadway at Ground Zero, July 2006. Signs control expressions of mourning so that covert communication with the dead, such as written messages and gifts, have been stymied by 2006. Photo by Andrea Frohne.

continue to be discouraged and discarded. Yet it is these offerings that are absolutely crucial in marking the space, rendering it sacred. In their stead, official memorials begin to take their place.

To conclude, this chapter illustrates that artworks and offerings demarcate a space of spirituality, thereby contributing to the production of spirituality and reclamation of space at the African Burial Ground in the twentieth and twenty-first centuries. Artworks represent the ancestors and African-based spirit worlds, and offerings personalize the sacred. David Rashid Gayle incorporates crossroads and kente cloth (fig. 41), and *The New Ring Shout* contains the Kongo cosmogram, Yorùbá crossroads, and Gullah ring shout among others (plate 8). Moreover, Gayle and Clyde Lynds (fig. 44) illustrate conflicts and connections between the U.S. government and the African Burial Ground in their pieces. Such conflict over space is evident with personal offerings for the ancestors versus a hegemonic urban space aesthetic. The varied commemorations in the chapter illustrate tensions and productions of spirituality during efforts to visually remember and represent the African Burial Ground. In so doing, the artworks document spiritually, as well as historically and politically, the formation of a New York City African diaspora linked directly to the African Burial Ground.

6

Late Commemorative Artworks, 1998–2007

Pan-African Arts and the Body Politic

The late commemorative artworks were installed in and around the Ted Weiss Federal Building through three separate government commissions between 1998 and 2007. Following the first round of Art-in-Architecture program GSA commissions discussed in chapter 5, a second round of commemorative artworks was organized for the building lobby. This occurred because grassroots activists insisted upon more involvement in the commemoration process and called for greater visual acknowledgement of the African Burial Ground within the office building. The three artworks were funded through $3 million approved by Congress and President George H. W. Bush in 1992 for artists Barbara Chase-Riboud, Tomie Arai, and Melvin Edwards (not built). Funded through Percent for Art and installed in 2000, the next government commission was made by the New York City Department of Parks and Recreation to Lorenzo Pace for an outdoor sculpture fountain half a block away in Foley Square. Finally, the GSA exterior memorial competition was realized, with the National Park Service first managing and then taking over the project. After Congress appropriated funds in 2003, the commission was awarded to Rodney Léon, and the African Burial Ground National Monument opened in 2007 behind the office building.

All of the artworks express pan-African perspectives in which their visual narratives about Africa play a significant role in recognizing,

275

representing, and spiritualizing the African Burial Ground. I identify the implications of pan-African narratives in the artworks to suggest here that they manifest a representation of Africa at the same time that the African Burial Ground is recuperated.

What do the artworks emblematize for the African Burial Ground? In drawing upon my interviews, dialogues, and attendance at public meetings, I consider the complex processes by which pan-African identity was articulated at the African Burial Ground amid tensions, competing voices, contested terrains, and counternarratives. I discuss the selection, design, and installation methods for many of the artworks to explore the intricacy, layered narratives, and great struggle that figured into defining and recognizing the burial ground. The process was literally a history in the making with an unknown outcome.

In attending the events, I witnessed conflict, anger, frustration, and hard work toward respectful commemoration. All those who attended the public meetings seemed to understand the stakes. If dissenting voices did not challenge GSA in order to fight for a production of sacred memory, particularly from an African perspective, then the reclamation of the African Burial Ground and its ancestors could be minimalized or tokenized. Yet, a range of discourses, voices, and agendas both competed and coalesced so that the commemorations do not present a coherent collective identity. Despite the site's moments of marginalization, I ultimately conclude that grassroots efforts and government involvement have repositioned the burial ground and its artworks within United States' national identity as well as the body politic.

Pan-African Artistic Expression

A pan-African narrative has continued to emerge and shape identity, history, and memory of the site.[1] In particular, the burial ground has been commemorated through a pan-African perspective in primarily two interrelated ways. The first approach can be characterized as Afrocentric pan-Africanism, meaning it invokes a homogeneous

Africa and a generalized African spirituality with diasporic Africans in the United States enacting a unidirectional look back to Africa. In this case, Africa and diasporic Africans become one and the same in the United States. For instance, Afrocentrist Molefi Asante explains that "*we Africans* have been involved in making the modern world . . ." (emphasis mine).[2] Such an Afrocentric approach uses "African history and values, indeed the entire African cosmology, as the foundation of black Diaspora identity and the basis of self-affirmation."[3] Broadly speaking, the multiplicity of African cultural particulars become homogenized to present one overarching African culture (in the singular) or one general African spirituality.

The burial ground is also commemorated through what I identify as a second type of pan-Africanism, which is an assembly of several African arts and cosmologies from various but specific cultural groups. Here, transcultural flows between and within Africa, the Americas, and the Caribbean are recognized. Examples of pan-African articulations in all of the artworks include the Kongo cosmogram, Yorùbá crossroads, Gullah ring shout, quotes by pan-African leaders, Egyptian headrest, Akan stool and *adinkra*, Ifá divination tray, Kuba textiles, Mande *bogolan*, Bamana *Ciwara*, Haitian *vèvè* with Legba, and also Èsù, and a reproduced padlock of an enslaved ancestor. These specific cultural and spiritual artistic representations combine with each other, meaning that several are presented at the same time within any one commemorative artwork. The artworks at the burial ground express the two pan-African aspects in that they embody specific African world views as well as, and in relation to, Afrocentric discourse.

For over a decade, I commonly heard Afrocentric pan-African discourse during hearings, open houses, and vigils that I attended. For example, historian John Henrik Clarke was invited to give a testimony for a hearing in 1992 for which he contextualized the unearthing of the burial ground in the following way: "This is a beginning, a new beginning, not only for us but for the world. We have to stop looking at it as a New York thing. It's a holistic thing that touches the lives of *African* people in this country and might touch the lives of *African* people all over the world. When you look at us all over the world, we are not a minority. We're not a minority in this country either"[4] (emphasis mine). Clarke identified people of African descent in New York as African, thereby eschewing a connection to European America. Other activists drew clear connections with the deceased by calling them "our ancestors." Mayor David Dinkins stressed this in his remarks at the same hearing: "The African Burial Ground may be a small piece of Manhattan—but it links us directly to the great continent of Africa."[5] Such rhetoric evinces a return to Africa at the burial ground.

To summarize, the formulation of a pan-African discourse for representing and commemorating the site is *spatial* rather than *chronological*. The representations in the artworks are to Africa and its diaspora geographically, ethnically, and cosmologically. Africa understood as a place and a location rather than in time is central for recuperating the African Burial Ground.

At a 1993 public hearing in city hall, representatives of GSA, Art-in-Architecture, and 290 Broadway architects discussed the objectives for the second round of commissioning, including the content of the art. They stressed the importance of rendering the office building as a space of spirituality through artwork, which becomes key for articulating an Afrocentric pan-African discourse in the art. At this hearing, architect and consultant Herman H. Howard remarked, "throughout this building [the art] will have the opportunity to speak the heritage of *African* people . . . The art is somehow going to give to us the knowledge that this once was a burial ground" (emphasis mine).[6] Howard Dodson considered incorporating art into the office building "so that at the time that it opens, the sense of it as a part of a broader sacred universe that is indeed the nature of the Burial Ground can be communicated to all who come to it and come through it."[7] Indeed, a key guideline in selecting the short list of artworks was to "encourage the concept of sacred space," as expressed by Howard.[8] Federal Steering Committee member Herb Bennett explained, "Our ancestors are the authors and we must blend the reality of a world that we have inherited with the unfamiliar spiritual aspects that contemporary society seems to avoid . . . Here is an opportunity, however, to fuse the spirit into a structural equation that we can all relate to. If spirit is strange to us, then we must be about making the strange familiar."[9] Rather than one specific spiritual tradition or religious practice, this discussion called for a broad African-based spirituality honoring the ancestors in general.

There inevitably exists an element of idealization and utopia in framing the African Burial Ground through a pan-African articulation. At a time when academic scholarship is conceptualizing the notion of diaspora more along the lines of the transnational, what I found in New York may be read as essentialized or homogenized. Stuart Hall creates a space for such a reality when he explains that a holistic black experience or essence can be rooted in a singular identity, experience, and history. This collective identity has been powerful in anticolonial struggles, resistance against racism, and a resource for black identity, "offer[ing] a way of imposing an imaginary coherence on the experience of dispersal and fragmentation, which is the history of all enforced diapsoras."[10] Hall maintains that a return to roots is important for speaking of a past that was once denied a language and is now an act of speaking "hidden histories" and making "another place to stand in." It is a concept that offers empowerment, resistance, identity, and unity.[11]

This notion of collective memory and identity does not spare room for specific histories, cultures, locations, or differences. There is necessarily an element of imagining and mythologizing that occurs here in order to arrive at a homogeneous, essentialized sameness. Hall balances that mode of memory and identity with another equally important one, which is constantly in process and change in relation to heterogeneous factors such as explicit geographic location, ethnicity, gender, culture, religion, social class, politics, and power.[12]

In either case (collective cultural identity or discontinuous cultural identity), collective memories are not fixed, but are representations or constructions of reality constantly under revision. Because the former mode of memory making certainly occurs at the African Burial Ground and clearly holds continuing importance, one can critically consider its homogeneity and romanticization with-out doing away with it. Stuart Hall makes the important point that Africa is not in fact a fixed origin that can be found and returned to: an "original 'Africa' is no longer there" because it has also changed with time, and therefore, "we can't literally go home again."[13] In this sense, Hall recognizes the process of taking symbolic journeys and instead suggests returning to Africa, "but 'by another route': what Africa has *become* in the New World . . ."[14]

We can then apply Hall's solution to the African Burial Ground. How might the artworks function as a returning to Africa, but by another route? One answer to this is to consider specific contexts. In this chapter then, analyses of the commemorations concern a collective, pan-African memory but in relation to very specific histories of ruptured, politicized, and contested spaces. What has Africa become in the New World, how is Africa remembered at the African Burial Ground in New York City?

The words "commemoration" and "memorial" are both related to the Latin root *memor* (mindful), which is also the etymological root for "memory." All three words invoke the act and process of calling to mind or remembering. Memory occurs on several levels at the burial ground: through personal memory, collective memory, invented memory, and anamnesis. Anamnesia is the remembering of ideas stored in the soul, which have been carried from one life to the next. Socrates, via Plato, introduced the term when he reasoned that this ideal state, or knowledge of the soul, can be accessed through remembering. Phaedo recalls Socrates's explanation, "Is not what we call 'forgetting' simply the loss of knowledge? . . . So, as I maintain, there are two alternatives. Either we are all born with knowledge of these standards, and retain it throughout our lives, or else, when we speak of people learning, they are simply recollecting what they knew before. In other words, learning is recollection."[15] To this end, research and the pursuit of intellectual conversations are experiences of rediscovering previously possessed knowledge stored in the soul. And in conversation with Meno, Socrates added that for the pursuit of knowledge, "there is no reason why he should not find out all the rest, if he keeps a stout heart and does not grow weary of the search, for seeking and learning are in fact nothing but recollection."[16] This ancient philosophy and theory need by no means be considered "Western," but I would argue are just as much "African" because anamnesis is built in part upon Pythagoras's idea of the transmigration of the soul from Egypt.[17] Anamnesis may be understood in terms of divination in African contexts as well—a means for accessing forgotten or requested knowledge via the spirit world.

In terms of the means by which anamnesis operates at the African Burial Ground, the recalling of memory by African Americans has been an important process in the pan-African reclamation and reconceptualization of the space. Many informal conversations that I heard and numerous statements that were given at GSA open houses concerned the need to access the ancestors, to honor them from an African perspective, and to identify them as African. An example in which this was powerfully played out was during the weekend-long 2003 reburial in which a naming ceremony was held. In the absence of memory, an elder performed a ceremony in which she gave Swahili names to each of the excavated 419 unnamed through the course of the evening. It was so successful that she held a reenactment, performing another ceremony the next year at the anniversary of the reburial in October 2004. This invention of memory, both in terms of naming the deceased and in terms of creating a ritual that does not exist as a specific ceremony in Africa, functioned as an enacting of memory— an amnestic recollection of the past that was in part fictional.

Artist and art historian Moyo Okediji explores anamnesis to consider connections between Yorùbá and African American arts. In his discussion of three African American artists, Okediji writes, "Anamnesia allows the artists not only to *cognize* America, but also to *recognize* Africa and centrally (re)locate themselves and their (re) constructions in the pluralism of American art history . . . Because it is a construction of reality based on recollection—whatever could be snatched from the locked storehouse of memory—anamnesia is also a fictional form, fashioned on the artists' fabrication of a past engaged with nostalgia."[18]

In the case of the African Burial Ground, commissioned artists of varying heritage crossed cultures to access memories of the African experience. The commemorations are in part an expression of anamnesis; they recall African cosmologies, arts, and cultures, which facilitate in remembering, reclaiming, and reconstructing a severed Africa. Anamnesis assists in the recovery into the present of a geographically and chronologically remote past.[19]

Art Commissioned by GSA, Round Two

Following pressure from concerned citizens for increased recognition of the site, the Federal Steering Committee made a recommendation to Congress to federally fund a second group of artists. In addition to the three Art-in-Architecture commissions discussed in chapter 5, this new second round was realized with $3 million approved by Congress in October 1992. The process for selection, as described at the beginning of chapter 5, was the same one used to select artwork in 1993. This time, a broader public voice was included,[20] with the artworks explicitly commemorating the burial ground.[21] Barbara Chase-Riboud cast a piece in bronze entitled *Africa Rising*, Tomie Arai created a mural named *Renewal*, and Melvin Edwards was selected to design a gate entitled *Gate of Thanks and Appreciation* (not built), all for the lobby of the building (both installed 1998).

Barbara Chase-Riboud, Africa Rising,
Commissioned 1995, Installed 1998

Barbara Chase-Riboud's *Africa Rising*, installed at 290 Broadway, is a monumental 15½-foot-high, 8⅗-foot-wide, and 4⅖-foot-deep sculpture made of bronze through the lost-wax process and coated with a silver patina (fig. 49). The piece is an amalgam of pan-African and classical Western themes that echoes the artist's own life.

Chase-Riboud was born in Philadelphia, where she earned a degree from Tyler School of Fine Arts, affiliated with Temple University

(1957). In 1958, she studied and exhibited in Rome, an experience that sparked her great love for the Baroque style, and traveled to Egypt for three months. She then earned a Masters from Yale (1960) and moved to Paris (1961). While at Yale, Chase-Riboud studied with artists, architects, and authors whose works were emblematic of Western modernism: Josef Albers, Vincent Scully, Philip Johnson, Paul Rand, and Louis Kahn. Through her years in Europe, Chase-Riboud participated in and interacted again with key figures of the modernist movement, including Max Ernst, Jean Tinguely, Ben Shahn, Man Ray, Alexander Calder, Roberto Matta, Victor Brauner, and Wilfredo Lam. In 1966, she exhibited at the First African Festival of Art in Senegal and met Négritude poet and president of Senegal Léopold Senghor; and she attended the First Pan-African Festival in Algiers and met Huey Newton and high ranking members of the Black Panthers. She attended the Pan-African Festival in Nigeria in 1969 and traveled to Greece in 1973. Chase-Riboud's passion for African American art and history led her to design, among other works, a monument for the Middle Passage (1994, 1997); the Malcolm X series (1970); the Cleopatra series (1973–94), which was in part inspired by Edmonia Lewis's *the Death of Cleopatra* (1876); and the Zanzibar series (1970).

These varied experiences straddling Europe and the United States elucidate the convergence of classical European and pan-African ideals represented in *Africa Rising*. As seen in figure 49, the lower half of the sculpture is based on headrests found throughout the African continent, with a focus on Egypt and Ethiopia in particular.[22] Headrests are a part of quotidian life, but also important in honoring the dead when used in burials, such as in ancient Egypt. The basic shape of *Africa Rising*'s lower half also evokes an Akan stool from Ghana, Dogon architecture from Mali, an Egyptian boat that carries the dead across the river to the next world, and a ship of the Middle Passage.[23] Though not visible in the photograph, several coins or medallions bearing images of famed people of African descent lie along the base:

Figure 49. Barbara Chase-Riboud, *Africa Rising*, 1998. Bronze, 15½ × 8⅗ × 4⅖ ft. The sculpture in the lobby of the office building presents a complex convergence of European and pan-African arts. They include African headrests, an Akan stool, Nike of Samothrace, a Boccioni sculpture, and Sarah Baartman. Photographs in the Carol M. Highsmith Archive, Library of Congress, Prints and Photographs Division.

West end coins	East end coins
Malcolm X	All Colored Troops of the Civil War
W.E.B. DuBois	Frederick Douglas
John VI, King of Portugal	Sojourner Truth
Abraham Hannibal	Alessandro de Medici
Edmonia Lewis	Joseph Cinqué
Alexander Pushkin	Alexandre Dumas
Josephine Baker	Marcus Garvey
Toussaint L'Overture	

Pushkin and Dumas, who represent iconic national identity for their Russian and French nation-states, are here repositioned within a pan-African context emphasizing their African descent. Other figures have led lives that bestride both the African and European continents, reflecting the mix found within the artwork itself. Specifically, King John VI (1769–1826) established a royal court in Brazil and was in part African via his aunt; Abraham Hannibal (or Gannibal) (1696–1781) was of Abyssinian royalty (from today's Eritrea), was kidnapped into slavery, and once in Russia became a general under Peter the Great; Alexander Pushkin (1799–1837), hailed as one of Russia's greatest poets and a founder of modern Russian literature, was of African heritage on his mother's side because his great-grandfather was the aforementioned Hannibal; Alessandro de Medici's mother was Amazigh (Berber) of Morocco, making this Duke of Florence (1530) one of the earliest black heads of state in the modern Western world (he was buried in Michelangelo's famous tomb); Joseph Cinqué of Sierra Leone led the revolt on the *Amistad* in 1839 and then won his case in the U.S. Supreme Court with the advocacy of John Quincy Adams for being enslaved illegally; and Alexandre Dumas, the French novelist who wrote *The Three Musketeers* (1844) and *The Count of Monte Cristo* (1845–46), was of African and Dominican descent by his mother, Marie Césette.

The strongly classical upper half of *Africa Rising* is modeled after the famous Nike of Samothrace sculpture.[24] The third century BCE Greek monument commemorated a naval victory won by the powerful maritime state of Rhodes. After the winged goddess descended from the sky to stand on the prow of a ship, she was so carved in honor of the triumphal fleets. The statue was made as an offering by the people to the goddess Nike (Victory). Before it was taken to the Louvre Museum, the sculpture belonged to a pan-Hellenic religious temple complex on the island of Samothrace, where she overlooked the Sanctuary of the Great Gods. Chase-Riboud evokes Nike of Samothrace but also appropriates her within the context of the slave trade and pan-African identity. Nike on the prow of a battle ship is converted to the mast of a slave ship so that Nike's naval victory becomes victory of pan-African identity, as evidenced in the title *Africa Rising*. The figure manifests "liberty both from bondage and death, an overcoming of adversity and defeat, and a resurrection in both the Christian and African sense of the word."[25]

The piece depicts not only Nike of Samothrace, but also Sarah Baartman. An earlier rendition, Chase-Riboud's bronze scale model number 6 for *Africa Rising*, is entitled *Sarah Baartman/Africa Rising* (1996).[26] The body of Nike takes on the shape of Sarah Baartman from southern Africa, pejoratively nicknamed the Hottentot Venus in Europe. Baartman's buttocks, genitalia, and body became a point of fascination and exoticism when she was taken from South Africa and was exhibited in London and Paris beginning in 1810 until her untimely death in 1816 at age twenty-five. Her marginalized, sexualized body was used by scientists of the time to further construct taxonomies of "race" to such an extent that her genitalia remained on display in the Museé de l'Homme until 1989. Chase-Riboud's convergence of Nike and Sarah Baartman becomes a positive reclamation of the tragic treatment of Baartman to proclaim victory over adversity. This convergence also Africanizes Nike so that ancient Greek power and beauty are balanced with African ideals of beauty.

Finally, Chase-Riboud's figure is also based on the sculpture *Unique Forms of Continuity in Space* (1913) by Italian Futurist Umberto Boccioni, in which he attempted to portray motion in his static bronze sculpture.[27] The leader and manifesto writer of Futurism, F. T. Marinetti, contrasted in 1909 the artistic movement against the Nike of Samothrace in his efforts to proclaim the death of classical art and the celebration of the machine, urban life, and European modernity: "a roaring automobile which seems to rush over exploding powder is more beautiful than the *Victory of Samothrace*."[28] There are, in effect, two sets of antithetical aesthetics operating here: Marinetti's Futurism against Nike, and Sarah Baartman against Nike.

Thus, what are the implications of a Western artistic presence in relation to a pan-African one at the African Burial Ground? Chase-Riboud herself explains that she strives to make her work accessible to all:[29] "I want to use everything I know, from . . . my knowledge of Greek and Roman art. I'm as passionate about politics as any black woman, but I want my art to be universal."[30] She explained in an interview with me that her piece is like the Statue of Liberty. Liberty was an African woman sculpted in a Western neoclassical style of sculpture, and *Africa Rising* is an African woman cast in the style of the Hellenistic Nike.[31] Chase-Riboud's title is reminiscent of Meta Warrick Fuller's *Ethiopia Rising* (ca. 1910), a pan-African bronze piece carved in the neoclassical style and so important to the Harlem Renaissance. *Africa Rising* veers away from Molefi Asante's Afrocentrism, in which he explains, "The Afrocentric analysis reestablishes the centrality of the ancient Kemetic (Egyptian) civilization . . . as points of reference for an African perspective in much the same way that Greece and Rome serve as reference points for the European world."[32] The incongruity of incorporating the West into the pan-African artwork, as perceived from an Afrocentric lens, illustrates that a seamless collective memory of the African Burial Ground necessarily remains an impossibility.

A poem written by Chase-Riboud accompanies the artwork.[33] The poem is pan-African in content, linking together histories of several specific African nations.

. . . Out of Omega, rending the cosmos
Groaning across deserts and pyramids of Kush.
A lunar landscape of brimstone
Basalt and Obsidian, biotite and barium.

From undergrounds pebbled with diamonds and gold scum
We came, into the Hell of deathly White,
In eclipsed sun, the negation of time.
Conned and even bankrupt and ravished kingdom.
Zeila & Somaliland. Galla & Abyssinia. Tigre & Shoa
Niger & Nile. Orange & Congo. Cubango & Kasai
Strung out in caravans, we came, a stunned string of
Black pearls like a hundred year centipede: one thousand.
One thousand thousand. one million. three. six. nine. thirty
    million.
Torn from their roots, like belladonna lilies we came.
Death in every heart. sprawling over the badlands.
The red flag of slavery blotted out sky, hope and memory
Lashing the hot sand of Ogaden
. . . .
With the sea and slavery before us.
The Race. resplendent unto itself dissolves and
All biographies become One.

The final line of Chase-Riboud's poem is indicative of the conclusion of Jean-Paul Sartre's *Black Orpheus* (1948), in which universality is achieved through a dialectical melding of whiteness and Négritude. She may well have been familiar with it, given her involvement in pan-African festivals and meeting Senghor, a founder of Négritude. Like Sartre's conclusion, the poem's final lines explicate the artist's integration of African and Western components in her artworks.

Tomie Arai, Renewal, Commissioned 1995, Installed 1998

Artist Tomie Arai created a 7½ x 38-foot silkscreen entitled *Renewal* (1998) that hangs in the open lobby of the office building opposite the elevators (plate 9). *Renewal* is an effective combination of pan-African motifs and key moments in the formation of a New York City African diaspora. Arai incorporated the pan-African liberation colors of red, black, green, and gold into the print.[34]

Arai used a variety of language systems and textiles to reflect the varied heritages of so many living in New York. These are alphabetic (English and Dutch) and ideographic (concept or idea) modes of communication, as expressed by adinkra (Ghana), bogolan (Mali), and wampum (Iroquois). They point to rich and varied means for retelling histories, information, and cultural identities.[35] On either side of the right pillar, there are Iroquois nation wampum belts. The belts are a writing system formed by purple and white seashells woven together to document treaties and agreements. Arai's other communication systems illustrate African world views and history-telling. Inside of the right pillar, thin horizontal bands of Kuba textiles from central Africa separate sections that retell the institution of slavery: slave fort in Africa, slave ship, cross section of a slave ship, and escaped slave in the waves of the ocean (plate 9). The ship cross section in the middle of the right pillar is surrounded by *bogolan*, mud cloths from Mali, as if to protect its human cargo.[36] The symbols on the actual bogolan traditionally express, through visual language, songs of praise for historic heroes such as hunters, expansionists of the Malian empire, or famed resistors against colonialism. Triangular shards of Kuba and bogolan textiles along with wampum are scattered throughout *Renewal*. For instance, in plate 10, a strip of Kuba textile lies on the left side, and a shard of bogolan on the right side next to the laboring figure.

Along with graphic communication systems, the silkscreen bears the well-known alphabetic system of writing. In the left pillar, we see bricks with text that spell the names of the first eleven male Africans brought to New Amsterdam in 1626, as documented in European American archives (chapter 1, n. 1). Arai positions the early ancestors Anthony Portuguese, Simon Congo, Big Manuel, Peter Santomee (likely phonetic spelling of Sao Thome), Manuel de Gerrit de Reus, and Paulo Angola as the actual foundation of the modern Manhattan skyline rising above them.

Finally, and most famously, the left pillar of the silkscreen bears a heart-shaped adinkra from Ghana, an ideographic writing system made up of proverbs traditionally stamped onto clothing of those mourning the dead. The sankofa adinkra in particular was thought to be tacked into Burial 101's coffin lid (plate 9 and fig. 31). There is another sankofa in plate 10 underneath the tree. The proverb advises, "Look to the past to inform the future."

Arai explained to me that the sankofa operates as the basis for *Renewal*, with visualized histories mapped in layers: on top of, through, and adjacent to each other.[37] In this typically African conceptualization of cyclical time, layers of New York history, many of which are related to slavery, are displayed throughout the piece. Arai likens the temporal component in the sankofa to the process of memory; they can be both selective and anachronistic.[38] Specifically, Arai appropriated the following details from colonial prints and arranged them syncretically rather than chronologically (plate 9):

- *Freedom's Journal*, the first African American owned and operated newspaper published in the United States, beginning in 1827.
- New York African Free School founded by the Manumission Society in 1787. Its white, wealthy male members advocated full abolition and provided education for children of enslaved and freed people. Located below the sankofa.
- A.M.E. Zion Church or African Methodist Episcopal Zion. Founded in 1796, it was the oldest black church in the United States and was a stop on the Underground Railroad.
- Cover of the *Journal of the Proceedings of the Detection of the Conspiracy*. This journal presents Judge Daniel Horsmanden's account of the court case of the 1741 Conspiracy, in which the enslaved population allegedly conspired to take over New York City (detail in plate 10, see end of chapter 3).
- 1817 Manumission Certificate freeing the forty-five-year-old slave named George, who was owned by John DeLancey.
- "Am I not a Man and a Brother" design, the earliest and most identifiable image for the eighteenth-century abolitionist

movement in Britain and then in the United States. This image was circulated by a Quaker led society in 1787 and then reproduced in the Wedgewood pottery factory by Josiah Wedgewood.

- Engraving of Fraunces Tavern, which was owned by a free black and was the site of George Washington's final address at the close of the Revolutionary War.
- Seneca Village (1825–57), the black community in today's Central Park.
- Maerschalck Plan of 1755, one of the few colonial documents acknowledging the existence of the cemetery, as outlined in chapter 1 (plate 10 and fig. 7). The Federal Steering Committee's renaming of the "Negros Burial Ground" to the "African Burial Ground" powerfully conveys the politics of race and space imbued in the sacred site.

Arai has represented varying African arts from several regions of the continent to create a space of transculturality that reinforces a pan-African articulation grounded in New York City history. We have seen the bogolan, Kuba, and sankofa textiles along with wampum, all of which suggest the weaving of history.

Added to this, in the apex of the triangle, there is a Yorùbá divination tray (called *opon ifa*) in which Arai placed funerary objects excavated from the African Burial Ground (plate 10). Specifically, they are copper pins that fastened white shrouds around the deceased, coins placed on eyes of the deceased, waist beads placed around a female elder in Burial 340, light blue enamel cuff links bearing an undeciphered design, and buttons used for clothing or as funerary remains (each analyzed in chapter 3). With the suggestion of a divination taking place, the tray illustrates communication in process with the ancestors to access knowledge about their past. The tray represents a continuity of Africa in the Atlantic diaspora as well as a specific Yorùbá system to engage the ancestors of the African Burial Ground.

A detail of the 1755 Maerschalck Plan lies directly under the Yorùbá tray (plate 10). With this placement, secular cartography of the cemetery has now been rendered sacred. The map is recontextualized to celebrate rather than obfuscate a colonial and contemporary African presence, hovering directly beneath a communication in process with the ancestors.

In Nigeria and its diasporas, Ifá divination is performed by a diviner, or *babaláwo*, who sprinkles powder onto the tray, traces two perpendicular, intersecting lines as a crossroads in the powder to visually depict *ayé* (spirit world) and *òrun* (physical world), and then throws sixteen palm nuts into the tray. The inscribed cross expresses paths of life and death as well as open "channels of communication" between the worlds (also seen in *The New Ring Shout* and Gayle's painting).[39] The babaláwo then interprets the configuration of the palm nuts and correlates them to a body of oral literature called *odu*, which becomes the reading for the client.[40] As Arai illustrates, the top central section of the divination tray usually bears the carved eyes or face of Èsù. The òrìshà Èsù is acknowledged first in divination in order to prevent disorder or mischief since he is also a trickster. He communicates information from the babaláwo to the spirit world and back.[41] Èsù can also assist with decision-making processes for the client.

Arai's Ifá tray asserts a connection generally speaking of African concepts of spirituality in the diaspora while it simultaneously reminds us of specific Yorùbá roots. She uses the Ifá tray in tandem with the sankofa proverb of recalling and reclaiming the past in order to inform the future to create a transcultural means of honoring the ancestors of the African Burial Ground.

In this transcultural sense, *Renewal* concerns Asian and Asian diasporic experiences because the artist herself is third-generation Asian American. She understands diasporas and migration, as her family moved from Japan to the United States. The entire silkscreen is in the shape of a mountain based on the Chinese words *Gum Saan*, or Gold Mountain, a phrase that means America.[42] The term came into use when Chinese laborers traveled to California, beginning in the 1850s, carrying hopes and dreams of a mythic gold mountain prior to their arrival. California, which was considered the land of golden opportunity, became a land of exploitation for migrants, who were used as cheap labor in mines and on the railroads. This racist treatment of Chinese immigrants was repeated in the Caribbean and in Latin America, where the gradual abolition of African slavery led to an increasingly larger number of "coolies," or contract laborers. Between 1847 and 1874, up to 225,000 Chinese contract laborers worked the plantations of Peru and Cuba, at times alongside Africans.[43] The British increasingly replaced Africans with Asian contract laborers (primarily Indian, and secondly Chinese) from 1806 to 1884, particularly in Jamaica, Trinidad, today's Guyana, and today's Belize. In fact, it can be said that Chinese, Japanese, and East Indian immigrants contributed significantly to "economic, social, and political development of the Caribbean and Latin America."[44]

In developing *Renewal*, Arai conducted extensive interviews, particularly at OPEI, to identify significant points for commemorating the African Burial Ground. She asked herself, "How can I talk about the singular space of one people?" and at the same time, have "the awesome responsibility of representing and portraying African Americans in all their diversity."[45] Having received many responses concerning African arts and spiritual systems as well as African American history in New York, she noted to me that the mountain "is a common symbol in many cultures for a sacred site. It is spiritual."[46] Thus, her project is centered on transcultural pan-African identity, but expands to a global dimension by cleverly incorporating her own Asian American diasporic identity and then locating important ties between African, African American, Asian, and Asian American histories, which in effect become united through the narrative of slavery as recounted above. *Renewal* is multidimensional, containing spatial, metaphysical, and temporal modes of mapping such as the Maerschalck Plan, Ifá tray, sankofa, African textiles, African American history in New York City, the slave trade, and new diasporas. Arai's piece invokes specific New York histories, slavery, and African arts and cosmologies to arrive at a pan-African commemoration.

Melvin Edwards, Gate of Thanks and Appreciation, Not Built

The third artwork funded by GSA was awarded to Mel Edwards for The Gate of Thanks and Appreciation, which was not in fact finalized or installed. The twenty foot wide gate made of stainless steel with bronze images laid into it would have closed off a portion of the lobby to house an interpretive center.[47] The gate would allow the general public to visit the Interpretive Center after building hours while keeping the rest of the lobby blocked off.

Art Commissioned by Parks Department, through Percent for Art

Lorenzo Pace, Triumph of the Human Spirit
in Foley Square, Installed 2000

Triumph of the Human Spirit (2000) is an outdoor memorial separate from GSA's commissions. It was designed by Lorenzo Pace and funded by the New York City Department of Parks and Recreation (plate 11). Open to the public and located in Foley Square (Block 122, formerly Collect Pond), it lies one block northeast of the GSA property, and both are visible from each other (fig. 1). The 50-foot tall, 62-foot long, 300-plus-ton work in black granite contrasts starkly against the neoclassical government buildings that surround it. Standing amid the Supreme Courthouse (as depicted in Gayle's painting, fig. 41), the County Courthouse, the Sanitation Department, and the Jacob Javits Convention Center, *Triumph of the Human Spirit* is literally imbricated in the scape of the body politic. The public walks around it, eats lunch on its benches, poses for tourist photos, and reads the explanatory text on the monument. Aesthetically and conceptually, the piece becomes a pan-African interruption within the Civic Center.

Pace's $750,000 piece was part of an $18 million urban renovation project headed by the city's parks and recreation department.[48] The monument was funded through Percent for Art, both a law and a program initiated by Mayor Edward Koch in 1983. One percent of the city's budget in construction projects funds site specific public art.

It was only as a result of African American activists and Peggy King Jorde that the final design ultimately incorporated the local history of Foley Square through the centuries. The Department of Parks and Recreation initially considered a centralized globe with tents and marquees spread throughout the public space. In reaction, an external committee formed, and it was decided that a call for designs would be issued, with strong leadership from Peggy King Jorde.[49] As a result, through community activism and public concern, multivalent histories impacting what is today Foley Square have been remembered and visualized.

In the final built design, architect R. G. Roesch laid five large bronze medallions, designed by Rebecca Darr of the parks department, into the ground throughout the park, which are connected by a network of paths. Historical events from Foley Square are depicted in each of the inlaid bronze circles (table 5).

In 1992, the city's parks department and its Office of Cultural Affairs issued a call to design a monument for the center of the square. Lorenzo Pace was selected from a pool of over four hundred applicants.[50] Pace initially designed a horizontal line of workers in front of a government office building to illustrate the labor involved in building New York.[51] The committee pushed for a closer tie to the historical significance of the area with particular interest in the African Burial Ground. This time, Pace submitted a design in 1994 for a black granite sculpture based on the antelope Ciwara headdress of Mali rising out of a boat that represents diasporic communities. Ground was broken on 16 October 1997, and the entire urban project was completed 19 May 2000, taking eight years to finish. The sculpture was assembled on site in fifteen 22-ton pieces.

The work is an abstracted Ciwara antelope headdress from Mali (plate 11). In Africa, Ciwara, or farming wild animal, taught humans to farm (fig. 50). It has been venerated in varying ways through time and in different areas of Mali. An initiation society honors Ciwara,

Table 5

Five Medallions Laid into Foley Square around Lorenzo Pace Sculpture

Medallion	Dates	Historical Event
1	Before 1600	Lenape and Munsee Native Americans with three totem animals, the turtle, wolf, and turkey.
2	1712–1794	The African Burial Ground with skeletons from Burial 336 and 354 of a mother and baby, along with the African Free School, Maya Angelou's "Still I Rise," and adinkra symbols of Ghana.
3	1700–1800	The Dutch presence and Dutch West India Company, Powder House for the city's gun powder, gallows built in 1742 during the so called Negro Plot Conspiracy to hang eighteen blacks and three whites, and Bridewell city prison for American revolutionaries during British occupation.
4	1800–1900	A shot tower for making lead cannon balls, the site of Collect Pond, which was leveled and filled in, and the dangerous Five Points neighborhood that housed new immigrants.
5	1900–2000	Construction of the subway or Interborough Rapid Transit, building the Civic Center, unearthing the African Burial Ground, the reconstruction of Foley Square described above, and Lorenzo Pace's monument.

Source: From Rebecca Darr and R. G. Roesch, "Schematic of Medallions" (photocopy, New York City Department of Parks and Recreation, 7 Oct. 1996).

requests blessings for fertile earth and successful harvests, and asks for protection against snake bites in the fields. The champion farmer and heroic dancer are given emphasis in performances.[52] Masqueraders may dance wearing male and female headdresses to parallel fertility, planting, and harvesting. The male headdress is carved with an intricate serrated mane, while the female is recognizable by the baby antelope she carries on her back (fig. 50). It is this female version that was the inspiration for Lorenzo Pace upon visiting the Metropolitan Museum of Art.[53]

Lorenzo Pace recognizes in his monument the importance of nurturing and solidarity that are necessary for survival.[54] He understands the male and female Ciwara as integral to reproduction and survival, and he considers the baby on the female Ciwara's back the link to fertility necessary for farming. Pace uses the notion of fertility, as seen by the mother and baby, to signify rebirth. Farming the earth sustains humanity just as a mother cares for her offspring; "as nurturers of the young, they have great responsibility for ensuring the continuation of the next generation."[55]

The piece can be understood as pan-African in a variety of ways. Based on his research as well as consultation with African art historian Barbara Frank, Pace invokes cultural specificity of Ciwara. In addition, he uses the notion of fertility, as exemplified by the mother and baby along with a successful harvest by farmers, to parallel the endurance, survival, and rebirth of those in the diasporas.[56] Pace also views the Ciwara as an iconic symbol representing Africa by reiterating that it is "a recognizable and respectable image in the diaspora and so it is pan-African."[57] The piece can be considered a reclamation of African identity and a generic embodiment of Africa or the motherland, literally depicted here as a mother.

As well as the Ciwara, the sculpture concerns slavery so that the commemoration brings together African art with African American history. In this piece, the boat refers to enslaved people who were transported to New York City and to immigrants in general: "part of our history is devastating but we have to realize that we're [almost] all

Figure 50. Unknown artist, Ciwara headdress (female), nineteenth to early twentieth century. Wood, metal bands, 28 × 12⅛ × 2⅛ in. A female Ciwara in the Metropolitan Museum of Art made in Mali inspired Pace's sculpture *Triumph of the Human Spirit*. Courtesy of The Metropolitan Museum of Art, The Michael C. Rockefeller Memorial Collection, Gift of Nelson A. Rockefeller, 1964. (1978.412.436).

immigrants, and we need to celebrate our diversity, and our struggle, and use it as a stepping stone to carry on in the name of our ancestors."[58] As in *The New Ring Shout*, water is clearly the means by which people, cultures, histories, cosmologies, memories, and ideas have traveled to form diasporas in New York City (plate 11).

Pace adds his personal history of slavery, which is a singular component within the formation of a New York City diaspora. As explained in the engraved text of the granite monument, he buried beneath it a replica of a lock that shackled his enslaved great-great-grandfather. The lock has been passed down through generations of the Pace family, so that Lorenzo is now the keeper of the lock, which is 150 years old. Before the foundation of the *Triumph* monument was laid, the replica was buried during a ceremony in which the earth was spiritually cleansed by Dòwòti Désir.

Since Pace invoked a specific African spirituality to honor the dead, we can explore and understand the commemorative artwork through an indigenous Malian world view. There are two concepts crucial to Mande (the West African linguistic group that includes Bamana) aesthetics known as *badenya* and *fadenya* through which Ciwara can be understood.[59] The Mande conception of badenya, which stands for solidarity, support of others, unity, and farming for the community, functions very similarly to Lorenzo Pace's intentions in *Triumph of the Human Spirit*. Badenya is a concept that refers to society, convention, harmony, and order. It promotes cooperation and compliance with authority and is important for maintaining stability and group order in society.

The counterpart of badenya is fadenya, which also exists in Ciwara and in Pace's monument. Among Mande people, fadenya concerns heroism and the drive to attain recognition and renown by surpassing the accomplishments and ambition of one's parent and ultimately one's ancestors. Fadenya can cause disequilibrium, jealousy, rivalry, aggrandizement, individuality, and competition for power in an attempt to break away from conformity. In Ciwara, fadenya exists through competitive dancing and farming—the desire to achieve the status of a heroic performer and physically strong farmer. For instance, an excerpt from a praise song is as follows:

Hey Chi Wara
Champion farmer come farm here
   Sung by one singer
The field has become a competition
Come farm here before us all[60]

Fadenya and badenya are held in tension with each other but also operate as complementary qualities that balance the universe—both are needed to maintain equilibrium.

There is certainly a component of fadenya to *Triumph of the Human Spirit*. The monument stands out in Foley Square against a slew of neoclassical buildings that include the Supreme Courthouse, New York City Hall, Tweed Courthouse, U.S. Courthouse, U.S. Appeals Court, and U.S. District Court. Pace realizes the difficulty in competing with Greek/Roman architecture, and decided to show, "You got your thing, I got mine."[61] So now, a monument to Africa, slavery, Ciwara, and African diasporas lies in the center of New York City's government district.

Unveiling the Sculpture

Pace resisted governmental authority in the vein of fadenya. After the piece had been assembled and installed in Foley Square, it was wrapped in a green tarp for at least six months until an official unveiling ceremony and city dedication could be held. The press, who had been instrumental in pressing politics related to the African Burial Ground previously, raised the question here. *New York Post* journalist Maria Alvarez wrote a piece asking why the memorial remained wrapped in a green tarp, and questioning why she had been shuffled from Mayor Giuliani's office to Senator Moynihan's office to the parks department with still no answer.[62] The unveiling of the sculpture was arranged between government officials Mayor

Giuliani and Senator Moynihan for 12 October 2000, which was Columbus Day. For Pace, the holiday marked the beginning "of persecution for American Indians and slavery" and would be inappropriate for the dedication of a piece celebrating those same people.[63] Pace commented in a *New York Times* article, "I don't want to pull out the race card, but I'm a realist. Let's get to the real deal here: this should be a day for healing. We've all got our scars. Racism is a cancer that's eaten away at our society, let's face it. We've got to stop the madness. Maybe it won't happen in my lifetime, but I'd like to see it start happening here."[64]

In response, Moynihan's chief of staff Tony Bullock answered, "I think this fellow needs to be a little more reasonable. To equate Christopher Columbus with slavery is being ridiculous."[65] Department of Parks and Recreation Commissioner Henry Stern added, "I think it's political correctness run amok. It is an attempt to delegitimize traditional American institutions similar to the war on Thanksgiving."[66] As was the case previously with politics concerning the African Burial Ground, government officials reacted differently to issues concerning race in relation to national identity. With holidays at stake that are so integral to defining and mythologizing the national identity of the United States, Eurocentrically minded politicians could not afford subversion. Other New York City officials found politics surrounding the African Burial Ground to be a fitting means to challenge such historically racist notions. To this end, city council member Kathryn Freed and Manhattan Borough President Virginia Fields requested a change of date for the city dedication. Amazingly, Moynihan was unable to attend the originally planned 12 October ceremony. Pace also did not attend. He boycotted his own event, and then, along with GSA's OPEI office, organized a separate dedication a few days later for 19 October. The day included poetry reading by Amiri Baraka, including, "Why Is We Americans." In attendance were Senator David Paterson, Councilpeople Bill Perkins and Wendell Foster, and Reverends Herbert Daughtry, and Calvin Butts. Pace fought politics of space and memory in order to control his own memory-making in the present.

The pan-African articulation in *Triumph of the Human Spirit* includes specific contexts; namely, a Bamana worldview in conjunction with slavery and the New York African diaspora. On top of this, I asked Pace about the notion of spirituality, and he spoke about it in terms of a generalized Africa, affirming that it is "very basic for African people. It is the African way of thinking and I can't do anything without bringing that in. Ancestors are very important."[67] For the final design, Pace attested, "And to be honest with you, I think the ancestors took my hand and did this: boom, boom, boom. I was led."[68] Thus, the artwork reclaims a general Africa through the specificity of Ciwara in order to honor ancestors of the African Burial Ground while also paying homage to all descendants of enslaved Africans living in its diaspora. Pace says, "We need to celebrate our diversity, and our struggle, and use it as a stepping stone to carry on in the name of our ancestors."[69]

Because Pace's monument was commissioned by a government agency and occupies the heart of the Civic Center, *Triumph of the Human Spirit* becomes a construction of national memory with global ramifications. The $18 million project entailed the implementation of a new subway entrance so that as people ascend the stairs and exit the station in Foley Square, they directly face Pace's monument. Unlike 290 Broadway, Foley Square invites engagement and, even in his design, Pace envisioned the area being used and occupied by people.[70] The public sits on the granite wall surrounding the sculpture fountain or on World's Fair benches under shade trees.

The project eventually came to fruition, but only after struggles for commemoration, selection of the design, and installation of the artwork. Today, it seems almost seamlessly enveloped into the body politic. Tourists regularly walk up to the fountain or rest on its wall to read their guidebooks, the Grayline bus tour circles around Foley Square, the *Law and Order* and *Blue Bloods* television shows have been regularly filmed here, and an "Occupy Wall Street" protest with thousands of people took place here in November 2011.

Exterior Memorial, Organized by NPS

The exterior memorial was the final piece to officially honor the cemetery. The memorial lies behind the office building on the former pavilion site along Duane Street where two hundred burials remain in situ. Details of the selection, design, construction, and management process of the memorial illustrate some cohesion as well as competing voices, contested terrain, and counternarratives that occurred through the years. As such, the outdoor monument does not reflect a coherent collective identity. Ultimately, the chronology of the events summarized below illustrates struggles in the production of memory and spirituality of space at the African Burial Ground. Through those struggles, many of which were political, the final monument has been embraced nationally and opened to the public locally.

The Exterior Memorial Design Competition

The competition for the exterior memorial took over a decade to be realized and was among the most delayed in the whole African Burial Ground project, caught in GSA politics, lack of leadership, and conflict with community activists. Initially, GSA planned for an exterior memorial competition and an interpretive center competition, as stipulated in the amended 1991 Memorandum of Agreement. Also, the community-based Federal Steering Committee submitted specific recommendations to Congress and GSA in 1993 for the two projects. (The exterior memorial, finalized in 2007, is considered in this chapter, and the interpretive center is discussed in chapter 4.)

The exterior memorial was organized as a competition by GSA; it began in 1997 and reached the beginning of phase 2, then stalled around 1998 with no short list or final winner declared. A public forum and preproposal conference were held early on 4 February 1998, during which potential competitors could ask questions and network prior to assembling a design/build proposal (this means that the winning team, with funding, was entirely responsible for designing, engineering, and building the project). Community members' comments at the roundtable were telling in terms of their frustration over a sense of exclusivity about who had access to participation in the production of memory for the memorial. The forms, maps, blueprints, documents, and instructions for the design/build guidelines were difficult to understand unless one was trained or experienced. To this end, attendees at the preproposal conference wondered aloud how the memorial would function collectively and successfully in honoring the dead:

> I'm an architect here in New York . . . I can't help but feel that the ball's been missed with this project so far in that the purpose of the project I think is to honor the people that were buried there and all the people from African descent around the world, not just America. But somehow from all this paperwork, what's really missing is the spirit of creativity to do that . . . I really don't know that in the end we'll be able to get a monument that's really going to serve its purpose that well . . . Somehow all of this paperwork is making that very hard. I think there are a lot of people who have great ideas who will not meet the criteria for either the design part of it or the construction part of it. And in that sense, I think a disservice has been done to the actual community that it's focusing on. . . . [applause].[71]

> I'm a historical researcher and planner. I was involved in the early parts of this African Burial Ground Review Committee that was established after a great deal of activism on the part of the community. I'm very concerned, having read through all of this, having spent seven years in the Corps of Engineers . . . there's a lot that needs to be said . . . I think that if, especially if a minority community is able to apply itself to this process, it needs to do it by having a fair shot at reading very specific instructions and not in a sense be over-advantaged by folks who have years and years of experience dealing with GSA . . . [applause].[72]

> I am a graphic designer, sculptor . . . I found this document [130 page Call for Proposals] to be rather intimidating for someone who

has not had the kind of experience that architects or other designers in here have had. Commissions do not come easily, and specifically with reference to minorities . . . But you have all this stuff
in there dealing with soil. And it talks about using architects and
contractors and what have you. And I'm sure a lot of artists didn't
show up for that reason. Because frankly, most minorities that are
artists have not had this experience. And it's like the usual here's
the government slamming the door in creative people's faces. It's
just not right.[73]

The Project Executive of Memorialization, Peggy King Jorde,
responded to these issues laid on the table by acknowledging that
memory is infrequently produced by a nonhegemonic entity. "It is
not very often that the African-American community or the African
community has an opportunity to look at or discuss how it is that
we speak to our story in the built environment. And there are not
very many people who know how to do that."[74] The implications
of these conversations were that the exterior memorial and its collective identity would seemingly be produced by those educated in
navigating GSA's system of production. How could others be a part
of the memorialization process? This would be the most transparent
dialogue surrounding the exterior competition up to this point.

Later in 1998, a short list of finalists was recommended to GSA
by an advisory panel made up of architects, artists, and public art
specialists.[75] The short list was not released to the public. No development of the proposals occurred, and no winner was decided upon.
From that time onward the project seems to have virtually come to a
stop for reasons that are unclear, though GSA was certainly caught
in a vicious cycle. In May 1998, GSA discontinued funding the African Burial Ground project. At the beginning of 2000, with monies
depleted, scientific research was shut down and funding cut entirely,
as described in chapter 4.

Perhaps because of a change in administration in the federal
branch of GSA in Washington, DC, the competition resurfaced when
five short-listed finalists for phase 2 were quite suddenly announced

publicly in February 2003. It seems that a concentrated effort was made beginning in 2003 to complete the exterior memorial, which coincided with Stephen Perry's appointment as GSA administrator.

In September 2003, GSA entered into an interagency agreement with the National Park Service (NPS) under the U.S. Department of the Interior, which would then take over managing the interpretive center and exterior memorial competitions.[76] As the presence of NPS grew, and its staff introduced themselves each time at a community event, the public realized that the new NPS management had been put into place by GSA without any civic knowledge. Once again, people were upset that an aspect of memorialization had occurred seemingly in secret by an entity of the federal government without input from descendants of those buried in the cemetery directly related to African American history and identity. An example of this frustration played out at a community meeting I attended that was held by the National Park Service in February 2004. Ayo Harrington had founded a group called Friends of the African Burial Ground in the fall of 1998 due to a growing concern about the status of the project. She now explained to NPS, "So we don't want you to come in here again, another group, not you know, we don't want another group coming in here, you know, telling us where we should start and what we should do and what you want to hear. We want to tell you the way it should be. That's what we want. This is the only kind of relationship that we can have with the NPS that is going to be positive."[77]

Activist and elder Mother Franklin stressed the importance of what was at stake: "But learn your history, your history. Nobody can learn your history for you. You got to learn your own history, and when you know it, you know it yourself."[78] This comment was made in reference to the presumed understanding that NPS could swoop in at the end of nearly a decade of activism and resistance, claiming leadership and therefore, necessarily, knowledge of the project, which there was no way that they could possess at this point in the memorial process. Again, questions of narrativizing memory were at stake: would GSA, NPS, or African American activists be the primary voices in shaping memory and history at the site? These instances of contention emphasized the multiplicity of voices expressed during the exterior memorial process with no collective identity being constituted.

As progress commenced again toward memorialization, but this time under the National Park Service, the agency made a concerted effort to include the public because concerned citizens had been excluded by GSA in the past, resulting in contentiousness that had lasted years. NPS was therefore particularly sensitive to inclusivity, and they held successive events related to the design of the memorial. A public workshop was held in May 2004 at Medgar Evers College and the Schomburg Center to gather public input. The five finalists presented their initial designs, and then their redeveloped designs, during a series of public forums held throughout the five boroughs in June and September 2004.

At each of these events, response forms were handed out to the public for feedback. Many of the comments called for or praised pan-African representations in the memorials. One person noted about a design, "It incorporates the flavor, accents, and feeling of African heritage."[79] Comments on another short-listed design: "It has a feeling of a village in Africa"; "Add more African symbolism . . . let benches look like African drums"; and, "it shows the designs of our African Ancestors." One of the team finalists included pyramids, which garnered the following responses: "Pyramid effect. Reminds me of the motherland"; and "The design has the closest, out of all, [a] look to our home 'Africa,' which would be a respective [respectful] look for it." Only two responders questioned the pyramid motif meant to function as a pan-African symbol, stating, "Get rid of the pyramid, it's a cliché that has little, if anything to do with 20,000 West Africans buried there," and "Too Egyptian. Not reflective of my feeling of the Diaspora." Except for the second to last one, these comments from across the five boroughs express an Afrocentric discourse that recuperates a generalized Africa to represent the African Burial Ground.

Next, NPS produced recommendations to the community for how they would manage the memorial and interpretive center. To do so, they wrote the *Draft Management Recommendations for the African Burial Ground* in 2005 that was mailed out to involved community members. It listed four management alternatives, which the public commented upon through a handout or on a website. The result was that NPS would take over from GSA in managing and operating the memorial and the visitor center, now housed inside the lobby of the 290 Broadway building (formerly OPEI and the interpretive center). NPS assumed responsibility on 1 November 2006.

Rodney Léon, Ancestral Libation Chamber, 2007

In April 2005, Rodney Léon, a Haitian American architect with AARRIS Architects, was declared the winner of the five short-listed proposals and was awarded the commission for the exterior memorial, which he entitled *Ancestral Libation Chamber* (plate 12). The memorial's symbols and overall design embodied Africa spatially and metaphysically through a large geopolitical map on the floor and a variety of religious symbols on the wall.

A ceremonial groundbreaking was held on 28 September 2005. At the outdoor ceremony that involved government officials, Peggy King Jorde, school children, and GSA administrator Steven Perry acknowledged to some extent the now-eight-year delay: "It indeed has been a long way, but we have finally come to the day when real progress [is evident]."[80] He understood that the memorial would "not only be an inspiration to people in New York, it will be an inspiration to people throughout this country and indeed throughout the world." With a dedication ceremony, the monument opened on 5 October 2007.

The 250-foot monument combines slavery with many global cosmologies (plate 12). The enclosed triangle that comprises the right half of the monument is inscribed with a heart-shaped Ghanaian sankofa, the ideographic symbol that has remained central to the African Burial Ground. It visually recounts the proverb, "Look to the past to inform the future." Next to this, a libation text written by Léon reads:

> For all those who were lost
> For all those who were stolen
> For all those who were left behind
> For all those who were not forgotten

The Akan sankofa becomes pan-African as it refers simultaneously to Africa in a generalized way (rather than to Ghana specifically), to the African Burial Ground, and finally to slavery as explicated by the text alongside it. The memorial's entrance to the far right of the sankofa mimics the Door of No Return, the door to the ocean known by that name in slave forts in Africa. It was the last point of exit before boarding slave ships. This collective enslaved experience links together ancestors of those in the diasporas.

As an alternative to this door, one can enter the memorial by following an outer Spiral Processional Ramp that gradually descends into the lower court recessed below ground (plate 12). It is an integrated space that, as Léon explained to me in an interview, "commemorates diversity of diasporic culture, tying all together who were dispersed."[81] The black wall, called the Circle of the Diaspora, depicts symbols of African and diasporic cosmologies. The piece illustrates transcultural and transspiritual flows, with Africa mapped as the point of origin.

As one walks the spiral to descend below ground along the Circle of the Diaspora, symbols encountered at the halfway point are of particular relevance. Not pictured here, three symbols create a tripartite configuration with, first, the Haitian vèvè for Baron (a ground drawing done in white chalk to call a *lwa*, or deity, to that earthly point); second the Kongo cosmogram; and third, the Haitian vèvè for Manman Brigitte of Haiti. Baron and Manman Brigitte are married lwa who guard the cemetery. In his physical manifestation, Baron typically dresses as an undertaker in a black top hat and dress coat and wears sunglasses because his eyes are sensitive to light since he is underground among the tombs.[82] The Kongolese cosmogram between these lwa outlines a guiding principle of the monument— that a boundary exists between the land of the living and the land of the dead. This fluid boundary is transgressed as we walk the descending spiral into the cemetery. Because Africans from the Kongo were brought not only to New York but also to Haiti, Kongolese spiritual systems are an integral component of Vodoun in Haiti, particularly the *petwo*, or Haitian Kongo side, of Vodoun. Interestingly, both *The Ancestral Libation Chamber* and *The New Ring Shout* invoke spirals as incarnations of the Kongo cosmogram, thus enacting an intentional dialogue between the two artworks.

Symbols in the last third of the descent to the bottom of the memorial relate to God and nature in a spiritual sense. The Tanit, Latin Cross, and Medicine Wheel in plate 12 concern Islam, Christianity, and Native Americans, all encountered by Africans in Africa and the New World. Following the Medicine Wheel in plate 12, the Egyptian Ankh is a hieroglyph meaning life. Next, there are three adinkra (ideographic symbols traditionally worn on funerary clothes in Ghana): Hye Won Hye (imperishability and endurance), Asase Ye Duru (divinity of Mother Earth), and Nsoromma (guardianship).

The third symbol from the end in plate 12 is a chalk drawing of Nkisi Sarabanda from Cuba. The drawing, or *firma* (as it is known in Cuba), is made at the point that an nkisi should be placed, and is the specific signature of an invoked spirit. Some of the deceased in the Burial Ground were probably buried with minkisi. Here, the Cuban firma drawing contains the Kongo cosmogram within it, and therefore stands as a powerful example of its Kongolese extension in the New World. The second-to-last symbol at the end of the ramp is the Akan adinkra Gye Nyame, or Supremacy of God.

The last symbol as one enters the lowest court of the memorial is a vèvè or Haitian chalk drawing to invoke Legba, the lwa of the crossroads (plate 12). Legba takes on a pan-African identity: he is known as Èsù or Esu-Elégba in Nigeria (as represented by Arai in plate 10), Echú or Eleguá in Cuba, Exu in Brazil, and Legba among

Fon people in Benin. He is the mediator, communicator, and trick-ster, opening or blocking pathways of life. The detail is not visible in the photograph, but Legba's vèvè at the end of the memorial wall consists of a major crossroads (horizontal and vertical line perpen-dicular to each other: +) with two small Kongo cosmograms at the end of the vertical axis, a small crossroads in the center, and a cane over the right hand axis, with which the elderly Legba can often be seen walking. Because of the slave trade, the deity is a geospiritual and therefore pandiasporic entity, present in several cultures and geographic spaces, including New York City.

As the keeper of the crossroads between the physical and spirit worlds, Legba is the one who "opens the gate," providing or deny-ing permission to speak with or enter the spirit world.[83] Léon placed Legba at the final point of transition before reaching the greatest depth of the memorial and the closest point to the African Burial Ground ancestors.[84] Rather than a memorial stretching to the sky, this is recessed into the ground to create a metaphorical and metaphysical meeting with the ancestors. Léon explained to me in an interview that at the bottom of the court, a visitor is "isolated physically and psychologically from the street level," allowing one to "think about the ancestors and their contributions without distrac-tion."[85] As one turns around to ascend the spiral to reenter the land of the living, Legba is the first in walking the gateway as one begins to exit the memorial.

The floor of the memorial is covered with a world map, with Africa in the middle, and the coast of West Africa at its very center (upside down in plate 12). This reinscription of a Eurocentric map-ping decenters Europe by reclaiming Africa. The map visually unites the disseminated African world on a global level with transatlantic and trans-Indian diasporic routes demarcated by radial lines that emanate from the center, or West Africa, to North, South, and Cen-tral America, Europe, India, and the Caribbean.

Léon uses more than one system of mapping in his memorial. First, the conventional Western system of cartography illustrates geo-political relationships between Africa and its diasporas. Second, the memorial is situated on an easterly axis of the eighteenth-century ancestral world, in the direction that New York Africans were buried rather than the grid system of urban downtown New York surrounding it.[86] Within the memorial, the three-dimensional spiral, akin to the Kongo cosmogram, performs a transition back and forth between the living and the afterlife. Descent and ascent, or the directions "down" and "up" (as opposed to east or west), become the spatial means for mapping this confluence of physical and metaphysical worlds. Finally, the symbols surrounding the spiral ramp create a transspiritual space. This transspirituality becomes a complex linking of multiple cosmological systems through and beyond Africa into diasporas.

Through these various kinds of mapping, the memorial casts Africa and the African Burial Ground in a positive light, privileging complex systems of writing and language that counter Enlightenment notions of an uncivilized Africa. Léon endeavored to consciously break a system of education that located Africa and its diasporas as pessimistic, and instead designed an interactive piece that would invoke curiosity and respect for the ancestors and spiritualities.[87] Ultimately, Léon sees the memorial as initiating education: "No longer should one be able to walk past this site or throughout Lower Manhattan and not be provided the opportunity to know, understand, acknowledge, and respect the important contributions that ancestral Africans have made to this district. Our generation has been entrusted with this awesome responsibility, and we're honored . . . We embrace it for our children and for all future generations so that they may come to know, understand, acknowledge, respect, and be proud of their history."[88]

As can be seen, the memorial resonates with a clear narrative celebrating African and African descendant identity and spirituality that was in line with much of the activist discourse. Nonetheless, several citizens rejected the memorial project itself. This is because European American involvement in the project elicited anger, on the one hand, as well as a fundamental resistance to the presence of an American government at the sacred site on the other. The memorial has been contested by some because the earth beneath it is contaminated; first when this area of Manhattan was leveled at the beginning of the nineteenth century and the colonial cemetery was covered under 25 feet of fill, and then again at the end of the twentieth century when the remains were excavated in order to build the office building. At a prayer vigil following an OPEI open house held on 22 May 1999, Miss Eloise Dicks expressed, "This is not sacred ground. It has been disturbed and contaminated because earth was moved here and dug into by Europeans." Another key activist named Adunni Oshupa Tabasi explained that she had no interest in reclaiming the office building built on the cemetery, but would rather it be "leveled to the ground."[89] And some have resisted the basic notion of a memorial on the land, preferring it be left undisturbed as a sacred space. One anonymous public comment collected by NPS on the five final designs explained, "Nothing should be constructed here. There has been enough desecration! Shame!"; another said, "No. This disturbs the ground. Too much digging!" Betty Dobson, co-chair of the Committee to Eliminate Media Offensive to African People (CEMOTAP) also explained, "A lot of people feel that this monument is a very nice piece of work: it's upscale, it's modern. Well, I'm not a judge of architecture, but I just don't think this memorial should be placed on top of a cemetery."[90]

Government involvement has been seen as a counternarrative to the production of narrative and memory at the African Burial Ground. Initially, GSA approached the project insensitively so that from the outset, a disconnect existed between a branch of the government and descendant African Americans. Philosopher David Theo Goldberg has argued that the state typically denies the existence of race, using homogeneity in an attempt to "trump the perceived threat of heterogeneous states of being."[91] Grassroots intervention, however, insisted that the first two designs at the site of Foley Square be changed, that a second round of commissions be made for the lobby of 290 Broadway, that an exterior memorial be constructed onsite, and that African Americans be involved as stipulated by Section 106. The African-based discourse so crucial to commemorating and reclaiming the African Burial Ground was therefore articulated in government-sponsored artworks with community input while activists were in direct conflict with the government and GSA. Thus, the monument presents an interesting paradox in that it espouses pan-African ideals, but does so through governmental processes.

The *Ancestral Libation Chamber* stands as the first national monument permanently dedicated to people of African descent. The dedication of the monument entailed a proclamation by President George W. Bush and keynote remarks by Secretary of the Interior Gale Norton, at the very least suggesting federal acceptance of the African Burial Ground. This proclamation was made because, in order for the management decision to go into effect allowing the National Park Service to take over the memorial from GSA, it must officially be designated a national monument, and this designation could only be accomplished by the president of the United States.[92] The decision was endorsed by Mayor Michael Bloomberg, which he expressed in a letter sent to President Bush.[93] Accordingly, George W. Bush made the proclamation on 27 February 2006 for the Establishment of the African Burial Ground National Monument. The next day, GSA and NPS officials as well as former Mayor David Dinkins, Congressperson Jerry Nadler, and Howard Dodson listened to Gale Norton give keynote remarks clearly situating the burial ground within the body politic and within national identity:

> The President's proclamation that the African Burial Ground will be set apart and preserved as a National Monument of the United States ensures that as a nation we will not forget the mothers and daughters, fathers and sons buried here.
>
> As a nation we will not allow a steel and glass tower to cover holy ground.
>
> As a nation we give to persons of African descent a place of reconnection with their beginnings, ancestry, culture and heritage.
>
> As a nation we ask young people to learn the lessons taught here.
>
> As a nation we give to future generations the responsibility to forever preserve the sacred ground.[94]

Instead of shunning African and African American identity as part of New York's civic identity, government officials had reached a point where they officially embraced and accepted the African Burial Ground.

Finally, the memorial opened on 5 October 2007 with a formal dedication after a decade long process at a total cost of $5 million.[95] The weekend dedication event organized by the National Park Service serves as a case in point for incorporating the burial ground into American identity. To welcome the African Burial Ground National Monument as the newest addition to the National Parks of the New York Harbor, a torch carrying a flame traveled from the Statue of Liberty (also managed by NPS) to the shore of Manhattan. Then, a candlelight procession began at Battery Park and traveled into Foley Square led by 419 drummers (one for each of the deceased). Performances were held all of the next day, including one by Maya Angelou with Mayor Michael Bloomberg and Senator Chuck Schumer in attendance.

While the final monument itself may appear to depict a seamless collective memory, the many narratives surrounding it speak to politics of the state, power, capital, and civilians. Can the varying predominantly pan-African narratives at the African Burial Ground be incorporated into daily life of downtown lower Manhattan? Their appropriation in part by government agencies suggests so. Through the commemorative process, the burial ground and Rodney Léon's memorial become a part of the body politic, if tenuously. The works are inevitably and necessarily interconnected to this body politic through intricate relationships of history and power.

I close with an example in which a competing narrative was partially resolved and differences were bridged. One day in 2007, I walked into the African Burial Ground Visitor Center now overseen by NPS, which occupies a section inside the office building at 290 Broadway. The greeter at the desk was none other than Adunni Tabasi, a staunch resistor to the construction of the building and to GSA. I jokingly said, "Why are you in here?" She smiled and answered, "I had to come inside to fight." She made the decision to bring her narrative into GSA's office building and an NPS office in order to continue her important participation in the creation of memory at the African Burial Ground.

The narrativizing of memory is far from static. During all of the open hours of the monument, which are Monday to Sunday from 9:00 a.m. to 5:00 p.m., an NPS ranger remains on site, giving well-informed tours to school children and answering questions for visitors. Rather than the former fixed text on a sign behind a fence, as depicted in figure 45, visitors now interact with different rangers each time they visit. These public hours are a vast improvement over the locked fence through which no one could enter for a decade prior to the existence of the exterior memorial unless a special occasion was organized. Moreover, there is no fence at all now. A simple low wall surrounds the perimeter of the space to guide visitors to the entrance rather than prohibit "trespassers" as before. The fact that a fence does not deny entry onto sacred space is one of the most important features of the memorial.

How is the space engaged spiritually? With the memorial in place, I find that there are no more impromptu offerings left at the site. The memorial's original design invited visitors to pour libations into the center of the deeply recessed map, but this was quickly aborted as physical objects were being placed into the cavity, as well as damaging liquids such as oils.[96] The absence of this feature, which is articulated in the very name of the *Ancestral Libation Chamber* itself, points to politics of memorialization in relation to spirituality of space. The space has become an official means of honoring the dead and provides less of an impromptu, personal connection with the ancestors. In attempting to represent a collective identity, a kind of exclusive performance of spirituality emerges. In *Commemorations: The Politics of National Identity*, John Gillis writes, "Commemorative activity is by definition social and political, for it involved the coordination of individual and group memories, whose results may appear consensual when they are in fact the product of processes of intense contest, struggle, and, in some instances, annihilation."[97]

As Gillis describes, all of the commemorative artworks and the memorial came into existence through contemporary politics, tensions, and controversies over race, space, national identity, and power in an extreme effort to honor the dead. Such issues over politics of space stretch back even to the colonial era. The site was enveloped in layers of land disputes before the twentieth century, reaching all the way back to 1661 when the Janeway Land was deeded to two different people and in 1673 when the Van Borsum Patent belonging to the City was awarded concurrently to Sara Roeloff. Despite this detailed knowledge concerning European American ownership of the land, we know little about the cemetery. There are two images that depict the land only prior to and after its use as the African Burial Ground, and four civic maps label the eighteenth-century cemetery. In terms of who is buried out of the estimated fifteen thousand deceased, we know the initials of one individual, H. W., tacked onto the coffin lid of Burial 332.

How was the African Burial Ground recuperated, reclaimed, and represented? In light of missing memories, I argue that the dozen or so art projects and personal offerings are a means for constituting an invention of memory at the African Burial Ground in the late twentieth and twenty-first centuries. Africa itself becomes a means for recalling the African Burial Ground through assorted arts and cosmologies. The implications of these varied means of representation are that the African Burial Ground is not commemorated so much through specific content from the cemetery. Rather, a general pan-African framing in the artworks commemorates the site.

Managed by GSA and NPS with community input, the arts, along with grassroots activism, begin to subvert a secular office building in recuperating the sanctified space of the dead. The commemorative works interrupt mainstream hegemonic American histories by giving voice to once-lost ancestors. Through complex relationships of space, spirituality, and memory, the African Burial Ground is and continues to become a part of the body politic, a part of the everyday landscape of lower Manhattan.

Appendix

Chronology
of Contemporary
Political Events

Notes

Bibliography

Index

African Burial
Ground Final Reports

In this volume, citations from the African Burial Ground final reports derive from the 2006 and 2004 versions that were formerly posted on the GSA website at http://www.africanburialground.gov. The reports are no longer available at that URL. The final reports were reformatted with a new copyright date of 2009 and are now located at http://www.gsa.gov /portal/content/249941. Page numbers cited in this book correspond to the earlier edition, which I accessed, rather than those in the currently posted 2009 versions. Below is a list of the chapters from each of the final reports cited in this book, presented here to facilitate a correspondence between my citations and the current internet posting.

New York African Burial Ground Archaeology Final Report, edited by Warren R. Perry, Jean Howson, and Barbara A. Bianco. Washington, DC: General Services Administration and Howard Univ., 2006

Volume 1

Chapter 2. "Documentary Evidence on the Origin and Use of the African Burial Ground," by Jean Howson, Barbara A. Bianco, and Steven Barto
Chapter 3. "The Archaeological Site," by Jean Howson and Leonard G. Bianchi
Chapter 4. "Relative Dating," by Jean Howson, Warren R. Perry, Augustin F. C. Holl, and Leonard G. Bianchi
Chapter 5. "Overview of Mortuary Population, Burial Practices, and Spatial Distribution," by Warren R. Perry and Jean Howson

Chapter 6. "The Early Group," by Warren R. Perry, Jean Howson, and Augustin F. C. Holl

Chapter 7. "The Middle Group," by Warren R. Perry, Jean Howson, and Augustin F. C. Holl

Chapter 8. "The Late-Middle Group," by Warren R. Perry, Jean Howson, and Augustin F. C. Holl

Chapter 9. "The Late Group," Warren R. Perry, Jean Howson, and Augustin F. C. Holl

Chapter 10. "Coffins," by Jean Howson and Leonard G. Bianchi, with Iciar Lucena Narvaez and Janet L. Woodruff

Chapter 11. "Pins and Shrouding," by Jean Howson, with Shannon Mahoney and Janet L. Woodruff

Chapter 12. "Buttons and Fasteners," by Leonard G. Bianchi and Barbara A. Bianco, with Shannon Mahoney

Chapter 13. "Beads and Other Adornment" by Barbara A. Bianco, Christopher R. DeCorse, and Jean Howson

Chapter 14. "Coins, Shells, Pipes, and Other Items," by Warren R. Perry and Janet L. Woodruff

Chapter 15. "Summary and Conclusions," by Warren R. Perry, Jean Howson, and Barbara Bianco

Volume 2: "Descriptions of Burials 1–200," by Jean Cerasale, Jean Howson, Iciar Lucena Narvaez, Ruth Mathis, Warren R. Perry, and Janet L. Woodruff

Volume 3: "Descriptions of Burials 201–435," by Jean Cerasale, Jean Howson, Iciar Lucena Narvaez, Ruth Mathis, Warren R. Perry, and Janet L. Woodruff

The New York African Burial Ground Skeletal Biology Final Report, edited by Michael L. Blakey and Lesley M. Rankin-Hill. Washington, DC: General Services Administration and Howard Univ., 2004

Volume 1

Chapter 3. "Theory: An Ethical Epistemology of Publicly Engaged Biocultural Research," by Michael Blakey

Chapter 5. "Origins of the New York African Burial Ground Population: Biological Evidence of Geographical and Macroethnic Affiliations

Chronology
of Contemporary
Political Events

10 Dec. 1987 Congressional Committee on Public Works and Transportation authorized GSA to investigate the need to buy two plots of land in a Resolution.

1 Mar. 1988 Under Public Law 100-102, GSA submits prospectus to Congressional Committee on Public Works and Transportation outlining the land development plans.

11 Mar. 1988 Memorandum of Agreement signed between GSA and Mayor Koch (the City) stating their intent to construct a courthouse and office building.

5 May 1988 Committee on Public Works and Transportation accepts prospectus.

1988 Edwards & Kelsey contracted to prepare an EIS.

Sept. 1988–Mar. 1991 GSA competition for design/build team.

15 Mar. 1989 Memorandum of Agreement signed between GSA and ACHP. SHPO does not sign.

Sept. 1989 Stage 1A Cultural Resource Survey of Foley Square by HCI published. Revised in May 1990.

July 1990 HCI hired by GSA to do salvage archaeology.

7 July 1990 EIS draft published. Two to three pages out of two volumes discuss the burial ground.

12 Dec. 1990 GSA purchases two lots of land for $104 million. The Broadway block was $54.3 million.

Apr. 1991 Design/build team HOK/Tishman/Linpro

secures commission to construct office building.

May 1991 GSA rehires HCI to excavate alley.

20 May 1991 Archaeological fieldwork begins. Human remains are identified.

June 1991 Linpro/HOK receive permission to begin construction on building.

29 July 1991 MFAT agrees to analyze burials.

12 Sept. 1991 Full excavation of burials.

15 Sept. 1991 GSA, HCI, and MFAT all recognize there are more than an early estimate of fifty burials.

Sept. 1991 ACHP meets with GSA, NPS, & LPC. Mayor requests amendment of Memorandum of Agreement.

8 Oct. 1991 GSA Regional Administrator Bill Diamond holds press conference at the site. This is GSA's first public announcement about the burial ground.

Oct. 1991 Construction on the office building begins at 290 Broadway. Dr. Michael Blakey is contacted by New York City community.

5 Dec. 1991 Rossi announces expedited excavation. *New York Times* describes

excavation as coroner's method in early edition.

Dec. 1991 Senator Paterson establishes Task Force made up of community.

23 Dec. 1991 Memorandum of Agreement is amended. LPC also signs.

31 Dec. 1991 Amended MOA goes into effect.

10 Jan. 1992 Deadline for GSA's research design under amended MOA.

Jan. 1992 Peggy King Jorde contacts Dr. Blakey.

14 Feb. 1992 Digging accident with concrete damages approximately twenty burials. Diamond stops construction in the pavilion area until archaeology complete. GSA invites Blakey and Howard students for tour of excavations.

19 Feb. 1992 LPC Archaeologist Pagano first allowed to enter site to review 14 February damage.

6 Mar. 1992 Vandalism occurs at the site because guard is off duty and rounds not performed.

17 Mar. 1992 GSA authorizes production of a documentary film.

30 Mar. 1992 Brathwaite and community block concrete trucks at site.

Mar. 1992 GSA begins open, public meetings. Blakey works with MFAT assessing skeletons. Under GSA, HCI submits research design.

Apr. 1992 Blakey begins to draft a research plan. Dinkins establishes Mayor's Advisory Committee.

Apr.–June 1992 Blakey works with MFAT.

21 Apr. 1992 Hearing held at city hall.

23 Apr. 1992 Town meeting held at Trinity Church.

10 June 1992 ACHP rejects GSA's research plan.

11 June 1992 Blakey submits research plan.

July 1991 John Milner Associates (JMA) takes over HCI for archaeological aspect of Burial Ground project.

13 July 1992 ACHP meets with GSA and JMA to discuss research design and status of archaeology. JMA assesses it needs six weeks to devise a plan.

16 July 1992 Dinkins writes a letter to GSA outlining many concerns.

Mid-July 1992 GSA pays JMA $50,000 to hire consultants to write a research design.

27 July 1992 Hearing in Washington, DC, called by

Illinois Representative Gus Savage.

29 July 1992 GSA head office in DC suspends excavation on pavilion area.

30 July 1992 Meeting in Gracie Mansion during which decisions from hearing are implemented.

31 July 1992 Senate Appropriations Committee allocates $3 million for memorialization of burial ground.

9 Aug. 1992 Twenty-six-hour vigil begins.

13 Aug. 1992 LPC notices flooding in the site. They write a letter to GSA, and it is corrected.

Mid-Aug. 1992 JMA gathers a team of archaeologists for consulting in order to write the research design.

21 Aug. 1992 ACHP asks GSA to excavate the eleven exposed burials.

27 Aug. 1992 GSA writes to LPC requesting permission to excavate exposed burials.

Aug.–Sept. 1992 African American anthropologists are contracted via JMA to work on the project.

1 Sept. 1992 Second open public forum held concerning historic site designation of Burial Ground.

18 Sept. 1992 Blakey is contracted with GSA as scientific director.

22 Sept. 1992 LPC visits Lehman to affirm proper storage facilities of remains. Head GSA administrator Austin establishes Federal Steering Committee.

Sept. 1992 Archaeological lab established at World Trade Center. HCI's records are transferred to the new lab.

1 Oct. 1992 African American project leaders contracted in collaboration with JMA.

9 Oct. 1992 (began Sept. 28) Completion of excavation of eleven skeletons. The African Burial Ground excavation site closes.

15 Oct. 1992 JMA and Blakey submit a research design.

16 Oct. 1992 LPC's deadline for Blakey's submittal of research design.

26 Oct. 1992 Federal Steering Committee is chartered. President Bush signs a law that no building will be constructed on the pavilion area of 290 Broadway. Three million dollars is approved for second round of commemorative artworks.

Nov. 1992 Director Taylor of MFAT sends Blakey's draft research design to 120 colleagues for comment on race determination.

17 Nov. 1992 Public presentation of Blakey's research design.

1 Dec. 1992 Deadline for National Historic Landmark application.

22 Dec. 1992 Under Federal Steering Committee recommendations, ACHP agrees the remains will go to Howard and that MFAT's work is finished.

15 Jan. 1993 Closing date for comments on Blakey's research design.

25 Jan. 1993 Federal Steering Committee approves its seven resolutions.

3 Feb. 1993 Official federal landmark designation of site.

14 Feb. 1993 Con Ed digs up bones on Chambers Street.

25 Feb. 1993 LPC votes unanimously to designate the Burial Ground and common historic district a New York landmark.

19 Apr. 1993 The African Burial Ground is designated a National Historic Landmark by Secretary of the Interior Bruce Babbitt.

22 Apr. 1993 Revised research design submitted by JMA/ Howard.

20 May 1993 OPEI opens.

2 June 1993 City Council confirms the historic district.

14 June 1993 Public forum held at city hall concerning Federal Steering Committee recommendations that will be submitted to Congress.

6 Aug. 1993 Final Federal Steering Committee recommendations report submitted to Congress.

16 Aug. 1993 Howard contracts with GSA.

16 Aug.–3 Nov. African Burial Ground remains are shipped to Howard University in Washington, DC.

13 Sept. 1993 First test group of thirteen remains is successfully sent to Howard.

7 Oct. 1993 Idea memorial competition held.

23 Oct. 1993 First volunteer training session held by OPEI.

4 Nov. 1993 Ceremony in New York Mariner's Baptist church for sending final remains to DC.

5 Nov. 1993 "Ties That Bind" symposium and celebration at Howard University for the reception of final remains.

5 Feb. 1994 Con Ed digs up bones on Reade St. near Broadway while repairing a steam line.

July 1994 GSA disbands Federal Steering Committee as group is unproductive by now—too much fighting. Suggestion for a museum is rejected.

Dec. 1994 290 Broadway construction finishes. The federal office building opens.

Aug. 1996 Dr. Warren Perry appointed archaeological director of project.

May 1998 GSA asks Blakey for detailed proposals for remainder of Burial Ground research. Blakey writes an updated budget as requested by GSA.

Oct. 1996 Peggy King Jorde contracted to head memorialization and reinterment.

12 May 1998 GSA refuses to fund further research. GSA does not submit the budget for final research to Congress. Consequently, funding is projected to finish in April 1999.

5 Aug. 1998 Draft skeletal biology report is submitted to GSA.

By Nov 1998 Lisa Wager appointed executive project director.

Fall 1998 Friends of the African Burial Ground is established with Ayo Harrington as head.

Jan 1999 Jorde's office operates at 50 percent.

Feb.–July 26 1999 Burials at City Hall Park unearthed.

30 Apr. 1999 Project money is predicted to run out. Project would be over.

12 May 1999 Wager's position is dissolved due to public pressure. WTC lab is now open following asbestos abatement.

12 May 1999 GSA asks for second revised budget proposal, which will be submitted to the DC office.

22 May 1999 Bill Lawson and Ron Law of GSA hired.

12 Aug. 1999 Exposed city hall burials are covered over by bulldozers.

1 Oct. 1999 Budget submitted to oversight committee. Jorde's three-year contract runs until October 1999. Due to GSA delays, her work is about two years behind schedule.

2 Oct. 1999 First public forum held by GSA since 1994.

Nov. 1999 Budget approved by DC office. Asbestos abatement finishes, lab opens.

Dec. 1999 GSA has no more money for the project and there is no budget. Blakey has $30,000 left.

Jan. 2000 Contract between GSA and Blakey expires Bill Lawson leaves the project after less than one year.

Feb. 2000 WTC lab closes because of no contract. IDI is informed they are the Interpretive Center competition winners.

12 Mar. 2000 IDI hired to implement Interpretive Center. They are unable to progress with much work because they lack access to scientific research since the researchers are no longer salaried by GSA.

31 Sept. 2000 Oversight committee decides on budget.

21 Dec. 2000 Clinton signs a law mandating that GSA complete the burial ground project.

10 Jan. 2001 Peggy King Jorde receives notice her contract expires and will not be renewed after her involvement for a decade.

31 Jan. 2001 Peggy King Jorde's last day on the project.

By Mar. 2001 Cassandra Henderson and Lana Turner hired at GSA.

11 Sept. 2001 Artifacts stored in the WTC laboratory are lost. Some will be recovered. The OPEI office in building 6 is demolished.

Apr. 2003 The Federal Office Building is renamed Ted Weiss Federal Building

30 Sept.–4 Oct. 2003 Remains travel from Howard Univ.

through several cities and return to 290 Broadway during Rites of Ancestral Return. Reburial of all remains behind the office building during weekend-long ceremony.

1–3 Oct. 2004 One year anniversary commemoration of reburial hosted by GSA and the Schomburg Center. City renames Elk Street as African Burial Ground Way.

27 Feb. 2006 President George W. Bush issues proclamation for a national monument at burial ground.

28 Feb. 2006 Secretary of the Interior Gale Norton gives keynote in New York.

5 Oct. 2007 Exterior memorial by Rodney Léon opens behind office building.

27 Feb. 2010 Visitor Center designed by Amaze opens inside 290 Broadway.

Notes

Introduction

1. This estimate is based on two approaches. The first approach examines the density of the graves from the excavated area, populated with burials three layers deep at times. The second approach draws on historical census data, which suggests a similar numerical estimate. However, if infants and newborns were undercounted in the census and mortality bills, which was typically the case, then Howson and Bianchi add that "the total population of the African Burial Ground may have been well over 15,000." Jean Howson and Leonard G. Bianchi, "The Archaeological Site," in *New York African Burial Ground Archaeology Final Report*, eds. Warren Perry, Jean Howson, and Barbara Bianco (Washington, DC: General Services Administration and Howard Univ., 2006), 1:87. See Appendix for explanation of final report citations.

2. Prior to the inception of this large communal African Burial Ground, Africans could have been buried in Governor Stuyvesant's chapel yard on his bowerie (farm), or in the north yard of Trinity Church, the Reformed Dutch Church graveyard, or other religious institutions. See Jean Howson, Barbara A. Bianco, and Steven Barto, "Documentary Evidence on the Origin and use of the African Burial Ground," in *New York African Burial Ground Archaeology Final Report*, eds. Warren R. Perry, Jean Howson, and Barbara A. Bianco (Washington, DC: General Services Administration and Howard Univ., 2006), 1:40–44.

3. William D. Piersen, *From Africa to America: African American History from the Colonial Era to the Early Republic, 1526–1790* (New York: Twayne Publishers, 1996), 63.

4. For a detailed description of the boundaries, see U.S. Department of the Interior, National Park Service, *African Burial Ground National Historic Landmark Registration Form*, prepared by the New York City Landmarks Preservation Commission (Jean Howson and Gale Harris) (New York, 9 Nov. 1992), 32–35.

5. Ibid. 4.

6. See Allen Roberts, "Is 'Africa' Obsolete?" *African Arts* 33, no. 1 (Spring 2000): 6.

7. Erik R. Seeman, "Reassessing the 'Sankofa Symbol' in New York's African Burial Ground," *William and Mary Quarterly* 67, no. 1 (2010): 101. For useful distinctions between diasporas, see Kim D. Butler, "Defining Diaspora, Refining a Discourse," *Diaspora* 10, no. 2 (2001): 189–219.

8. James Clifford, "Diasporas," *Cultural Anthropology* 9, no. 3 (1994): 311.

9. Stuart Hall, "Cultural Identity and Diaspora," in *Diaspora and Visual Culture: Representing Africans and Jews*, ed. Nicholas Mirzoeff (New York and London: Routledge, 2000), 23.

10. David Chidester and Edward T. Linenthal, eds., "Introduction," in *American Sacred Space* (Bloomington and Indianapolis: Indiana Univ. Press, 1995), 15–16.

11. Don Mitchell, *Cultural Geography. A Critical Introduction* (Oxford and Malden, MA: Blackwell Publishers, 2000), 233.

12. For definitions of place, see Nigel Thrift, "Space: The Fundamental Stuff of Human Geography," in *Key Concepts in Geography*, eds. Sarah Holloway, Stephen Rice, and Gill Valentine (Sage Publications, 2003), 103; Noel Castree, "Place: Connections and Boundaries in an Interdependent World," in *Key Concepts*; and John R. Short, *Alternative Geographies* (Upper Saddle River, NJ: Prentice Hall, 2000).

13. For definitions of space, see Mitchell, *Cultural Geography*, 214; and Phil Hubbard et al., *Thinking Geographically: Space, Theory, and Contemporary Human Geography* (London and New York: Continuum, 2002), 14.

14. Hubbard, *Thinking Geographically*, 14.

15. Hall, "Cultural Identity and Diaspora," 26.

16. Piersen, *From Africa to America*, 63.

17. Excerpts from the document released after the twenty-fourth meeting of the IMBISA Standing Committee at Mahalapye (Botswana), 16–20 Sept. 1996, published by AMECEA Documentation Service, Nairobi (Kenya). Quoted in Chidi Denis Isizoh, "Who Is an Ancestor in African Traditional Religion?" *African Traditional Religion Special Topics* (17 Apr. 1999), http://www.afrikaworld.net/afrel/atr-ancestor.htm (accessed 21 July 2010).

18. Jack Goody, "Foreword," in *Cosmologies in the Making: A Generative Approach to Cultural Variation in Inner New Guinea*, ed. Fredrik Barth (Cambridge and New York: Cambridge Univ. Press, 1987), xi. Quoted in Mary H. Nooter, *Secrecy: African Art that Conceals and Reveals* (New York and Munich: The Museum for African Art and Prestel, 1993), 143.

19. R. Dona Marimba Richards, *Let the Circle Be Unbroken: The Implications of African Spirituality in the Diaspora* (Trenton, NJ: Red Sea Press, 1980), 43, 50.

20. Malidoma Patrice Somé, *Of Water and the Spirit* (New York: Penguin Books, 1994), 8.

21. W. Emmanuel Abraham, "A Paradigm of African Society," in *Readings in African Philosophy: An Akan Collection*, ed. Safro Kwame (Lanham, MD, and London: Univ. Press of America, 1995), 49.

22. Kwasi Wiredu, "African Philosophical Tradition," *Philosophical Forum* 24 (Fall-Spring 1992–93): 50, 52.

23. Emmanuel M. P. Edeh, *Towards an Igbo Metaphysics* (Chicago: Loyola Univ. Press, 1985), 73.

24. Henry John Drewal and John Pemberton III with Rowland Abiodun, *Yoruba: Nine Centuries of African Art and Thought* (New York: Center for African Art and Harry N. Abrams, 1989), 14.

25. Bolaji Idowu, *Olodumare: God in Yoruba Belief* (New York: The African Islamic Publications, 1994), 39. Anyone with an abnormality or deformation is understood as a sacred child of Obàtálá. So Obàtálá came to be the òrìshà who molds children in their mothers' wombs (J. Omasade Awolalu, *Yoruba Beliefs and Sacrificial Rites* [London: Longman Group Limited, 1979], 21).

26. Drewal and Abiodun with Pemberton, *Yoruba*, 15.

27. Rowland Abiodun, "Understanding Yorùbá Art and Aesthetics: The Concept of *Àse*," *African Arts* 27, no. 3 (July 1994): 68–78.

28. Roland Hallgren, *The Good Things in Life: A Study of the Traditional Religious Culture of the Yoruba People* (Löberöd, Sweden: Bokförlaget Plus Ultra, 1988), 8.

29. Kwabena Amponsah, *Topics on West African Traditional Religion* (Accra: Adwinsa Publications Ltd, 1977), 26. Quoted in J. O. Kayode, *Understanding African Traditional Religion* (Ile Ife: Univ. of Ife Press, 1984), 27.

30. Kwame Gyekye, *An Essay on African Philosophical Thought* (Cambridge: Univ. of Cambridge Press, 1987), 70.

31. Kofi Asare Opoku, "The World View of the Akan," *Tarikh* 7, no. 2 (1982): 62.

32. J. G. Platvoet, *Comparing Religions: A Limitative Approach. An Analysis of Akan, Para-Creole, and IFO-Sananda Rites and Prayers* (Hague: Mouton Publishers, 1982), 41.

33. Helaine K. Minkus, "The Concept of Spirit in Akwapim Akan Philosophy," *Africa* 50, no. 2 (1980): 182.

34. Kwasi Wiredu, *Cultural Universals and Particulars: An African Perspective* (Bloomington and Indianapolis: Indiana Univ. Press, 1996), 47.

35. Opoku, "The World View of the Akan," 65.

36. Anthony Ephirim-Donkor, *African Spirituality. On Becoming Ancestors* (Trenton, NJ, and Asmara, Eritrea: Africa World Press, 1997), 38. For a clear, detailed explanation of the ancestors and how the living relate to them, see A. K. Quarcoo, "Akan Visual Art and the Cult of the Ancestors," *Research Review* 9, no. 3 (1973): 48–82.

37. *Asomdwee Fie, Shrine of the Abosom and Nsamanfo Inc. (AFSANI)*, http://members.aol.com/afsani/spirituality.htm (accessed 9 Apr. 2002). The group explained on their homepage, "We are Africans born in the Diaspora who have willingly and excitedly chosen to follow in the footsteps of our ancestors . . . they were able to reach these shores thus we, the members of AFSANI, are here honoring them by following the cultural and spiritual traditions as we are taught from the various Palaces and Shrines in Ghana." Interestingly, their motto is the sankofa symbol that was possibly tacked into a coffin lid at the African Burial Ground and that translates into "learn from the past as you move into the future."

38. Anita Jacobsen-Widding, *Red-White-Black as a Mode of Thought* (Uppsala: Almquist & Wiskell International, 1979), 49.

39. K. K. Bunseki Fu-Kiau, "Natangu-Tandu-Kolo: The Bantu-Kongo Concept of Time," in *Time in the Black Experience*, ed. Joseph K. Adjaye (Westport, CT, and London: Greenwood Press, 1994), 18.

40. Katharine Hodgkin and Susannah Radstone, eds., *Contested Pasts: The Politics of Memory* (New York: Routledge, 2003), 2.

41. Stokes noted that the petition was found in a metal file labeled "Petitions, 1700–1795" in the city clerk's office and was not recorded in the minutes of the Common Council. Quoted here from *The African Burial Ground and the Commons Historic District Archaeological Sensitivity Study*, prepared for the New York City Department of General Services, Hunter Research, Inc., Mesick-Cohen-Waite Architects, 1994, 1–14. Originally cited in Isaac Newton Phelps Stokes, *The Iconography of Manhattan Island, 1498–1909* (New York: Robert H. Dodd, 1915–28), 6:46.

42. Quoted in Warren Perry, Jean Howson, and Augustin Holl, "The Late Group," in *New York African Burial Ground Archaeology Final Report*, eds. Warren R. Perry, Jean Howson, and Barbara A. Bianco (Washington, DC: General Services Administration and Howard Univ., 2006), 228.

43. On 16 February 1788, the author was made anonymous by the publication ostensibly to protect him or her. The author also raised the idea of passing a law to prohibit dissection on all but criminals. She or he wrote again on 28 February 1788, obviously out of frustration that the theft of the dead had not discontinued, warning the "students of physick" that their lives may be forfeited "should they dare to persist in their robberies." Quoted in Perry, Howson, and, Holl, "The Late Group," 228.

44. Claude Heaton, "Body Snatching in New York City," *The New York State Journal of Medicine* 43 (1943): 1863.

45. Edwin G. Burrows and Mike Wallace, *Gotham: A History of New York City to 1898* (New York: Oxford Univ. Press, 2000), 387.

1. Colonial Prints and Civic Cartographies

1. New York Colonial Manuscripts, 25 Feb. 1644. 4: 183–84 and Arnold J. F. Van Laer, ed. and trans., *New Netherland Council Minutes, 1638–1649* (Albany: Univ. of the State of New York, 1939), 4:212–13. Quoted in Jaap Jacobs, *New Netherland: A Dutch Colony in Seventeenth-Century America* (Leiden and Boston: Brill, 2005), 384.

2. John Thornton, *Africa and Africans in the Making of the Atlantic World, 1400–1800*, 2nd ed. (New York: Cambridge Univ. Press, 1998), 254.

3. For details concerning his life, see Henry B. Hoff, "A Colonial Black Family in New York and New Jersey: Pieter Santomee and his Descendants," *Journal of the Afro-American Historical and Genealogical Society* 9 (1988): 101–135.

4. Robert J. Swan, "First Africans into New Netherland, 1625 or 1626?" *Halve Maen* 66, no. 4 (Winter 1993): 78.

5. Edwin G. Burrows and Mike Wallace, *Gotham: A History of New York City to 1898* (New York: Oxford Univ. Press, 2000), 12.

6. Graham Russell Hodges, *Root and Branch: African Americans in New York and East Jersey, 1613–1863* (Chapel Hill and London: Univ. of North Carolina Press, 1999), 10. For the WIC involvement with white laborers, see Landon G. Wright, "Local Government in Colonial New York," (PhD diss., Cornell Univ., 1974), 18, 24–26. Additionally, for a history of blacks owning other blacks and Native Americans as slaves, see Sherrill D. Wilson, *New York City's African Slaveowners: A Social and Material Culture History* (New York and London: Garland Publishing, Inc., 1994).

7. Vivienne L. Kruger, "Born to Run: The Slave Family in Early New York, 1626–1827" (PhD diss., Columbia Univ., 1985), 35.

8. Thomas Joseph Davis, "Slavery in Colonial New York City" (PhD diss., Columbia Univ., 1974), 34.

9. Berthold Fernow, ed., *The Records of New Amsterdam from 1653 to 1674* (New York, 1897), 4:56–57. Quoted in Joyce D. Goodfriend, *Before the Melting Pot: Society and Culture in Colonial New York City, 1664–1730* (Princeton: Princeton Univ. Press, 1992), 114.

10. David S. Cohen, "How Dutch Were the Dutch of New Netherland?" *New York History* 62, no. 1 (Jan. 1981): 51.

11. The enigmatic relationship between the couple opens the engraving up for additional gender-based interpretations, none of which have been explored in scholarship and which are beyond the scope of this project.

12. The volumes discussed in this section can be viewed in full in Rare Books at the New York Public Library. Sample illustrations, including the ones described here, are reproduced in Isaac Newton Phelps Stokes, *The Iconography of Manhattan Island, 1498–1909* (New York: R. H. Dodd, 1915–28), vol. 6, as well as Gloria Gilda Deák, *Picturing America: Prints, Maps, and Drawings Bearing on the New World Discoveries and on the Development of the Territory that Is Now the United States* (Princeton: Princeton Univ. Press, 1988).

13. Pieter van der Aa's book had two earlier incarnations. Initially, the project contained European cities and fortresses with a French concentration that was mapped, engraved, and published in 1693–97 by Nicolas de Fer, the French Geographer to the King. The volumes were reissued in Amsterdam by Pierre Mortier ca. 1702. Mortier copied and then augmented the series from eight volumes and 176 plates to fourteen volumes and 319 plates. Pieter van der Aa then bought all of Mortier's plates and added sixteen plates of America that had mostly been published before in separate places. The newly assembled set contained 509 plates published in Paris and Leiden in 1726. Philip Lee Phillips, *A List of Geographical Atlases in the Library of Congress* (Washington, DC: Washington Printing Office, 1909), I:274 and 1046.

14. Thelma Wills Foote, *Black and White Manhattan: The History of Racial Formation in Colonial New York City* (New York: Oxford Univ. Press, 2004), 38.

15. Wilson, *New York City's African Slaveowners*, 37.

16. Dennis J. Maika, "Slavery, Race, and Culture in Early New York," *Halve Maen* 73, no. 2 (Summer 2000): 31.

17. Hodges, *Root and Branch*, 9.

18. Leslie M. Harris, *In the Shadow of Slavery: African Americans in New York City, 1626–1863* (Chicago and London: Univ. of Chicago Press, 2003), 15.

19. Davis, "Slavery in Colonial New York City," 49.

20. Willie F. Page, *The Dutch Triangle: The Netherlands and the Atlantic Slave Trade, 1621–1664* (New York: Garland Publishers, 1997), 199.

21. Taken from Evarts B. Greene and Virginia D. Harrington, *American Population Before the Federal Census of 1790* (1932, rpt. Gloucester, MA, 1966), 94–104, and Davis, "Slavery in Colonial New York City," 2. Quoted in "African Burial Ground and the Commons Historic District Designation Report," prepared by Gale Harris, Jean Howson, and Betsy Bradley, ed. Marjorie Pearson (New York: Landmarks Preservation Commission, 1993). Appendix in *Memorialization of the African Burial Ground*, prepared by Peggy King Jorde, and Weil, Gotshal and Manges Counsel, and the Federal Steering Committee (August 6, 1993), 17.

22. Eric Homberger, *The Historical Atlas of New York City* (New York: Henry Holt and Co., 1994), 55.

23. Morton Wagman, "Corporate Slavery in New Netherland," *Journal of Negro History* 65, no. 1 (1980): 40.

24. Hodges, *Root and Branch*, 10.

25. For instances in which such images are examined in detail, see the following: G. N. G. Clarke, "Taking Possession: The Cartouche as Cultural Text in Eighteenth-Century American Maps," *Word and Image* 4, no. 2 (Apr.–June 1988): 455–74; John Rennie Short, *Representing the Republic: Mapping the United States, 1600–1900* (London: Reaktion Books, 2001); Benjamin Schmidt, "Mapping an Empire: Cartographic and Colonial Rivalry in Seventeenth-Century Dutch and English North America," *William and Mary Quarterly* 54, no. 3 (July 1997): 549–78; Wilson, *New York City's African Slaveowners.*

26. Schmidt, "Mapping an Empire," 551; Clarke, "Taking Possession," 456; and J. B. Harley, "Silences and Secrecy: The Hidden Agenda of Cartography in Early Modern Europe," *Imago Mundi* 40 (1988): 57.

27. Denis Cosgrove, ed., *Mappings* (London: Reaktion Books, 1999), 10.

28. J. B. Harley, "Maps, Knowledge, and Power," in *The Iconography of Landscape*, eds. Denis Cosgrove and Stephen Daniels (Cambridge: Cambridge Univ. Press, 1988), 277.

29. Cosgrove, *Mappings*, 10; and Harley, "Maps, Knowledge, and Power," 297.

30. Clarke, "Taking Possession," 456.

31. Short, *Representing the Republic*, 36.

32. Jacobs, *New Netherland*, 381.

33. Stokes, *Iconography of Manhattan Island*, 4:116. Cited in Joep M. J. de Koning, "Dating the Visscher, or Prototype, View of New Amsterdam," *Haelve Moon* 71, no. 3 (Fall 1999): 53.

34. The structures on this Block F are delineated in the Castello Plan (1660) and detailed by Stokes in volume 2 of *The Iconography of Manhattan Island*. It is interesting that physician and surgeon Dr. Hans Kierstede resided in the first house of Block F just a few doors down from the WIC buildings from 1647 to 1666. As is explained in chapter 2, his wife Sara Roeloff owned a portion of the African Burial Ground. The twentieth-century office building at 290 Broadway would be built on her land.

35. Harley, "Silences and Secrecy," 57.

36. Schmidt, "Mapping an Empire," 556.

37. Cohen, "How Dutch Were the Dutch," 32.

38. Schmidt, "Mapping an Empire," 554.

39. Ibid.

40. Ibid., 555. According to Schmidt, the British did not possess a developed production of cartography, and certainly not one that could rival the Dutch: "English printed maps of America were inadequate: limited, derivative, or just plain inferior" (563). Because of the change in power structure, the British could appropriate the engravers' plates that had been previously used by the Dutch (565).

41. Ibid., 556.

42. Margaret Pritchard and Henry Taliaferro, *Degrees of Latitude: Mapping Colonial America* (Williamsburg, VA, and New York: The Colonial Williamsburg Foundation and Harry N. Abrams, 2002), 86.

43. Robert Macdonald, "The City of New Amsterdam Located on the Island of Manhattan in New Netherland c. 1650," nd, http://www.mcny.org/newview .htm (accessed 6 Nov. 1998), p. 4. Thank you to Eileen Morales of the Museum of the City of New York for sending me relevant material.

44. Cosgrove, *Mappings*, 4.

45. de Koning, "Dating the Vissher," see especially p. 53 and p. 56.

46. The Duke of York's investment in the predecessor to the Royal African Company, the Company of Royal Adventurers Trading to Africa, encouraged the British slave trade to New York.

47. Schmidt, "Mapping an Empire," 573n37.

48. James Duncan, "Sites of Representation: Place, Time and the Discourse of the Other," in *Place/Culture/Representation*, eds. James Duncan and David Ley (London and New York: Routledge, 1994), 39.

49. Ibid., 43.

50. John A. Kouwenhoven, *The Columbia Historical Portrait of New York* (Garden City, NY: Doubleday & Company, 1953), 47. This image is also reproduced in Stokes, *Iconography of Manhattan Island*, 1:pl. 19. Stokes includes in his commentary that the Danckaerts views of New York are "undoubtedly the most accurate and valuable pictorial records of the period which we possess, and are a mine of information to the careful student" (Stokes, *Iconography of Manhattan Island*, 1:caption for pl. 17).

51. Kouwenhoven, *The Columbia Historical Portrait of New York*, 47. The right half of the drawing depicts the North River, or Hudson River. Although difficult to identify, a sailboat and aquatic creature like a whale spouting water verify this. Broadway (still a path and not yet a roadway) runs diagonally from the windmills in the bottom left corner to the fort.

52. Jasper Danckaerts, *Journal of Jasper Danckaerts, 1679–1680*, trans. Henry C. Murphy, eds. Bartlett Burleigh James and J. Franklin Jameson (1867, 1913; rpt. New York: Barnes and Noble, Inc., 1946), 136.

53. The African neighborhood is documented in several sources. The most comprehensive map of African-owned lands can be found in Stokes, *The Iconography of*

Manhattan Island, 6:69, plate 84B. This map is reproduced in Jean Howson, Barbara A. Bianco, and Steven Barto, "Documentary Evidence on the Origin and Use of the African Burial Ground," in *New York African Burial Ground Archaeology Final Report*, eds. Warren R. Perry, Jean Howson, and Barbara A. Bianco (Washington, DC: General Services Administration and Howard Univ., 2006), 1:46. Murray Hoffman published the written grants deeded to "the Free Negroes" and assembled a map showing ownership in *A Treatise upon the Estate and Rights of the Corporation of the City of New York as Proprietors* (New York: Edmund Jones and Co., 1862), 2:195–201 and Diagram 6. Additionally, I located a hand-drawn sketch by John H. Innes in the New-York Historical Society made between 1880 and 1920, entitled "The Manumitted Negroes [and their plots in New Amsterdam. ca. 1644]" (NS13 M5.2.63). Finally, Graham Russell Hodges drew his own map in *Root and Branch*, 14.

54. Stokes, *Iconography of Manhattan Island*, 4:224.

55. Davis, "Slavery in Colonial New York City," 52.

56. Wagman, "Corporate Slavery," 39, and Hodges, *Root and Branch*, 34–36. Granted a deed between one and twenty acres of land, freed Africans owned their own farms for growing produce. Provisions were also made initially: any living or yet to be born children of freed slaves were still slaves to the West India Company, and 22½ bushels of maize, wheat, peas, beans, and one hog had to be paid each year to the company. Such an unrealistic list suggests that these provisions were not consistently enforced. In 1650, no more than three of the many children were employed by the company (William Stuart, "Servitude and Slavery in New York and New Jersey" [master's thesis, Univ. of Chicago, 1921], 66). The second recorded manumission in 1646 only asked for eight bushels of wheat and nothing else (Wagman, "Corporate Slavery," 39). Also see Hodges, *Root and Branch*, 34–36, and Peter R. Christoph, "The Freedmen of New Amsterdam," *Journal of the Afro-American Historical & Genealogical Society* (Fall 1983): 139–54. Jacobs makes the point that this arrangement could just as well have been called half slavery instead of half freedom (384).

57. Emphasis mine. Hoffman, *A Treatise upon the Estate and Rights*, 2:214.

58. Foote, *Black and White Manhattan*, 150.

59. Christoph, 150.

60. Edgar J. McManus, *A History of Negro Slavery in New York* (Syracuse: Syracuse Univ. Press, 1966), 80.

61. William Bradford, "The Laws of His Majesties Colony of New-York. Acts Passed by the General Assembly of the Colony of New-York" (New York: William Bradford, 1719), microfiche, 52–54.

62. *Trinity Church Vestry Minutes*, 25 Oct. 1697, I:11. Trinity Church Archives, New York City. Foote (*Black and White Manhattan*, 146) cites the

1773–74 burial of a black Anglican who was buried within the Trinity Churchyard, explaining that Evert Bancker paid for Mary's funeral, burial plot, gravedigger, white gloves for the pallbearers, and ringing of the church bell that winter (quoted in House Expense Book of Evert Bancker, 1760 to 1775). A separate black Anglican cemetery was planned in July 1774 by Church, Reade, and Chapel Streets. Despite the guideline, perhaps it could be bypassed.

63. King William III in England sent a founding charter and land grant for an Anglican church on 6 May 1697. The church building would not be completed until 1698.

64. Rev. William Berrian, *An Historical Sketch of Trinity Church, New-York* (New York: John R. M'Gown, 1847), 367. Digital copy at http://www.archive.org /stream/historicalsketc00berr/historicalsketc00berr_djvu.txt (accessed 2010).

65. Quoted in *First Recorded Minutes Regarding the Building of Trinity Church in the City of New York 1696–99*, forward by John Heuss, 1964. The Parish of Trinity Church in the City of New York.

66. Quoted in *First Recorded Minutes Regarding the Building of Trinity Church*. Also, the minutes list a building contract on 3 June 1697, wherein it was discussed how the managers would furnish their enslaved. See Morgan Dix, *A History of the Parish of Trinity Church in the City of New York*, vol. 1 (New York: G. P. Putnam's Sons, 1898; reprint [New York]: Parish of Trinity, 1984), 109. Additionally, "Mr. Mayor and Mr. Emott Capt. Tothill & Capt. Wilson have each of them lent a Negro to worke on Wensday Next for y Opening the Ground for the foundation. Agreed Nemine Contra Dicente that ye twelve Managers of the Church building do each find A Negro or Labourer to be Imploy'd on the Sd building for fourteen days at their own proper Charge over & Above their Subscriptions (23 March 1696)."

67. Details are provided in chapter 2. Marjorie Ingle, Jean Howsen, and Edward S. Rutsch, S.O.P.A. of Historic Conservation and Interpretation, Inc., *A Stage IA Cultural Resource Survey of the Proposed Foley Square Project in the Borough of Manhattan, New York, NY*, for Edwards & Kelcey Engineers, Inc. (Sept. 1989, revised May 1990), 69.

68. Berrian, *Historical Sketch of Trinity Church*, 30, 34, 40, and 49. Huddleston's many contributions to Trinity Church were compared to those of Elias Neau, who was director of the SPG and also instructed Africans.

69. Letter to David Humphreys, Secretary of the SPG, 27 Dec. 1726. Quoted in Berrian, *Historical Sketch of Trinity Church*, 50.

70. John Sharpe, "Proposals for Erecting a School, Library and Chapel at New York [1712–1713]," *New-York Historical Society Collections* 13 (1880): 355. Among the chief impediments the SPG believed it faced was the small regard whites gave slaves for Christian sacraments, including the conducting of weddings and funerals. The full paragraph reads: "In Religious respects there is but little regard had

to them, their marriages are performed by mutual consent without the blessing of the Church and they are buried in the Common by those of their country and complexion without the office, on the contrary, the Heathenish rites are performed at the grave by their countrymen, and there is no notice given of their being sick that they may be visited and many other such deficiencys there are to discourage them" (355).

71. *The New York African Burial Ground Archaeology Final Report*, eds. Warren R. Perry, Jean Howson, and Barbara A. Bianco (Washington, DC: General Services Administration and Howard Univ., 2006), discusses several highly viable possibilities for where Africans buried their dead prior to the known existence of the burial ground. The possibilities included Governor Stuyvesant's chapel yard on his bowerie (farm), the north yard of Trinity Church, the Reformed Dutch Church graveyard, other religious institutions, or the African Burial Ground. See Jean Howson, Barbara A. Bianco, and Steven Barto, "Documentary Evidence on the Origin and Use of the African Burial Ground," 40–44.

72. Sharpe, "Proposals for Erecting a School," 352–53.

73. Hodges, *Root and Branch*, 65.

74. Jill Lepore, "The Tightening Vise: Slavery and Freedom in British New York," in *Slavery in New York*, eds. Ira Berlin and Leslie M. Harris (New York: New Press, 2005), 78.

75. Lepore, "The Tightening Vise," 79.

76. See Hodges, *Root and Branch*, 66–67, for details.

77. Rev. John Sharpe to the Secretary of the Society for the Propagation of the Gospel in Foreign Parts, New York, June 23, 1712, *New York Genealogical and Biographical Record* XXI (1890): 162–63.

78. Davis, "Slavery in Colonial New York City," 100.

79. Gene Fein, "The New York City Slave Rebellion of 1712 Revisited: Through the Optic of the Akan" (1999, email file), 39. A shorter version of this paper was presented at the Conference on New York State History at Fordham University in June 2000. I would like to thank the author for sharing his work with me.

80. Anne Hilton, *The Kingdom of the Kongo* (Oxford: Clarendon Press, 1985), 62 and 195. Cited in Pamela McClusky, *Art from Africa: Long Steps Never Broke a Back* (Seattle and Princeton: Seattle Art Museum with Princeton Univ. Press, 2002), 146, 150.

81. Lepore, *New York Burning*, 239. The list of participants and their owners is in Lepore, "The Tightening Vise," 80.

82. Hodges, *Root and Branch*, 55. For a detailed recounting of Neau's life and suffering as a galley slave and prisoner, see Sheldon S. Cohen, "Elias Neau, Instructor to New York's Slaves," *New-York Historical Society Quarterly* 55, no. 1 (Jan. 1971): 6–27. Also, Jon Butler, *The Huguenots in America: A Refugee People in New World Society* (Cambridge, MA, and London: Harvard Univ. Press, 1983).

83. Sharpe, "Proposals for Erecting a School," 354.

84. Hodges, *Root and Branch*, 60, and Frank Klingberg, *Anglican Humanitarianism in Colonial New York* (Philadelphia: Church Historical Society, 1940), 144. Call-and-response in letter from Elias Neau to Dr. Woodward, 5 Sept. 1705 in *Letterbooks of the Society for the Propagation of the Gospel in Foreign Parts* (Widener Library, Harvard Univ.), microfilm. Example in Foote, *Black and White Manhattan*, 239.

85. Interestingly, months prior to the 1712 Insurrection, Governor Hunter had issued an official proclamation to send all slaves to Neau's Anglican catechism classes to instruct them "in the Knowledge of Jesus Christ" (Proclamation of Governor Hunt, 1711. Housed in the New-York Historical Society and reproduced in Hodges, *Root and Branch*, 61). Then, just before the insurrection occurred, Trinity Rector William Vesey actually refused to read the proclamation aloud in his church (although the proclamation ordered this), and he would not baptize a woman of mixed African and European descent. Vesey had baptized some enslaved without their owners' knowledge and commented that there were those who now wished him ill. Perhaps he was under specific pressure not to baptize, or had decided not to place himself in such a position again. (See Klingberg, 127, 130, 132. Cited in Hodges, *Root and Branch*, 58–59.) In this case, matters of race and class dictated policies of the parent, Trinity Church, which did not support its own offshoot organization, the SPG.

86. Sharpe, "Proposals for Erecting a School, 353.

87. Hodges, *Root and Branch*, 62.

88. Hodges, *Root and Branch*, 54.

89. Robert Hunter to the Lords of Trade, 23 June 1712, in *Documents Relative to the Colonial and Revolutionary History of New York*, ed. E. B. O'Callaghan (Albany: Weed, Parsons, 1855–61), 5:342. Although Hunter believed the laws too strict, it seems he was pressured to comply with the general white New York population.

90. Kruger, "Born to Run," 596.

91. "A Law for Regulating Negro's & Slaves in the Night Time," *Minutes of the Common Council of the City of New York*, 1675–1776 (New York: Dodd, Mead, 1905), 4:51–52.

92. Cohen, "Elias Neau," 21.

93. Denis Cosgrove, ed., *Mappings* (London: Reaktion Books, 1999), 4.

94. J. B. Harley, "Silences and Secrecy: The Hidden Agenda of Cartography in Early Modern Europe" *Imago Mundi* 40 (1988): 57.

95. Anthony D. King, *Spaces of Global Cultures. Architecture Urbanism Identity* (London and New York: Routledge, 2005), 142.

96. Although not exhaustive, the following published maps offer an idea of the number of examples that did not demarcate the African Burial Ground, with their date of publication: Lyne-Bradford Plan (1730), A Plan of NY by James Lyne

(1730), Carwitham Plan (1740), Montresor Plan (1767), Ratzen Plan (1776), Ratzer Map (1776), Holland Map (1776), British Headquarters Map (ca. 1782), Hills Plan (1785), Directory Plan of 1789, Taylor-Roberts Plan (1797).

97. Deák, *Picturing America*, 1:54.

98. The Fresh Water Pond served as a natural boundary between the town and the countryside, and supplied the purest and largest amount of drinking water for the city. It was also known as Collect Pond because "Collect" derived from Kalchook, or the Dutch word Kolch, meaning a small body of water (Deák, *Picturing America*, 149). It would eventually be drained and covered over just after the turn of the nineteenth century.

99. Foote, *Black and White Manhattan*, 141.

100. David Humphreys, *An Historical Account of the Incorporated Society for the Propagation of the Gospel in Foreign Parts to Instruct Negroes* (1730; rpt., New York: Arno Press, 1969), 93–95.

101. David T. Valentine, "History of Broadway," *Manual of the Common Council of New York* (New York: D. T. Valentine, 1865), 567.

102. City of New York, *Minutes of the Common Council of the City of New York, 1675–1776* (New York: Dodd, Mead, and Co., 1905), 4:447.

103. City of New York, *Minutes of the Common Council*, 3:296.

104. See Deák, *Picturing America*, 54. The photograph of this plan that I purchased from the Print Collection of NYPL in the late 1990s is also labeled on the back as "anonymous."

105. Paul Cohen and Robert Augustyn, *Manhattan in Maps, 1527–1995* (New York: Rizzoli International Publications, 1997), 60.

106. Length and type of wood handwritten on the back of David Grim's map in 1819. Cited in Howson, Bianco, and Barto, "Documentary Evidence," 57n14.

107. Jean Howson and Leonard G. Bianchi, "The Archaeological Site," in *New York African Burial Ground Archaeology Final Report*, eds. Warren R. Perry, Jean Howson, and Barbara A. Bianco (Washington, DC: General Services Administration and Howard Univ., 2006), 1:84, 88.

108. Kalk Hook Farm, which was on the northern part of the burial ground, belonged to Rutgers. South of the dashed or unbroken line existed what was called the Van Borsum Patent, which was deeded to the Van Borsum/Roeloff family. This same line was mapped on the Ratzen Plan of 1767. See Jean Howson, Warren R. Perry, Augustin F. C. Holl, and Leonard G. Bianchi, "Relative Dating," in *New York African Burial Ground Archaeology Final Report*, eds. Warren R. Perry, Jean Howson, and Barbara A. Bianco (Washington, DC: General Services Administration and Howard Univ., 2006), 1:105, 106.

109. Frances Maerschalck petitioned to be the city surveyor on 31 March 1732, was appointed as such on 8 June 1733, and died in 1776. His plan depicted

for the first time the beginnings of the street grid system as the town expanded northward (Cohen and Augustyn, *Manhattan in Maps*, 64).

110. Cohen and Augustyn, *Manhattan in Maps*, 65. The new streets both north and south of the pond were once portions of large holdings of the Rutgers and Bayard families, respectively, that had recently been parceled out (64). He also surveyed George Janeway's land near the Collect Pond and burial ground, as remarked upon by William Cockburn. See chapter 2n33.

111. The Lyne-Bradford Plan, surveyed by James Lyne, was the first printed map of the city, as well as the first to be printed in New York City. The printer was William Bradford, a British Anglican buried in Trinity Churchyard whose grave can still be visited today. Maerschalck's newly added section is evident on the right, as can be seen by the vertical line or joint through Fresh Water Pond (see plate 3) (Cohen and Augustyn, *Manhattan in Maps*, 65). The Lyne-Bradford Plan is illustrated in Cohen and Augustyn.

112. Cohen and Augustyn, *Manhattan in Maps*, 65. Similarly, the Lyne-Bradford Plan was promoted once by city publisher William Bradford in the newspaper he published in 1731, and three copies of the map remain today (54).

113. Seymour Schwartz and Ralph Ehrenberg, *The Mapping of America* (New York: Harry Abrams, 1980), 166. Interestingly, a plan of New York City had not been published for England since 1730, leaving a large lapse of time between then and this 1763 publication (Cohen and Augustyn, *Manhattan in Maps*, 57). This certainly differed from the Dutch, who mapped the city many times. Additionally, the 1763 Maerschalck Plan was republished in David T. Valentine's *Manual of the Corporation of New York* in 1850 (facing p. 220), and in Daniel Curry's book *New-York: A Historical Sketch of the Rise and Progress of the Metropolitan City of America* in 1853 (facing p. 109) (Daniel C. Haskell, ed., *Manhattan Maps. A Co-operative List* [New York: New York Public Library, 1931], 22).

114. Philip Lee Phillips, *A List of Geographical Atlases in the Library of Congress* (Washington, DC, Washington Printing Office, 1914), III:31.

115. Haskell, *Manhattan Maps. A Co-operative List*, 40. A facsimile of Kirkham's Plan (fig. 9) in the NYPL Map Division led its chief, Alice Hudson, to contact the Library of Congress, where the full logbook was said to be housed. Senior reference librarian Mike Klein in the Geography and Map Division of the Library of Congress eventually located the logbook. Thanks to Araba Dawson-Andoh at Ohio University Library for then purchasing a microfilm of the logbook from the Library of Congress.

116. P. Lee Phillips, "A Descriptive List of Maps and Views of New York City in the Library of Congress, 1639–1865" (unpublished manuscript, Library of Congress, 1920), 211.

117. Illustrated in Cohen and Augustyn, *Manhattan in Maps*, 94–97.

118. The name of the mapmaker, Lieutenant Bernard Ratzer, was misspelled by the engraver on the smaller edition of the two maps published by Faden and Jefferys in London in 1776. Because Ratzen was written in the cartouche, it is known as the Ratzen Plan. The larger version is properly named the Ratzer Map (Cohen and Augustyn, *Manhattan in Maps*, 73).

119. Cohen and Augustyn, *Manhattan in Maps*, 73. Ratzer was a Swiss-born military engineer recruited by the British to go to America for the French and Indian War.

120. *Smith, ex. dem. Teller, v. G.& P. Lorillard*, 10 Johnson Reports 182 (N.Y. Sup. Ct.), 355. Cited in Stokes, *Iconography of Manhattan Island*, 4:394.

121. Grim, "Notes on the City of New York," New-York Historical Society. Quoted in Jill Lepore, *New York Burning: Liberty, Slavery, and Conspiracy in Eighteenth-Century Manhattan* (New York: Alfred A. Knopf, 2005), 105. David's father, Philip Grim, emigrated from Bavaria in 1739, so David would have arrived in New York City just two years earlier at the age of two. Perhaps the culture shock of experiencing a new country contributed to the strength of his memory, although four is a young age despite any childhood experiences.

122. William Smith Pelletreau, *Historic Homes and Institutions and Genealogical and Family History of New York* (New York: Lewis Publishing Company, 1907), 1:394.

123. Italics are my emphasis. John Fanning Watson, *Annals and Occurrences of New York City and State in the Olden Time* (Carlisle, MA: Applewood Books, 1846), 184–85. Additionally, Jill Lepore quotes Grim, "I made for my Amusement, with the intent that it be on a future day presented to the New-York Historical Society" ("The Tightening Vise," 59).

124. Watson, *Annals and Occurrences*, 183. Also, a historical dictionary lists David Grim as "known for his series of sketches of Revolutionary period New York City. All of the sketches were made from memory later in Grim's life." (Terry M. Mays, *Historical Dictionary of Revolutionary America* [Lanham, MD: Scarecrow Press, 2005], 121).

125. Daniel Horsmanden, *Journal of the Proceedings in the Detection of the Conspiracy Formed by Some White People, in Conjunction with Negro and Other Slaves for Burning the City of New-York in America, and Murdering the Inhabitants* (New York: James Parker, 1744; rpt. [Boston]: Beacon Press, 1971), 64. For further details and accounts concerning the 1741 Conspiracy or the Great Negro Plot, see Lepore, *New York Burning*; Foote, *Black and White Manhattan*; Herbert Aptheker, *American Negro Slave Revolts* (New York: International Publishers, 1967); Mike Fearnow, "Theatre for an Angry God: Public Burnings and Hangings

in Colonial New York, 1741," *The Drama Review* (Summer 1996): 15–36; and Horsmanden. A detailed review of literature can be found in Lepore, *New York Burning*, 275 and 279–81, n11.

126. Edwin G. Burrows and Mike Wallace, *Gotham: A History of New York City to 1898* (New York: Oxford Univ. Press, 2000), 151, 159.

127. "African Burial Ground and the Commons Historic District Designation Report," 17.

128. Harris, *In the Shadow of Slavery*, 43.

129. Fearnow, "Theatre for an Angry God," 22.

130. Lepore, "The Tightening Vise," 87.

131. Burrows and Wallace, *Gotham*, 162. The Supreme Court, the trial, and a basement makeshift jail were all located inside of City Hall. It was located on 26 Wall Street at the corner of Nassau, which is number 7 on the Grim Plan, fig. 10.

132. Lepore, *New York Burning*, 201.

133. Complete lists of the accused and owners can be found in Appendix B and Appendix C of Lepore, *New York Burning*.

134. Lepore, *New York Burning*, 132, 264–65.

135. Horsmanden, *Journal*, 273. Jill Lepore documented that Hughson was executed along with the rest of the Africans on the island of Little Collect Pond on the east border of the African Burial Ground (*New York Burning*, 120). From his personal memory, David Grim mapped a different site for Hughson's body not near the African Burial Ground, but along the East River on the north side of the palisades at number 57, "Plot Hughson Gibbeted," on the Grim Plan, fig. 10.

136. Dorinda Outram, *The Enlightenment* (Cambridge Univ. Press: Cambridge, 1995), 76.

137. Quoted in Audrey Smedley, *Race in North America: Origin and Evolution of a Worldview* (Boulder and Oxford: Westview Press, Inc., 1993), 184.

138. Ibid.

139. Quoted in Foote, *Black and White Manhattan*, 172.

140. Thanks to Alessandra Raengo for sharing with me an analysis of this spectacle. See also Foote, *Black and White Manhattan*, 183.

141. Lepore, *New York Burning*, 239.

142. Davis, "Slavery in Colonial New York City," 68.

143. Cohen and Augustyn, *Manhattan in Maps*, 63.

2. Ownership Disputes, Land Surveys, and Urban Developments

1. Murray Hoffman, *A Treatise upon the Estate and Rights of the Corporation of the City of New York as Proprietors*, vol. 2 (New York: Edmund Jones and Co., 1862), Diagram 8.

2. U.S. Department of the Interior, National Park Service, *African Burial Ground National Historic Landmark Registration Form*, prepared by the New York City Landmarks Preservation Commission (Jean Howson and Gale Harris) (New York, 9 Nov. 1992), 9–10. It was the lower, more southern portion of Kalk Hook Farm that was therefore part of the African Burial Ground.

3. Damen owned a "West Indian servant maid" named Cicilje whom he freed upon his death. She did not have to make any payments as a free woman. Jaap Jacobs, *New Netherland: A Dutch Colony in Seventeenth-Century America* (Leiden and Boston: Brill, 2005), 383. The four lots are detailed in Hoffman, *Treatise upon the Estate*, 214–16, with a map in Diagram 9 depicting the subdivisions of Damen's farm. The southeastern quadrant, or Lot 2, comprises in large part the northern half of today's Block 154 around Duane Street where burials were found. See also Isaac Newton Phelps Stokes, *The Iconography of Manhattan Island, 1498–1909* (New York: R. H. Dodd, 1915–28), 6:82–83.

4. In relation to the excavation, see Jean Howson, Barbara A. Bianco, and Steven Barto, "Documentary Evidence on the Origin and Use of the African Burial Ground," in *New York African Burial Ground Archaeology Final Report*, eds. Warren R. Perry, Jean Howson, and Barbara A. Bianco (Washington, DC: General Services Administration and Howard Univ., 2006), 1:47.

5. It was the southwest quadrant of Kalk Hook Farm, or Lot 1. Marjorie Ingle, Jean Howsen, and Edward S. Rutsch, S.O.P.A. of Historic Conservation and Interpretation, Inc., *A Stage IA Cultural Resource Survey of the Proposed Foley Square Project in the Borough of Manhattan, New York, NY*, prepared for Edwards & Kelcey Engineers, Inc. (Sept. 1989, revised May 1990), 69.

6. Rev. William Berrian, *An Historical Sketch of Trinity Church, New-York* (New York: John R. M'Gown, 1847), 30, 34, 40, 49, http://www.archive.org/stream /historicalsketc00berr/historicalsketc00berr_djvu.txt (accessed 2010).

7. In 1726, Anthony Rutgers purchased Verplanck's land (Lot 1) through a combination of deeds with grantors Hill, Lewis, and Kiersted, as detailed in New York County Deeds, Liber 31:115–25 (cited in Ingle, Howson, and Rutsch, *Stage IA Cultural Resource*, 69). Anthony Rutgers purchased Lot 2 in 1723 (owned by Jan Vigne and then Wolfort Webber) and Lot 3 in 1725 (Howson, Bianco, and Barto, "Documentary Evidence," 51n12). The Rutgers farm stretched from the large chalk hill on the western side of Kalk Hook pond (or Collect Pond) to just south of Duane Street.

8. Cited in *Reconstruction of Foley Square: Historical and Archaeological Resources Report*, prepared for the New York Department of Parks and Recreation by Joan H. Geismar, (Dec. 1993), 8; and David T. Valentine, "History of Broadway," in *Manual of the Common Council of New York* (New York: D. T. Valentine, 1865), 566–67.

9. Henry Barclay, *Map of Land Surveyed for Henry Barclay, Leonard Lispenard and Anthony Rutgers Lying Near the Fresh Water Pond*, [1763] 1860. M29.1.9. "Copied from the original now in the possession of Mr. Henry Barclay of Morristown Queens Count, and this day compared by me and found correct. NY Oct 27 1860. J.M. Martin."

10. This is corroborated in Jean Howson and Leonard G. Bianchi, "The Archaeological Site," in *New York African Burial Ground Archaeology Final Report*, eds. Warren R. Perry, Jean Howson, and Barbara A. Bianco (Washington, DC: General Services Administration and Howard Univ., 2006), 1:84. They add that houses built along the eastern side of Broadway in the 1760s could have truncated some burials.

11. Howson and Bianchi, "The Archaeological Site," 84, 88.

12. The Dongan Charter read: "all the waste, vacant, unpatented, and unappropriated land lying and being within the said city of New York, and on Manhattan's Island aforesaid, extending and reaching to the low water mark" (quoted in Hoffman, *Treatise upon the Estate*, 1:121). The British substantiated this with the Montgomerie Charter, extending the grant further north beyond city limits. The Dongan Charter was based on a 1658 conveyance made by Governor Stuyvesant and the Council of the New Netherland to New Amsterdam Burgomasters of vacant lands south of the city wall ("African Burial Ground and the Commons Historic District Designation Report," prepared by Gale Harris, Jean Howson, and Betsy Bradley, ed. Marjorie Pearson [New York City: Landmarks Preservation Commission, 1993], Appendix in *Memorialization of the African Burial Ground*, prepared by Peggy King Jorde, and Weil, Gotshal and Manges Counsel, and the Federal Steering Committee [6 Aug. 1993], 6).

13. Howson, Bianco, and Barto suggest the latter, with the word "possible" in italics ("Documentary Evidence," 57). The size of the almshouse burial ground was "the length of two Boards" (City of New York, *Minutes of the Common Council of the City of New York, 1675–1776* [New York: Dodd, Mead, and Co., 1905], 6:85). Also, see Marilyn Anderson, "Under City Hall Park" *Archaeology*, 25 Feb. 2000, http://archive.archaeology.org/online/features/cityhall/.

14. Howson and Bianchi, "The Archaeological Site," 84n3.

15. The patent stretches from present-day Chambers Street to Duane Street between Broadway and Centre Street. It is possible that the enslaved Native American Ande who worked for Roeloff assisted with the translations. Roeloff also had two enslaved African boys, a girl, and two adults.

16. Hoffman, *Treatise upon the Estate*, 2:205.

17. New York County, Wills Liber 5–6:1–6. Quoted in Howson, Bianco, and Barto, "Documentary Evidence," 47. Seven of Roeloff's children were by her first husband, a surgeon named Hans Kiersted. He lived next to the West India Company complex where enslaved Africans resided (see chap. 1, n33). Roeloff's eighth child

was with Van Borsum. She married a third time to Elbert Stouthoff, and made a prenuptial contract with him in which she maintained ownership of her own land.

18. New York State, Patents Liber 7:11. Quoted in "African Burial Ground and the Commons Historic District Designation Report," 7.

19. "African Burial Ground and the Commons Historic District Designation Report," 7.

20. City of New York, *Minutes of the Common Council*, 5:416. Specifically, the heirs were John Teller, Jacobus Stoutenburgh, and Maria Van Vleck.

21. "African Burial Ground and the Commons Historic District Designation Report," 7.

22. Detailed in Hoffman, *Treatise upon the Estate*, 1:121–26.

23. Edwin G. Burrows and Mike Wallace, *Gotham: A History of New York City to 1898* (New York: Oxford Univ. Press, 2000), 129.

24. U.S. Department of the Interior, National Park Service, *African Burial Ground National Historic Landmark*, 33.

25. City of New York, *Minutes of the Common Council*, 6:238. Quoted in "African Burial Ground and the Commons Historic District Designation Report," 7n10; and Howson, Bianco, and Barto, "Documentary Evidence," 57 and 59.

26. See Howson, Bianco, and Barto, "Documentary Evidence," 59n16.

27. *Smith, ex. dem. Teller, v. G.& P. Lorillard*, 10 Johnson Reports 182 (N.Y. Sup. Ct.), 355. Cited in Stokes, *Iconography of Manhattan Island* 4:394.

28. Howson, Bianco, and Barto, "Documentary Evidence," 61. The cemetery is marked by small crosses in the 1782 British Headquarters Map located in the Map Division of the New York Public Library.

29. Thank you to Ron Becker, Head of Special Collections, Rutgers University Libraries for his weeklong perseverance in searching for and then unearthing the heretofore lost Janeway Papers. Replicas of these papers at the New-York Historical Society are lost and have not been found.

30. Detailed in Hoffman, *Treatise upon the Estate*, 2:206–7.

31. Stokes, *Iconography of Manhattan Island*, 6:108. Or, a slightly different version was recorded in 1765 in the Janeway Papers at Rutgers in which widow Mary Teller (the successor of Paulus Schrick) conveyed the land herself to Jacob Kip. James Duane recorded this. He was presumably the attorney who would become mayor of the City of New York in 1783 and who would have Duane Street named after him, which was laid across the African Burial Ground. James Duane, Drawer 8, Folder 6 of "The Janeway Papers," in Special Collections, Rutgers University Libraries.

32. *Reconstruction of Foley Square*, 14. This seems to contradict Hoffman's account and Duane's summary, which state that in 1698 the land passed from William Merritt to William Janeway (Liber 9:103) and then there was an exchange

between Janeway and the Corporation of New York in 1708. Hoffman concludes, " . . . and it is impossible to reconcile all the lines and courses" (*Treatise upon the Estate*, 2:207).

33. As part of the rectification, Cockburn drew up on 22 Jan. 1768 "Remarks on Mr. Maerschalk's Map of George Janeway's Lott at Freshwater," which affirms that Maerschalck was surveying this area of the city and therefore knew the existence of the burial ground intimately for his plan, as argued in chapter 1 (William Cockburn, Drawer 8, Folder 5, Item 59 of "The Janeway Papers," in Special Collections and University Archives, Rutgers University Libraries).

34. Jean Howson, Warren R. Perry, Augustin F. C. Holl, and Leonard G. Bianchi, "Relative Dating," in *New York African Burial Ground Archaeology Final Report*, eds. Warren R. Perry, Jean Howson, and Barbara A. Bianco (Washington, DC: General Services Administration and Howard Univ., 2006), 1:107.

35. "African Burial Ground and the Commons Historic District Designation Report," 27. For instance, the dead had been removed by 1833 from the French Episcopal Church on Pine Street and the Presbyterian burial ground on Nassau Street. For the Lutheran burying ground at the corner of Broadway and Rector Street, the "bones in open box carts [were carted off] promiscuously, and fragments of bones and coffins were dumped into the North River" in 1805–06 for the construction of Grace Church (Stokes, *Iconography of Manhattan Island*, 5:1717. Cited in "African Burial Ground and the Commons Historic District Designation Report," 27n100). Similarly, interments of the Quaker burial ground were carried away in carts. The Jewish burying ground on Oliver Street, which had been mapped by Maerschalck, Grim, and Kirkham, was excavated. Finally, the old Dutch cemetery on lower Broadway had been sold off as lots for development as early as 1677.

36. Howson, Bianco, and Barto, "Documentary Evidence," 62.

37. Survey from New York County Register's Office, Deeds (Liber 46:139). "African Burial Ground and the Commons Historic District Designation Report" mistakenly dated this survey to 1785. The earliest survey I know that depicts the first division of land into lots on the African Burial Ground predates fig. 14 by three years. I uncovered the document, dated 8 September 1784 by Gerrit Ochleberg, in the Bancker Plans boxes in the New York Public Library. The survey illustrates the precise moment of transformation from a sacred site to secular lots prepared for profit and development. No recipients' names are written; simply the division of lots into three city blocks. Land disputes had not been resolved and so ownership is not yet mapped. At the top lies a diagonal line of dashes and the label "Mrs. Barclays," that is, Kalk Hook Farm. Evart Bancker Jr., Box 1, Folder 44, of the "Bancker Plans," in the Manuscripts Collection of the NYPL.

38. Ingle, Howson, and Rutsch, *Stage IA Cultural Resource*, 71. See New York County Register's Office, Deeds (Liber 45:198).

39. Howson, Bianco, and Barto, "Documentary Evidence," 63.

40. Ibid., 62.

41. Howson, Perry, Holl, and Bianchi, "Relative Dating," 125.

42. *The African Burial Ground and the Commons Historic District Archaeological Sensitivity Study*, prepared for the New York City Department of General Services (Hunter Research, Inc., Mesick-Cohen-Waite Architects, 1994), 89.

43. Howson and Bianchi, "The Archaeological Site," 90.

44. This 1845 copy of a 1792 original in the New-York Historical Society is entitled *Map of Lots between Duane/Anthony and Thomas St. at Ann St. Copy of an Original Done by the Request of Egbert Benson Esqr 1792*.

45. Howson and Bianchi, "The Archaeological Site," 84.

46. Valentine, "History of Broadway," 434.

47. Stokes, *Iconography of Manhattan Island*, 5:1480. Cited in *Reconstruction of Foley Square*, 9.

48. Howson, Bianco, and Barto, "Documentary Evidence," 59. It was located near the southeast corner of today's Chambers Street and Broadway.

49. A print made from the watercolor was later used as an inset for a map by H. M. Hale in the New-York Historical Society (M29.5.75A). The print was made in 1939 and presented to commemorate the completion of the new Criminal Courts Building foundation. The caption for the print reads, "View of Collect Pond in 1798 after Alexander Robertson, looking southwest (from Baxter and Bayard Streets)." However, Stokes maintains that the scene corresponds "even more possibly [with] a point just north of the small hill near present Centre and Canal St" (Stokes, *Iconography of Manhattan Island*, 3:539–41).

50. Howson and Bianchi, "The Archaeological Site," 80.

51. Stokes, *Iconography of Manhattan Island*, 3:539–41. Walter M. Aikman later made an engraving, giving one in 1920 to the Society of Iconophiles to which he belonged. The image was published in *History of the Society of Iconophiles* in 1930. The society was founded in 1895 by William Loring Andres in order to publish views of New York and to retain a process of engraving by hand on copper (Stokes, 6:44).

52. Gloria Gilda Deák, *Picturing America: Prints, Maps, and Drawings Bearing on the New World Discoveries and on the Development of the Territory that is Now the United States* (Princeton: Princeton Univ. Press, 1988), 1:149.

53. I located the first in Evart Bancker Jr., Box 1, Folder 44, of the "Bancker Plans," in the Manuscripts Collection of the New York Public Library. The second, finalized version, not depicted here, is in the Division of Land Records (formerly the New York County Register's Office), *Survey of the Van Borsum Patent Showing Lots Divided among the Heirs*, Deeds (Liber 195:405, Filed Map 76J) and can be seen in Howson, Bianco, and Barto, "Documentary Evidence," 66.

54. "African Burial Ground and the Commons Historic District Designation Report," 20.

55. Ingle, Howson, and Rutsch, *Stage IA Cultural Resource*, 70–71. Heirs and claimants included Henry H. Kip, Abraham I. Van Vleck, John Kip, Samuel Kip, Samuel Breese, Aaron Burr, Samuel Bay, Theophilis Beekman, Isaac Van Vleck and Elizabeth Matthews, and Daniel Denniston.

56. City of New York, *Minutes of the Common Council of the City of New York, 1784–1831* (New York: The City of New York, 1917), 2:112. Quoted in Howson, Bianco, and Barto, "Documentary Evidence," 65.

57. Ibid., 2:137.

58. Ibid., 2:158–159. A portion of the petition is reproduced in Howson, Bianco, and Barto, "Documentary Evidence," 67. The original lies in the Municipal Archives of the City of New York, Papers of the Common Council, Petitions (Isaac Fortune, June 19, 1795).

59. *Trinity Church Vestry Minutes*, 15 Sept. 1773. Trinity Church Archives, New York City.

60. Hoffman, *Treatise upon the Estate*, 2:206.

61. *City of New York, Minutes of the Common Council, 1784–1831*, 2:252.

62. Ibid., 2:548–49, 615, 626.

63. Unknown surveyor, *A Copy of a Survey of Streets and Lots in New York City between Broadway and the Fresh Water, some lots of which are to be given by the Corporation of New York to George Janeway and others to be given by Janeway to the Corporation of New York for the better laying out of streets*, nd, Drawer 8, Folder 5, Item 9 of "The Janeway Papers," Deeds and Indentures Collection. Special Collections and University Archives, Rutgers University Libraries.

64. Unfortunately, Cockburn's survey is undated. It seems to be a copy of an original (it states at the bottom, "as by original Survey to be Less [in scale]") and could have been created posthumously. On the map, lots had not yet been drawn over the burial ground, and Chambers and Reade Streets were not yet laid. However, Augustus Street is included, which was not named until 1786. Thus, I would date the document to 1786 or later.

65. "African Burial Ground and the Commons Historic District Designation Report," 21.

66. Howson and Bianchi, "The Archaeological Site," 90. See Table 3.2, p. 95 for a list of burials and how they were damaged historically.

67. Interestingly, the woman was intentionally interred in her red cedar, hexagonal coffin, but entirely within the grave shaft of an earlier grave dug for a forty-year-old male (Burial 247). The bones of his disturbed skeleton were carefully placed at the end of her coffin and surrounded by pieces of his coffin. See "Descriptions of Burials 201 Through 250," in Warren R. Perry, Jean Howson,

and Barbara A. Bianco, eds., *New York African Burial Ground Archaeology Final Report* (Washington, DC: General Services Administration and Howard Univ., 2006), 3: Burial 213.

68. Henry Moscow, *The Street Book: An Encyclopedia of Manhattan's Street Names and Their Origins* (New York: Fordham Univ. Press, 1978), 37.

69. Howson and Bianchi, "The Archaeological Site," 89. In between, it was known as Barley Street around 1800.

70. Lepore, *New York Burning*, 264–65. John Chambers was also a slave-holder and prosecutor against Africans in the 1741 Conspiracy.

71. *Smith, ex. dem. Teller, v. Burtis & Woodward*, 9 Johnson Reports 182 (N.Y. Sup. Ct., 1812). Quoted in "African Burial Ground and the Commons Historic District Designation Report," 28n104.

72. Ingle, Howson, and Rutsch, *Stage IA Cultural Resource*, 90.

73. "African Burial Ground and the Commons Historic District Designation Report," 37.

74. Foley Square Federal Courthouse and Office Building, *Research Design for Archeological, Historical, and Bioanthropological Investigations of the African Burial Ground (Broadway Block, New York, NY)*, prepared by Howard University and John Milner Associates, Inc., 22 Apr. 1993, 18. For instance, in the mid-1860s, 3-story federal-style homes along Broadway were converted into commercial structures, and larger buildings were added in order to support the dry-goods trade there. The commercial building at 60 Duane Street on the corner of Elk (formerly Elm) Street stood from 1867 to 1991. Designed in 1860, 66–68 Duane Street was a store and loft building with a cast-iron facade. A 5-story structure at the corner of Republican Alley and Elk in 1899 was torn down for the federal office building.

75. "African Burial Ground and the Commons Historic District Designation Report," 37.

76. U.S. Department of the Interior, National Park Service, *African Burial Ground National Historic Landmark*, 14.

77. "African Burial Ground and the Commons Historic District Designation Report," 28.

78. Ingle, Howson, and Rutsch, *Stage IA Cultural Resource*, 88.

79. "African Burial Ground and the Commons Historic District Designation Report," 36.

80. The pottery business was on Reade Street, but there is a discrepancy as to whether it was on the north or south side of Reade, which would determine if it was in present day Block 153 or 155. Most recently, Howson, Bianco, and Barto ("Documentary Evidence," 51) located the pottery on Block 153 (south side), while the "African Burial Ground and the Commons Historic District Designation Report" (38) had positioned it on the southern half of Block 155 or the north side.

81. "African Burial Ground and the Commons Historic District Designation Report," 39. Prior to the construction of these two buildings, the block was used for foundries. Morris and Cummings opened an iron foundry and millstone here in the early 1840s. D. D. Badger Iron Works and Turner and Lane glass cutting businesses stood next to each other at 42–46 Duane Street during the 1850s. The Connor type foundry took up much of the block at the end of the nineteenth century.

82. U.S. Department of the Interior, National Park Service, *African Burial Ground National Historic Landmark*, 14.

83. See *Report of the New York City Improvement Commission to the Honorable Geo. B. McClellan, Mayor of the City of New York, and to the Honorable Board of Aldermen of the City of New York* (New York, 1904), 15.

84. "African Burial Ground and the Commons Historic District Designation Report," 30.

3. Burying the Dead

1. Dr. Michael L. Blakey is an anthropologist at the College of William and Mary. Dr. Warren R. Perry at Central Connecticut State University was the director of archaeology. The third team was led by Dr. Edna Greene Medford at Howard University as director of history. Additional African Burial Ground project directors were Dr. Sherrill Wilson for the Office of Public Education and Interpretation, Dr. Lesley Rankin-Hill as director of skeletal biology, Dr. Alan Goodman as director of chemical studies, Dr. Fatimah Jackson as director of genetics, Dr. Jean Howson as associate director for archaeology, Leonard Bianchi as the archaeology laboratory director, and Mark Mack as the Cobb Laboratory director at Howard University.

2. Citations from the African Burial Ground final reports derive from the 2006 and 2004 versions that were formerly posted on the GSA website at http:// www.africanburialground.gov. The reports are no longer available at that URL. The final reports were reformatted with a new copyright date of 2009 and are now located at http://www.gsa.gov/portal/content/249941. Page numbers cited in this book correspond to the earlier edition, which I accessed, rather than those in the currently posted 2009 versions. The appendix at the end of this book entitled African Burial Ground Final Reports lists the chapters from each of the final reports cited in this book, which will facilitate a correspondence between my citations and the current internet posting.

3. Michael L. Blakey, "Theory: An Ethical Epistemology of Publicly Engaged Biocultural Research," in *The New York African Burial Ground Skeletal Biology Final Report*, eds. Michael L. Blakey and Lesley M. Rankin-Hill (Washington, DC: General Services Administration and Howard Univ., 2004), 1:105.

4. Blakey, "Theory: An Ethical Epistemology," 99, 104.

5. Additionally, European, Native American, and Caribbean influences likely impacted funerary traditions, although African and African descendant practices are the focus here. Few African cemeteries are known to exist in the Americas. The only other excavated eighteenth-century urban cemetery for enslaved people is St. Peter's Cemetery in New Orleans, where twenty-nine people were exhumed. Quite a few nineteenth-century urban African cemeteries, usually related to churches, are known. Not many have been excavated, although the First African Baptist Church cemetery in Philadelphia was. The site dated from the 1820s to the 1840s, with over 140 burials. A small number of burials have been excavated from rural sites (usually associated with plantations), save the Newton Plantation in Barbados. It dates from the seventeenth to nineteenth century and had at least 101 people in it (U.S. Department of the Interior, National Park Service, *African Burial Ground National Historic Landmark Registration Form*, prepared by the New York City Landmarks Preservation Commission [Jean Howson and Gale Harris] [New York, 9 Nov. 1992], 21–22).

6. Two significant texts that carefully develop this point are Edward Said, "Representing the Colonized: Anthropology's Interlocutors," *Critical Inquiry* 15, no. 2 (1989): 205–225; and James Clifford, "Traveling Cultures," in *Cultural Studies*, eds. Lawrence Grossberg, Cary Nelson, and Paula Treichler (New York and London: Routledge, 1992), 96–116.

7. Warren R. Perry et al., "The African Burial Ground: Mortuary Complex in Diasporic Perspective" (paper presented at the 14th Congress of Anthropological and Ethnological Sciences, Williamsburg, VA, 28 July 1998), 4.

8. Jean Howson, Leonard G. Bianchi, and Warren R. Perry, "Introduction," in *New York African Burial Ground Archaeology Final Report*, eds. Warren R. Perry, Jean Howson, and Barbara A. Bianco (Washington, DC: General Services Administration and Howard Univ., 2006), 1:10.

9. Warren Perry, Jean Howson, and Barbara Bianco, "Summary and Conclusions," in *New York African Burial Ground Archaeology Final Report*, eds. Warren R. Perry, Jean Howson, and Barbara A. Bianco (Washington, DC: General Services Administration and Howard Univ., 2006), 1:447–48.

10. Warren R. Perry and Jean Howson, "Overview of Mortuary Population, Burial Practices, and Spatial Distribution," in *New York African Burial Ground Archaeology Final Report*, eds. Warren R. Perry, Jean Howson, and Barbara A. Bianco (Washington, DC: General Services Administration and Howard Univ., 2006), 1:133.

11. Ross Jamieson, "Material Culture and Social Death: African American Burial Practices," *Historical Archaeology* 29, no. 4 (1995): 52. Quoted in Perry and Howson, "Overview of Mortuary Population," 134.

12. Jean Howson and Leonard Bianchi, with Iciar Lucena Narvaez and Janet L. Woodruff, "Coffins," in *New York African Burial Ground Archaeology Final Report*, eds. Warren R. Perry, Jean Howson, and Barbara A. Bianco (Washington, DC: General Services Administration and Howard Univ., 2006), 1:250.

13. Ibid., 256.

14. Ibid., 258.

15. Ibid., 253.

16. We know the initials, H. W., placed on the coffin in figure 28, and the first names of those executed in the 1741 Conspiracy.

17. Howson and Bianchi, "Coffins," 251.

18. Perry et al., "The African Burial Ground: Mortuary Complex in Diasporic Perspective," 12.

19. Howson and Bianchi, "Coffins," 274. Strike marks are visible on the back from hand forging.

20. Jean Cerasale, Jean Howson, Iciar Lucena Narvaez, Ruth Mathis, Warren R. Perry, and Janet L. Woodruff, "Descriptions of Burials 1–200," in *New York African Burial Ground Archaeology Final Report*, eds. Warren R. Perry, Jean Howson, and Barbara A. Bianco (Washington, DC: General Services Administration and Howard Univ., 2006), 2: Burial 176.

21. L. M. Rankin-Hill, J. Gruber, P. Allen, and A. Barrett, "Burial Descriptions," in *The New York African Burial Ground Skeletal Biology Final Report*, eds. Michael L. Blakey and Lesley M. Rankin-Hill (Washington, DC: General Services Administration and Howard Univ., 2004), Section 4, 63.

22. Howson and Bianchi, "Coffins," 271.

23. Jean Howson, with Shannon Mahoney and Janet L. Woodruff, "Pins and Shrouding," in *New York African Burial Ground Archaeology Final Report*, eds. Warren R. Perry, Jean Howson, and Barbara A. Bianco (Washington, DC: General Services Administration and Howard Univ., 2006), 1:288.

24. David R. Watters, "Mortuary Patterns at the Harney Site Slave Cemetery, Montserrat, in Caribbean Perspective," *Historical Archaeology* 28, no. 3 (1994): 62.

25. See for example, Abdurahman Juma, "Muslim Burial Customs on the East African Coast," *Tor* (Uppsala) 28 (1996): 351.

26. Howson, with Mahoney and Woodruff, "Pins and Shrouding," 290.

27. Ibid., 295. Cited in Rita S. Gottesman, *The Arts and Crafts in New York, 1726–1776: Advertisements and News Items from New York City Newspapers* (New York: New-York Historical Society, 1938), 142.

28. Ibid., 297 (Table 11.6) and 298.

29. David R. Roediger, "And Die in Dixie: Funerals, Death and Heaven in the Slave Community, 1700–1865." *Massachusetts Review* 22, no. 1 (Spring 1981): 169.

30. Ibid., 166.

31. Robert Farris Thompson and Joseph Cornet, *The Four Moments of the Sun: Kongo Art in Two Worlds* (New Haven: Eastern Press, 1981), 52.

32. Daniel Mato, "Clothed in Symbol: The Art of Adinkra among the Akan of Ghana," (PhD diss., Indiana Univ., 1986), 69.

33. Perry and Howson, "Overview of Mortuary Population," 146.

34. Jean Howson and Leonard G. Bianchi, "The Archaeological Site," in *New York African Burial Ground Archaeology Final Report*, eds. Warren R. Perry, Jean Howson, and Barbara A. Bianco (Washington, DC: General Services Administration and Howard Univ., 2006), 1:98.

35. City of New York, *Minutes of the Common Council of the City of New York, 1675–1776* (New York: Dodd, Mead, and Co., 1905), 4:447.

36. Eugene Genovese, *Roll, Jordan, Roll* (New York: Pantheon Books, 1972), 197.

37. David T. Valentine, "History of Broadway," in *Manual of the Common Council of New York* (New York: D. T. Valentine, 1865), 567. The full quote is, "Many of them were native Africans, imported hither in slave ships, and retaining their native superstitions and burial customs, among which was that of burying by night, with various mummeries and outcries."

38. Michael Mullin, *Africa in America: Slave Acculturation and Resistance in the American South and the British Caribbean, 1736–1831* (Urbana: Univ. of Illinois Press, 1992), 65.

39. Ibid.

40. Ibid., 66.

41. Kimpianga Mahaniah, "The Religious and Medicinal Functions of the Cemetery Among the Bakongo of Zaire," 1977. Quoted in Thompson and Cornet, *The Four Moments*, 95.

42. Thompson and Cornet, *The Four Moments*, 194.

43. Warren R. Perry and Janet L. Woodruff, "Coins, Shells, Pipes, and Other Items," in *New York African Burial Ground Archaeology Final Report*, eds. Warren R. Perry, Jean Howson, and Barbara A. Bianco (Washington, DC: General Services Administration and Howard Univ., 2006), 1:419.

44. The other burial numbers are 214, 230, and 242. Additional coins were found in the African Burial Ground excavation but could not be definitively associated with burials. For details, see Perry and Woodruff, "Coins, Shells, Pipes," 421–22n4.

45. Watters, "Mortuary Patterns," 64.

46. William D. Piersen, *From Africa to America: African American History from the Colonial Era to the Early Republic, 1526–1790* (New York: Twayne Publishers, 1996), 97. This belief continued into the nineteenth century. In his 1837

narrative as a slave, Charles Ball described an infant's funeral that he attended in which a miniature canoe and small paddle were buried with the child. The father told him the objects would enable him "to cross the ocean to his own country." Also buried with the child was some food, a small bow and arrows, and an iron nail. Charles Ball, *Fifty Years in Chains* (New York: Dover Publications, 1970), 265. Quoted in Albert J. Raboteau, *Slave Religion: The 'Invisible Institution' in the Antebellum South* (New York: Oxford Univ. Press, 1978), 44.

47. Perry and Woodruff, "Coins, Shells, Pipes," 426.

48. Perry and Howson, "Overview of Mortuary Population," 150, 151.

49. Perry and Woodruff, "Coins, Shells, Pipes," 429. To ascertain this identification, the piece was sent to the American Museum of Natural History, the New York Aquarium, the Smithsonian Museum of Natural History, and then the Geology Department at the University of Iowa.

50. Thompson and Cornet, *The Four Moments*, 95.

51. Ibid.

52. Anne Hilton, *The Kingdom of the Kongo* (Oxford: Clarendon Press, 1985), 62, 195. Cited in Pamela McClusky, *Art from Africa: Long Steps Never Broke a Back* (Seattle and Princeton: Seattle Art Museum with Princeton Univ. Press, 2002), 146, 150.

53. Perry and Woodruff, "Coins, Shells, Pipes," 432.

54. Perry, Howson, and Bianco, "Summary," 452.

55. Ibid.

56. Perry and Woodruff, "Coins, Shells, Pipes," 432. She was from the Middle Group section of the Burial Ground and had been buried directly in the ground with no coffin. Her arms were crossed and above her head, which was an unusual position.

57. Robert Farris Thompson, *Flash of the Spirit: African and Afro-American Art and Philosophy* (New York and Toronto: First Vintage Books, 1984).

58. Since the crystal was not found until the skeleton was in the laboratory, it is not known whether it was placed in the grave or if it was in the soil used to fill the grave (Perry and Woodruff, "Coins, Shells, Pipes," 436).

59. Laurie A. Wilkie, "Secret and Sacred: Contextualizing the Artifacts of African-American Magic and Religion," *Historical Archaeology* 31, no. 4 (1997): 100.

60. Judy Sterner, "Sacred Pots and 'Symbolic Reservoirs' in the Mandara Highlands of Northern Cameroun," in *An African Commitment: Papers in Honour of Peter Lewis Shinnie*, eds. Judy Sterner and Nicholas David (Calgary: Univ. of Calgary Press, 1992), 175.

61. Thompson, *Flash of the Spirit*, 84.

62. Perry and Woodruff, "Coins, Shells, Pipes," 438.

63. Cerasale et al., "Descriptions of Burials 201–435," 3: Burial 328.

64. Leland Ferguson, "The Cross Is a Magic Sign: Marks on Eighteenth-Century Bowls from South Carolina," in *I, Too, Am America: Archaeological Studies of African-American Life*, ed. Theresa Singleton (Charlottesville: Univ. Press of Virginia, 1999), 116.

65. Thompson and Cornet, *The Four Moments*, 179.

66. Monica Blackmun Visona, Robin Poyner, and Herbert M. Cole, *A History of Art in Africa* (New York: Prentice Hall and Harry N. Abrams, 2001), 92.

67. Barbara A. Bianco, Christopher R. DeCorse, and Jean Howson, "Beads and Other Adornments," in *New York African Burial Ground Archaeology Final Report*, eds. Warren R. Perry, Jean Howson, and Barbara A. Bianco (Washington, DC: General Services Administration and Howard Univ., 2006), 1:382.

68. Ibid., 398.

69. Ibid., 404. A larger bead produced the same way was found in Barbados at the Newton Plantation Burial Ground. Furthermore, anthropologist and bead specialist Chris DeCorse excavated such beads from Elmina, but only in the eighteenth and nineteenth centuries. See Jerome S. Handler, "An African-Type Healer/Diviner and His Grave Goods: A Burial from a Plantation Slave Cemetery in Barbados, West Indies," *International Journal of Historical Archaeology* 1, no. 2 (1997): 91–130.

70. Perry et al., "The African Burial Ground: Mortuary Complex in Diasporic Perspective," 7.

71. Perry and Howson, "Overview of Mortuary Population," 132. The older male of Burial 221 had bone scarring in his lower limbs as a result of inflammation from bacterial infection or an injury (periostitis) and osteoarthritis in his knee, ankle, and hand (Rankin-Hill, Gruber, Allen, and Barret, "Burial Descriptions," section 4, 78).

72. Bianco, DeCorse, and Howson, "Beads," 399. For the latter, see Amanda Gilvin, "'The Fire Is Too Hot for Them': Gender and Change in the Krobo Bead Industry," (MA thesis, Cornell Univ., 2006). The burial ground beads range in size from a 2.2 mm. diameter to 7 mm., and one large bead in Burial 250 at 13.6 mm. in size. (Christopher R. DeCorse, personal communication with author, 16 Mar. 2000; and Bianco, DeCorse, and Howson, "Beads," 399.)

73. Bianco, DeCorse, and Howson, "Beads," 390.

74. Ibid., 403.

75. Cerasale et al., "Descriptions of Burials 1–200," 2: Burial 187. He was buried in the very northern part of the cemetery, so he died after 1776.

76. Rankin-Hill, Gruber, Allen, and Barret, "Burial Descriptions," section 4, 67.

77. Bianco, DeCorse, and Howson, "Beads," 385.

78. Rankin-Hill, Gruber, Allen, and Barret, "Burial Descriptions," section 4, 40.

79. Cerasale et al., "Descriptions of Burials 201–435," 3: Burial 428.

80. Rankin-Hill, Gruber, Allen, and Barret, "Burial Descriptions," section 4, 144.

81. Bianco, DeCorse, and Howson, "Beads," 413.

82. Bianco, DeCorse, and Howson, "Beads," 411. Rings were frequently dispersed to relatives, friends, executors, clergy, and pallbearers at European American funerals. Called mourning rings, they were gold or enameled tokens from the deceased worn in remembrance of him or her. Kenneth Scott, "Funeral Customs in Colonial New York," *The Staten Island Historian* 22, no. 1 (Jan.–Mar. 1961): 6, 7.

83. Bianco, DeCorse, and Howson, "Beads," 387.

84. Ibid., 413.

85. Ibid., 414.

86. Perry and Howson, "Overview of Mortuary Population," 151.

87. Ibid.

88. Bianco, DeCorse, and Howson, "Beads," 414.

89. Ibid., 390.

90. Ibid.

91. Howson and Bianchi, "Coffins," 275.

92. Leonard G. Bianchi and Barbara A. Bianco with Shannon Mahoney, "Buttons and Fasteners," in *New York African Burial Ground Archaeology Final Report*, eds. Warren R. Perry, Jean Howson, and Barbara A. Bianco (Washington, DC: General Services Administration and Howard Univ., 2006), 1:327.

93. See figure 5 in Allison Manfra McGovern, "Rocky Point's African American Past: A Forgotten History Remembered through Historical Archaeology at the Betsey Prince Site," *Long Island History Journal* 22, no. 1 (2011), https://lihj .cc.stonybrook.edu/2011/articles/rocky-point's-african-american-past-a-forgotten -history-remembered-through-historical-archaeology-at-the-betsey-prince-site/ (accessed 17 Aug. 2012); and Mark LoRusso, "The Betsey Prince Site: An Early Free Black Domestic Site on Long Island," in *Nineteenth- and Early Twentieth-Century Domestic Site Archaeology in New York State*, eds. John P. Hart and Charles L. Fisher (New York State Museum Bulletin 495) (Albany: Univ. of the State of New York and New York State Education Dept., 2000), 195–224. Thanks to Mark LoRusso for introducing the pin to me.

94. Rankin-Hill, Gruber, Allen, and Barret, "Burial Descriptions," section 4, 5. Strontium isotope is explained in n144.

95. Ibid.

96. Perry, Howson, and Bianco, "Summary," 450.

97. The varieties consisted of: fourteen light gold, transparent, circular beads; twenty-five circular, transparent blue green/turquoise beads; fifty-nine transparent, cobalt blue (oblate to barrel-shaped) beads; one barrel-shaped, opaque black

bead with three white wavy lines encircling it perpendicular to the hole, which was just over 8 mm. in size; six transparent, light gold beads; one opaque blue bead with a wavy gilt stripe at either end of the irregular barrel shape; and one red-faceted bead made of amber. Cheryl J. LaRoche, "Beads from the African Burial Ground, New York City: A Preliminary Assessment," *Beads: Journal of the Society of Bead Researchers* 6 (1994): 10–11.

98. Bianco, DeCorse, and Howson, "Beads," 403.

99. Linda France Stine, Melanie Cabak, and Mark Groover, "Blue Beads as African-American Cultural Symbols," *Historical Archaeology* 30, no. 3 (1996): 50.

100. LaRoche, "Beads from the African Burial Ground," 16.

101. Edna Greene Medford, Warren Perry, Selwyn Carrington, Linda Heywood, Fatimah Jackson, S. O. Y. Keita, Richard Kittles, and John Thornton, "The Transatlantic Slave Trade to New York City: Sources and Routing of Captives" (paper presented at the 14th Congress of Anthropological and Ethnological Sciences, Williamsburg, VA, 28 July 1998).

102. William Hugh Grove, 1732. Quoted in L. Baumgarten, "Clothes for the People. Slave Clothing in Early Virginia," *Journal of Early Southern Decorative Arts* 14, no. 2 (Nov. 1988): 28.

103. Daniel Mato, "Clothed in Symbol: The Art of Adinkra among the Akan of Ghana" (PhD diss., Indiana Univ., 1986): 53.

104. Cerasale et al., "Descriptions of Burials 1–200," 2: Burial 158.

105. Handler, "An African-Type Healer," 113–14.

106. J. Taylor, *Historie of His Life and Travels in America: Containing a Full Geographical Description of the Island of Jamaica* (Ms., National Library of Jamaica, Kingston, 1688), 544. Quoted in Handler, "An African-Type Healer," 113.

107. Wilkie, "Secret and Sacred," 99.

108. Augustin F. C. Holl, "The Cemetery of Houlouf in Northern Cameroun (AD 1500–1600): Fragments of a Past Social System," *African Archaeological Review* 12 (1994): 139.

109. N. K. Dzobo, "African Symbols and Proverbs as Sources of Knowledge and Truth," in *Person and Community*, eds. Kwasi Wiredu and Kwami Gyekye (Washington, DC: Council for Research in Values and Philosophy, 1992), 84.

110. J. B. Danquah, *The Akan Doctrine of God: A Fragment of Gold Coast Ethics and Religion*, 2nd ed. (London: Frank Cass and Co., 1968), xxxvii.

111. Medford et al., "The Transatlantic Slave Trade"; Howson and Bianchi, "Coffins," 273; and Warren R. Perry, Jean Howson, and Augustin F. C. Holl, "The Late-Middle Group," in *New York African Burial Ground Archaeology Final Report*, eds. Warren R. Perry, Jean Howson, and Barbara A. Bianco (Washington, DC: General Services Administration and Howard Univ., 2006), 222. The proverb in Twi is *se wo were fi na wo sankofa a yenkyi*. Already proposed in the Final Report

in the citations preceding this sentence, Seeman also challenged the identification of the sankofa on Burial 101's coffin lid in a journal article that was highlighted in the *New York Times*. He leans towards an Anglo-American appropriation instead. Nevertheless, an African-based relationship with the ancestral realm could still be pertinent. See Sewell Chan, "Coffin's Emblem Defies Certainty," *New York Times* 27 Jan. 2010, C1, drawn from a journal article: Erik R. Seeman, "Reassessing the '*Sankofa* Symbol' in New York's African Burial Ground," *William and Mary Quarterly* 67, no. 1 (Jan. 2010): 101–22.

112. Seeman "Reassessing the '*Sankofa* Symbol,'" 116–17; Howson and Bianchi, "Coffins," 273.

113. Howson and Bianchi, "Coffins," 272.

114. Michael Blakey, Open House, 21 Nov. 1998.

115. Mack, Educator Symposium, 20 Nov. 1999 and F.L.C. Jackson, A. Mayes, M.E. Mack, A. Froment, S.O.Y. Keita, R.A. Kittles, M. George, K. Shujaa, M. L. Blakey, and L.M. Rankin-Hill, "Origins of the New York African Burial Ground Population: Biological Evidence of Geographical and Macroethnic Affiliations Using Craniometrics, Dental Morphology, and Preliminary Genetic Analyses," in *The New York African Burial Ground Skeletal Biology Final Report*, eds. Michael L. Blakey and Lesley M. Rankin-Hill (Washington, DC: General Services Administration and Howard Univ., 2004), 1:194.

116. Perry, Howson, and Holl, "The Late-Middle Group," 223.

117. Blakey, Open House, 22 May 1999 and Perry, Howson, Bianco, "Summary," 451. Yaws is a contagious bacterial disease that forms yellowish or reddish tumors on the skin resembling raspberries. Yaws was contracted by those born in Africa because it is a tropical disease and no outbreak of the disease was reported in New York at that time. One court case in New York concerned an African with yaws, so it is evident that people with yaws lived in New York. C. C. Null, M. L. Blakey, K. J. Shujaa, L. M. Rankin-Hill, and S. H. H. Carrington, "Osteological Indicators of Infectious Disease and Nutritional Inadequacy," in *The New York African Burial Ground Skeletal Biology Final Report*, eds. Michael L. Blakey and Lesley M. Rankin-Hill (Washington, DC: General Services Administration and Howard Univ., 2004), 1:378.

118. Perry, Howson, and Holl, "The Late-Middle Group," 219.

119. Cerasale et al., "Descriptions of Burials 1–200," 2: Burial 108.

120. Perry, Howson, Bianco, "Summary," 451.

121. Perry, Howson, Holl, "The Late-Middle Group," 223.

122. Seeman, "Reassessing the '*Sankofa* Symbol,'" 101.

123. Rodger Taylor, "Inside the Lab . . . Putting It All Back Together," *Update: Newsletter of the African Burial Ground and Five Points Archaeological Projects* 1, no.1 (Spring 1993), 8.

124. Jean Howson, Warren R. Perry, Augustin F.C. Holl, and Leonard G. Bianchi, "Relative Dating," in *New York African Burial Ground Archaeology Final Report*, eds. Warren R. Perry, Jean Howson, and Barbara A. Bianco (Washington, DC: General Services Administration and Howard Univ., 2006), 1:112.

125. Warren R. Perry, Jean Howson, and Augustin F. C. Holl, "The Early Group," in *New York African Burial Ground Archaeology Final Report*, eds. Warren R. Perry, Jean Howson, and Barbara A. Bianco (Washington, DC: General Services Administration and Howard Univ., 2006), 1:196.

126. Warren R. Perry, Jean Howson, and Augustin F. C. Holl, "The Middle Group," in *New York African Burial Ground Archaeology Final Report*, eds. Warren R. Perry, Jean Howson, and Barbara A. Bianco (Washington, DC: General Services Administration and Howard Univ., 2006), 1:197.

127. Ibid., 204.

128. Cerasale et al., "Descriptions of Burials 1–200," 2: Burials 142, 144, 149.

129. Perry, Howson, and Holl, "The Late-Middle Group," 207.

130. Ibid., 218, 220.

131. In the westernmost area of excavation, a ditch north of the ostensible fence suggested yet another property marker (U.S. Department of the Interior, *African Burial Ground National Historic Landmark Registration Form*, 9–10).

132. Howson, Perry, Holl, and Bianchi, "Relative Dating," 107, 109. My uncovering of the lost Janeway Papers confirms that the fence did exist, and that it was still in place in 1766, as depicted in William Cockburn's survey. See figure 13.

133. Howson, Perry, Holl, and Bianchi, "Relative Dating," 109.

134. Warren R. Perry, Jean Howson, and Augustin F. C. Holl, "The Late Group," in *New York African Burial Ground Archaeology Final Report*, eds. Warren R. Perry, Jean Howson, and Barbara A. Bianco (Washington, DC: General Services Administration and Howard Univ., 2006), 1:242.

135. John Fanning Watson, *Annals and Occurrences of New York City and State in the Olden Time* (Carlisle, MA: Applewood Books, 1846), 362.

136. Perry, Howson, and, Holl, "The Late Group," 241.

137. Ibid., 248.

138. Ibid., 227.

139. Ibid., 249.

140. M. L. Blakey, L. M. Rankin-Hill, A. Goodman and F. Jackson, "Discussion," in *The New York African Burial Ground Skeletal Biology Final Report*, eds. Michael L. Blakey and Lesley M. Rankin-Hill (Washington, DC: General Services Administration and Howard Univ., 2004), 1:442. I would like to thank my colleague Dr. Nancy Stevens in the Department of Biomedical Sciences at Ohio University for her generous assistance in editing this section of the chapter on skeletal and bone analysis.

141. Of the 301 recovered burials for which age could be determined, 171 (56.8 percent) were adults and 130 (43.2 percent) were children under the age of fifteen. L. M. Rankin-Hill, M. L. Blakey, J. Howson, E. Brown, S. H. H. Carrington, and K. Shujaa, "Demographic Overview of the African Burial Ground and Colonial Africans of New York," in *The New York African Burial Ground Skeletal Biology Final Report*, eds. Michael L. Blakey and Lesley M. Rankin-Hill (Washington, DC: General Services Administration and Howard Univ., 2004), 1:271.

142. Rankin-Hill, Blakey, Howson, Brown, Carrington, and Shujaa, "Demographic Overview," 275.

143. The two analytical chemistry approaches, strontium isotope analysis of tooth enamel calcification and secondly, LA-ICP-MS Elemental Signature Analysis that identifies elements in tooth enamel, were used to reveal clusters of burials born either in Africa or born in New York. Those below the age of eight were equivalent to the isotopic signature linked with Manhattan for the strontium isotope analysis of tooth enamel calcification. Blakey, Rankin-Hill, Goodman, and Jackson, "Discussion," 542. Also, A. Goodman, J. Jones, J. Reid, M. Mack, M. L. Blakey, D. Amarasiriwardena, P. Burton, and D. Coleman, "Isotopic and Elemental Chemistry of Teeth: Implications for Places of Birth, Forced Migration Patterns, Nutritional Status, and Pollution," in *The New York African Burial Ground Skeletal Biology Final Report*, eds. Michael L. Blakey and Lesley M. Rankin-Hill (Washington, DC: General Services Administration and Howard Univ., 2004), 1:218.

144. M. Blakey, M. Mack, A. R. Barrett, S. S. Mahoney and A. H. Goodman, "Childhood Health and Dental Development," in *The New York African Burial Ground Skeletal Biology Final Report*, eds. Michael L. Blakey and Lesley M. Rankin-Hill (Washington, DC: General Services Administration and Howard Univ., 2004), 1:306, 313.

145. Blakey, Rankin-Hill, Goodman, and Jackson, "Discussion," 543.

146. Blakey, Mack, Barrett, Mahoney, and Goodman, "Childhood Health," 326.

147. Goodman et al., "Isotopic and Elemental Chemistry," 262. This was ascertained through Elemental Signature Analysis. The amount acceptable today before neurological damage occurs varies from 5 ppm to 10 ppm.

148. S. K. Goode-Null, K. Shujaa, and L. M. Rankin-Hill, "Subadult Growth and Development," in *The New York African Burial Ground Skeletal Biology Final Report*, eds. Michael L. Blakey and Lesley M. Rankin-Hill (Washington, DC: General Services Administration and Howard Univ., 2004), 1:488.

149. Ibid., 512.

150. Ibid., 495.

151. Ibid., 498.

152. Ibid., 511.

153. Ibid., 501.

154. Mark Mack, presenter at the "African Burial Ground Project Fall 1999 Educators Symposium," New York City, 20 Nov. 1999.

155. Rankin-Hill, Gruber, Allen, and Barret, "Burial Descriptions," section 4, 18.

156. The child was buried in a hexagonal coffin made with fifteen nails from the rarely used yew wood (only one other coffin was made of yew). Straight pins at the head and pelvis indicate he or she was shrouded. M. E. Mack, A. H. Goodman, M. L. Blakey, and A. Mayes, "Odontological Indicators of Disease, Diet, and Nutrition Inadequacy," in *The New York African Burial Ground Skeletal Biology Final Report*, eds. Michael L. Blakey and Lesley M. Rankin-Hill (Washington, DC: General Services Administration and Howard Univ., 2004), 1:347.

157. Cerasale et al., "Descriptions of Burials 1–200," 2: Burials 12 and 14. The shroud pins from Burial 12 are photographed in figure 21. A slight discrepancy in age, the archaeological team dated Burial 14 as less than six months old, and the skeletal team dated the child as zero to three years of age. Rankin-Hill, Gruber, Allen, and Barret, "Burial Descriptions," section 4, 9.

158. Perry and Howson, "Overview of Mortuary Population," 141, 142.

159. Blakey, Rankin-Hill, Goodman, and Jackson, "Discussion," 544.

160. Ibid., 545.

161. Rankin-Hill, Blakey, Howson, Brown, Carrington, and Shujaa, "Demographic Overview," 272.

162. Ibid.

163. Ibid., 282.

164. Ibid., 283.

165. Ibid., 287.

166. Mack, Goodman, Blakey, and Mayes, "Odontological Indicators," 339.

167. Ibid., 350.

168. Null, Blakey, Shujaa, Rankin-Hill, and Carrington, "Osteological Indicators," 353.

169. Ibid., 380. Periostitis is also associated with treponemal infection. Forty had a treponemal infection that likely results from yaws. See n117 for a description of yaws. Furthermore, researchers compared which of the 275 adults exhibited evidence of both porotic hyperostosis and periostitis (lesions on the surface of bones in response to disease or an infectious agent), and they found that more than one-third, or 34.2 percent (94 people) shared the two (Ibid., 395).

170. Ibid., "Osteological Indicators," 362.

171. Blakey, Rankin-Hill, Goodman, and Jackson, "Discussion," 546.

172. C. Wilczak, R. Watkins, C. Null, and M. L. Blakey, "Skeletal Indicators of Work: Musculoskeletal, Arthritic and Traumatic Effects," in *The New York African Burial Ground Skeletal Biology Final Report*, eds. Michael L. Blakey and

Lesley M. Rankin-Hill (Washington, DC: General Services Administration and Howard Univ., 2004), 1:403, 407.

173. Ibid., 408, 414.

174. Ibid., 415.

175. Ibid., 419.

176. Rankin-Hill, Gruber, Allen, and Barrett, "Burial Descriptions," section 4, 7.

177. Wilczak, Watkins, Null, and Blakey, "Skeletal Indicators," 441.

178. Ibid., 448.

179. Ibid., 457.

180. Ibid., 450.

181. Ibid., 454.

182. Cerasale et al., "Descriptions of Burials 201–435," 3: Burial 205.

183. Wilczak, Watkins, Null, and Blakey, "Skeletal Indicators," 455. Both Burial 180 and 205 belong to the Late Group in terms of relative dating.

184. Rankin-Hill, Gruber, Allen, and Barrett, "Burial Descriptions," section 4, 65.

185. Wilczak, Watkins, Null, and Blakey, "Skeletal Indicators," 458.

186. Perry, Howson, and Holl, "The Middle Group," 202.

187. Cerasale et al., "Descriptions of Burials 1–200," 2: Burial 25.

188. Goodman et al., "Isotopic and Elemental Chemistry," 245. The burial numbers are 47, 23, 6, 114, 326, 366, 377, 101, 241, 367, 397, 68, 194, 243, 403, 115, 384, 9, 106, 151, 192, 266, 270, 340, 281, 165.

189. Jerome Handler's excavation of the Newton plantation cemetery in Barbados, which was roughly contemporaneous with the African Burial Ground, revealed five people with filed teeth. Handler concludes "with a certain degree of confidence that such persons were born in Africa and not in the New World." Handler was a member of the burial ground Federal Steering Committee originated by Congress, discussed in chapter 4. Jerome S. Handler, "Determining African Birth from Skeletal Remains: A Note on Tooth Mutilation," *Historical Archaeology* 28, no. 3 (1994): 114, 118.

190. Michael Blakey, presenter at the "African Burial Ground Project Fall 1998 Educators Symposium," New York City, 21 Nov. 1998; and Goodman et al., "Isotopic and Elemental Chemistry," 244.

191. Mark E. Mack and M. C. Hill, "Notes from the Howard University Biological Anthropology Laboratory: Dental Observations of the New York African Burial Ground Skeletal Population" *Update: Newsletter of the African Burial Ground and Five Points Archaeological Projects* 1, no. 6 (Winter 1995): 4; and also Wilczak, Watkins, Null, and Blakey, "Skeletal Indicators," 449.

192. Goodman et al., "Isotopic and Elemental Chemistry," 246.

193. Cerasale et al., "Descriptions of Burials 1–200," 2: Burial 137.

194. F. L. C. Jackson, A. Mayes, M. E. Mack, A. Froment, S. O. Y. Keita, R. A. Kittles, M. George, K. Shujaa, M. L. Blakey, and L. M. Rankin-Hill, "Origins of the New York African Burial Ground Population," in *The New York African Burial Ground Skeletal Biology Final Report*, eds. Michael L. Blakey and Lesley M. Rankin-Hill (Washington, DC: General Services Administration and Howard Univ., 2004), 1:166. The chapter discusses the historical complexities of such an analysis.

195. Ibid., 185.

196. Ibid., 197.

197. Luanda in Angola was particularly important for the Portuguese. The area provided more Africans for America than anywhere during the seventeenth century (Hugh Thomas, *The Slave Trade: The Story of the Atlantic Slave Trade, 1440–1870* [New York: Touchstone, 1999], 140). In fact, between 1597 and 1637, an estimated 84 percent were taken from there.

198. After several attempts, the Dutch captured Elmina on the Gold Coast from the Portuguese in 1637. The Dutch also took a portion of Angola, including the major port of Luanda, from the Portuguese in 1641. Additionally, Sao Thome was taken from the Portuguese from 1642 to 1648.

199. The Dutch took over Curaçao from Spaniards in 1634 in order to create a military base and attack Spanish fleets and islands. Jan Rogozinski, *A Brief History of the Caribbean: From the Arawak and the Carib to the Present*, rev. ed. (New York and Oxford: Facts on File, 1999), 65.

200. Joyce D. Goodfriend, "Burghers and Blacks: The Evolution of a Slave Society at New Amsterdam," *New York History* (Apr. 1978): 137.

201. Willie F. Page, *The Dutch Triangle: The Netherlands and the Atlantic Slave Trade, 1621–1664* (New York: Garland Pub., 1997), 199. Before moving to Curaçao, Stuyvesant lived three years in Pernambuco and had thus witnessed Brazil's dependence on slavery.

202. Robert J. Swan, "The Other Fort Amsterdam: New Light on Aspects of Slavery in New Netherland," *Afro-Americans in New York Life and History* 22, no. 2 (1998): 27.

203. Ibid.

204. Vivienne L. Kruger, "Born to Run: The Slave Family in Early New York, 1626–1827" (PhD diss., Columbia Univ., 1985), 44. Additionally, Africans who received land grants between 1647 and 1659 were given names such as Anna d'Angola, Anthony Congo, Domingo Angola, Assento Angola, Francisco Cartagena, Christoffel Santomie (whose name had been recorded earlier in 1656 as Christoffel Crioelle [creole]), and Van St. Thomas (Kruger, 45, 206–7).

205. John Thornton, *Africa and Africans in the Making of the Atlantic World, 1400–1800* 2nd ed. (New York: Cambridge Univ. Press, 1998), 254.

206. Kruger, "Born to Run," 53.

207. Cathy Matson, *Merchants and Empire: Trading in Colonial New York* (Baltimore and London: Johns Hopkins Univ. Press, 1998), 202.

208. New York inhabitants endorsed trading with Madagascar because it evaded the English Royal African Company monopoly. The East India Company halted these relations twice because their monopoly in that area was disrupted. Virginia Platt, "The East India Company and the Madagascar Slave Trade," *William and Mary Quarterly* 26, no. 4 (Oct. 1969): 548–77.

209. Jacob Judd, "Frederick Philipse and the Madagascar Trade," *New-York Historical Society Quarterly* 55, no. 4 (Oct. 1971): 357.

210. Joyce D. Goodfriend, *Before the Melting Pot: Society and Culture in Colonial New York City, 1664–1730* (Princeton: Princeton Univ. Press, 1992), 112.

211. Sherrill D. Wilson, *New York City's African Slaveowners: A Social and Material Culture History* (New York and London: Garland Publishing, 1994), 22.

212. Kruger, "Born to Run," 79.

213. James G. Lydon, "New York and the Slave Trade, 1700–1774," *William and Mary Quarterly* 35, no. 2 (Apr. 1978): 383.

214. E. R. Shipp, "Black Cemetery Yields Wealth of History," *New York Times*, 9 Aug. 1992, 41.

4. Contemporary Politics and Grassroots Efforts

1. For a detailed timeline of events, see "Chronology of Contemporary Political Events" following chapter 6. For narratives up to 1993, see Spencer Harrington, "Bones and Bureaucrats: New York's Great Cemetery Imbroglio," *Archaeology* (Mar.–Apr. 1993): 30–38; and Christopher Moore, *The African Burial Ground: An American Discovery*, part 3, directed and produced by David Kutz (U.S. General Services Administration, 1994), DVD, 30 min.

2. *GSA Public Buildings Service*, http://www.gsa.gov/pbsintro.htm (accessed 29 July 2000).

3. For more information, see Rebecca Yamin, ed., *Tales of Five Points: Working-Class Life in Nineteenth Century New York*. Prepared by John Milner Associates for Edwards and Kelcey Engineers and General Services Administration, Region 2, 2000; and Rebecca Yamin, "New York's Mythic Slum," *Archaeology* 50, no. 2 (Mar.–Apr. 1997). The popular film *The Gangs of New York* (2002) concerns this neighborhood.

4. Spencer Harrington, "Bones and Bureaucrats," 31.

5. During the 1992 hearing cited here in which Gus Savage unraveled these details, he questioned GSA, "Then why didn't you bring that information back to the attention of Congress . . . that there's a burial ground that may be considered

the most important archeological discovery in this century . . . So don't put it on Congress. It's on GSA. You did not tell us." *Foley Square Construction Project and the Historic African Burial Ground, New York, NY: Hearing before the Subcommittee on Public Buildings and Grounds of the Committee on Public Works and Transportation*, 102nd Cong., 2nd sess., 27 July 1992, 68–69.

6. *Foley Square Construction Project*, House subcommittee hearings, 27 July 1992, 45.

7. A complete copy of this MOA can be found in *Foley Square Construction Project*, House subcommittee hearings, 27 July 1992, 111, 114–11.

8. Jean Howson, Leonard G. Bianchi, and Warren R. Perry, "Introduction," in *New York African Burial Ground Archaeology Final Report*, eds. Warren R. Perry, Jean Howson and Barbara A. Bianco (Washington, DC: General Services Administration and Howard Univ., 2006), 1:1, 3.

9. *Foley Square Construction Project*, House subcommittee hearings, 24 Sept. 1992, 327; and Howson, Bianchi, and Perry, "Introduction," 3. For HCI's complete document, see Marjorie Ingle, Jean Howson, and Edward S. Rutsch, S.O.P.A. of Historic Conservation and Interpretation, Inc., *A Stage 1A Cultural Resource Survey of the Proposed Foley Square Project in the Borough of Manhattan, New York, NY*, prepared for Edwards & Kelcey Engineers, Inc. (Sept. 1989, revised May 1990).

10. *Foley Square Construction Project*, House subcommittee hearings, 27 July 1992, 77.

11. Ibid., 65.

12. GSA would organize the construction of both the Foley Square Courthouse and the Ted Weiss Federal Building through design/build teams. The process consisted of teams of architects and contractors working collaboratively under fixed-cost design and construction proposals. GSA opened up the competition in September 1988 by soliciting proposals from teams and then hired independent estimators to review the figures that were submitted by the competing teams.

13. Bradford McKee, "Federal Design/Build: Six Projects Reveal How the Government Has Succeeded—and Failed—by Teaming Architects and Contractors," *Architecture* 83, no. 10 (Oct. 1994): 4. HOK was ranked the second-largest architectural firm in the world by *World Architecture Magazine* in 2001. Chair Gyo Obata is a Japanese American who studied under Eero Saarinen and joined the Skidmore, Owings and Merrill firm before joining HOK in the 1950s. *HOK*, http://www.architectureasia.com/HONG-KONG/architects/hok.htm (accessed 9 Apr. 2002).

Linpro, later known as LCOR, is a national real estate development, investment, and management company specializing in the structuring and implementing of public/private developments. They have been involved with the International

372 • Notes to Pages 180–85

Air Terminal Building at JFK; the Warwick House, a 533-unit, two-tower high-rise rental apartment community in Arlington, Virginia; and Queensport, a commercial and recreational development in Queens. *LCOR,* http://www.lcor.com /foleysquare1.html (accessed 9 Apr. 2002).

14. McKee, "Federal Design/Build," 4.

15. Edward Rutsch, telephone conversation with Andrea Frohne, 11 Aug. 2000.

16. Robert Ingrassia, "$21 Million Plan Mired in Woe: Researchers, Feds Wrangle over African Burial Ground," *New York Daily News,* 5 Feb. 2001.

17. Rutsch, telephone conversation.

18. Rutsch, telephone conversation.

19. Philip Perazio, "Archaeological Monitoring," 27 Apr. 1997 in ACRA-L archive (American Cultural Resources Association), http://lists.gardencity.net/list-proc/archives/acra-l/9704/0134.html (accessed 17 Oct. 2000).

20. Ibid.

21. Spencer Harrington, "Bones and Bureaucrats," 31.

22. Howson, Bianchi, Perry, "Introduction," 3.

23. Sherrill Wilson and Jean Howson, "Modern Myths of the African Burial Ground" (photocopy, Office of Public Education and Interpretation, New York City), 8–9.

24. *Foley Square Construction Project,* House subcommittee hearings, 27 July 1992, 112.

25. Susan C. Pearce, "Africans on this Soil: The Counter-Amnesia of the New York African Burial Ground (Ph.D. diss., New School for Social Research, 1996), 62.

26. Wilson and Howson, "Modern Myths," 8–9.

27. U.S. General Services Administration, *New York African Burial Ground: Skeletal Biology Report—First Draft,* prepared by the African Burial Ground Project-The W. Montague Cobb Biological Anthropology Laboratory-Howard Univ., Washington, DC (5 Aug. 1998), 10.

28. David W. Dunlap, "Excavation Stirs Debate on Cemetery," *New York Times,* 6 Dec. 1991, B4. See Pearce, "Africans on this Soil," 207–13, for a discussion of differences between the early and late edition versions of the story.

29. *Foley Square Construction Project,* House subcommittee hearings, 24 Sept. 1992, 237 and 317.

30. Spencer Harrington, "Bones and Bureaucrats," 35.

31. Ibid.

32. Tureka Turk, "Dispute Stops Progress on African Burial Study," *Michigan Citizen,* 22 May 1993, A1. *Ethnic Watch,* CD-ROM, Softline Information, 1995, 3.

33. "African Burial Ground and the Commons Historic District Designation Report," by Gale Harris, Jean Howson, and Betsy Bradley, ed. Marjorie Pearson

(New York City: Landmarks Preservation Commission, 1993). Appendix in *Memorialization of the African Burial Ground*, prepared by Peggy King Jorde, Weil, Gotshal and Manges Counsel, and the Federal Steering Committee (6 Aug. 1993), 4. A complete copy of the amended 1991 MOA can be found in *Foley Square Construction Project*, House subcommittee hearings, 27 July 1992, 118–24.

34. *Foley Square Construction Project*, House subcommittee hearings, 27 July 1992, 9.

35. Figure 3 of Section 106, entitled "Public Participation Principles," explains that members of the public with information about a historic property should be enlisted; professionals and practitioners with knowledge such as history, landscape architecture, and archaeology can be utilized; Indian cultural groups or neighborhood associations whose "immediate interests may be affected" are to be involved; and viewpoints offered by interested persons will be considered (Ibid., 143).

36. Spencer Harrington, "Bones and Bureaucrats," 33. Many burials were damaged by massive architectural footings in the eastern part of the construction site and the southeastern section (which was particularly dense with graves), and also by a perimeter wall built in 1991. Jean Howson and Leonard G. Bianchi, "The Archaeological Site," in *New York African Burial Ground Archaeology Final Report*, eds. Warren R. Perry, Jean Howson, and Barbara A. Bianco (Washington, DC: General Services Administration and Howard Univ., 2006), 1:98.

37. Pearce, "Africans on this Soil," 199.

38. "Statement of Mr. William Diamond, Regional Administrator U.S. GSA, Regarding the Disturbance of Six Burial Sites in the Negroes Burial Ground at 290 Broadway New York, NY," 7 Mar. 1992. Filed in Municipal Library, New York City. See also James Rutenberg, "Black Politicians Fight Fate of Old 'Negro Burial Ground' Downtown," *Manhattan Spirit* 28 Apr. 1992, 9.

39. *Foley Square Construction Project*, House subcommittee hearings, 24 Sept. 1992, 301.

40. Rutenberg, "Black Politicians," 7.

41. Moore, *The African Burial Ground: An American Discovery*.

42. Ibid.

43. Ibid.

44. Pearce, "Africans on this Soil," 122–23. OPEI was GSA's Office of Public Education and Interpretation for the burial ground. See p. 202.

45. Ibid., 122.

46. Spencer Harrington, "Bones and Bureaucrats," 34.

47. *Foley Square Construction Project*, House subcommittee hearings, 27 July 1992, 170. Statement prepared by Howard Dodson.

48. Moore, *The African Burial Ground: An American Discovery*.

49. Ibid.

50. Ibid.

51. David W. Dunlap, "New York Dig Unearths Early Cemetery for Blacks," *New York Times*, 9 Oct. 1991.

52. Rutenberg, "Black Politicians," 9.

53. Ibid.

54. Spencer Harrington, "Bones and Bureaucrats," 34.

55. ACHP letter to GSA Regional Administrator Bill Diamond, 10 June 1992. In *Foley Square Construction Project*, House subcommittee hearings, 27 July 1992, 125.

56. *Foley Square Construction Project*, House subcommittee hearings, 27 July 1992, 156.

57. *Foley Square Construction Project*, House subcommittee hearings, 24 Sept. 1992, 247.

58. Mayor David Dinkins, letter to GSA Regional Administrator Bill Diamond, New York City, 16 July 1992. Filed in OPEI.

59. Mayor David Dinkins to Congressperson Floyd H. Flake, U.S. House of Representatives, St. Albans, NY, 17 July 1992. Filed in the Municipal Archives, New York City.

60. Spencer Harrington, "Bones and Bureaucrats," 36. In Part 3 of Christopher Moore's video *African Burial Ground: An American Discovery*, Diamond stated that he would not act contrary to "our responsibility," but continue to work until Congress directed him otherwise without being pushed or blackmailed.

61. Gus Savage became his district's first African American Representative in South Side Chicago in 1981 and held office for six terms. Throughout his career, he worked as a civil rights advocate speaking out against racial inequality and challenging housing, employment, and labor union discrimination. It was he, as a journalist, who had first printed the shocking photograph of fourteen-year-old Emmett Till's body in 1955, bringing attention to the murder.

62. James Barron, "Dinkins Seeks to Halt Work at Site of a Black Cemetery," *New York Times*, 21 July 1992, B3.

63. *Foley Square Construction Project*, House subcommittee hearings, 27 July 1992, 6.

64. Ibid., 166.

65. Ibid., 79.

66. Ibid., 80.

67. Ibid.

68. Ibid., 187.

69. Herb Boyd, "Gus Savage: The Ancestral Burial Ground Should Be Covered Only by 'Dirt and Sunshine,'" *New York Amsterdam News*, 22 Aug. 1992, 5. As per John Milner's advice, it was agreed by ACHP, LPC, and the Mayor's Advisory

Council that already partially exposed and excavated burials be exhumed after the site was closed down. LPC was directed to monitor the site weekly afterwards.

70. *Foley Square Construction Project*, House subcommittee hearings, 24 Sept. 1992, 198–99.

71. *Foley Square Construction Project*, House subcommittee hearings, 24 Sept. 1992, 279.

72. "Sen. D'Amato gets $3 Million to Protect 'Negro' Cemetery," *New York Amsterdam News*, 8 Aug. 1992.

73. *Foley Square Construction Project*, House subcommittee hearings, 24 Sept. 1992, 207, 249. See the subcommittee hearing for details about this contract. Blakey was brought onto the project through a variety of disparate avenues. He was contacted by community members in October 1991, telephoned by Peggy King Jorde of the Mayor's Office and Burial Ground liaison in December or January, written to by Rutsch and HCI , and assessed skeletal remains at Lehman College for MFAT in March 1992.

74. Warren R. Perry, "New York City's African Burial Ground," *Africa Update: Quarterly Newsletter of the Central Connecticut State University African Studies Program* 3, no. 4 (Fall 1996), http://www.ccsu.edu/afstudy/fall96.html#lk7 (accessed July 2000).

75. "Transforming Sankofa: Black Anthropologists Interpret Life in 1700s New York through African Burial Ground Project," *About . . . Time Magazine* 24 (28 Feb 1996): 19.

76. General Services Administration Region 2, *Comments on the Draft Research Design for Archeological, Historical, and Bioanthropological Investigations of the African Burial Ground and Five Points Area New York, NY*, for Foley Square Project (Federal Courthouse and Federal Office Building New York, NY, 1992).

77. Ibid.

78. K. Cook, "Black Bones, White Science: The Battle over New York's African Burial Ground," *Village Voice*, 4 May 1993, 27. Quoted in Terrence W. Epperson, "The Politics of 'Race' and Cultural Identity at the African Burial Ground Excavations, New York City," *World Archaeological Bulletin* 7 (1997): 115.

79. Ibid.

80. *Response to the GSA's Comments and Suggestions of the Draft New York African Burial Ground Skeletal Biology Report*, prepared by Michael Blakey, to Mr. William Lawson, Deputy Regional Administrator, 21 Dec. 1999, 5.

81. The committee members were: Dr. Howard Dodson, Chair, Robert McCadams, Laurie Beckelman, J. Max Bond, Elombe Brath, Richard Brown, Robert Bush, Dr. John Henrik Clarke, Ron Conroy, Rev. Suzan Johnson Cook, Rev. Herbert Daughtry, Barbara J. Fife, Miriam B. Francis, Verna M. Francis, Raenice Goode, Dr. Jerome S. Handler, Rev. Dr. M. William Howard Jr., Robert

Macdonald, Mary Lacey Madison, Joan Maynard, Ollie McClean, Christopher Moore, Paul O'Dwyer, Senator David Paterson, Noel Pointer, Carolyn Sherry, Adunni Oshupa Tabasi, Howard Wright. Handler donated his documents to the University of Virginia Library, http://ead.lib.virginia.edu/vivaxtf/view?docId=uva-sc/viu01226.xml;query=; (accessed 11 Dec. 2013).

82. Debbie Officer, "Burial Grounds Meeting Ends in Uproar," *New York Amsterdam News*, 4 Apr. 1993, 32, 34.

83. For a recounting of its rocky start, see *Foley Square Construction Project*, House subcommittee hearings, 24 Sept. 1992, 228. The FSC approved its seven resolutions on 25 Jan. 1993 and held a public forum at city hall about them on 14 June 1993.

84. Marilyn Anderson, "Valid Permits: Inside City Hall," *Archaeology*, 25 Feb. 2000, http://archive.archaeology.org/online/features/cityhall/bones.html (accessed 29 July 2000).

85. Debbie Officer, "Outrage over Desecration of Ancestral Burial Ground," *New York Amsterdam News*, 20 Feb. 1993, 1.

86. "Con Edison Crew Unearths Bones Near Early Black Graveyard," *New York Times*, 14 Feb. 1993, 43.

87. Artifacts from the burial ground and the Five Points site had previously been housed in the private New Jersey home/office of Edward Rutsch of HCI and also in the conservation laboratory of the South Street Seaport Museum. They were eventually transferred to a laboratory in the World Trade Center. These dispersions of sacred bones also caused alarm and dismay among African American activists.

88. Debbie Officer, "Con Ed Digs into African Burial Ground with New York City 'Emergency' Permits," *New York Amsterdam News*, 19 Feb. 1994, 2.

89. Ibid., 2.

90. David W. Dunlap, "African Burial Ground Made Historical Site," *New York Times*, 26 Feb. 1993, B31.

91. Ibid.

92. Initially, the African Burial Ground archives were to be housed at the Schomburg Center, but the institution did not have adequate space to house everything (Steve Laise, NPS Chief of Cultural Resources, personal communication with Andrea Frohne, 19 Feb. 2015). GSA then partnered with the Army Corps of Engineers for the conservation and curation of the materials. Everything was sent to St. Louis to the Corps' Center of Expertise for the Curation and Management of Archeological Collections (Paul Rubenstein, Army Corps Federal Preservation Officer, email to Andrea Frohne, 24 Feb. 2015). Following that, GSA transferred all of the archives to NPS, which has housed them offsite in Federal Hall. The public does not have access to visit the documents or images, but may request to view specific ones.

93. Howard Dodson, *A Public Forum on the Draft Proposal to the U.S. Congress for Commemorating the African Burial Ground* (New York: S & S Reporting Co., 14 June 1993), 165.

94. Moore, *The African Burial Ground: An American Discovery.*

95. Pearce, "Africans on this Soil," 2.

96. Lula N'zinga Strickland, "Update 2000 on the ABG," *Caribbean Life Queens/Long Island Edition*, 4 Apr. 2000, 8. Reprinted in *Daily Challenge*, 13 Apr. 2000 and 14–16 Apr. 2000.

97. Ibid.

98. Brent Staples, "Manhattan's African Dead: Colonial New York, from the Grave," *New York Times*, 22 May 1995, A14.

99. General Services Administration Region 2, *Comments on the Draft Research Design.*

100. Ibid.

101. *Foley Square Construction Project*, House subcommittee hearings, 24 Sept. 1992, 272.

102. Debbie Officer, "Uproar and Protest at African Burial Ground Meeting," *New York Amsterdam News*, 21 Apr. 1999.

103. Zita Allen, "Meet our Ancestors: Members Play a Key Role. The African Burial Ground: The Making of a Landmark," *Public Employees Press* (nd): 10–11.

104. Gil Noble, Sherrill Wilson, Noel Pointer, and David Paterson, "Negro Burial Ground," *Like It Is*, television show on WABC TV (2 Aug. 1992).

105. Turk, "Dispute Stops Progress," 3.

106. Sharon Fitzgerald, "Sacred Ground." *Essence* 24, no. 5 (Sept. 1993). http://referenc.lib.binghamton.edu:2076 . . . Fmt=3&Sid=4&Idx=43&Deli=1&R QT=309&Dtp=1 (accessed 13 Oct. 2000).

107. Moore, *The African Burial Ground: An American Discovery.*

108. Herb Boyd, "Hundreds Pay Respects to their Ancestors in Burial Ground Vigil," *New York Amsterdam News*, 15 Aug. 1992, 3, 35.

109. "African Burial Ground Commemoration," *New York Voice* 34, no. 36 (16 Dec. 1992): 14. http://referenc.lib.binghamton.edu:2095/s . . . tate=f8ev5p.18 .softTemplate.w&softtpl=toc.

110. Moore, *The African Burial Ground: An American Discovery.*

111. "Visiting Royal African Delegation," *New York Beacon*, 9 Aug. 1995, 23. http://referenc.lib.binghamton.edu:2095/s...tate=olmviq.11.softTemplate.w&softt pl=toc.

112. Patrice Gaines, "Bones of Forebears: Howard University Study Stirs Ghanaian Chiefs to Honor Ages-Old Link to U.S. Blacks," *Washington Post*, 3 Aug. 1995, B11.

113. John Gregerson, "From Red Tape to Blue Ribbons," *Building Design and Construction* 36, no. 8 (Aug. 1995): 5. *Expanded Academic ASAP*, http://reference.lib.binghamton.edu:2088/i . . . M_O_A17284173&dyn=70!ar_fmt?sw_aep=bingul (accessed 31 July 2000).

114. The following documentation has not been published; I have constructed a narrative based on oral histories, dialogues, and presentations. These were gathered from my interviews and my attendance to open houses, hearings, and educational symposia. Oral histories culled from journalists that fill hundreds of newspaper articles are also relied upon.

115. Jonathan Shaw, "Life by Design," *Harvard Magazine* (Jan.–Feb. 1998): 3, http://harvardmagazine.com/1998/01/loeb.html (accessed 29 July 2000); and Rodger Taylor, "The Site Seer: Guardian of the People with No Names," *The City Sun*, 18–24 Mar. 1992, 2.

116. Michael Blakey, presenter at the "African Burial Ground Project Fall 1998 Educators Symposium," New York City, 21 Nov. 1998.

117. Michelle Collison, "Disrespecting the Dead: DNA Research on Remains from the African Burial Ground Project May Be Lost Forever Because of a Financial Feud," *Black Issues in Higher Education*, 1 Apr. 1999, 4. During this time, another controversy ensued in which geneticist Rick Kittles of Howard University, who had been working on the African Burial Ground project, began a private enterprise for DNA testing for African Americans. See Tanu Henry, "Controversy Brews over DNA Testing Plan," *Africana.com*, http://www.africana.com (accessed 26 Aug. 2000); and Arthur Allen, "Flesh and Blood and DNA," *Salon.com* (12 May 2000), http://www.salon.com/2000/05/12/roots_2/ (accessed 8 Oct. 2000).

118. Charles Brooks, "African Burial Ground Project Denied Needed Funding," *New York Amsterdam News*, 20 Jan. 1999, 3.

119. Status of the African Burial Ground Project Community Hearing, New York City, 23 Jan. 1999.

120. Ayo Harrington, "Friends of the African Burial Ground," *Update: Newsletter of the African Burial Ground and Five Points Archaeological Projects* 2, no. 10 (Spring 1999): 8. Ayo Harrington, letter to Congressman Charles Rangel, 15 Mar. 1999.

121. Michael L. Blakey, "African Burial Ground in Jeopardy: Continue the Research and Preservation or 'Business as Usual?'" *About . . . Time Magazine*, 28 Feb. 1999: 38. Also published in *Update: Newsletter of the African Burial Ground and Five Points Archaeological Projects* 2, no. 8.

122. Dr. Michael Blakey and Dr. Sherrill Wilson to Peggy King Jorde, 7 Apr. 1999.

123. Officer, "Uproar and Protest," 4.

124. Ayo Harrington, "Friends of the African Burial Ground," 12.

125. A Public Update on the New York African Burial Ground Project, New York City, 2 Oct. 1999.

126. To clarify, there was a widespread, if not near unanimous desire for reburial among concerned citizens in New York City. There have been differing opinions about the approach to reburial. The Committee of Descendants of the Afrikan Ancestral Burial Ground continued its demands for reburial. On 26 December 1999 and the first day of Kwanzaa, the thirty members of the committee gathered at the burial ground site to press for reburial and lament that the remains had been exhumed for eight years. The group returned on 26 December 2000 during Ramadan and Kwanzaa for the same purpose. Nana Okomfo Ansaa Atei poured a libation and spoke in Twi and English, "We pray to all the deities and the ancestors to be honored by name and the unnamed" (Ali Rahman, "Lest we Forget! Our Ancestors' Bones Still Call to Us from the Empty Graves in Lower Manhattan," *New York Beacon*, 12 Jan. 2000, 16). The group brought red carnations shaped in an Egyptian cross (ankh), which remained on the property for many months afterwards.

127. Sherrill Wilson, communication with Andrea Frohne, New York City, 10 Mar. 2001.

128. Perry had performed 80 percent of his analysis. He worked in the WTC laboratory only for the last three months because it had closed for asbestos abatement in January 1999. When the WTC collapsed one and a half years later, some of the funerary objects and original in situ photos were unrecoverable.

129. See Ingrassia, "$21 Million Plan Mired in Woe."

130. Lula N'zinga Strickland, "Burial Scientist Blasts *Daily News* Report," *New York Amsterdam News*, 8 Mar. 2001, 33.

131. They were all stipulated in the amended 1991 Memorandum of Agreement and the community-derived Federal Steering Committee recommendations to Congress in 1993.

132. "Symposium for the Design Competition for the African Burial Ground," notes compiled by Lacey Torge, http://www.nyu.edu/classes/tourist/abglacey (accessed 25 Nov. 1998).

133. "Public Forum for African Burial Ground Interpretive Center," New York City, 8 Apr. 1999.

134. [Peggy King Jorde], "The African Burial Ground Design Competitions. Brochure" (New York: U.S. General Services Administration, 1997), 3 http://r2.gsa.gov/afrburgro/brochure.html (accessed 29 July 2000). Included in mailings for design teams.

135. "Symposium for the Design Competition."

136. Karen Juanita Carrillo, "Community Elders Don't Want Any Buildings on African Burial Ground," *New York Amsterdam News*, 20 Apr. 2006.

137. Teams submitted designs in June 1998 following two extensions. For phase two, teams received $10,000 to produce models of their designs. Seven professionals were contracted by GSA to serve on a Team Selection Committee to make individual recommendations for a finalist. The seven were Dr. Michael Blakey of Howard University, who was scientific director of the African Burial Ground project; Dr. Rex Ellis of the National Museum of American History at the Smithsonian; Dr. T. J. Davis of History at Arizona State University; Sylvia Harris, exhibit designer at Yale University; Dr. Fath Davis Ruffins of the National Museum of American History; and Gretchen Sullivan Sorin of the Graduate Program in History Museum Studies at SUNY Cooperstown (U.S. General Services Administration News Release, "GSA Announces Finalists for African Burial Ground Interpretive Center," New York City, 15 Mar. 1999. Also at http://r2.gsa.gov/afrburgro/PressReleases.html.

138. First, the shortlisted designs for the interpretive center were exhibited on large boards during a GSA public update held on 23 January 1999 at the Schomburg Center for Black Studies in Harlem. Next, a forum was held to introduce the short listed teams on 8 April.

139. IDI is a New York–based African American/African/Caribbean multidisciplinary team that consisted of: Trevor Prince, Atim Oton, Saleem Kahtri, Jacqueline Hamilton, Paula Griffith, Antonio Cox, Stephan Carriglio, Jasper Whyte, Deirdre Scott, Phillipe Bailey, Elliott Hardie, Elizabeth Geary-Archer, Dr. A. J. Williams-Myers, and Dr. Lee Baker.

140. IDI Design Presentation at CUNY, 17 June 2000.

141. This initial interagency agreement was for a three-year period. It stated, "At the request of GSA, NPS will provide technical assistance services set forth below to GSA relating to the planning, design, programming and operations of African Burial Ground related interpretive facilities and assign representatives to participate on the GSA African Burial Ground Exterior Memorial Existing Source Selection Board." *Interagency Agreement for African Burial Ground Technical Assistance Between the National Park Service and the General Services Administration* (Northeast Region, Sept. 2003), 1, http://www.africanburialground.gov/Documents/GSA_NPS_Interagency_Agreement.pdf (accessed 12 Aug. 2008; site discontinued).

142. The minutes from these meetings, as well as supporting documents related to this second attempt to produce an interpretive center, were available online at http://www.africanburialground.gov/ABG_InterpretiveCenter.htm (site discontinued).

143. This is because the northern boundary of the 6.7-acre cemetery was likely around Duane Street, and to the east lay Collect Pond, and to the west, Broadway. Thus, the only direction the cemetery could extend its 6.7 acres would be south

into City Hall Park (fig. 1). Marilyn Anderson, "Under City Hall Park," *Archaeology* 25 (Feb. 2000), 2, http://archive.archaeology.org/online/features/cityhall (accessed 29 July 2000).

144. Howson and Bianchi, "The Archaeological Site," 84n3.

145. Graves in situ faced all directions. Bone fragments were scattered throughout the park. Secondary fragments were studied at the Smithsonian by physical anthropologist Marilyn London (Anderson, "Under City Hall Park," 3). Exposed burials were covered over 12 Aug. 1999.

146. The coffin manufacturer was Dallytex in Ghana. The wood for the coffins was cut to size in Accra, transported to Aburi to be carved, and then sent back to Accra for assembly. The carving took up to one and one half days per coffin, with over one hundred carvers working on the project. The larger crypts that held the coffins were manufactured by Premier Restoration and Interior Maintenance in New York City. "GSA African Burial Ground Coffin/Crypt Fact Sheet" (photocopy, GSA, New York City, Sept. 2002).

147. For instance, I collected a postcard announcing the Shepsu Day Committee in Brooklyn, which was founded upon ancient Egypt or Khemet. The postcard depicts the Old Kingdom sculpture (ca. 2500 BCE) of Menkaure and Khamernebty, along with two nineteenth-century Benin Kingdom bronzes from Nigeria and three nineteenth or twentieth-century central African masks, all of which represent an Africa.

148. Amy Goodman and Juan González, "Remains of 419 Enslaved Africans Re-Buried at the African Burial Ground in New York City," *Democracy Now*, 6 Oct. 2003. http://www.democracynow.org/2003/10/6/remains_of_419_enslaved_africans_re.

149. Deborah S. Morris, "Resting Place: History/Slave Remains Return to NYC Burial Grounds," *Newsday*, 4 Oct. 2003.

5. Early Commemorative Artworks, 1992–1995

1. Spirituality is understood here as pertaining to or consisting of the spirit realm and includes a broad spectrum of practices including personal and collective engagement with the spirit world.

2. David Rashid Gayle, telephone interview with Andrea Frohne, 30 Mar. 2015.

3. Ibid.

4. Ibid.

5. Ibid.

6. Emilyn Brown, "An Important Postscript . . . ," *Update: Newsletter of the African Burial Ground and Five Points Archaeological Projects* 1, no. 10 (Winter 1996): 9.

7. Gayle, telephone interview.

8. Gayle, telephone interview.

9. The kente cloth is traditionally made by Akan and Ewe people in Ghana and neighboring Côte d'Ivoire and Togo. With Kwame Nkrumah (1909–72) as a leader of Pan-Africanism and anticolonialism and the first president of Ghana, kente cloth has become synonymous with Pan-African ideals. It has been appropriated in the United States to represent a collective Africa as well as African identity.

10. Gayle, telephone interview.

11. Gayle, telephone interview.

12. *LCOR*, http://www.lcor.com/foleysquare1.html (accessed 11 Mar. 2002). Linpro is now known as LCOR.

13. Senator David Paterson, letter to Regional Director William Diamond, New York City, 4 Oct. 1992. Located in OPEI Binder entitled "Documents: African Burial Ground Project. Book 1 of 1,A."

14. The group, which had originally intended to file a lawsuit against the federal government, was comprised of the New York Coalition of Black Architects (NYCOBA), the National Organization of Minority Architects (NOMA), the Municipal Art Society of New York, the City Club of New York, Metropolitan Black Bar Association, Minority Environmental Lawyers Association, New York City Environmental Justice Alliance, and Professional Archaeologists of New York City (PANYC). Submissions are illustrated in the accompanying publication. Edward Kaufman, ed., *Reclaiming Our Past, Honoring Our Ancestors: New York's 18th Century African Burial Ground and the Memorial Competition* (New York: Ragged Edge Press, 1994), 24, 25.

15. William Davis, telephone conversation with Andrea Frohne, 1 Aug. 1997.

16. The other members of the jury were architectural critic Robert Campbell, expert on African American architecture Richard Dozier, Cuban born printmaker and educator Ofelia Garcia, sculptor Richard Hunt, architect and urban designer M. David Lee, and Ghanaian historic preservation architect D. D. Kpodo-Tay. The jury was led by artist and art historian Dr. Leslie King-Hammond, Dean of Graduate Studies at the Maryland Institute College of Art (Kaufman, *Reclaiming Our Past*, 25, 82–85).

17. *Portfolio Management Division. Southeast Sunbelt Region 4. Fine Arts. Art-in-Architecture*, http://r4.gsa.gov/4p/4ptart.htm (accessed 23 Mar. 1999).

18. *GSA—Art in Architecture Program*, http://www.gsa.gov (accessed 19 July 2008). According to the GSA website at the time of the 290 Broadway commissioning, between 0.5 and 2 percent of the estimated building cost or purchase price of federal buildings was allocated for art work.

19. The panel was comprised of five professionals in the visual arts and five representatives of the community, all of whom formed a diverse group to represent a

variety of constituencies including the mayor's office and the African Burial Ground Federal Steering Committee (Susan Harrison, telephone interview with Andrea Frohne, 23 Mar. 1999. Harrison was manager of the Art-in-Architecture program).

20. U.S. General Services Administration, "*The New Ring Shout*" brochure.

21. Commissioned in 1993, the piece was initially planned for the outside of the pavilion adjoining the office building (Joseph De Pace, interview with author, New York City, 29 Oct. 1998). The change in plan caused a tension between HOK architectural firm, which had not intended an artwork to occupy its central rotunda, and the commissioned artists. A successful piece, employees and visitors constantly move across it as they walk to the elevators throughout the day.

22. Samuel Miller Lawton, "The Religious Life of South Carolina Coastal and Sea Island Negroes" (Ph.D. diss. George Peabody College for Teachers, Nashville, TN, 1939), 77–79. Quoted in Betty M. Kuyk, *African Voices in the African American Heritage* (Bloomington: Indiana Univ. Press, 2003), 93.

23. Houston Conwill, Joseph De Pace, and Estella Conwill Majozo, "*The New Ring Shout* Public Art Project Design Proposal" (photocopy, GSA, New York City, 25 May 1994), [1].

24. Cited in Conwill et al., "*The New Ring Shout* Public Art Project Design Proposal," 3.

25. A. Fu-Kiau, *Le Mukongo et le monde qui l'entourait (N'Kongo y nza yakun' zungidila* (Kinshasa: Office National de la Recherche et du Developpement, 1969), 26, 28, 30. Quoted in Wyatt MacGaffey, *Modern Kongo Prophets: Religion in a Plural Society* (Bloomington: Indiana Univ. Press, 1983): 127.

26. MacGaffey, *Modern Kongo Prophets*, 116.

27. Conwill et al., "*The New Ring Shout* Public Art Project Design Proposal," [1].

28. If an *nganga* (Kongolese divination specialist) draws a cosmogram, the line of communication has been opened with the otherworld. During this process called "singing the point," Kikongo words are sung to ensure a meeting with the *simbi* (ancestor). The nganga may position himself at a crossroads, and then outline a cosmogram in the earth or draw one on the ground with white chalk. Bunseki Fu-Kiau, interview with Robert Farris Thompson, winter 1978, quoted in Robert Farris Thompson, *Flash of the Spirit: African and Afro-American Art and Philosophy* (New York and Toronto: First Vintage Books, 1984), 110; and Wyatt MacGaffey, *Religion and Society in Central Africa: The BaKongo of Lower Zaire* (Chicago: Univ. of Chicago Press, 1986), 107, which was quoted in Shannen Hill, "Minkisi Do Not Die: The Survival of Kongo Cosmology in the Visual Culture of Modern Christian Zaire" (MA thesis, Univ. of Wisconsin, 1994), 17.

29. The four phases of life can also be conceived of as following the path of the sun. Birth parallels the sunrise, the zenith of life is reached at noon, changes in life

occur around sunset, and death transpires at midnight (Robert Farris Thompson and Joseph Cornet, *The Four Moments of the Sun* [Washington, DC: National Gallery of Art, 1981], 28). The spirit then travels from dusk to dawn to prepare for rebirth.

30. Conwill et al., "*The New Ring Shout* Public Art Project Design Proposal," [4]. In Yorùbáland, the upper half of the cosmological system is the realm of *ayé* or the spirit world where God (Olódùmarè), deities (òrìshà), and ancestors dwell. The bottom half of the circle is the area of *òrun* or the world of the living. Henry John Drewal and John Pemberton III with Rowland Abiodun, *Yoruba: Nine Centuries of African Art and Thought* (New York: Center for African Art and Harry N. Abrams, 1989), 14.

31. Houston Conwill, telephone interview with Andrea Frohne, 16 May 2000.

32. Details concerning the research process can also be found here. "Searching for Enoch Sontonga," *South Africa.info*, 23 Sept. 2002, http://www.southafrica .info/about/history/sontonga.htm#.VZHAwkYrTfc (accessed 1 July 2008).

33. Gage Averill, *A Day for the Hunter, A Day for the Prey: Popular Music and Power in Haiti* (Chicago: Univ. of Chicago Press, 1997), 137.

34. Conwill et al., "The New Ring Shout Public Art Project Design Proposal," [1].

35. Ibid, [3].

36. Ibid., [5].

37. Joseph De Pace, interview with Andrea Frohne, New York City, 29 Oct. 1998.

38. See Richard J. Powell, "Art History and Black Memory: Toward a 'Blues Aesthetic,'" in *History and Memory in African-American Culture*, eds. Geneviève Fabre and Robert O'Meally (New York: Oxford Univ. Press, 1994), 228–43.

39. Conwill, telephone interview. Also explicated in Conwill et al., "The New Ring Shout Public Art Project Design Proposal," [2–3].

40. U.S. General Services Administration, "*The New Ring Shout*: A Tribute to the African Burial Ground," brochure available in lobby of 290 Broadway. Poem printed in Estella Conwill Majozo, *Blessings for a New World* (Chicago: Third World Press, 2007).

41. See Martin Munro, *Different Drummers: Rhythm and Race in the Americas* (Berkeley: Univ. of California Press, 2010).

42. U.S. General Services Administration, "The New Ring Shout" brochure; poem printed in Majozo, *Blessings for a New World*, 5–6, 9.

43. Dòwòti Désir, interview with Andrea Frohne, New York City, 18 Aug. 1999.

44. Peggy King Jorde, interview with Andrea Frohne, New York City, 16 Mar. 1999; and Peggy King Jorde, "An Open Invitation to the Community," *Update:*

Newsletter of the African Burial Ground and Five Points Archaeological Projects 2, no. 9 (Winter 1999): 12.

45. U.S. General Services Administration, "The Roger Brown Mosaic at Foley Square, New York." Brochure available in lobby of 290 Broadway.

46. Ibid.

47. Clyde Lynds, *"American Song* [sic]. A Sculpture Proposal for the Federal Office Building at 920 [sic] Broadway, New York, NY. General Services Administration Art-in-Architecture Program Public Buildings Service" (photocopy, Sept. 1993), [3]; and U.S. General Services Administration, "Art-in-Architecture. *America Song*. Clyde Lynds's Sculpture for the Entrance of the Federal Office Building in New York City." Brochure available in 290 Broadway.

48. Clyde Lynds, email to Andrea Frohne, 24 July 2008.

49. Lynds, "American Song,"[3].

50. Ibid.

51. Clyde Lynds, email to Andrea Frohne, 24 July 2008. The GSA brochure cites the quotation as written by an anonymous African poet.

52. The first Statue of Liberty was conceived by Édouard René Lefèbvre de Laboulaye of France as a tribute to the recently freed enslaved people in the United States. His friend, sculptor Frederick Auguste Bartholdi, took on the project. The monument was of an African woman with broken chains on her hand and at her feet. The American Committee on the Statue of Liberty rejected this model. However, the chains at her feet still remain in today's version. A model of the first version is housed at the Museum of the City of New York. James I. Newsom, "The Black History of the Statue of Liberty," *Black Web Portal* (24 Jan 2002), http://www.blackwebportal.com/wire/DisplayArticle.cfm?ArticleID=529 (accessed 18 Mar. 2002). See also Laboulaye, *New York Times Magazine* (18 May 1986) and *New York Post* (17 June 1986).

Bartholdi's model derived from one that he had proposed to the Egyptian government in the 1860s for the entrance to the Suez Canal. His *Egypt Bringing Light to Asia* was never approved (Caterina Pierre, "Black Statue of Liberty Bibliography," http://www2.h-net.msu.edu/~women/bibs/bibl-blackliberty.html [accessed 18 Mar. 2002]).

53. Dòwòti Désir, interview by Andrea Frohne, New York City, 18 Aug. 1999.

54. See Marina Peterson, "Patrolling the Plaza: Privatized Public Space and the Neoliberal State in Downtown Los Angeles," *Urban Anthropology* 35, no. 4 (2006): 356, 373.

55. Marita Sturken, "The Wall, the Screen and the Image: The Vietnam Veterans Memorial," in *The Visual Culture Reader,* ed. Nicholas Mirzoeff (New York: Routledge, 1998), 173.

56. Thomas B. Allen, *Offerings at the Wall: Artifacts from the Vietnam Veterans Memorial Collection* (Atlanta: Turner Publishing, Inc., 1995).

6. Late Commemorative Artworks, 1998–2007

1. The word pan-African is used not in reference to the specific movement (capital P) beginning with the Pan-African Congress of 1900, but as a general ideology (small p) that may, for example, be the focus in church organizations, community groups, or pressure groups. This distinction, originally made by George Shepperson, is analyzed by Brent Hayes Edwards in "The Uses of Diaspora," *Social Text* 66 (Spring 2001): 50.

2. Molefi Asante, *The Afrocentric Idea* (Philadelphia: Temple Univ. Press, 1998), 9.

3. Tunde Adeleke, *The Case Against Afrocentrism* (Jackson: Univ. Press of Mississippi, 2009), 87.

4. *Foley Square Construction Project and the Historic African Burial Ground, New York, NY: Hearing before the Subcommittee on Public Buildings and Grounds of the Committee on Public Works and Transportation*, 102nd Cong., 2nd sess., 27 July 1992, 71.

5. *Foley Square Construction Project*, House subcommittee hearings, 24 Sept. 1992, 192.

6. Howard Dodson, *A Public Forum on the Draft Proposal to the U.S. Congress for Commemorating the African Burial Ground* (New York: S & S Reporting Co., 14 June 1993), 30.

7. Ibid., 45. The pieces were not installed until 1998.

8. Ibid., 30.

9. Ibid., 19.

10. Stuart Hall, "Cultural Identity and Diaspora," in *Diaspora and Visual Culture: Representing Africans and Jews*, ed. Nicholas Mirzoeff (New York: Routledge, 2000), 23.

11. Stuart Hall, "The Local and the Global: Globalization and Ethnicity," in Anthony D. King, *Culture, Globalization and the World-System* (Minneapolis: Univ. of Minnesota, 1997), 35.

12. This second perspective allows for instance for the consideration of New African diasporas, or Africans of varying nationalities immigrating to New York City today who live transnational, transcultural lives. See Isidore Okpewho and Nkiru Nzegwu, eds., *The New African Diaspora: Assessing the Pains and Gains of Exile* (Bloomington: Indiana Univ. Press, 2010); and Khalid Koser, *New African Diasporas* (New York and London: Routledge, 2003).

13. Hall, "Cultural Identity," 28.

14. Ibid., 29.

15. Edith Hamilton and Huntington Cairns, eds., *The Collected Dialogues of Plato* (New York: Pantheon Books, 1961), 58, 59. *Phaedo*, 75d, 76a.

16. Ibid., *Meno*, 81d.

17. The notion of transmigration of the soul, or reincarnation of the soul, was put forward by Pythagoras and the Pythagoreans after he lived in Egypt for twenty years during the fourth century BCE, studying intensively with Egyptian priests there. This transmigration of the soul precursor informs anamnesis: "[Transmigration of the soul] of course, is an allusion to the Orphists and Pythagoreans, but in logical terms the doctrine of *anamnesis* is derived from this religious doctrine" (Wolfgang Detel, *Foucault and Classical Antiquity: Power, Ethics and Knowledge* [Cambridge: Cambridge Univ. Press, 2005], 209). Alternatively, Ohio State University professor Fritz Graff suggested during an invited guest lecture at Ohio University in 2008 that transmigration of the soul traveled from India to Samos via the Persians. Thus, transmigration of the soul and its successor anamnesis would not be solely Greek, but mixed, if not African.

18. Moyo Okediji, "Semioptics of Anamnesia: Yoruba Images in the Works of Jeff Donaldson, Howardena Pindell, and Muneer Bahauddeen" (PhD diss., Univ. of Wisconsin, 1995), 284.

19. Moyo Okediji, *The Shattered Gourd: Yoruba Forms in Twentieth-Century American Art* (Seattle: Univ. of Washington Press, 2003), 19.

20. The Federal Steering Committee created a subcommittee and panel involved in selecting the final short list of artists. Members of the panel were representatives of the community such as architects, professors, museum staff from MoMA and the Bronx Museum of Art, and members of the Federal Steering Committee including Herb Bennett, Noel Pointer, Gracie Stanislaus, Dòwòti Désir, and Cheryl LaRoche. Dodson, *A Public Forum on the Draft Proposal*, 15.

21. Peggy King Jorde, interview with Andrea Frohne, New York City, 31 July 1997.

22. Barbara Chase-Riboud, telephone interview with Andrea Frohne, 16 Nov. 1998.

23. *Chase-Riboud: African Rising* [sic], catalog at the Stella Jones Gallery, 17 Jan.–21 Feb. 1998 (New Orleans: Professional Printing Services, 1997).

24. Chase-Riboud, telephone interview; and Peter Selz and Anthony F. Janson, *Barbara Chase-Riboud: Sculptor* (New York: Harry N. Abrams, 1999), 66–68.

25. *Chase-Riboud: African Rising.*

26. See image on page 68 in Selz and Janson, *Barbara Chase-Riboud*. Chase-Riboud would go on to publish a novel about Baartman entitled *The Hottentot Venus* (2003).

27. Selz and Janson, *Barbara Chase-Riboud*, 66–68.

28. Quoted in Herschel B. Chipp, *Theories of Modern Art: A Source Book by Artists and Critics* (Berkeley: Univ. of California Press, 1968), 286.

29. Barbara Chase-Riboud, telephone interview.

30. Chris Waddington, "Expatriate Gains," *The Times-Picayune*, 14 Feb. 1998.

31. See the Statue of Liberty explanation chapter 5, n. 52.

32. Asante, *The Afrocentric Idea*, 11.

33. Originally entitled "Harrar" and written in 1991, the poem inspired her Middle Passage Monument sculpture, but when she revisited the poem, it also formed the basis for the current commemoration (Selz and Janson, *Barbara Chase-Riboud*, 70). The poem is retitled "Africa Rising" and is printed in full in the GSA brochure in the lobby of 290 Broadway. It is published in Barbara Chase-Riboud, *Everytime a Knot Is Undone a God Is Released: Collected and New Poems, 1974–2011* (New York: Seven Stories Press, 2014). Copyright © 2014 by Barbara Chase-Riboud. Reprinted with the permission of The Permissions Company, Inc., on behalf of Seven Stories Press, www.sevenstories.com.

34. Tomie Arai, telephone interview with Andrea Frohne, 1 Apr. 1999.

35. See Mary Nooter Roberts, Elizabeth Harney, Allyson Purpora, and Christine Kreamer, "Inscribing Meaning: Ways of Knowing," in *Inscribing Meaning: Writing and Graphic Systems in African Art* ([Washington, DC]: Smithsonian National Museum of African Art, 2007), 13–27.

36. See Victoria Rovine, *Bogolan: Shaping Culture through Cloth in Contemporary Mali* (Washington, DC: Smithsonian Institution Press), 2001.

37. Tomie Arai, telephone interview.

38. Ibid.

39. Henry John Drewal and John Pemberton III with Rowland Abiodun, *Yoruba: Nine Centuries of African Art and Thought* (New York: The Center for African Art and Harry N. Abrams, 1989), 14.

40. Wande Abimbola and Barry Hallen, "Secrecy and Objectivity in the Methodology and Literature of *Ifá* Divination," in *Secrecy. African Art that Conceals and Reveals*, ed. Mary H. Nooter (New York: The Museum for African Art, 1993), 217.

41. A person's spiritual essence is located in one's inner head (*orí inú*). Thus, every person has a spiritual origin because of her or his arrival from the ancestral realm, or òrun. A client may visit a babaláwo for assistance in recovering or

rediscovering one's life purpose or destiny. Abimbola writes that when a person visits a diviner, "He is simply trying to find out through Ifá the wishes of his own Orí who is his personal divinity who regulates the affairs of his own life" (`Wande Abimbola, *Ifá: An Exposition of Ifá Literary Corpus* [Ibadan: Oxford Univ. Press, 1976], notes on plates between 4 and 5).

42. Tomie Arai, telephone interview.

43. Evelyn Hu-DeHart, "Chinese in the Caribbean and Latin America," in *Tomie Arai: Double Happiness*, ed. Lydia Yee (New York: Bronx Museum of the Arts, 1998), 34.

44. Hu-DeHart, "Chinese in the Caribbean," 34.

45. Tomie Arai, telephone interview.

46. Ibid.

47. Lorraine Haucke, Property Development Office of GSA, personal communication with Andrea Frohne, New York City, 26 Sept. 1997.

48. Constructed by Coe Lee Robinson Roesch, Inc. (CLRR), it combined Thomas Paine Park and Foley Square as well as some other pieces of land (see northeast corner in fig. 1), enhanced automobile and pedestrian traffic flows, and created a park for public assembly, rest, and relaxation. Foley Square is bounded by Worth Street, Lafayette Street, Pearl Street, and Duane Street. Collect Pond existed here formerly. "Foley Square Officially Opened after a Massive Three Year, $18 Million Redesign and Reconstruction," *Media Advisory for New York City Department of Parks and Recreation*, http://www.nycgovparks.org/sub_news room/media_advisories/media_advisories.php?id=7764 (accessed 12 July 2008).

49. Lorenzo Pace, interviews with Andrea Frohne, New York City, 3 Aug. 1998 and 20 July 2006.

50. Caroline Brewer, "Soaring Tribute, Montclair State Professor's Monument Honors Slaves Buried in Manhattan," *The Record*, 12 Feb. 2000; and Robin Finn, "Public Lives: With Memorial, a Monument Predicament," *New York Times*, 27 Sept. 2000, B2.

51. Lorenzo Pace, interview, 3 Aug. 1998.

52. Pascal James Imperato, "The Dance of the Tyi Wara," *African Arts* 4, no. 1 (1970): 13.

53. Lorenzo Pace, "Concept of Design for the African Burial Ground and Foley Square," 21 Mar. 1997 (photocopy)and Lorenzo Pace, interview, 20 July 2006.

54. Pace, "Concept."

55. Ibid.

56. Ibid.

57. Lorenzo Pace, interview, 20 July 2006.

58. Brewer, "Soaring Tribute," 2.

59. See Patrick McNaughton, *Mande Blacksmiths: Knowledge, Power, and Art in West Africa* (Bloomington: Indiana Univ. Press, 1988), 14; and Stephen Wooten, *The Art of Livelihood: Creating Expressive Agri-Culture in Rural Mali* (Durham: Carolina Academic Press, 2009), 18–33.

60. Imperato, "The Dance of the Tyi Wara," 77.

61. Lorenzo Pace, interview, 20 July 2006.

62. Maria Alvarez, "Slave Memorial Bound in Slavery," *New York Post*, 31 July 2000.

63. "Foley Square Unveiling," *Downtown Express*, 10 Oct. 2000.

64. Robin Finn, "Public Lives," B2.

65. Josh Rogers, "Division Grows as Foley Unveiling Finally Is Scheduled," *Downtown Express*, 26 Sept. 2000.

66. Josh Rogers, "One Statue, Two Ceremonies at Foley Square," *Downtown Express*, 25 Oct. 2000.

67. Lorenzo Pace, telephone interview with Andrea Frohne, 24 Feb. 1998.

68. Brewer, "Soaring Tribute," 3.

69. Ibid., 2.

70. Lorenzo Pace, interview, 3 Aug. 1998.

71. "GSA Roundtable–Q & A," Pre-Proposal Conference for the Exterior Memorial, New York City, 4 Feb. 1998 (photocopy), 43–44.

72. Ibid., 28, 30.

73. Ibid., 31–32.

74. Ibid., 36.

75. The memorial advisors were Herb Bennett, Steven Campbell, Dòwòti Désir, Gene Norman, and Grace Stanislaus. Extensions for final submission occurred many times: 6 March 1998, 30 April, 12 May, and finally the closing date of 2 June 1998. Originally, the award was slated for up to $1 million for the design, fabrication, and installation of the memorial.

76. This initial interagency agreement was for a three-year period. See chapter 4, n141 for the agreement.

77. "African Burial Ground National Park Service Listening Session Held at 250 Broadway NY, NY," 25 Feb. 2004, 6:18 p.m., transcript, reported by Marc Russo, 76–77.

78. "African Burial Ground National Park Service Listening Session," 65.

79. "Memorial: Public Comments, Design by: GroundWorks," http://www.africanburialground.gov/Memorial/ABG_Memorial_Comments_02_Ground works.htm (accessed 4 Feb. 2011; site discontinued).

80. Tanangachi Mfuni, "Emotional Burial Ground Memorial Groundbreaking," *New York Amsterdam News*, 29 Sept. 2005, 5.

81. Rodney Léon, telephone interview with Andrea Frohne, 5 Aug. 2008.

82. Donald J. Cosentino, "ENVOI: The Gedes and Bawon Samdi," in *Sacred Arts of Haitian Vodou*, ed. Donald J. Cosentino, 405 (Los Angeles: UCLA Fowler Museum of Cultural History, 1995).

83. Sharon Caulder-Hounon, "A Tribute to Mami Wata Vodun Supreme Chief Daagbo Hounon Houna," in *Sacred Waters: Arts for Mami Wata and Other Divinities in Africa and the Diaspora*, ed. Henry John Drewal (Bloomington: Indiana Univ. Press, 2008), 196.

84. Rodney Léon, telephone interview, 5 Aug. 2008.

85. Ibid.

86. Ibid.

87. Ibid.

88. "Rodney Léon's Statement on the African Burial Ground," *African Burial Ground News* 4, no. 1 (Fall 2005), 2.

89. Remark made during "A Public Update on the New York African Burial Ground Project," Schomburg Center for Black Studies, New York City, 2 Oct. 1999.

90. Karen Juanita Carrillo, "Community Elders Don't Want Any Buildings on African Burial Ground," *New York Amsterdam News*, 20 Apr. 2006.

91. David Theo Goldberg, *The Racial State* (Malden, MA, and Oxford: Blackwell Publishers, 2002), 6.

92. Monamma Al-Ghuiyy, personal communication with Andrea Frohne, 29 July 2008. Al-Ghuiyy was the Supervisory Park Ranger under NPS for the African Burial Ground monument.

93. "Update: National Park Service (NPS)," *African Burial Ground News* 4, no. 2 (Winter 2005): 4.

94. "Update: National Park Service," *African Burial Ground News* 5, no. 2 (Winter 2006): 4.

95. Elias E. Lopez, "Nameless Are Memorialized at Old African Burial Site," *New York Times*, 2 Oct. 2007.

96. Rodney Léon, telephone interview, 5 Aug. 2008.

97. John R. Gillis, ed., "Memory and Identity: The History of a Relationship," Introduction to *Commemorations. The Politics of National Identity* (Princeton: Princeton Univ. Press, 1994), 5.

Bibliography

Abimbola, `Wande. *Ifá: An Exposition of Ifá Literary Corpus*. Ibadan: Oxford Univ. Press, 1976.

Abimbola, `Wande, and Barry Hallen. "Secrecy and Objectivity in the Methodology and Literature of Ifá Divination." In *Secrecy: African Art that Conceals and Reveals*, edited by Mary H. Nooter, 213–22. New York and Munich: The Museum for African Art and Prestel, 1993.

Abiodun, Rowland. "Understanding Yoruba Art and Aesthetics. The Concept of *Ase*." *African Arts* (July 1994): 68–78.

Abraham, Emmanuel, W. "A Paradigm of African Society." In *Readings in African Philosophy: An Akan Collection*, edited by Safro Kwame. Lanham, MD and London: Univ. Press of America, 1995.

Adegbola, E. A. *Traditional Religions in West Africa*. Ibadan: Daystar Press, 1983.

Adeleke, Tunde. *The Case Against Afrocentrism*. Jackson: Univ. Press of Mississippi, 2009.

Adjaye, Joseph K., ed. "Time, Identity, and Historical Consciousness in Akan." In *Time in the Black Experience*. Westport, CT, and London: Greenwood Press, 1994.

African Burial Ground, The. New York: Municipal Archives of the City of New York, New York City Dept. of Records and Information Services, 1994.

African Burial Ground and the Commons Historic District Archaeological Sensitivity Study, The. Prepared for the New York City Department of General Services. Hunter Research, Inc., Mesick-Cohen-Waite Architects, 1994.

"African Burial Ground and the Commons Historic District Designation Report." Prepared by Gale Harris, Jean Howson, and Betsy Bradley. Edited by Marjorie Pearson. New York City: Landmarks Preservation

Commission, 1993. Appendix in *Memorialization of the African Burial Ground: Recommendations to the Administrator, General Services Administration, and the United States Congress*. Prepared by Peggy King Jorde, Weil, Gotshal and Manges Counsel, and the Federal Steering Committee. 6 Aug. 1993.

"African Burial Ground National Park Service Listening Session Held at 250 Broadway NY, NY." 25 Feb. 2004, 6:18 p.m. Reported by Marc Russo.

Allen, Arthur. "Flesh and Blood and DNA." *Salon.com*, 12 May 2000. http://www.salon.com (accessed 8 Oct. 2000).

Allen, Thomas B. *Offerings at the Wall: Artifacts from the Vietnam Veterans Memorial Collection*. Atlanta: Turner Publishing, 1995.

Allen, Zita. "Meet our Ancestors: Members Play a Key Role. The African Burial Ground: The Making of a Landmark." *Public Employees Press* (nd): 10–11.

Alvarez, Maria. "Slave Memorial Bound in Slavery." *New York Post*, 31 July 2000.

Anderson, Marilyn. "Under City Hall Park." *Archaeology*, 25 Feb. 2000. http://archive.archaeology.org/online/features/cityhall/.

———. "Valid Permits: Inside City Hall." *Archaeology*, 25 Feb. 2000. http://archive.archaeology.org/online/features/cityhall/bones.html (accessed 29 July 2000).

Aptheker, Herbert. *American Negro Slave Revolts*. New York: International Publishers, 1967.

Asante, Molefi. *The Afrocentric Idea*. Philadelphia: Temple Univ. Press, 1998.

Averill, Gage. *A Day for the Hunter, A Day for the Prey: Popular Music and Power in Haiti*. Chicago: Univ. of Chicago Press, 1997.

Awolalu, J. Omasade. *Yoruba Beliefs and Sacrificial Rites*. London: Longman Group Limited, 1979.

Balfe, Judith, and Margaret Wyszomirski. "The Commissioning of a Work of Public Sculpture." In *Writings About Art*, edited by Carole Gold Calo. Englewood Cliffs, NJ: Prentice-Hall, 1994.

Bancker Jr., Evart. Bancker Plans, Box 1, Folder 44. Manuscript Collections. The New York Public Library, Astor, Lenox and Tilden Foundations.

Baumgarten, L. "Clothes for the People: Slave Clothing in Early Virginia," *Journal of Early Southern Decorative Arts* 14, no. 2 (Nov. 1988): 27–61.

Berrian, Rev. William. *An Historical Sketch of Trinity Church, New- York.* New York: John R. M'Gown, 1847.

Bianchi, Leonard G., and Barbara A. Bianco, with Shannon Mahoney. "Buttons and Fasteners." In *New York African Burial Ground Archaeology Final Report*, edited by Warren R. Perry, Jean Howson, and Barbara A. Bianco, vol. 1, chap. 12. Washington, DC: General Services Administration and Howard Univ., 2006.

Bianco, Barbara A., Christopher R. DeCorse, and Jean Howson. "Beads and Other Adornment." In *New York African Burial Ground Archaeology Final Report*, edited by Warren R. Perry, Jean Howson, and Barbara A. Bianco, vol. 1, chap. 13. Washington, DC: General Services Administration and Howard Univ., 2006.

Blackburn, Robin. *The Making of New World Slavery: From the Baroque to the Modern, 1492–1800.* London and New York: Verso, 1998.

Blakey, Michael L. "African Burial Ground in Jeopardy: Continue the Research and Preservation or 'Business as Usual?'" *About . . . Time Magazine*, 28 Feb. 1999: 38.

———. "The New York African Burial Ground Project: An Examination of Enslaved Lives, A Construction of Ancestral Ties." *Transforming Anthropology* 7, no. 1 (1998): 53–58.

———. "Theory: An Ethical Epistemology of Publicly Engaged Biocultural Research." In *The New York African Burial Ground Skeletal Biology Final Report*, edited by Michael L. Blakey and Lesley M. Rankin-Hill, vol. 1, chap. 3. Washington, DC: General Services Administration and Howard Univ., 2004.

Blakey, Michael L., Jean Howson, Selwyn Carrington, M. C. Hill, S. O. Y. Keita, Mark Mack, Lesley Rankin-Hill, and Kenya Shujaa, "Biocultural Approaches to the Health and Demography of Africans in Colonial New York." Paper presented at the 14th Congress of Anthropological and Ethnological Sciences, Williamsburg, Virginia, 28 July 1998.

Blakey, M. L., M. Mack, A. R. Barret, S. S. Mahoney, and A. H. Goodman. "Childhood Health and Dental Development." In *The New York African Burial Ground Skeletal Biology Final Report*, edited by Michael L. Blakey and Lesley M. Rankin-Hill, vol. 1, chap. 8. Washington, DC: General Services Administration and Howard Univ., 2004.

Blakey, Michael L. and Lesley M. Rankin-Hill, eds. *The New York African Burial Ground Skeletal Biology Final Report.* Washington, DC: General Services Administration and Howard Univ., 2004.

Blakey, Michael L., Lesley M. Rankin-Hill, Alan Goodman, and Fatimah Jackson. "Discussion." In *The New York African Burial Ground Skeletal Biology Final Report,* edited by Michael L. Blakey and Lesley M. Rankin-Hill, vol. 1, chap. 14. Washington, DC: General Services Administration and Howard Univ., 2004.

Bockie, Simon. *Death and the Invisible Powers: The World of Kongo Belief.* Bloomington and Indianapolis: Indiana Univ. Press, 1993.

Bogart, Michele H. "Public Space and Public Memory in New York's City Hall Park." *Journal of Urban History* 25, no. 2 (Jan. 1999): 226–57.

Boiarsky, Carolyn, and Margot Soven. *Writings from the Workplace: Documents, Models, Cases.* Boston and London: Allyn and Bacon, 1995.

Bolster, W. Jeffrey. *Black Jacks: African American Seamen in the Age of Sail.* Cambridge, MA and London: Harvard Univ. Press, 1997.

Boyd, Herb. "Artists, Musicians and Activists Join Forces in Tribute to their Ancestors." *New York Amsterdam News,* Aug. 1992, 3,8.

———. "Gus Savage: The Ancestral Burial Ground Should Be Covered Only by 'Dirt and Sunshine.'" *New York Amsterdam News,* 22 Aug. 1992, 5.

———. "Hundreds Pay Respects to their Ancestors in Burial Ground Vigil." *New York Amsterdam News,* 15 Aug. 1992, 3, 35.

Bradford, William. "The Laws of His Majesties Colony of New-York. Acts Passed by the General Assembly of the Colony of New-York." New York: William Bradford, 1719. Microfiche.

Brewer, Caroline. "Soaring Tribute, Montclair State Professor's Monument Honors Slaves Buried in Manhattan." *The Record,* 12 Feb. 2000.

Brodhead, John. *History of the State of New York: First Period 1609–1664.* 15 vols. Albany: Weed, Parsons, Printers, 1853–87.

Brooks, Charles. "African Burial Ground Project Denied Needed Funding." *New York Amsterdam News,* 20 Jan. 1999, 3.

Broomfield, John. *Other Ways of Knowing.* Rochester, VT: Inner Traditions, 1997.

Brown, Emilyn. "An Important Postscript . . ." *Update: Newsletter of the African Burial Ground and Five Points Archaeological Projects* 1, no. 10 (Winter 1996): 9.

Brown, Henry Collins. *The Story of Old New York*. New York: E. P. Dutton and Co., 1934.

Browne, J. Zamgba. "Pols Demand Burial Ground be Made an Historical Site." *New York Amsterdam News*, 25 Apr. 1992, 58.

Burrows, Edwin G. and Mike Wallace. *Gotham: A History of New York City to 1898*. New York: Oxford Univ. Press, 2000.

Butler, Jon. *The Huguenots in America: A Refugee People in New World Society*. Cambridge, MA, and London: Harvard Univ. Press, 1983.

Butler, Kim D. "Defining Diaspora, Refining a Discourse." *Diaspora* 10, no. 2 (2001): 189–219.

Cantwell, Ann-Marie, and Diana di Zerega Wall. *Unearthing Gotham: The Archaeology of New York City*. Princeton: Yale Univ. Press, 2001.

Carmichael, David, et al., eds. *Sacred Sites, Sacred Places*. London and New York: Routledge, 1994.

Carrillo, Karen Juanita. "Community Elders Don't Want Any Buildings on African Burial Ground." *New York Amsterdam News*, 20 Apr. 2006.

Caulder-Hounon, Sharon. "A Tribute to Mami Wata Vodun Supreme Chief Daagbo Hounon Houna." In *Sacred Waters: Arts for Mami Wata and Other Divinities in Africa and the Diaspora*, edited by Henry John Drewal. Bloomington: Indiana Univ. Press, 2008.

Cerasale, Jean, Jean Howson, Iciar Lucena Narvaez, Ruth Mathis, Warren R. Perry, and Janet L. Woodruff. "Descriptions of Burials 1–200," vol. 2, and "Descriptions of Burials 201–435," vol. 3. In *New York African Burial Ground Archaeology Final Report*, edited by Warren R. Perry, Jean Howson, and Barbara A. Bianco. Washington, DC: General Services Administration and Howard Univ., 2006.

Chan, Sewell. "Coffin's Emblem Defies Certainty." *New York Times*, 27 Jan. 2010, C1.

Chase-Riboud. African [sic] *Rising*. At the Stella Jones Gallery, 17 Jan.–21 Feb. 1998. New Orleans: Professional Printing Services, 1997.

———. *Everytime a Knot Is Undone a God Is Released: Collected and New Poems, 1974–2011*. New York: Seven Stories Press, 2014.

Cheek, Charles D., and Daniel G. Roberts, eds. *The Archeology of 290 Broadway*. 4 vols. Westchester, PA: John Milner Associates, Inc., 2009. http://s-media.nyc.gov/agencies/lpc/arch_reports/1294.pdf (accessed 1 Jan. 2015).

Chidester, David, and Edward T. Linenthal, eds. "Introduction." In *American Sacred Space*. Bloomington: Indiana Univ. Press, 1995.

Chipp, Herschel B. *Theories of Modern Art: A Source Book by Artists and Critics*. Berkeley and Los Angeles: Univ. of California Press, 1968.

Christoph, Peter R. "The Freedmen of New Amsterdam." *Journal of the Afro-American Historical and Genealogical Society* (nd): 139–54.

City of New York. *Minutes of the Common Council of the City of New York, 1675–1776*. 8 vols. New York: Dodd, Mead, and Co., 1905.

City of New York. *Minutes of the Common Council of the City of New York, 1784–1831*. 19 vols. New York: The City of New York, 1917.

Clarke, G. N. G. "Taking Possession: The Cartouche as Cultural Text in Eighteenth-Century American Maps." *Word and Image* 4, no. 2 (Apr.–June 1988): 455–74.

Clifford, James. "Diasporas." *Cultural Anthropology* 9, no. 3 (1994): 302–38.

———. "Traveling Cultures." In *Cultural Studies*, edited by Lawrence Grossberg, Cary Nelson, and Paula Treichler, 96–116. New York and London: Routledge, 1992.

Cockburn, William. "Remarks on Mr. Maerschalk's Map of George Janeway's Lott at Freshwater." The Janeway Papers, Drawer 8. Deeds and Indentures Collection. Special Collections and University Archives. Rutgers University Libraries.

Cohen, David. "How Dutch Were the Dutch of New Netherland?" *New York History* 62, no. 1 (Jan. 1981): 43–60.

Cohen, Paul, and Robert Augustyn. *Manhattan in Maps: 1527–1995*. New York: Rizzoli International Publications, 1997.

Cohen, Sheldon S. "Elias Neau, Instructor to New York's Slaves." *New-York Historical Society Quarterly* 55 (Jan. 1971): 7–27.

Cole, Herbert M., and Doran H. Ross. *The Arts of Ghana*. Los Angeles: Museum of Cultural History, 1977.

Collison, Michelle. "Disrespecting the Dead: DNA Research on Remains from the African Burial Ground Project May Be Lost Forever Because of a Financial Feud." *Black Issues in Higher Education*, 1 Apr. 1999, 4.

Condon, Thomas J. *New York Beginnings: The Commercial Origins of New Netherland*. New York: New York Univ. Press; London: Univ. of London Press Limited, 1968.

Conwill, Houston, Joseph De Pace, and Estella Conwill Majozo. "*The New Ring Shout* Public Art Project Design Proposal." GSA, New York City, 25 May 1994. Photocopy.

Cook, Karen. "Skeletons Haunt American Race Debate." *The Weekly Journal*, 27 May 1993, n.p. *Ethnic Watch.* CD-ROM. Softline Information, 1995.

Cosentino, Donald J. "ENVOI: The Gedes and Bawon Samdi." In *Sacred Arts of Haitian Vodou*, edited by Donald J. Cosentino. Los Angeles: UCLA Fowler Museum of Cultural History, 1995.

Cosgrove, Denis ed. *Mappings.* London: Reaktion Books, 1999.

Cottman, Michael. "Burial Site Set for a Vigil in Black History." *Newsday*, 4 Aug. 1992, 32.

Cronin, Anne. "The Ghosts of Graveyards." *New York Times*, 23 May 1993, 32.

Daly, Michael. "Brass Tacks of Slavery Revealed." *New York Daily News*, 7 Dec. 1997, 8.

Danckaerts, Jasper. *Journal of Jasper Danckaerts, 1679–1680.* Edited by Bartlett Burleigh James and J. Franklin Jameson. New York: Barnes and Noble, Inc., 1946.

Danquah, J. B. *The Akan Doctrine of God: A Fragment of Gold Coast Ethics and Religion.* 2nd ed. London: Frank Cass & Co., 1968.

Davis, Thomas Joseph. "Slavery in Colonial New York City." PhD diss., Columbia Univ., 1974.

Deák, Gloria Gilda. *Picturing America: Prints, Maps, and Drawings Bearing on the New World Discoveries and on the Development of the Territory that Is Now the United States.* 2 vols. Princeton: Princeton Univ. Press, 1988.

DeCorse, Christopher R. "Historical Archaeological Research in Ghana 1986–1987." *Nyame Akume* no. 29 (Dec. 1987): 27–31.

De Koning, Joep M. J. "Dating the Vissher, or Prototype, View of New Amsterdam." *Haelve Moon* 71, no. 3 (Fall 1999): 47–56.

Delaney, Jill. "Public Space or Publicity?" *Architecture/Research/Criticism* no. 5 (1994–95): 2–5.

Delaplaine, Joshua. Joshua Delaplaine Papers, 1721–1779. Collection of the New-York Historical Society.

Detel, Wolfgang. *Foucault and Classical Antiquity: Power, Ethics and Knowledge.* Cambridge: Cambridge Univ. Press, 2005.

Deyle, Steven. "'By Farr the Most Profitable Trade': Slave Trading in British Colonial North America." In *Slave Trades, 1500–1800: Globalization of Forced Labour*, edited by Patrick Manning. Brookfield, VT: Variorum, 1996.

Dix, Morgan. *A History of the Parish of Trinity Church in the City of New York*. Vol. 1. GP Putnam's Sons. Knickerbocker Press, 1898; reprint [New York]: Parish of Trinity, 1984.

Dodson, Howard. *A Public Forum on the Draft Proposal to the U.S. Congress for Commemorating the African Burial Ground*. New York: S & S Reporting Co., 14 June 1993.

Donnan, Elizabeth, ed. *Documents Illustrative of the History of the Slave Trade to America*. 4 vols. New York: Octagon Books, 1965.

Duane, James. The Janeway Papers, Drawer 8. Deeds and Indentures Collection. Special Collections and University Archives. Rutgers University Libraries.

Drewal, Henry John, and John Mason. *Beads Body and Soul: Art and Light in the Yoruba Universe*. Los Angeles: UCLA Fowler Museum of Cultural History, 1998.

Drewal, Henry John, and John Pemberton III with Rowland Abiodun. *Yoruba: Nine Centuries of African Art and Thought*. New York: Center for African Art and Harry N. Abrams, 1989.

Duncan, James. "Sites of Representation: Place, Time and the Discourse of the Other." In *Place/Culture/Representation*, edited by James Duncan and David Ley. London and New York: Routledge, 1994.

Duncan, James, and David Ley, eds. *Place/Culture/Representation*. London and New York: Routledge, 1993.

Dunlap, David W. "African Burial Ground Made Historical Site." *New York Times*, 26 Feb. 1993, B31.

———. "Excavation Stirs Debate on Cemetery." *New York Times*, 6 Dec. 1991, B4.

———. "New York Dig Unearths Early Cemetery for Blacks." *New York Times*, 9 Oct. 1991.

Dzobo, N. K. "African Symbols and Proverbs as Sources of Knowledge and Truth." In *Person and Community*, edited by Kwasi Wiredu and Kwami Gyekye, 73–84. Washington, DC: Council for Research in Values and Philosophy, 1992.

Echo-Hawk, Roger, and Walter. *Battlefields and Burial Grounds: The Indian Struggle to Protect Ancestral Graves in the United States*. Minneapolis: Lerner Publications Company, 1994.

Edeh, Emmanuel M. P. *Towards an Igbo Metaphysics*. Chicago: Loyola Univ. Press, 1985.

Edwards, Brent Hayes. "The Uses of Diaspora." *Social Text* 66 (Spring 2001): 45–73.

Egyir, William. "Elaborate Rites are Being Planned for Burial of 24 Skeletons in Ghana." *New York Amsterdam News*, 14 Jan. 1995, 4.

Eisenstadt, Peter, ed. *The Encyclopedia of New York State*, 1st ed., s.v. "beaver." Syracuse: Syracuse Univ. Press, 2005.

Ephirim-Donkor, Anthony. *African Spirituality: On Becoming Ancestors*. Trenton, NJ, and Asmara, Eritrea: Africa World Press, Inc., 1997.

Epperson, Terrence W. "The Politics of 'Race' and Cultural Identity at the African Burial Ground Excavations, New York City." *World Archaeological Bulletin* 7 (1997): 108–117.

Fabre, Geneviève and Robert O'Meally, eds. *History and Memory in African-American Culture*. New York and Oxford: Oxford Univ. Press, 1994.

Fearnow, Mark. "Theatre for an Angry God: Public Burnings and Hangings in Colonial New York, 1741." *Drama Review* 40, no. 2 (Summer, 1996): 15–36.

Fein, Gene. "The New York City Slave Rebellion of 1712 Revisited: Through the Optic of the Akan." 1999. Email file.

Ferguson, Leland. "The Cross Is a Magic Sign: Marks on Eighteenth-Century Bowls from South Carolina." In *I, Too, Am America: Archaeological Studies of African-American Life*, edited by Theresa Singleton, 116–31. Charlottesville: Univ. Press of Virginia, 1999.

———. *Uncommon Ground: Archaeology and Early African America, 1650–1800*. Washington, DC: Smithsonian Institution Press, 1992.

Fernow, Berthold, ed. *The Records of New Amsterdam from 1653 to 1674*. 7 vols. New York, 1897.

Finn, Robin. "Public Lives: With Memorial, a Monumental Predicament." *New York Times*, 27 Sept. 2000, B2.

First Recorded Minutes Regarding the Building of Trinity Church in the City of New York, 1696–99. Foreword by John Heuss. The Parish of Trinity Church in the City of New York, 1964.

Fitzgerald, Sharon. "Sacred Ground." *Essence* 24, no. 5 (Sept. 1993).

Foley Square Construction Project and the Historic African Burial Ground, New York, NY: Hearing before the Subcommittee on Public Buildings and Grounds of the Committee on Public Works and Transportation, 102nd Cong., 2nd sess., 27 July 1992 and 24 Sept. 1992.

Foley Square Federal Courthouse and Office Building New York, New York. *Research Design for Archeological, Historical, and Bioanthropological Investigations of the African Burial Ground (Broadway Block) New York, New York.* Prepared by Howard Univ., Washington, DC, and John Milner Associates, Inc., PA, 22 Apr. 1993.

"Foley Square Officially Opened after a Massive Three Year, $18 Million Redesign and Reconstruction." *Media Advisory for New York City Department of Parks and Recreation.* http://www.nycgovparks.org/sub _newsroom/media_advisories/media_advisories.php?id=7764 (accessed 12 July 2008).

Foote, Thelma Wills. "Black Life in Colonial Manhattan, 1664–1786." PhD diss., Harvard Univ., 1991.

———. *Black and White Manhattan: The History of Racial Formation in Colonial New York City.* New York: Oxford Univ. Press, 2004.

Frankel, Bruce. "Black Cemetery in NYC New Key to Colonial Times." *USA Today,* 15 Sept. 1992.

Freeman, Rhoda Golden. "The Free Negro in New York City in the Era Before the Civil War." PhD, diss., Columbia Univ., 1966.

Freifeld, Karen. "Bones Dug Up Near Historic Cemetery." *Newsday,* 15 Feb. 1993, 21.

Frohne, Andrea E. "The African Burial Ground in New York City: Manifesting and Representing Spirituality of Space." PhD diss., SUNY Binghamton, 2002.

———. "Commemorating the African Burial Ground in New York City: Spirituality of Space in Contemporary Art Works." *Ijele Art eJournal* 1, no. 1 (Mar. 2000). http://www.ijele.com.

———. *The Encyclopedia of New York State,* 1st ed., s.v. "African Burial Ground." Syracuse: Syracuse Univ. Press, 2005.

———. "Reclaiming Space: The African Burial Ground in New York City." In *"We Shall Independent Be": African American Place-Making and the Struggle to Claim Space in the United States,* edited by Leslie Alexander and Angel Nieves. Boulder: Univ. Press of Colorado, 2008.

Fu-Kiau, K. K. Bunseki. "Natangu-Tandu-Kolo: The Bantu-Kongo Concept of Time." In *Time in the Black Experience*, edited by Joseph K. Adjaye, 17–34. Westport, CT and London: Greenwood Press, 1994.

Gaines, Patrice. "Bones of Forebears: Howard University Study Stirs Ghanaian Chiefs to Honor Ages-Old Link to U.S. Blacks." *Washington Post*, 3 Aug. 1995, B11.

Gbadegesin, Segun. *African Philosophy: Traditional Yoruba Philosophy and Contemporary African Realities*. New York: Peter Lang, 1991.

Geismar, Joan H. "Digging into a Seaport's Past." *Archaeology* 40 (Jan./Feb. 1987): 30–35.

General Services Administration. Request for Proposal. *The African Burial Ground Interpretive Center Design and Fabrication: A Project in Cultural Storytelling through the Environment*. New York, 1997.

———. Request for Proposal. *The African Burial Ground Memorial Design and Fabrication: A Project in Cultural Storytelling through the Environment*. New York, 1997.

———. "Brochure for the African Burial Ground Memorial and Interpretive Center." 1997. Photocopy.

———. "GSA Roundtable—Q&A." Pre-Proposal Conference for the Interpretive Center, New York City, 4 Feb. 1998. Photocopy.

General Services Administration Region 2. *Comments on the Draft Research Design for Archeological, Historical, and Bioanthropological Investigations of the African Burial Ground and Five Points Area, New York, NY*. For Foley Square Project. Federal Courthouse and Federal Office Building. New York, NY, 1992.

Genovese, Eugene. *Roll, Jordan, Roll*. New York: Pantheon Books, 1972.

Gillis, John R., ed. "Memory and Identity: The History of a Relationship." Introduction to *Commemorations: The Politics of National Identity*. Princeton: Princeton Univ. Press, 1994.

Gilvin, Amanda. "'The Fire Is Too Hot for Them': Gender and Change in the Krobo Bead Industry." MA thesis, Cornell Univ., 2006.

Goldberg, David Theo. *The Racial State*. Malden, MA, and Oxford: Blackwell Publishers, 2002.

Goode-Null, S. K., K. Shujaa, and L. M. Rankin-Hill. "Subadult Growth and Development." In *The New York African Burial Ground Skeletal*

Biology Final Report, edited by Michael L. Blakey and Lesley M. Rankin-Hill, vol. 1, chap. 12. Washington, DC: General Services Administration and Howard Univ., 2004.

Goodfriend, Joyce D. *Before the Melting Pot*. Princeton: Princeton Univ. Press, 1992.

———. "Burghers and Blacks: The Evolution of a Slave Society at New Amsterdam." *New York History* (Apr. 1978): 125–44.

Goodman, Amy, and Juan González. "Remains of 419 Enslaved Africans Re-Buried at the African Burial Ground in New York City." *Democracy Now*, 6 Oct. 2003. http://www.democracynow.org/2003/10/6 /remains_of_419_enslaved_africans_re.

Goodman, A., J. Jones, J. Reid, M. Mack, M. Blakey, D. Amarasiriwardena, P. Burton, and D. Coleman. "Isotopic and Elemental Chemistry of Teeth: Implications for Places of Birth, Forced Migration Patterns, Nutritional Status, and Pollution." In *The New York African Burial Ground Skeletal Biology Final Report*, edited by Michael L. Blakey and Lesley M. Rankin-Hill, vol. 1, chap. 6. Washington, DC: General Services Administration and Howard Univ., 2004.

Gould, Kira. "On Hallowed Ground: The African Burial Ground Competition." *Competitions* (Fall 1994): 28–33.

Gregerson, John. "From Red Tape to Blue Ribbons." *Building Design and Construction* 36, no. 8 (Aug. 1995).

"GSA African Burial Ground Coffin/Crypt Fact Sheet." GSA, New York City, Sept. 2002. Photocopy.

"GSA Pre-Proposal Conference: Phase One for African Burial Ground Solicitation." 1 Federal Plaza, New York City, 6 Oct. 1997.

Gyekye, Kwame. *An Essay on African Philosophical Thought: The Akan Conceptual Scheme*. Cambridge: Cambridge Univ. Press, 1987.

Gyekye, Kwame, and Kwasi Wiredu. *Person and Community: Ghanaian Philosophical Studies*. Washington, DC: The Council for Research in Values and Philosophy, 1992.

Hackett, Thomas. "Remains of African Slaves to be Reburied." *New York Daily News*, 11 Mar. 2001, 2.

Hall, Stuart. "Cultural Identity and Diaspora." In *Diaspora and Visual Culture: Representing Africans and Jews*, edited by Nicholas Mirzoeff, 21–33. New York: Routledge, 2000.

———. "The Local and the Global: Globalization and Ethnicity." In *Culture, Globalization and the World-System*, edited by Anthony D. King, 19–40. Minneapolis: Univ. of Minnesota, 1997.

Hallgren, Roland. *The Good Things in Life: A Study of the Traditional Religious Culture of the Yoruba People*. Löberöd, Sweden: Bokförlaget Plus Ultra, 1988.

Hamilton, Edith, and Huntington Cairns, eds. *The Collected Dialogues of Plato*. New York: Pantheon Books, 1961.

Handler, Jerome S. "An African-Type Healer/Diviner and His Grave Goods: A Burial from a Plantation Slave Cemetery in Barbados, West Indies." *International Journal of Historical Archaeology* 1, no. 2 (1997): 91–130.

———. "Determining African Birth from Skeletal Remains: A Note on Tooth Mutilation." *Historical Archaeology* 28 no. 3 (1994): 113–19.

Handler, Jerome S., and Frederick Lange. *Plantation Slavery in Barbados: An Archaeological and Historical Investigation*. Cambridge, MA and London: Harvard Univ. Press, 1978.

Hansen, Joyce, and Gary McGowan. *Breaking Ground, Breaking Silence: The Story of New York's African Burial Ground*. New York: Henry Holt and Co., 1998.

Harley, J. B. "Maps, Knowledge, and Power." In *The Iconography of Landscape*, edited by Denis Cosgrove and Stephen Daniels. Cambridge: Cambridge Univ. Press, 1988.

———. "Silences and Secrecy: The Hidden Agenda of Cartography." *Imago Mundi* 40 (1988): 57.

Harrington, Ayo. "Friends of the African Burial Ground." *Update: Newsletter of the African Burial Ground and Five Points Archaeological Projects* 2, no. 10 (Spring 1999): 8.

———. Letter to Congressperson Charles Rangel, 15 Mar. 1999.

Harrington, Spencer. "Bones and Bureaucrats: New York's Great Cemetery Imbroglio." *Archaeology* (Mar.–Apr. 1993): 30–38.

Harris, Leslie M. *In The Shadow of Slavery: African Americans in New York City, 1626–1863*. Chicago and London: Univ. of Chicago Press, 2003.

Haskell, Daniel C., ed. *Manhattan Maps: A Co-operative List*. New York: The New York Public Library, 1931.

Hawkins, Denise. "Howard Scientists 'Listen' to Bones: 1991 Manhattan Dig Still Yielding Priceless Data on Colonial-Era Africans." *Black Issues in Higher Education*, 19 Oct. 1995.

Heaton, Claude. "Body Snatching in New York City." *The New York State Journal of Medicine* 43 (1943): 1863.

Henry, Tanu. "Controversy Brews over DNA Testing Plan." *Africana.com*. http://www.africana.com (accessed 26 Aug. 2000).

Hill, Shannen. "Minkisi Do Not Die: The Survival of Kongo Cosmology in the Visual Culture of Modern Christian Zaire." MA thesis, Univ. of Wisconsin, 1994.

Hodges, Graham Russell. *Root and Branch: African Americans in New York and East Jersey, 1613–1863*. Chapel Hill and London: Univ. of North Carolina Press, 1999.

Hodgkin, Katharine, and Susannah Radstone, eds. *Contested Pasts: The Politics of Memory*. New York: Routledge, 2003.

Hoff, Henry B. "A Colonial Black Family in New York and New Jersey: Pieter Santomee and His Descendants." *Journal of the Afro-American Historical and Genealogical Society* 9 (1988): 101–135.

Hoffman, Murray. *A Treatise upon the Estate and Rights of the Corporation of the City of New York as Proprietors*. 2 vols. New York: Edmund Jones and Co., 1862.

Holl, Augustin F. C. "The Cemetery of Houlouf in Northern Cameroun (AD 1500–1600): Fragments of a Past Social System." *African Archaeological Review* 12 (1994): 133–70.

Holloway, Sarah, Stephen Rice, and Gill Valentine, eds. *Key Concepts in Geography*. Sage Publications, 2003.

Homberger, Eric. *The Historical Atlas of New York City*. New York: Henry Holt and Co., 1994.

Horsmanden, Daniel. *The New York Conspiracy, or, A History of the Negro Plot with the Journal of the Proceedings against the Conspirators at New York in the Years 1741–1742*. New York: Southwick & Pelsue, 1810; Reprint, New York: Negro Universities Press, 1969.

Howson, Jean, and Leonard G. Bianchi. "The Archaeological Site." In *New York African Burial Ground Archaeology Final Report*, edited by Warren R. Perry, Jean Howson, and Barbara A. Bianco, vol. 1, chap. 3. Washington, DC: General Services Administration and Howard Univ., 2006.

Howson, Jean, and Leonard G. Bianchi, with Iciar Lucena Narvaez and Janet L. Woodruff. "Coffins." In *New York African Burial Ground Archaeology Final Report*, edited by Warren R. Perry, Jean Howson, and Barbara A. Bianco, vol. 1, chap. 10. Washington, DC: General Services Administration and Howard Univ., 2006.

Howson, Jean, Barbara A. Bianco, and Steven Barto. "Documentary Evidence on the Origin and Use of the African Burial Ground." In *New York African Burial Ground Archaeology Final Report*, edited by Warren R. Perry, Jean Howson, and Barbara A. Bianco, vol. 1, chap. 2. Washington, DC: General Services Administration and Howard Univ., 2006.

Howson, Jean, Warren R. Perry, Augustin F. C. Holl, and Leonard G. Bianchi, "Relative Dating." In *New York African Burial Ground Archaeology Final Report*, edited by Warren R. Perry, Jean Howson, and Barbara A. Bianco, vol. 1, chap. 4. Washington, DC: General Services Administration and Howard Univ., 2006.

Howson, Jean, with Shannon Mahoney and Janet L. Woodruff. "Pins and Shrouding." In *New York African Burial Ground Archaeology Final Report*, edited by Warren R. Perry, Jean Howson, and Barbara A. Bianco, vol. 1, chap. 11. Washington, DC: General Services Administration and Howard Univ., 2006.

Hu-DeHart, Evelyn. "Chinese in the Caribbean and Latin America." In *Tomie Arai: Double Happiness*, edited by Lydia Yee. New York: Bronx Museum of the Arts, 1998.

Hubbard, Phil, et al., *Thinking Geographically: Space, Theory, and Contemporary Human Geography*. London and New York: Continuum, 2002.

Humphreys, David. *An Historical Account of the Incorporated Society for the Propagation of the Gospel in Foreign Parts to Instruct Negroes*. 1730. Reprint, New York: Arno Press, 1969.

IDI Construction Team. "IDI Construction Team for the African Burial Ground." IDI, New York City, Oct. 1999.

Idowu, E. Bolaji. *Oludumare: God in Yoruba Belief*. New York: The African Islamic Publications, 1994.

Imperato, Pascal James. "The Dance of the Tyi Wara." *African Arts* 4, no. 1 (1970).

Ingle, Marjorie, Jean Howson, and Edward S. Rutsch, S.O.P.A. of Historic Conservation and Interpretation, Inc. *A Stage IA Cultural Resource*

Survey of the Proposed Foley Square Project in the Borough of Manhattan, New York, NY. Prepared for Edwards & Kelcey Engineers, Inc. Sept. 1989, revised May 1990.

Ingrassia, Robert. "$21 Million Plan Mired in Woe: Researchers, Feds Wrangle over African Burial Ground." *New York Daily News,* 5 Feb. 2001.

Interagency Agreement for African Burial Ground Technical Assistance between the National Park Service and the General Services Administration (Northeast Region, Sept. 2003), 1.

Isizoh, Chidi Denis. "Who is an Ancestor in African Traditional Religion?" *African Traditional Religion Special Topics* (17 Apr. 1999). http:// www.afrikaworld.net/afrel/atr-ancestor.htm (accessed 21 July 2010).

Jackson, F. L. C., A. Mayes, M. E. Mack, A. Froment, S. O. Y. Keita, R. A. Kittles, M. George, K. Shujaa, M. L. Blakey, and L. M. Rankin-Hill. "Origins of the New York African Burial Ground Population." In *The New York African Burial Ground Skeletal Biology Final Report,* edited by Michael L. Blakey and Lesley M. Rankin-Hill, vol. 1, chap. 5. Washington, DC: General Services Administration and Howard Univ., 2004.

Jackson, Kenneth. *The Encyclopedia of New York City.* New Haven: Yale Univ. Press, 1995.

Jacobs, Jaap. *New Netherland: A Dutch Colony in Seventeenth-Century America.* Leiden and Boston: Brill, 2005.

Jacobsen-Widding, Anita. *Red-White-Black as a Mode of Thought.* Uppsala: Almquist & Wiskell International, 1979.

Jameson, John Franklin, ed. *Narratives of New Netherland, 1609–1664.* New York: Charles Scribner's, 1909; Reprint, New York: Barnes and Noble, 1959.

Janeway Family. The Janeway Papers, Drawer 8. Deeds and Indentures Collection. Special Collections and University Archives. Rutgers University Libraries.

Johnson, Kirk A. "The History in 'Dem Bones.'" *Heart and Soul* (Feb.– Mar. 1996): 77–80.

[Jorde, Peggy King]. "The African Burial Ground Design Competitions. Brochure." New York: U.S. General Services Administration, 1997. Included in mailings for design teams. http://r2.gsa.gov/afrburgro/bro chure.html (accessed 29 July 2000).

Jorde, Peggy King. "An Open Invitation to the Community." *Update: Newsletter of the African Burial Ground and Five Points Archaeological Projects* 2, no. 9 (Winter 1999): 12.

Judd, Jacob. "Frederick Philipse and the Madagascar Trade." *New-York Historical Society Quarterly* 55, no. 4 (Oct. 1971): 354–74.

Juma, Abdurahman. "Muslim Burial Customs on the East African Coast." *Tor* (Uppsala) 28 (1996): 349–55.

Kaufman, Edward, ed. *Reclaiming Our Past, Honoring Our Ancestors: New York's 18th Century African Burial Ground and the Memorial Competition*. New York: African Burial Ground Competition Coalition, 1994.

Kayode, J. O. *Understanding African Traditional Religion*. Ile Ife: Univ. of Ife Press, 1984.

King, Anthony D. *Spaces of Global Cultures: Architecture Urbanism Identity*. New York and London: Routledge, 2005.

Kirkham, Major A. *Private Log Book Kept on Board Different Ships, 1798–1820*. Library of Congress. Microfilm.

Klein, Herbert. *The Atlantic Slave Trade: New Approaches to the Americas*. Cambridge: Cambridge Univ. Press, 1999.

Klingberg, Frank. *Anglican Humanitarianism in Colonial New York*. Philadelphia: Church Historical Society, 1940.

Kobrin, David. *The Black Minority in Early New York*. Albany: State Education Department, 1971; Reprint, Albany: New York State American Revolution Bicentennial Commission, 1975.

Koser, Khalid. *New African Diasporas*. New York and London: Routledge, 2003.

Kouwenhoven, John A. *The Columbia Historical Portrait of New York*. Garden City, NY: Doubleday & Company, Inc., 1953.

Kruger, Vivienne L. "Born to Run: The Slave Family in Early New York, 1626–1827." PhD diss., Columbia Univ., 1985.

Krüger-Kahloula, Angelika. "On the Wrong Side of the Fence: Racial Segregation in American Cemeteries." In *History and Memory in African-American Culture*, edited by Geneviève Fabre and Robert O'Meally, 130–49. New York: Oxford Univ. Press, 1994.

———. "Homage and Hegemony: African American Grave Inscription and Decoration." In *Slavery in the Americas*, edited by Wolfgang Binder, 317–35. Würzburg: Koenigshausen and Newman, 1993.

Kuyk, Betty M. *African Voices in the African American Heritage*. Bloomington: Indiana Univ. Press, 2003.

Kwame, Safro. *Readings in African Philosophy: An Akan Collection*. Lanham, MD: Univ. Press of America, 1995.

Lang, Joel. "The Sankofa Man." *Hartford Courant* (15 Feb. 1998): 10–16.

LaRoche, Cheryl J. "Beads from the African Burial Ground, New York City: A Preliminary Assessment." *Beads: Journal of the Society of Bead Researchers* 6 (1994): 3–20.

LaRoche, Cheryl J., and Michael L. Blakey. "Seizing Intellectual Power: The Dialogue at the New York African Burial Ground." *Historical Archaeology* 31, no. 3 (1997): 84–106.

Lawton, Samuel Miller. "The Religious Life of South Carolina Coastal and Sea Island Negroes." PhD diss., George Peabody College for Teachers, Nashville, TN, 1939.

Léon, Rodney. "Rodney Léon's Statement on the African Burial Ground." *African Burial Ground News* 4, no. 1 (Fall 2005), 2.

Lepore, Jill. *New York Burning: Liberty, Slavery, and Conspiracy in Eighteenth-Century Manhattan*. New York: Alfred A. Knopf, 2005.

———. "The Tightening Vise: Slavery and Freedom in British New York." In *Slavery in New York*, edited by Ira Berlin and Leslie M. Harris. New York: New Press, 2005.

Long, Claramae B. "History of Negro Education in New York City, 1701–1853." MS thesis, New York City College, 1935.

Lopez, Elias E. "Nameless Are Memorialized at Old African Burial Site." *New York Times*, 2 Oct. 2007.

LoRusso, Mark. "The Betsey Prince Site: An Early Free Black Domestic Site on Long Island." In *Nineteenth- and Early Twentieth-Century Domestic Site Archaeology in New York State*, edited by John P. Hart and Charles L. Fisher. New York State Museum Bulletin 495. Albany: Univ. of the State of New York Education Dept. 2000: 195–224.

Lydon, James G. "New York and the Slave Trade, 1700–1774." *William and Mary Quarterly* 35, no. 2 (Apr. 1978): 375–94.

Lynds, Clyde. "American Song. Sculpture Proposal for the Federal Office Building at 920 [sic] Broadway, New York, NY. *General Services Administration Art-in-Architecture Program Public Buildings Service*. Sept. 1993. Photocopy.

Macdonald, Robert. "Bad Blood at the Burial Ground." *New York Times* 12 Sept. 1992, 21.

———. "The City of New Amsterdam Located on the Island of Manhattan in New Netherland c. 1650." nd. http://www.mcny.org/newview.htm (accessed 6 Nov. 1998).

MacGaffey, Wyatt. *Art and Healing of the BaKongo Commented by Themselves: Minkisi from the Laman Collection*. Bloomington: Indiana Univ. Press, 1991.

———. *Religion and Society in Central Africa: The BaKongo of Lower Zaire*. Chicago: Univ. of Chicago Press, 1986.

———. *Modern Kongo Prophets: Religion in a Plural Society*. Bloomington: Indiana Univ. Press, 1983.

Mack, M. E., A. H. Goodman, M. L. Blakey, and A. Mayes. "Odontological Indicators of Disease, Diet, and Nutrition Inadequacy." In *The New York African Burial Ground Skeletal Biology Final Report*, edited by Michael L. Blakey and Lesley M. Rankin-Hill, vol. 1, chap. 9. Washington, DC: General Services Administration and Howard Univ., 2004.

Mack, M. E., and M. C. Hill. "Notes from the Howard University Biological Anthropology Laboratory: Dental Observations of the New York African Burial Ground Skeletal Population." *Update: Newsletter of the African Burial Ground and Five Points Archaeological Projects* 1, no. 6 (Winter 1995).

Mack, Mark, Edna Medford, M. C. Hill, Jean Howson, Lisa King, Warren Perry, and Lesley Rankin-Hill. "Toiling through Our Troubles: Exploitation and Resistance of African New Yorkers in the Eighteenth Century." Paper presented at the 14th Congress of Anthropological and Ethnological Sciences, Williamsburg, VA, 28 July 1998.

Maika, Dennis J. "Slavery, Race, and Culture in Early New York." *Halve Maen* 73, no. 2 (Summer 2000): 27–33.

Majozo, Estella Conwill. *Blessings for a New World*. Chicago: Third World Press, 2007.

Martens, Wendy. "Beyond the Graves: Vigil Traces the Spiritual Heritage Found in the African Burial Ground." *Downtown Express*, 17 Aug. 1992.

Mato, Daniel. "Clothed in Symbol: The Art of Adinkra among the Akan of Ghana." PhD diss., Indiana Univ., 1986.

Matson, Cathy. *Merchants and Empire: Trading in Colonial New York.* Baltimore: Johns Hopkins Univ. Press, 1998.

Mays, Terry M. *Historical Dictionary of Revolutionary America.* Lanham, MD: Scarecrow Press, 2005.

McClusky, Pamela. *Art from Africa: Long Steps Never Broke a Back.* Seattle and Princeton: Seattle Art Museum with Princeton Univ. Press, 2002.

McGovern, Allison Manfra. "Rocky Point's African American Past: A Forgotten History Remembered through Historical Archaeology at the Betsey Prince Site." *Long Island History Journal* 22, no. 1 (2011). https://lihj.cc.stonybrook.edu/2011/articles/rocky-point's-african-american-past-a-forgotten-history-remembered-through-historical-archaeology-at-the-betsey-prince-site/ (accessed 17 Aug. 2012).

McKee, Bradford. "Federal Design/Build: Six Projects Reveal How the Government Has Succeeded—and Failed—by Teaming Architects and Contractors." *Architecture* 83, no. 10 (Oct. 1994).

McManus, Edgar J. *Black Bondage in the North.* Syracuse: Syracuse Univ. Press, 1973.

———. *A History of Negro Slavery in New York.* Syracuse: Syracuse Univ. Press, 1966.

McNaughton, Patrick. *Mande Blacksmiths: Knowledge, Power, and Art in West Africa.* Bloomington: Indiana Univ. Press, 1988.

Medford, Edna Greene, Warren Perry, Selwyn Carrington, Linda Heywood, Fatimah Jackson, S. O. Y. Keita, Richard Kittles, and John Thornton. "The Transatlantic Slave Trade to New York City: Sources and Routing of Captives." Paper presented at the 14th Congress of Anthropological and Ethnological Sciences, Williamsburg, VA, 28 July 1998.

Mfuni, Tanangachi. "Emotional Burial Ground Memorial Groundbreaking." *New York Amsterdam News*, 29 Sept. 2005.

Minkus, Helaine K. "The Concept of Spirit in Akwapim Akan Philosophy." *Africa* 50, no. 2 (1980): 182–92.

Mitchell, Don. *Cultural Geography: A Critical Introduction.* Malden, MA: Blackwell Publishers, 2000.

Moore, Christopher. *The African Burial Ground: An American Discovery.* Parts 1–4. Directed and produced by David Kutz. Washington, DC: U.S. General Services Administration, 1994. DVD, 2 hrs.

Morris, Deborah S. "Resting Place: History/Slave Remains Return to NYC Burial Grounds." *Newsday*, 4 Oct. 2003.

Moscow, Henry. *The Street Book: An Encyclopedia of Manhattan's Street Names and Their Origins*. New York: Fordham Univ. Press, 1978.

Mullin, Michael. *Africa in America: Slave Acculturation and Resistance in the American South and the British Caribbean, 1736–1831*. Urbana and Chicago: Univ. of Illinois Press, 1992.

Munro, Martin. *Different Drummers: Rhythm and Race in the Americas*. Berkeley: Univ. of California Press, 2010.

Newman, Marc. "Slavery and Insurrections in the Colonial Province of New York." *Social Education* 59 (Mar. 1995): 125–29.

Newsom, James I. "The Black History of the Statue of Liberty." *Black Web Portal*, 24 Jan. 2002. http://www.blackwebportal.com/wire/Dis playArticle.cfm?ArticleID =529 (accessed 18 Mar. 2002).

Noble, Gil, Sherrill Wilson, Noel Pointer, and David Paterson. "Negro Burial Ground." *Like It Is*. WABC TV, 2 Aug. 1992.

Nooter, Mary H, ed. *Secrecy: African Art that Conceals and Reveals*. New York: The Museum for African Art, 1993.

Null, C. C., M. L. Blakey, K. J. Shujaa, L. M. Rankin-Hill, and S. H. H. Carrington. "Osteological Indicators of Infectious Disease and Nutritional Inadequacy." In *The New York African Burial Ground Skeletal Biology Final Report*, edited by Michael L. Blakey and Lesley M. Rankin-Hill, vol. 1, chap. 10. Washington, DC: General Services Administration and Howard Univ., 2004.

O'Callaghan, E. B., ed. *Documents Relative to the Colonial and Revolutionary History of New York*. Albany: Weed, Parsons, 1855–1861.

Officer, Debbie. "Burial Grounds Meeting Ends in Uproar." *New York Amsterdam News*, 4 Apr. 1993, 32, 34.

———. "Outrage over Desecration of Ancestral Burial Ground." *New York Amsterdam News*, 20 Feb. 1993, p. 1.

———. "African Burial Ground Opens Official Liaison Office in WTC." *New York Amsterdam News*, 29 May 1993, 10. *Ethnic Watch*. CD-ROM. Softline Information. 1993.

———. "Con Ed Digs into African Burial Ground with New York City 'Emergency' Permits." *New York Amsterdam News*, 19 Feb. 1994, 2.

———. "Last Rites." *African Voices* (Mar. 1994): 4–5.

————. "Uproar and Protest at African Burial Ground Meeting." *New York Amsterdam News*, 21 Apr. 1999.

Okediji, Moyo. "Semioptics of Anamnesia: Yoruba Images in the Works of Jeff Donaldson, Howardena Pindell, and Muneer Bahauddeen." PhD diss., Univ. of Wisconsin, 1995.

————. *The Shattered Gourd: Yoruba Forms in Twentieth-Century American Art*. Seattle: Univ. of Washington Press, 2003.

Okpewho, Isidore, and Nkiru, Nzegwu, eds. *The New African Diaspora: Assessing the Pains and Gains of Exile*. Bloomington: Indiana Univ. Press, 2009.

Olsen, J. P. "Paterson Bill Says Dig They Must Not." *Newsday*, 12 May 1993, 27M.

Opoku, Kofi Asare. "The World View of the Akan." *Tarikh* 7, no. 2 (1982): 61–73.

Outram, Dorinda. *The Enlightenment*. Cambridge Univ. Press: Cambridge, 1995.

Pace, Lorenzo. "Concept of Design for the African Burial Ground and Foley Square." 21 Mar. 1997. Photocopy.

Page, Willie F. *The Dutch Triangle: The Netherlands and the Atlantic Slave Trade, 1621–1664*. New York: Garland Pub., 1997.

Paterson, (Senator) David. Letter to Regional Director William Diamond, New York City, 4 Oct. 1992.

Pearce, Susan C. "Africans on This Soil: The Counter-Amnesia of the New York African Burial Ground." PhD diss., New School for Social Research, 1996.

Peek, Philip M., ed. *African Divination Systems: Ways of Knowing*. Bloomington and Indianapolis: Indiana Univ. Press, 1991.

Pelletreau, William Smith. *Historic Homes and Institutions and Genealogical and Family History of New York*. Vol. 1. New York: Lewis Publishing Co., 1907.

Perazio, Philip. "Archaeological Monitoring." 27 Apr. 1997 in ACRA-L archive. http://lists.gardencity.net/listproc/archives/acra-l/9704/0134.html.

Perry, Warren R. "New York City's African Burial Ground." *Africa Update: Quarterly Newsletter of the Central Connecticut State University African Studies Program* 3, no. 4 (Fall 1996). http://www.ccsu.edu/afstudy/fall96.html#lk7.

Perry, Warren R., et al., "The African Burial Ground: Mortuary Complex in Diasporic Perspective." Paper presented at the 14th Congress of Anthropological and Ethnological Sciences, Williamsburg, VA, 28 July 1998.

Perry, Warren R., and Jean Howson. "Overview of Mortuary Population, Burial Practices, and Spatial Distribution." In *New York African Burial Ground Archaeology Final Report*, edited by Warren R. Perry, Jean Howson, and Barbara A. Bianco, vol. 1, chap. 5. Washington, DC: General Services Administration and Howard Univ., 2006.

Perry, Warren R., Jean Howson, and Barbara A. Bianco, eds. *New York African Burial Ground Archaeology Final Report*. Washington, DC: General Services Administration and Howard Univ., 2006.

Perry, Warren R., Jean Howson, and Barbara Bianco. "Summary and Conclusions." In *New York African Burial Ground Archaeology Final Report*, edited by Warren R. Perry, Jean Howson, and Barbara A. Bianco, vol. 1, chap. 15. Washington, DC: General Services Administration and Howard Univ., 2006.

Perry, Warren R., Jean Howson, and Augustin F. C. Holl. "The Early Group." In *New York African Burial Ground Archaeology Final Report*, edited by Warren R. Perry, Jean Howson, and Barbara A. Bianco, vol. 1, chap. 6. Washington, DC: General Services Administration and Howard Univ., 2006.

———. "The Middle Group." In *New York African Burial Ground Archaeology Final Report*, edited by Warren R. Perry, Jean Howson, and Barbara A. Bianco, vol. 1, chap. 7. Washington, DC: General Services Administration and Howard Univ., 2006.

———. "The Late-Middle Group." In *New York African Burial Ground Archaeology Final Report*, edited by Warren R. Perry, Jean Howson, and Barbara A. Bianco, vol. 1, chap. 8. Washington, DC: General Services Administration and Howard Univ., 2006.

———. "The Late Group." In *New York African Burial Ground Archaeology Final Report*, edited by Warren R. Perry, Jean Howson, and Barbara A. Bianco, vol. 1, chap. 9. Washington, DC: General Services Administration and Howard Univ., 2006.

Perry, Warren R., and Janet L. Woodruff, "Coins, Shells, Pipes, and Other Items." In *New York African Burial Ground Archaeology Final*

Report, edited by Warren R. Perry, Jean Howson, and Barbara A. Bianco, vol. 1, chap. 14. Washington, DC: General Services Administration and Howard Univ., 2006.

Peterson, Marina. "Patrolling the Plaza: Privatized Public Space and the Neoliberal State in Downtown Los Angeles." *Urban Anthropology* 35, no. 4 (2006): 355–86.

Phillips, Philip Lee. *A List of Geographical Atlases in the Library of Congress.* 4 vols. Washington, DC: Washington Printing Office, 1909–1914.

Phillips, P. Lee. "A Descriptive List of Maps and Views of New York City in the Library of Congress, 1639–1865." Unpublished manuscript, Library of Congress, 1920.

Pierre, Caterina. "Black Statue of Liberty Bibliography." http://www2.h -net.msu.edu/~women/bibs/bibl-blackliberty.html.

Piersen, William D. *From Africa to America: African American History from the Colonial Era to the Early Republic, 1526–1790.* New York: Twayne Publishers, 1996.

Platt, Virginia. "The East India Company and the Madagascar Slave Trade." *William and Mary Quarterly* 26, no. 4 (Oct. 1969): 548–77.

Platvoet, J. G. *Comparing Religions: A Limitative Approach. An Analysis of Akan, Para-Creole, and IFO-Sananda Rites and Prayers.* The Hague: Mouton Publishers, 1982.

Powell, Richard J. "Art History and Black Memory: Toward a 'Blues Aesthetic.'" In *History and Memory in African-American Culture*, edited by Geneviève Fabre and Robert O'Meally, 228–43. New York: Oxford Univ. Press, 1994.

Pritchard, Margaret and Taliaferro, Henry. *Degrees of Latitude: Mapping Colonial America.* Williamsburg, VA, and New York: The Colonial Williamsburg Foundation and Harry N. Abrams, 2002.

Quarterly Report of the New York African Burial Ground Project. Submitted by Dr. Michael L. Blakey, Project Director [. . .], to Ms Miriam Lopez-Rivera, Contracting Officer, [. . .] GSA, 1999.

Raboteau, Albert J. *Slave Religion: The 'Invisible Institution' in the Antebellum South.* New York: Oxford Univ. Press, 1978.

Rahman, Ali. "Lest We Forget! Our Ancestors' Bones Still Call to Us from the Empty Graves in Lower Manhattan." *New York Beacon*, 12 Jan. 2000, 16.

Rankin-Hill, L. M., M. L. Blakey, J. Howson, E. Brown, S. H. H. Carrington, and K. Shujaa. "Demographic Overview of the African Burial Ground and Colonial Africans of New York." In *The New York African Burial Ground Skeletal Biology Final Report*, edited by Michael L. Blakey and Lesley M. Rankin-Hill, vol. 1, chap. 7. Washington, DC: General Services Administration and Howard Univ., 2004.

Rankin-Hill, L. M., J. Gruber, P. Allen, and A. Barrett. "Burial Descriptions." In *The New York African Burial Ground Skeletal Biology Final Report*, edited by Michael L. Blakey and Lesley M. Rankin-Hill, vol. 2, section 4. Washington, DC: General Services Administration and Howard Univ., 2004.

Rattray, R. S. *Ashanti*. New York: Clarendon Press, 1923. Reprint, New York: Negro Univ. Press, 1969.

———. *Religion and Art in Ashanti*. 1927. Reprint, Kumasi: Basel Mission Book Depot; London: Oxford Univ. Press, 1954.

Reconstruction of Foley Square: Historical and Archaeological Resources Report. Prepared for the New York Department of Parks and Recreation by Joan H. Geismar, Dec. 1993.

Report of the New York City Improvement Commission to the Honorable Geo. B. McClellan, Mayor of the City of New York, and to the Honorable Board of Aldermen of the City of New York. New York, 1904.

Research Design for Archaeological, Historical, and Bioanthropological Investigation of the African Burial Ground. Prepared by Howard Univ. and John Milner Associates. New York: Foley Square Federal Courthouse and Office Building, 22 Apr. 1993.

Response to the GSA's Comments and Suggestions of the Draft New York African Burial Ground Skeletal Biology Report. Prepared by Michael Blakey, to Mr. William Lawson, Deputy Regional Administrator, 21 Dec. 1999.

Richards, Dona Marimba. *Let the Circle Be Unbroken: The Implications of African Spirituality in the Diaspora*. Trenton, NJ: The Red Sea Press, 1980.

Richmond, Rev. J. F. *New York and Its Institutions, 1609–1873*. New York: E. B. Treat, 1872.

Rink, Oliver. "The People of New Netherland: Notes on Non-English Immigration to New York in the Seventeenth Century." *New York History* 62, no. 1 (Jan. 1981): 5–42.

Roberts, Allen. "Is 'Africa' Obsolete?" *African Arts* 33, no. 1 (Spring 2000): 1, 4–9, +93.

Roberts, Mary Nooter, Elizabeth Harney, Allyson Purpora, and Christine Kreamer. "Inscribing Meaning: Ways of Knowing." In *Inscribing Meaning: Writing and Graphic Systems in African Art*, 13–27. [Washington, DC]: Smithsonian National Museum of African Art, 2007.

Roediger, David R. "And Die in Dixie: Funerals, Death and Heaven in the Slave Community, 1700–1865." *Massachusetts Review* 22, no. 1 (Spring 1981): 163–83.

Rogers, Josh. "Division Grows as Foley Unveiling Finally Is Scheduled." *Downtown Express*, 26 Sept. 2000.

———. "One Statue, Two Ceremonies at Foley Square." *Downtown Express*, 25 Oct. 2000.

Rogozinski, Jan. *A Brief History of the Caribbean: From the Arawak and the Carib to the Present*. Rev. ed. New York and Oxford: Facts on File, 1999.

Rosenbaum, Art. *Shout Because You're Free: The African American Ring Shout Tradition in Coastal Georgia*. Athens, GA: Univ. of Georgia Press, 1998.

Rovine, Victoria. *Bogolan: Shaping Culture through Cloth in Contemporary Mali*. Washington, DC: Smithsonian Institution Press, 2001.

Rowlands, Penelope. "Cover Up?" *Art News* 97, no. 1 (Jan. 1998): 48, 50.

Rutenberg, James. "Black Politicians Fight Fate of Old 'Negro Burial Ground' Downtown." *Manhattan Spirit*, 28 Apr. 1992, 7, 9.

Said, Edward. *Culture and Imperialism*. New York: Alfred A. Knopf, 1993.

Salaam, Yusuf. "Ancestral Day Held at African Burial Ground," *New York Amsterdam News*, 6 Oct. 1999, 20.

Samford, Patricia. "The Archaeology of African-American Slavery and Material Culture." *William and Mary Quarterly* 53, no. 1 (Jan. 1996): 87–114.

Satchell, Michael. "Only Remember Us: Skeletons of Slaves from a New York Grave Bear Witness." *US News and World Report* 123, no. 4 (28 July 1997): 51(2).

Scarupa, Harriet Jackson. "Learning from Ancestral Bones: New York's Exhumed African Past." *American Visions* (Feb.–Mar. 1995): 19–21.

Schmidt, Benjamin. "Mapping an Empire: Cartographic and Colonial Rivalry in Seventeenth-Century Dutch and English North America." *William and Mary Quarterly* 54, no. 3 (July 1997): 549–78.

Schwartz, Seymour, and Ehrenberg, Ralph. *The Mapping of America*. New York: Harry Abrams, 1980.

Scott, Kenneth. "Funeral Customs in Colonial New York," *The Staten Island Historian* 22, no. 1 (Jan.–Mar. 1961): 6–8.

"Searching for Enoch Sontonga." *South Africa.info*, 23 Sept. 2002. http://www.southafrica.info/about/history/sontonga.htm#.VZHAwkYrTf.

Seeman, Erik R. "Reassessing the '*Sankofa* Symbol' in New York's African Burial Ground." *William and Mary Quarterly* 67, no. 1 (2010): 101–122.

Selz, Peter and Anthony F. Janson, *Barbara Chase-Riboud: Sculptor*. New York: Harry N. Abrams, Inc., 1999.

"Senator Paterson Announces Museum Plan for African Burial Ground." *New York Voice Inc./Harlem USA*, 6 Jan. 1993, 12.

Senie, Harriet F. *The Tilted Arc Controversy*. Minneapolis: Univ. of Minnesota Press, 2002.

Shabazz, Saed. "Howard U Scientists Make Historic DNA Breakthrough." *The Final Call Online*, 1 Jan. 2000. http://www.finalcall.com/national/dna1-4-2000.htm.

Sharpe, John. "Proposals for Erecting a School, Library and Chapel at New York [1712–1713]." *New-York Historical Society Collections* 13 (1880).

Sharpe, Rev. John. "To the Secretary of the Society for the Propagation of the Gospel in Foreign Parts, New York, June 23, 1712." *New York Genealogical and Biographical Record* 21 (1890): 162–63.

Shaw, Jonathan. "Life by Design." *Harvard Magazine* (Jan.–Feb. 1998): 3. http://harvardmagazine.com/1998/01/loeb.html (accessed 29 July 2000).

Shea, Richard. "Temples of Light." http://clydelynds.com/Shea.htm (accessed 21 July 2008).

Shipp, E. R. "Sign On to Honor Old Bones." *New York Daily News*, 23 Nov. 1994.

———. "Black Cemetery Yields Wealth of History." *New York Times*, 9 Aug. 1992: 41.

Short, John Rennie. *Alternative Geographies*. Upper Saddle River, NJ: Prentice Hall, 2000.

———. *Representing the Republic: Mapping the United States 1600–1900*. London: Reaktion Books, 2001.

Singleton, Theresa A. "The Archaeology of Slavery in North America." *Annual Review of Anthropology* 24 (1995): 119–140.

Singleton, Theresa A., ed. *I, Too, Am America: Archaeological Studies of African-American Life*. Charlottesville: Univ. Press of Virginia, 1999.

Smedley, Audrey. *Race in North America: Origin and Evolution of a Worldview*. Boulder: Westview Press, 1993.

Smith, Charles C. "In the Presence of the Ancestors." *Massachusetts* (Fall 1994): 10–13.

Somé, Malidoma Patrice. *Of Water and the Spirit*. New York: Penguin Books USA, 1994.

Stalling-Whited-Muniz, Barbara. *African Burial Ground "Tell the Story."* 2nd ed. N.p., 1992.

Staples, Brent. "Manhattan's African Dead: Colonial New York, from the Grave." *New York Times*, 22 May 1995, A14.

Sterner, Judy. "Sacred Pots and 'Symbolic Reservoirs' in the Mandara Highlands of Northern Cameroun." In *An African Commitment: Papers in Honour of Peter Lewis Shinnie*, edited by Judy Sterner and Nicholas David, 175. Calgary: Univ. of Calgary Press, 1992.

Sterner, Judy, and Nicholas David, eds. *An African Commitment: Papers in Honour of Peter Lewis Shinnie*. Calgary: Univ. of Calgary Press, 1992.

Stine, Linda France, Melanie Cabak, and Mark Groover. "Blue Beads as African-American Cultural Symbols." *Historical Archaeology* 30, no. 3 (1996): 49–75.

Stokes, Isaac Newton Phelps. *New York Past and Present: Its History and Landmarks, 1524–1939*. New York: R. H. Dodd, 1939.

———. *The Iconography of Manhattan Island, 1498–1909*. 6 vols. New York: R. H. Dodd, 1915–1928.

Stokes, Isaac Newton Phelps, and Daniel Haskell. *American Historical Prints: Early Views of American Cities, etc.* New York: New York Public Library, 1933. Reprint, Detroit: Gale Research Co, 1974.

Strickland, Lula N'zinga. "Update 2000 on the ABG." *Caribbean Life Queens/Long Island Edition*, 4 Apr. 2000, 8.

———. "Burial Scientist Blasts *Daily News* Report." *New York Amsterdam News*, 8 Mar. 2001, 33, 37.

Stuart, William. "Servitude and Slavery in New York and New Jersey." MA thesis, Univ. of Chicago, 1921.

Sturken, Marita. "The Wall, the Screen and the Image: The Vietnam Veterans Memorial." In *The Visual Culture Reader*, edited by Nicholas Mirzoeff, 357–70. New York: Routledge, 1998.

Swan, Robert J. "First Africans into New Netherland, 1625 or 1626?" *Halve Maen* 66, no. 4 (Winter 1993): 78–79.

———. "The Other Fort Amsterdam: New Light on Aspects of Slavery in New Netherland." *Afro-Americans in New York Life and History* 22, no. 2 (1998): 19–42.

Taylor, Rodger. "The Site Seer: Guardian of the People with No Names." *The City Sun*, 18–24 Mar. 1992.

Thomas, Hugh. *The Slave Trade: The Story of the Atlantic Slave Trade, 1440–1870*. New York: Touchstone, 1999.

Thompson, Robert Farris. *Flash of the Spirit: African and Afro-American Art and Philosophy*. New York and Toronto: First Vintage Books, 1984.

Thompson, Robert Farris, and Joseph Cornet. *The Four Moments of the Sun: Kongo Art in Two Worlds*. New Haven: Eastern Press, Inc., 1981.

Thornton, John. *Africa and Africans in the Making of the Atlantic World, 1400–1800*. 2nd ed. New York: Cambridge Univ. Press, 1998.

Trinity Church Vestry Minutes, 1694–1982. Trinity Church Archives, New York City.

Tuan, Yi-Fu. "Sacred Space: Explorations of an Idea." In *Dimensions of Human Geography: Essays on Some Familiar and Neglected Themes*, edited by Karl W. Butzer, 84–99. Chicago: Univ. of Chicago, 1978.

Turk, Tureka. "Dispute Stops Progress on African Burial Study." *Michigan Citizen*, 22 May 1993, A1.

"Update: National Park Service (NPS)," *African Burial Ground News* 4, no. 2 (Winter 2005).

U.S. Department of the Interior, National Park Service. *African Burial Ground National Historic Landmark Registration Form*. Prepared by the New York City Landmarks Preservation Commission (Jean Howson and Gale Harris). New York, 9 Nov. 1992.

U.S. General Services Administration. "Africa Rising." N.p., n.d. Brochure.

———. "The African Burial Ground Design Competitions." New York City, [1997].

————. "The African Burial Ground. Interpretive Center Design and Fabrication. A Project in Cultural Storytelling through the Environment [Design-Build Request for Proposals]." New York City, 1997. Booklet.

————. "The African Burial Ground. Memorial Design and Fabrication. A Project in Cultural Storytelling through the Environment [Solicitation, Offer and Award]." Issued by GSA, PBS, Property Development Division, New York City, 1997. Booklet.

————. "A Celebration of Public Art! Six Works Honoring the African Burial Ground. Program, the Artists, and Their Work." Produced by Public Buildings Service, New York City, 1998.

————. "Amendment [#3] of Solicitation/Modification of Contract [for] The African Burial Ground Memorial Design and Fabrication." New York City, 17 Feb. 1998.

————. "Art-in-Architecture. *America Song*. Clyde Lynds' Sculpture for the Entrance of the Federal Office Building in New York City." N.p., n.d. Brochure.

————. "GSA Announces Finalists for African Burial Ground Interpretive Center." New York City, 15 Mar. 1999. News Release.

————. "*The New Ring Shout*: A Tribute to the African Burial Ground." Brochure. Np, nd.

————. *New York African Burial Ground: Skeletal Biology Report—First Draft*. Prepared by the African Burial Ground Project—The W. Montague Cobb Biological Anthropology Laboratory—Howard Univ., Washington, DC, 5 Aug. 1998.

————. "The Roger Brown Mosaic at Foley Square, New York." N.p., n.d. Brochure.

Valentine, David. T. "History of Broadway." *Manual of the Common Council of New York*. New York: D. T. Valentine, 1865.

Van Laer, Arnold J. F., ed. and trans. *New Netherland Council Minutes, 1638–1649*. Albany: Univ. of the State of New York, 1939.

"Visiting Royal African Delegation." *New York Beacon*, 9 Aug. 1995, 23.

Visona, Monica Blackmun, Robin Poyner, and Herbert M. Cole. *A History of Art in Africa*. New York: Prentice Hall and Harry N. Abrams, 2001.

Waddington, Chris. "Expatriate Gains." *The Times-Picayune*, 14 Feb. 1998.

Wagman, Morton. "Corporate Slavery in New Netherland." *Journal of Negro History* 65, no. 1 (1980): 34–42.

Watson, John Fanning. *Annals and Occurrences of New York City and State in the Olden Time.* Carlisle, MA: Applewood Books, 1846.

Watters, David R. "Mortuary Patterns at the Harney Site Slave Cemetery, Montserrat, in Caribbean Perspective." *Historical Archaeology* 28, no. 3 (1994): 56–73.

Weathers, Natalie. *African Burial Ground of 1712.* New York: Manhattan Borough President's Office, 1993.

White, Shane. "Slavery in New York State in the Early Republic." *Australasian Journal of American Studies* 14 (Dec. 1995): 1–29.

Wiecek, William M. "The Origins of the Law of Slavery in British North America," *Cardozo Law Review* 17, no. 6 (May 1996): 1711–92.

Wilczak, C., R. Watkins, C. Null, and M. L. Blakey. "Skeletal Indicators of Work: Musculoskeletal, Arthritic and Traumatic Effects." In *The New York African Burial Ground Skeletal Biology Final Report*, edited by Michael L. Blakey and Lesley M. Rankin-Hill, vol. 1, chap. 11. Washington, DC: General Services Administration and Howard Univ., 2004.

Wilkie, Laurie A. "Secret and Sacred: Contextualizing the Artifacts of African-American Magic and Religion." *Historical Archaeology* 31, no. 4 (1997): 81–106.

Wilson, Mabel O. "The African Burial Ground Memorial." *Assemblage* 26 (1995): 88–93.

Wilson, Sherrill D. *New York City's African Slaveowners: A Social and Material Culture History.* New York and London: Garland Publishing, 1994.

Wilson, Sherrill, and Jean Howson. "Modern Myths of the African Burial Ground." Office of Public Education and Interpretation, New York City, n.d. Photocopy.

Wiredu, Kwasi. "African Philosophical Tradition: A Case Study of the Akan." *Philosophical Forum* 24 (Fall-Spring 1992–93): 35–61.

———. *Cultural Universals and Particulars: An African Perspective.* Bloomington and Indianapolis: Indiana Univ. Press, 1996.

———. *Philosophy and an African Culture.* Cambridge and New York: Cambridge Univ. Press, 1980.

Wooten, Stephen. *The Art of Livelihood: Creating Expressive Agri-Culture in Rural Mali.* Durham: Carolina Academic Press, 2009.

Wright, Roberta Hughes, and Wilbur B. Hughes III, et al. *Lay Down Body: Loving History in African American Cemeteries*. Detroit: Visible Ink Press, 1996.

Yamin, Rebecca. "New York's Mythic Slum." *Archaeology* 50, no. 2 (Mar.–Apr. 1997).

Yamin, Rebecca, ed. *Tales of Five Points: Working-Class Life in Nineteenth Century New York*. Prepared by John Milner Associates for Edwards and Kelcey Engineers and General Services Administration, Region 2, 2000.

Yeoh, Brenda. "The Control of 'Sacred' Space: Conflicts over the Chinese Burial Grounds." In *Contesting Space: Power Relations and the Urban Built Environment in Colonial Singapore*. New York: Oxford Univ. Press, 1996.

Young, Mahonri Sharp. "New York Patroons." *Apollo* 117, no. 255 (1983): 402–4.

Index

Page numbers in italics denote illustrations.

ANDREA E. FROHNE is Associate Professor of African art history at Ohio University. She teaches in the School of Interdisciplinary Arts and in the School of Art and Design, and she is an affiliate of African Studies. She is a co-editor of *At the Crossroads: Readings of the Postcolonial and* the *Global in African Literature and Visual Art* (Africa World Press, 2014) and is a contributor to several edited volumes.